# POETICS OF ARCHITECTURE
## Theory of Design

Anthony C. Antoniades

JOHN WILEY & SONS, INC.

New York   Chichester   Weinheim   Brisbane   Singapore   Toronto

*To my sister Maria Antoniadou*

This book is printed on acid-free paper. ☉

Copyright © 1992 by John Wiley & Sons, Inc. All rights reserved.

Published simultaneously in Canada.

No part of this publication may be reproduced, stored in a retrieval system or transmitted in any form or by any means, electronic, mechanical, photocopying, recording, scanning or otherwise, except as permitted under Sections 107 or 108 of the 1976 United States Copyright Act, without either the prior written permission of the Publisher, or authorization through payment of the appropriate per-copy fee to the Copyright Clearance Center, 222 Rosewood Drive, Danvers, MA 01923, (978) 750-8400, fax (978) 750-4744. Requests to the Publisher for permission should be addressed to the Permissions Department, John Wiley & Sons, Inc., 605 Third Avenue, New York, NY 10158-0012, (212) 850-6011, fax (212) 850-6008, E-Mail: PERMREQ@WILEY.COM.

This publication is designed to provide accurate and authoritative information in regard to the subject matter covered. It is sold with the understanding that the publisher is not engaged in rendering professional services. If professional advice or other expert assistance is required, the services of a competent professional person should be sought.

**Library of Congress Cataloging-in-Publication Data:**

Antoniades, Anthony C.
  Poetics of architecture: theory of design/Anthony C. Antoniades.
    p.   cm.
  Includes bibliographical references.
  ISBN 0-471-28530-7 (paperback)
  1. Architectural design.   I. Title.
NA2750.A65   1990
720'.1—dc20                                                         89-36617

Printed in the United States of America

20  19  18 17  16  15  14  13  12  11

# Contents

# Preface

This is a book about the theory of architecture. It addresses aspects of imagination and creativity and introduces the channels one can use to achieve creativity in architectural design. It is a product of several years of inquiry of a teacher-architect nurtured and educated in the Modern movement, who struggled with the pros and cons of the debates of the last fifteen years and contemplated the advantages and disadvantages of Postmodernism. The former, after all, was the prevailing attitude promoted by much of the architectural press; it shaped the work of many recent architects, and caused both student anxieties and faculty polarization.

As a lover of the creative act and a sincere critic of architecture, I could not remain silent about the good that I could see produced by some of the studios of my Postmodern colleagues in academia; on the other hand, I felt that many of their students were either copying the magazines unquestionably, or were generally at a loss, unable to recognize the purposes and goals of their explorations, often unable to adjust to other realities and more tangible, professional, expectations.

The climate of professional achievement of the recent decade, at least as presented in the fashionable media, closely resembled that of academia. The evolving reality included acclaimed works that often appeared out of place and time. Yet designs such as the Portland Building by Michael Graves, the Hong Kong and Shanghai Banking Corporation and the Lloyds Building in London, high-tech masterpieces by Norman Foster and Associates and Richard Rogers Partnership respectively, or the undeniably prolific creations by the Arquitectonica group and other "modernist" architects, are samples of undeniable notoriety within the "new reality" we have created, in which we live and which we have to challenge and understand. The task of the theoretician of this new reality is not one of Modernism vs. Postmodernism, but rather one of sorting out the good in both. Some of the best architects of our time have demonstrated the way; they have managed to synthesize the good, they have managed to stay "open-minded," and they have created works that we believe Le Corbusier and

Alvar Aalto, if they were still alive, would be receptive to and supportive of. I am inclined to think that if by some miracle Le Corbusier were to be reborn and run his office again, he would certainly be fascinated and perhaps envious of many recent projects, and he would certainly ask about the young people and the creative processes that made such works possible. He would be quick to reassure us that he himself, a Modernist, had initiated some of the "new channels" a long time ago.

But such miracles are not possible, and we do not need Corbu, Alvar Aalto, or Gunnar Asplund to bring us together again. We have to do the synthesis on our own. This has been explicitly demonstrated by architects such as Gunnar Birkerts, Antoine Predock, Ricardo Legorreta, Ralph Erskine, Juhani Pallasmaa, Kristian Gullichsen, Jörn Utzon, and Henning Larsen. All of them, though relatively quiet and occasionally remote, and although distinctively different from one another, have created works of what we have called synthetic inclusivity.

This book developed out of an effort to contribute to the debate in a constructive way, beyond petty polemics and destructive polarization. More, it is the product of my personal belief that architecture is desperately in need of a constructive theoretical representation, updated to meet the demands of the "new reality" of our time. After all, we have enough Modern, Postmodern, and inclusivist works all over the globe to permit us to draw conclusions and provide ourselves with critical standards. There is indeed a need for a constructive reorientation and collaborative continuation of whatever is good out of whatever we are creating, either as architects or in the place where it all starts, the architectural studio.

With that goal in mind, the book is designed to help the reader navigate the "channels of creativity" through which one can move in order to stimulate one's imagination and create design. These are the tangible channels, many of which were the core of modernism, as well as the intangible channels, many of which were developments of Postmodernism. In that sense, the book is a synthetic theoretical document which developed out of the need for a *reconciliation* of everything good bequeathed to us by Modernism and of everything good that we can retain out of recent Postmodernism. This reconciliation should result in a broader framework for design training and the progressive evolution of the inclusivist architect of the future.

We believe that the student, undergraduate or graduate, will find the book a handy guide. It will make it easier for the student to shape his or her expectations, to be prepared for what to expect in the architectural studios where varying channels to architectural creativity are attempted, and to make sure that he or she works out a plan of design exposure, either in school or early in life, that will bring the lens of inclusivity, the widest possible exposure and challenge, from which he or she will eventually graduate into an inclusivist architect, a good, solid designer whose work is relevant for the times. One could of course suggest (and hope) that architectural curriculums would also benefit, in that people might decide to explore channels of creative potential currently not substantially explored in many schools, or plan additions to the design curriculum on the basis of creativity channels that ought to be added.

Many of the premises of this book were challenged by me in my own architectural studios, at several design levels, at the University of Texas at Arlington. The constructive theoretical articulation was formulated through a course in architectural theory at the senior and graduate levels. The material was widely circulated and read prior to publication by many students, especially students from various design studios who, after reading the text, decided to stick with their studio directions, to try harder, and to give themselves the benefit of exposure to new and occasionally strange-sounding or initially incomprehensible studio expectations.

It is my strong conviction, however, that architectural design affects us all, whether done by architects or by each one of us separately whenever we make decisions about the spaces we live in and move about. I therefore hope that the book will be of benefit not only to my colleagues and to students of architecture and practicing architects, but to other creative artists as well. All of us live and will have to live together, and the quality of our collective lives will be greatly enhanced if we let our creative impulses operate within the widest possible framework of aesthetic appreciation and aesthetic decision making.

If I have managed to state in simple and explicit terms an account of the design philosophies and the theories of my time and if I have managed to weave a relevant reconciliatory framework out of all that, developing at the same time a comprehensive framework for creativity and a theory of the learning process, this was my intention. I hope I have suceeded, but it will be up to you to decide.

# Acknowledgments

I gratefully acknowledge the people that follow, for they provided platforms and support, and helped me articulate my points and communicate my messages which eventually resulted in the making of this book. Such people, all dedicated to the cause of architecture, have been for me the following:

Toshio Nakamura of *A + U*
Bruno Zevi of *L'architettura*
Donald Canty and Andrea O. Dean of *Architecture*
John Conron of *New Mexico Architecture*
Costas Karagounis of *Anthropos + Choros* (Man and space).

Ricardo Legorreta, has been my foremost inspirer, an architect par excellence, a friend and colleague in the broadest sense of the word. My very special thanks also go to the senior Greek architect Aristomenis Provelenghios, one of the most devoted Le Corbusier associates, who was most generous to me with his library and the original French editions of the Matila Ghyka studies referred to in the text, and directed my attention to the *3° Μάτι*, a short-lived Greek magazine of the 1930s and a treasure of discourse in aesthetics, which was unknown outside Greece. My special thanks also go to Nicholas Cholevas of the National Technical University in Athens, and to Savas Tsilenis, architect, who read and criticized earlier versions of the manuscript.

To the students of my design and theory classes, who critically read the manuscript and offered specific suggestions in several stages of its evolution, I am particularly indebted, especially to the following: David Breeding, Karen Caramela, Edward Dapper, Mark Fuentes, Edwin Harris, Teresa Hernandez, Crystal Linton, Filiz Oskan, and Joe Riley. Finally but not least, I am grateful to Professor Glenda Farvel Utsey of the School of Architecture, University of Oregon, for her open, candid, and constructive feedback throughout the evolution of the manuscript. Her continuous and enthusiastic support provided the strongest incentive for the making of this book.

The breadth of the subject, so much more easily conveyed in lecture settings via slides and blackboard drawings, made it necessary to adopt once again the method of the summarizing "drawing" fields used in my earlier basic introductory book *Architecture and Allied Design* (Kendall-Hunt, 2nd ed., 1986). All the drawings of these illustration "fields" were done by me, occasionally after illustrations, photographs, or drawings by other colleagues. Whenever a reduction of selected original drawings from other publications was used for commentary, it was treated as a "drawing quotation" and appropriate credits have been given. Further credit for copyrighted material is herewith acknowledged, with my thanks to editors for their permission to use material from these publications: *The Journal of Architectural Education, Architecture, A + U, Arkkitehti, Living Architecture, L'architettura,* and to the architects Ilmo Valjakka, Antoine Predock, Rodolfo Machado, and Rinaldo Petrini di Monforte, for the drawings and photographs they provided. You will note that titles of Greek books and journals appear in transliterated form in the reference sections of this book.

Cindy Smith, my secretary at the School of Architecture at the University of Texas at Arlington and all the people of Van Nostrand Reinhold who worked so hard to make this book have my sincere appreciation. But none of these people is responsible for any shortcomings of this work, for which I am solely responsible.

# Part 1 INTANGIBLE CHANNELS TO ARCHITECTURAL CREATIVITY

# Introduction

There is something mystical about the term *poetics*. From Plato and Aristotle to Gaston Bachelard and Igor Stravinsky, this word has been employed to address the aesthetics of genesis, the qualitative ingredients of space, the making of music. Poetics comes from a Greek verb that simply means "to make." The making of space, the making of music, the making of architecture . . . the making of poems . . . thus some of the confusion, since many people associate the term with poetry, which is only one of the forms of making—creating through words. Yet there is a lot more to the term poetics than mere semantics. All the books that have been written about poetics and the one at hand address "the making" of the work of art through the lens of aesthetics; that is, poetics has been tackled thus far as "the making" of art through the thoughtful, contemplative path of what is "good," or what would be the promises or subtle differences between the various possible ways of making, with regard to the "good."

## TYPES OF POETICS

A totally thoughtless poetics would have been the poetry of the arbitrary, which only a critic could perhaps classify, and even perhaps see merit in. Poetics that evolves out of a given tradition, "the way of doing things as our ancestors used to do," is the process of "making" that takes for granted the thought processes of our ancestors. It makes things that were resolved and contemplated by others, perhaps only endorsed by us, in a thoughtful way, which may or may not be the best solution for our current problems, such as the salvation of our historic settlements, and the conservation of deserving buildings. In this case we may distinguish two possibilities for this poetics: The mimetic and the dynamic. The first is considered inferior to the second, while the second is meritorious because it relies on the use of our own mind, sets its selective and critical faculty in motion, and exploits methods and technologies that fit the interest and the economy of the times.

There is a third case of poetics which is highly contemplative; rigorous; mentally, spiritually, and scientifically demanding; it aims at the creation of works that address a multitude of human needs and expectations, practical as well as spiritual. The making of architecture is a case par excellence of this category of complex poetics. Architecture through the ages has certainly experienced all three possible ways of poetics: *the arbitrary, traditional,* and *the contemplative.* Our focus will be the third category, because this has always been the conscious and systematic way of solving problems, especially within the demands of complex and multifaceted societal frameworks. This is of particular significance in a society as complex and diverse as ours is today. The desire to live in peace, the need for local identity as well as the need to qualify as members of the civilized community, and the expectation of arousing the chords of aesthetic emotion in all people, visually as well as spiritually, call for particular attention to the poetics of our focus. The poetics of today's architecture belongs to the most demanding category, which has as its goal the highest aesthetic aspirations and the satisfaction of the broader expectations of humanity.

## THE GOOD POETIC ATTITUDE IN ARCHITECTURE

What is "good" in architecture is obviously the most difficult thing to evaluate. It should certainly be the final goal of any creative architect. The concept of "good" has always been the central concern of aesthetics. It is clearly vested with a high degree of relativity: "good" for the architect? "good" for the individual user? or "good" for society? Architects, especially those who are gifted and creative, are generally ambitious human beings. Ambition is a motivating force. It is natural for creators to want to distinguish themselves. For many, the praise and publication of their work is their highest reward. Such ambitions make many architects risk the substance of architecture to seek distinction.

The "good" and the "virtuous" is the attitude that will generate works whose being depends on the resolution of all the parameters that affect it, be they internal, external, conceptual, technical, and of a detailed or general nature. The function and the construction, the interior and the exterior, the mechanical as well as the social, along with many other factors that may be at work, are among the major parameters of any architectural creation. The superficial architect will tackle only a few of them. The worst such cases are the façadist and the "style alone" architects. All these are examples of what is not good from the point of view of inclusivist architectural poetics. Because inclusivity should know no favorites; it should side with "the goal of the whole as a symphony" where the *building,* the *street,* the *town,* together contribute to the "good" of the whole, and are equally "good" within themselves and their parts, as well as with their *context,* everything that surrounds them.

It goes without saying that such "good" will be also good for the *user* and people at large. It will be good for them because the work will take into consideration their needs. The inclusivist architect is therefore confronted with a dilemma: whether to study the works of highly acclaimed architects who paid one-sided attention to architecture with no regard for the symphonic inclusivist attitude or to disregard them. Our unequivocal suggestion is that one should indeed pay attention to such architects, since, as we argue later, open-mindedness and the "benefit of the doubt" are important ingredients in the making of inclusivist judgments. Because proportions and façades can best be studied via the façadists, while an energy-biased composer will best teach others about the fundamentals of energy. In terms of inclusivity, the "monodimensionally" concerned architects of merit should be viewed like specialized consultants; the inclusivist architect should study, take into consideration, and finally synthesize their advice. The poetics of inclusivity should therefore also rely on noninclusivist works of merit, no matter how violently one may disagree about the noninclusivist attitude of such works. So the inclusivist poetics should aim at the advancement of the critical faculties of architects, and the upgrading of their selective and critical abilities.

In an earlier book, *Architecture and Allied Design* (Kendall/Hunt 1980, 1986), I defined architecture and the broad context of its appreciation as related to its allied design disciplines; this was certainly an introductory inquiry into inclusivity. It must have been clear then that I do not advocate a laissez-faire architecture of "plurality," or an architecture where "everything goes." On the contrary, I stand for an architecture that obeys and respects the rights and preferences of others. In this current volume I elaborate on a key concern of thoughtful architects and architectural educators over the years, the issue of "what is good" for architectural creativity and for design purposes. A theoretical overview of the various attitudes toward this central subject is presented later in this introduction. It is time now to elaborate on the concept and the types of inclusivity we have thus far taken for granted.

## INCLUSIVITY

In this volume, we will address the many possibilities through which the chances for the achievement of aesthetic emotion may be enhanced beyond the level of the concerns for the physical and visual aspects of design addressed earlier (see Antoniades 1980, 1986). The poetics that will have such goals in mind will be more creative, as it will give birth to works never conceived before and will be what we have decided to call here more inclusive. *Inclusivity means* the attitude of exploring ideas and the "making" of a work through many more points of contemplation (not only functional, not only formal, not only spiritual, not only as part of a historical/ traditional or contemporary milieu) than the limited or one-sided ones of the past. In this sense the poetics of architectural inclusivity is the making of architecture through a process of genesis (creativity) in which the aesthetic argument addresses a greater range of potential aesthetic constants, while at the same time operating on totally nondoctrinaire grounds while giving the benefit of the doubt to and exploring the advantages and disadvantages of the various creative possibilities and aesthetic systems.

Inclusivity is therefore a term denoting aesthetic and artistic license, only it offers the possibility of making sound judgments on what is "good" from the point of view of satisfying the constants of people and evoking the highest degree of aesthetic emotion—creating, that is, an architectural symphony. The idea of symphony is of particular significance in our times, since now, perhaps more than ever, we need agreement between the various instruments (various architects and theoreticians playing to their own tunes), so that we can experience harmony once again, as opposed to irrelevant, unrelated virtuoso performances.

It becomes clear, then, that the more complex, diverse, and sophisticated a society is, the more complex the task of the inclusivist architect. Further, the more architecture advances, the more the methods and techniques advance, the more complex the task of exploration may initially become. Yet as we will see, this may not be so grave a task for the future, since we have faith in the potential of computers, which will be capable of helping us and facilitating our tasks.

## THE CONTEXT OF THE CURRENT INCLUSIVIST FOCUS

"Inclusivity" can be treated through a number of approaches.

1. Through the inclusion of as many people as possible out of those who could participate in the making or in the enjoyment of the particular work of architecture. Such inclusivity is taken care of by considerations and research that address issues of society and the user—cultural anthropology, ethnography, sociology, and environmental psychology are obviously the best help to the architect about such matters.

2. Through the inclusion of as many diverse points of view as possible with regard to what has been perceived and appreciated as "good" in architecture, and the evaluation of the optimum for the purposes of optimum selection. Such inclusivity, although not alien to the architect, is generally understood to be take care of by those who study the various design methods—that is, the ways through which one can optimize the design process and come up with a more meaningful design.

3. Through the inclusion of as many ways of conception as possible —that is, tackling inclusivity at the stage on conception of the work of art, that very early stage Socrates called the "stage of creative pregnancy," where all the seeds of success (or not) are planted. Our study will focus on the third area of inclusivity, the first two have been covered by anthropological and user studies or design-oriented research. Our inquiry will explore the various channels through which one can approach the making of architecture to stimulate and fertilize the imagination as much as possible.

By *creativity* we should understand for preliminary introductory purposes all the processes, the state of mind and the "agony," perhaps the uneasiness and turmoil, the state of total emergence and the birth of nurturing mechanisms, through which the creator has to go during the stage of intellectual and design conception.

The concepts of *fantasy* and *imagination* are also paramount as ingredients in the creative process. The main body of the book covers an inclusive array of possible channels to architectural creativity, the theoretical overview of which constitutes the main contribution of this volume.

Most of the "channels" to architectural creativity have certainly existed for a long time, for they are nothing else but the various ways that have been argued by others in the past as problem-solving panaceas (the creation of the new based on the study of precedents, the study of history, or the creation of the new based solely on energy considerations, climate, etc.), along with several other possibilities that have perhaps been used but in haphazard and nonexplicit ways.

## THE MODERN VS. POSTMODERN PREDICAMENT

This book represents the efforts of one teacher/architect/author for "peace" and "evolution" for the benefit of architecture. The whole premise of this book is that architectural thought, methods of design exploration, and ultimately architecture as built today are much richer than they were during the earlier part of the century, the period of the Modern movement. Further on we assume that the period of Postmodernism, despite the objections one may have about some of its practices such as too much emphasis on historicism, gave strong theoretical impetus and offered a challenge through its polemic that did enrich the design process if seen with goodwill and a calm and critical mind during the inclusivist design process. Postmodernism opened many more possible channels to architectural creativity, all we need do now is reflect and synthesize them for constructive purposes.

This book therefore attempts to address the various preexisting channels to architectural creativity critically and to offer a synthesized overview of the crest of both Modern and Postmodern movements in complementary and inclusivist terms.

## STRUCTURE OF THE BOOK

Many of the channels to creativity that were developed as a result of the Modern movement (practices and methods of design, emphasis on structure, focus on materials, preference for geometry, distinct articulation of volumes, building as an object) represent recent memory to many people; they are better known and easy to comprehend. On the other hand, we believe that, although young architects and especially students are immersed in Postmodernism and its literature daily (through magazines and fashionable designs), they have a rather limited theoretical overview of what they thoughtlessly imitate. Because of that, it is more important, I believe, to approach our inquiry from the point of view of the recently emerged channels to architectural creativity—first, the intangible channels and then the tangible channels, those of the Modern movement. This, I hope, will offer a clearer picture of the advantages and disadvantages of what we are already doing, and it will also prepare the ground for a noncombative reevaluation of the values and concerns of a previous era that the current climate leaves largely unexplored.

Although it does not really matter what part of the book comes first, as at the end, whether we want it or not, all aspects of architectural consideration should be "included" in the making of architecture, we believe in the usefulness of the separation proposed above, and thus we have adopted it. The sequence of the various chapters, however, follows no particular rule of organization other than the author's goal of creating a stimulating narrative that will arouse the fantasies and the imagination of the readers, while convincing them that it will be only time, training, and exposure to as many channels as possible that will eventually make inclusivist architects, inclusivist appreciators, receptive users, or compassionate and well-rounded critics out of them.

It would certainly have been ideal if one could acquire "inclusivist" habits instantaneously, but this is a lifelong process. Multifaceted disposition and critical education are needed. An architect evolves into an "inclusivist" architect, while an architectural program or a design instructor may also so evolve. It is certainly my belief that inclusivity should be the goal of any school of architecture. At the very least all schools should plan to broaden their design curriculums and offer their students as many channels to architectural creativity as possible.

I also believe that one can offer a comprehensive overview of inclusivist design education without necessarily being pedantic, by offering the tangible and the basic design curriculum first (study of scale, proportions, rhythm), and leaving the "intangibles" for graduation. Yet experience has shown that most schools expose their students to the tangible channels first (geometry, materials, systems of proportion, exercises on rhythm). This tradition certainly has merit. It has proved helpful, yet I believe that it can be enhanced if the student gets an overall theoretical exposure to what design is all about as early as possible, rather than waiting for years for that to occur. This has been the fundamental reason for the ordering of the sequence of the units of this book and the precedence assigned to the intangibles. Still, the goal has been to present the material in such a manner that the reader can approach each chapter independently, without the necessity for a comprehensive or sequential reading. Although this book was written with the architectural student, the young architect, and the design instructor in mind, it will be the public that will probably benefit the most, as people will get the chance to "see" architecture through the lens of the essentials of its making, making them more compassionate, more sympathetic to the efforts of architects, and hopefully integral agents in the achievement of a more advanced and deserving architecture.

# Chapter 1 The Process of Creativity

Without an understanding of the relationships between the concepts of "real" and "unreal," "imagination" and "fantasy," it is impossible to have a clear understanding of the prerequisites for the creative process, or to embark on the task of cultivating and developing them. It is my belief that both imagination and fantasy, these two prerequisites for architectural creativity, can be cultivated and enhanced by the good will, the application, the training, and the discipline of the architect, even more than his or her inherent talent. The architect will become good or excellent in the real or in the theoretical arena only insofar as these two aspects of his or her work are developed.

The person who overemphasizes the development of fantasy alone will have little chance of seeing his or her visions built. Without the blessing of fantasy, he or she may produce projects of distinction, yet not blessed with the spark of life that only the really creative personality can produce. Only the architect who operates in both spheres, the sphere of fantasy and the sphere of imagination, will be able to realize truly extraordinary projects.

## FANTASY, IMAGINATION, REALITY

Figure 1-1 presents a very simplified introduction to an otherwise complex and highly demanding set of interrelationships. Let us look more closely at this diagram: If we refer to any child or adult, as someone who has a good sense of fantasy, we mean a person who has the mental ability to generate images of things or situations that have not existed before. To dream of castles in the clouds, to see angels performing a Mozart sonata in a celestial amphitheater, or to be able to see oneself walking on the water are encounters with the ability to fantasize. We define fantasy as the ability of a person to generate images that cannot become reality, no matter what the circumstance. Fantasy exists only in the mind. Dreams and visions are ingredients of fantasy; they are part of the act of fantasizing. We can fantasize asleep or awake, while working or relaxing, consciously or unconsciously. Imagination, on the other hand, refers to the ability of the mind to see what is there. It has a pragmatic connotation: "Go up the street, turn right after the church, go as far as the windmill, turn left, and around the mill, just behind the wall, plant the tree." The handyman with imagination who is about to follow these instructions will immediately see the image; he will create the

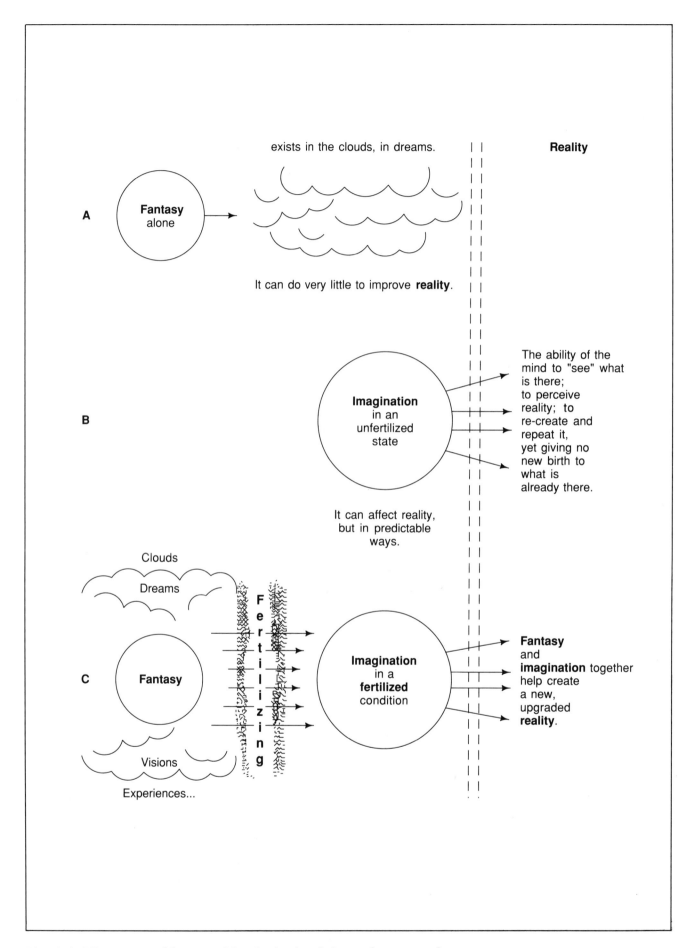

exists in the clouds, in dreams.

**Reality**

**A**

**Fantasy**
alone

It can do very little to improve **reality**.

**B**

**Imagination**
in an
unfertilized
state

The ability of the
mind to "see" what
is there;
to perceive
reality; to
re-create and
repeat it,
yet giving no
new birth to
what is
already there.

It can affect reality,
but in predictable
ways.

**C**

Clouds

Dreams

**Fantasy**

**F**
**e**
**r**
**t**
**i**
**l**
**i**
**z**
**i**
**n**
**g**

**Imagination**
in a
**fertilized**
condition

**Fantasy**
and
**imagination** together
help create
a new,
upgraded
**reality**.

Visions

Experiences...

**Fig. 1-1.** *The concepts of fantasy and imagination in relation to the concept of reality.*

church and the windmill in his mind, and he may even "see" the tree he is about to plant already blooming and shading the white wall.

The image of the blooming tree takes this person a bit beyond the level of basic imagination because the tree is not really there. It was because of his ability to fantasize that he has already planted it next to the white wall and given life to it. The fundamental distinction between fantasy and imagination becomes clear when we consider the concepts of real vs. unreal. Imagination is related to the real. Fantasy belongs to the sphere of the unreal, yet it possesses the power to see its effects on the real if it belongs to a person who has the power of imagination and the quality of being imaginative. Only when fantasy acts as a catalyst to the imagination is one able to create works of reality that are blessed with the new, the fresh vision, the never before tried: *Fantasy is the catalyst of imagination, while imagination is the filter through which fantasy must pass in order to become an ingredient of reality*. Imagination blessed with fantasy is therefore *the ability of the mind to see what is there in a way modified so that the ultimate mental construct is elevated to the sphere of the divine while at the same time being possible to realize*.

It should be clear that *reality* is inherent in clarifying the limitations of the term *imagination*. For the theater director, the imagination of an author is the prerequisite to the creation of the play. The imagination of the actor who reads the script is the prerequisite for entering into the characters and interpreting the play in reality. The whole play is the product of the imaginations of all three—author, actor, and director. Stanislavski wrote that "the dramatic Art is the product of the imagination, as the work of a dramatist should be. The aim of the actor should be to use his technique to turn the play into a theatrical reality." The architect could say that the work of an architectural act is the product of the imagination of the architect; contractor (and builder) use technique to turn the design into reality. Shifting back to Stanislavski, I ask you to make the architectural analogue yourselves. You could assume as universal his suggestion that

> Imagination creates things that can be or can happen, whereas fantasy invents things that are not in existence, which never have been or will be. And yet, who knows if they will come to be. When fantasy created the flying carpet, who would have thought that one day we should be winging our way through space? Both fantasy and imagination are indispensable to a painter.

## EXPONENTIAL SUBTLETIES

Louis Sullivan, who gave form to the American skyscraper (1856–1924), carefully avoided a direct definition of imagination. But concepts such as "real" and "unreal," "fantasy" and "imagination," were integrally interwoven in his mind. As he wrote: ". . . imagination, you may say anything about that suits your imagination; . . . it is the personal imagination that can grasp imagination." He addressed these topics peripherally, through poetic trips into the spheres of the real and the unreal, the physical and the metaphysical; life and death, or by addressing situations such as "the sound of the bird's song that can only be grasped by one hearing it." The metaphysics of Louis Sullivan brings us to a more complex sphere of understanding. When he says "imagination that can grasp imagination" he suggests an element of dynamism, an *exponentiality* of sorts in the concept of imagination.

When one has to first imagine the parameters of what one does not understand, perceive, or know from his or her tangible reality, and to then imagine that he is creating something for this imaginary world, he is operating on an exponential level of imagination. This was the concept of imagination understood by the ancient Gnostics, who accepted the notion of a "world of imagination." Recently, this concept has attracted groups of Western writers, aesthetes, and painters, as well as several architects and teachers. Massimo Scolari, the major proponent of explorations in the world of "imagined imagination," as well as others who share similar beliefs, "have proposed that we dematerialize forms and *immaginalizzare* (imagize) intelligible forms, proposing a 'visibility' of being and reality beyond sensation and conceptual abstraction."

Although we will return to the discussion of the possibilities, promises, and liabilities of such efforts later in our study, we declare at this point that our position, which we accept as the pivotal point for understanding the term imagination, is the nonexponential one, the "traditional" one if you will, the concept that understands imagination within the element of reality and gives fantasy the element of the doubt. After all, it is our belief that the ultimate goal of the architect is to build, so "reality" is undeniably related to this goal of architecture.

## REALITY AND THE ACT OF BUILDING

The architect has to build just like the actor has to act; and although the Sullivanesque attitude described above, perhaps intentional, certainly open-ended, may have caused some people to suggest that imagination and creativity cannot be taught, that one must be born with these qualities, it is my position here that such things can indeed be taught. Many other creative professionals also believe that it is possible to stimulate, cultivate, and elevate the imagination. Several among them have even developed methods and techniques that have produced legendary results. Stanislavski, for instance, realized that imagination may be inactive and can be put to work through appropriate techniques and coaching. The use of simple probing questions was the key with which Stanislavski elicited responses from students:

> If he responds thoughtlessly, I do not accept his answer. Then, in order to give a more satisfactory answer, he must either rouse his imagination or else approach the subject through his mind, by means of logical reasoning. Work on the imagination is often prepared and directed in this conscious, intellectual manner. The student then sees something, either in his memory or in his imagination: certain definite visual images are before him. For a brief moment, he lives in a dream. After that, another question and the process is repeated.

The process of continuous probing and focusing on imaginary constructs is the key to the final realization of the construct. This has been the experience of many people, and is certainly a well-known method among architectural instructors. The problem, however, is for the student to learn to probe such questions on his own.

In this respect the student is like any other person seeking a guide to self-improvement. The method is the same. Shakti Gawain, in her inspirational work on creative visualization, reaffirms the notion of the need for realistic implementation of the mental construct. On the other hand, she also reaffirms the notion that through continuous and regular probing, it becomes objective reality.

## THE GOAL OF FANTASY AND IMAGINATION

The continuous probing and the focusing of the architect can take several paths; all of them, probed appropriately, will eventually lead to the creative statement. In this sense, creativity may be understood as "the final goal of the imagination process . . . the state of realization of the visualization of an idea, a mental picture, or of a building." The composer Igor Stravinsky has stated it best: "What concerns us here is not imagination in itself, but rather creative imagination: the faculty that helps us to pass from the level of conception to the level of realization."

Imagination, therefore, belongs to the sphere of thought, while creativity refers to the sphere of making (the Greek "to make," or "poetics": everything one does in order to create). Aristotle was most explicit on the subject. In his *Metaphysics*, he wrote: "One phase of the productive process . . . is called thinking and another making: that which proceeds from the starting-point and from the form (*eidos*) is thinking; that which proceeds from the end-point of the thinking is making."

The Aristotelian concept of creativity and its relationship to imagination, along with the subtleties of reality vs. metaphysical application, all of them tied to the development of the being (the creator himself), have been dissected exhaustively in what exists today as an extraordinary literature on the subject. The history of philosophy, the history of aesthetics, as well as key works by philosophers such as Plato and Aristotle, Kant, Vico, and Descartes, or more recent ones such as Paul Valèry, Alfred North Whitehead, Jacques Maritain, Jean-Paul Sartre, and Ernst Cassirer, are the main sources on the subject. It would be simply redundant to attempt a recapitulation of the various theories here. It is important, however, for the purpose of our argument to point out that, in terms of creativity as applied to architecture, we will follow the treatment presented in the work of Ernst Cassirer. We consider his to have been the most "inclusivist" appreciation of creativity, and he will elaborate on it as necessary in support of our own beliefs about inclusivity or comprehensivity in architecture. At this point, it is important to mention the work of Ignacio L. Götz, who in his little-known publication *Creativity: Theoretical and Socio-Cosmic Reflections* has already presented the most inclusive summary of the positions of the various writers noted above. He has also provided valuable commentary on the qualitative and subtle differences between the various theories. Götz does not touch imagination and creativity as related to architecture; this task is attempted by the British architectural theoretician Broadbent in his *Design in Architecture* and by the design instructors Koberg and Bagnall in their *Universal Traveller*. Both books are reviews on creativity in the design studio and in the making of architecture.

## DEFINING CREATIVITY

A broader definition of creativity that will form the basis for further argument with reference to architecture can be crafted as a compendium of expressions including those of Ignacio Götz, Alfred North Whitehead, and my own, which can be credited to the inclusivist concepts of Cassirer. We therefore propose the following definition:

> *Creativity* is the process by which the imagination exists in the world. As process, creativity is indeed the ultimate; it is the universal of universals characterizing ultimate matter and fact. In a sense, creativity is synonymous with Aristotle's prime matter, except that creativity is neither passive nor receptive. But creativity may be seen as the absolute active

ground of all that comes to be, being in itself indescribable. Creativity . . . is that ultimate notion of the highest generality at the base of actuality. Creativity can be ever-present to include all the activities of man, be they scientific, artistic or cultural. All the elements of culture—language, myth, art, science, history, religion—contribute to its purest and wholesome evolution. (This is a composite based on Götz 1978, Whitehead in Götz 1978, and my own work.)

Some have argued in the past that creativity cannot be adequately defined because all the aspects of creativity are in fact more special than it is itself. This notion had been stated by Whitehead, and it may have been one of the reasons why architects in the past have argued that creativity cannot be taught. This, of course, has not been the prevailing notion among most architects. The truth of the matter is that the great majority of creative architects have not wanted to talk about their creative processes, or to reveal the secrets of their creativity. Although of course we must regard silence with suspicion, since it is often a cover-up for lack of originality and ignorance, a well-rewarded public relations strategy of the mediocrity, we must also respect the silence of true creators. Great creators will speak when they are ready. And usually when they speak they say so much with so little.

Louis Sullivan was the exception to the prevailing silence. He is the only one among the great creative architects to have left an explicit written account of his personal path to creativity; his *Kindergarten Chats*, a text full of emotion, is inspirational as well as didactic: A combination of prose and poetry in which the great architect and beloved master of Frank Lloyd Wright proves that sensitive, emotional, human, and sensual personality is perhaps a prerequisite for strong, robust, and constructively appropriate architecture. The literature on the subject of architectural creativity, scarce as it may have been, has made little reference to the enlightening work of Louis Sullivan. Any attempt to bring the subject home should start with paying credit to him.

## CREATIVITY IN ARCHITECTURE

### The Broader Framework

The study of creativity became a key concern of social scientists, psychologists, psychoanalysts, anthropologists, art critics, business people, behaviorists, educators, and doctors in the middle decade of this century. People after World War II were trying to rebuild the world. The goal was to increase productivity. Social scientists and human engineers saw "creativity" filtered through a concern for efficiency and productivity. Two bodies of literature on creativity developed: The first was a general, voluminous, and glorified presentation, the product of the "experts" and research scientists of the 1950s. It was a look at creativity through the lens of technocratic-quantitative efficiency. Its working focus centered on issues of cognitive and perceptual processes, both visual and mental, and it left behind a legacy of research and several useful findings to which we will refer as necessary in the appropriate chapters. The second body of research was rather timid, obscure, perhaps uncertain and unscientific, although in certain instances, it was human, emotional, and spiritually illuminating. This body of theoretical probing on creativity, almost forgotten and rarely referred to in recent years even by those who make their living through teaching, was developed by educators—general educators and architectural educators in particular.

A study of the two major bodies of research suggests a well-defined split between the various disciplines in the Western world following World War II. There were the professions that looked at creativity as a science that could further human performance on earth, and those professions that viewed their metier with a metaphysical focus that tolerated no scientific input in the creative process. Architects ignored the conferences and symposia on creativity that were organized in the mid-1950s by poets, writers, painters, sculptors, art historians, scientists, social scientists, and psychologists. So it is not surprising that much of the work on creativity bypassed architecture and offered minimal input on the subject. What input there was on architecture was either incidental or took architectural creativity for granted. We are skeptical of and astonished by this gross omission; we become even more skeptical about the findings and the theoretical foundations of the existing general literature which, by neglecting architecture, demonstrates the limitations of its foundations and the narrowness and monodimensionality of its approach to these fundamental subjects.

Architecture is, of course, a multidimensional, comprehensive discipline. As Alvar Aalto said, "Architecture is a synthetic phenomenon covering practically all fields of human activity." It is an art and a profession, and it is a state of mind. To be an imaginative and creative architect, therefore, you have to have imagination and to be creative at many levels, some purely artistic and intellectual, others scientific (technology, structures, materials, equipment) and professional (due process, ethics, business). The very nature of the art of architecture is to serve humanity; it is a utilitarian art, even in its most spiritual form. As such, it cannot exclude pragmatism and be one-sided, dogmatic, pure art (i.e., form alone). Most theories of imagination and creativity are either mostly scientific or mostly artistic; they tend to focus on one aspect, tend to be concerned at one level, and tend to support ideas of "instantaneity," "a particular spark," "divine inspiration," and "individuality," as opposed to "inclusion" and "comprehensivity" group work, and a studious attitude and involvement.

## The Comprehensivity of Cassirer

Ernst Cassirer was the exception; his thought conceived the mind as creative in all areas of culture—in language, myth, art, science, history, and religion. Yet architects had nowhere to go to find a theoretical explanation for experiences and concerns that were humanistic and cultural, like Cassirer's. Cassirer was largely unknown—difficult to understand, outside the mainstream. Had earlier architects found a model that would have included their own humanistic and cultural concern with regard to the making of architecture, they might have joined the body of research and they might have contributed to the evolution of thought on the subject. This did not happen, and official students of imagination and creativity missed the whole body of work that deals with the arts and the recent activities that are comprehensive, multilayered, and highly communal as far as the identity and the role of the creator are concerned. Architecture has not been alone in this respect; other synergistic arts, composites of many arts and professions, such as theater, filmmaking and space engineering and design, have been left outside the scope of inquiry of philosophers, and of social and psychoanalytic scientists. This was due perhaps to the fact that even the architects themselves preferred not to speak about creativity whenever they were asked, or preferred to appear indifferent to the efforts of those who were working on the study and theory of "creativity"; to them, the act of creation was holy, not to be spoken of lightly.

## Earlier Attitudes: Reverence for Creativity

Frank Lloyd Wright had called creative imagination "The manlight in mankind," and he had equated creative beings to gods. "A creative being is a

God. There will never be too many 'Gods.' " Wright did not respond to
an invitation to provide feedback for one of the very few studies undertaken
by the U.C. Berkeley psychologists in the 1950s on the traits of the creative
personality that included architects (Barron, 1969). Alvar Aalto took a
similar position on similar occasions: "They asked, among other things,
how one creates art. I replied, 'I don't know.' " On another occasion, Aalto
telegraphed to the dean of MIT that he was unable to produce "enough
architectural philosophy" to explain the Baker House, but that the dean
was free to publish his telegram instead, in which he quoted Sibelius: Sibelius said, "If you publish three words of explaining music, at least two
are wrong." Aalto further suggested that this might be true for architecture.
Aalto was echoing, in a sense, the beliefs of Louis Sullivan, who had written: "When the mind is actively and vitally at work, for its own creative
uses, it has not time for word-building: words are too clumsy. You have
no time to select and group them."

Le Corbusier's poem "Acrobat" shows perhaps in the clearest way the
concept he had of creators, a breed he knew well. If we substitute the word
"creator" for the word "acrobat," we get a comprehensive and candid
definition:

> An acrobat is no puppet
> He devotes his life to activities
> in which, in perpetual danger of death
> he performs extraordinary movements
> of infinite difficulty . . .
> nobody asked him to do this
> nobody owes him any thanks.
> . . . He does things
> which others cannot
> . . . Why does he do them?
> others ask. He is showing off;
> he's a freak; he scares us; we pity him;
> he's a bore.

But the "acrobat," the "creator," will go on, in spite of the pessimistic and
discouraging perceptions society might have of him. On another occasion,
while flying over the Nile delta Le Corbusier wrote in his sketchbook:
"Painting is a bitter struggle, terrifying, pitiless, unseen; a duel between
the artist and himself. The struggle goes on inside, hidden on the surface.
If the artist tells, he is betraying himself!" So as seen by Wright, Aalto, and
Le Corbusier, creation, creativity, and imagination were not only "holy,"
surrounded by a religious aura, but were conditions of constant encounter
and confrontation between creator and society. (Society may think of the
acrobat as a bore.)

We may now understand the reluctance of these people to respond to
psychological surveys that were attempting to quantify and explain imagination and creativity through scientific formulas. Creators of the caliber of
Wright, Aalto, and Le Corbusier never felt betrayed by letting their work
talk. Their numerous exhibitions, their buildings, books, and lectures, addressed the whole issue of creation and creativity, but in a "language" that
only creators could understand. We therefore might argue that the exclusion of architects from the psychoanalytic inquiry was due partly to the
language barrier between architects and social scientists, but also that it was
a result of the architects' attitude toward their art.

The creativity of architects had to be extracted from their own writings
and seen through the study of publications on their projects and their efforts
to develop them. Le Corbusier finally came close to offering suggestions,
even to the point of guidelines for the creative process. His books—and he
wrote a lot—his sketches, notebooks, and files, were studied after his death
by scholars working in the Le Corbusier Archives of the Fondation Le

Corbusier. They discovered that this body of work was not only the product of his creative effort, opening new directions to the world, but revealed the secrets of his creativity. According to the research of Daniele Pauly, Le Corbusier had written about his creative process and about his creative inventions. And as Pauly has argued, these inventions were not accidental, sudden and spontaneous, but the result of very long period of effort before he even picked up a pencil to draw. He used to store information in his memory and, as he said, use his "human brain" as a box in which he would let the "elements of a problem simmer." The multidimensionality and "synergistic" nature of architecture requires that the second part of the creative book will have to be written by multidimensionally and "synergistically" trained persons. Culture-oriented architects, filmmakers, and space scientists will have to write the part of the creativity literature that was not attempted by the psychoanalytic writers. This discussion makes it clear that architectural creativity is a touchy subject. Professional students of creativity, such as sociologists and psychoanalysts and professional architects with creative records and recognition, have long been at odds, so the chance to learn from them appears remote.

An additional oddity that inhibited the spread of learning regarding architectural creativity was the split that existed between the architectural profession and architectural education. An attitude of inexplicable arrogance/ignorance coupled with an attitude of intellectual elitism (Frank Lloyd Wright was perhaps the most glorious example in these respects) had caused occasional periods of tension between the architectural profession and architectural education. There were stereotyped, generalized perceptions such as "those architects practicing out there," or "those teachers who have never built anything." Because of such attitudes, some of the best research and findings of architectural educators, especially during the early 1950s, remained unnoticed, overshadowed by the success of the stars of the profession. And while students and perhaps architects were quoting references on creativity by technocratic and psychological experts, very few ever referred to the monumental efforts of the ACSA (Association of Collegiate Schools of Architecture) which tackled issues of architectural creativity on a rather consistent basis, especially during the first half of the 1960s.

## BROAD VS. NARROW CONCEPTS OF ARCHITECTURAL CREATIVITY

A study of the evolution of attitudes toward architectural creativity during our century reveals a model that could be described as a dialectic of the "narrow" versus the "broad." Europe nurtured the seeds of the Modern movement in architecture through a well-known sequence of events and manifestos that came about as an answer to the Beaux-Arts attitude. It was the United States that provided the platform for the challenge and the qualitative evolution of architecture as a didactic and creative affair. In this respect, perhaps the deepest (and since then unique) roots for thought on architectural creativity were planted in this country by Jean Labatut in an article entitled "An Approach to Architectural Composition," published in the *Journal of Architectural Education* in 1956. I consider Labatut's contribution the pivotal one around which to weave a theory of the "narrow" vs. "broad" interpretations of architectural creativity (see Fig. 1.2). His will be considered the key "broad" conception; others occupy the left and the right sides of the dialectic curve. Jean Labatut was the first advocate of "inclusivist" architecture in this century; he is largely unknown to those outside the profession of architectural education, his students and the few architects who knew and respected him.

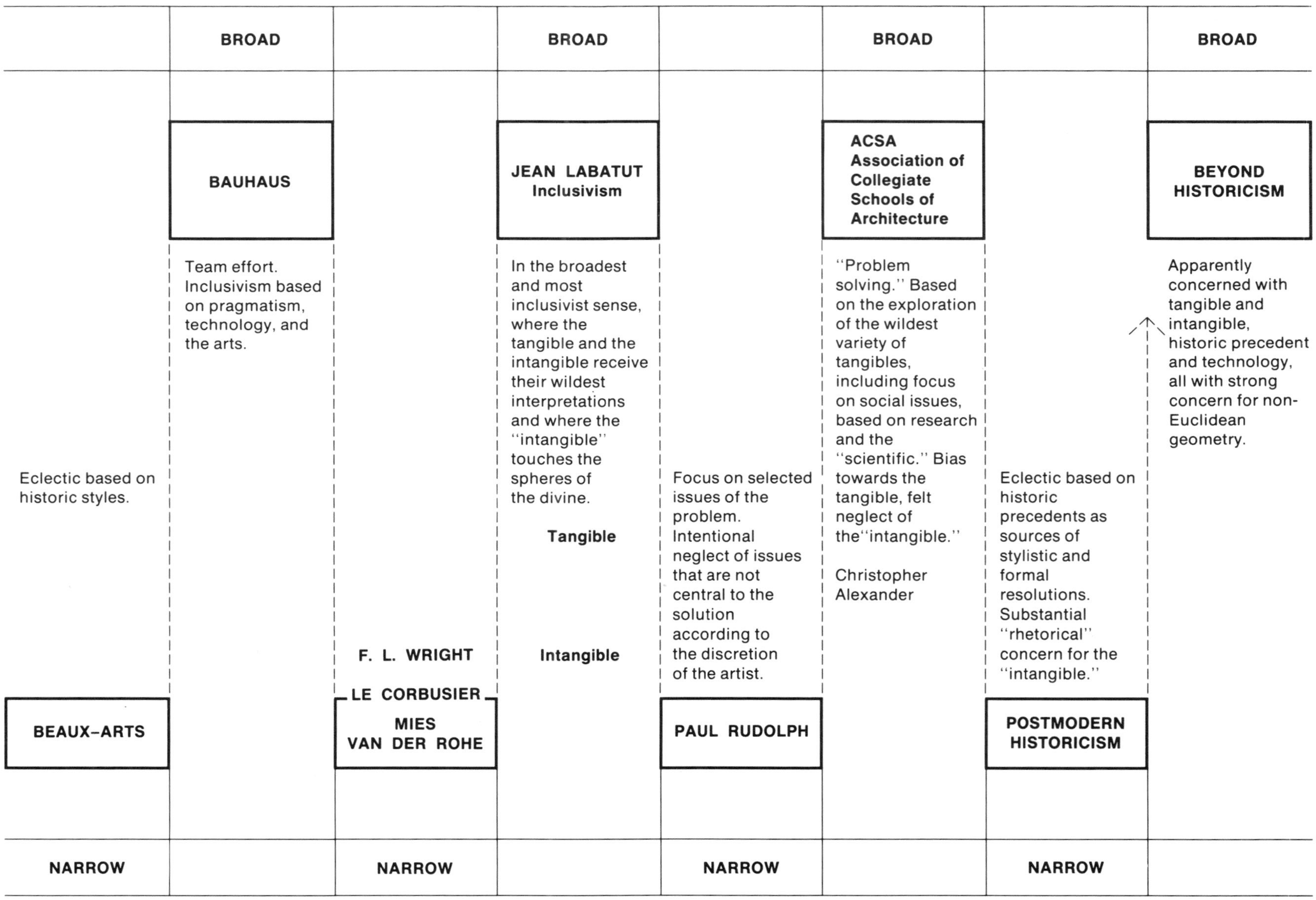

| NARROW | BROAD | NARROW | BROAD | NARROW | BROAD | NARROW | BROAD |
|---|---|---|---|---|---|---|---|

| BEAUX–ARTS | BAUHAUS | LE CORBUSIER MIES VAN DER ROHE / F. L. WRIGHT | JEAN LABATUT Inclusivism | PAUL RUDOLPH | ACSA Association of Collegiate Schools of Architecture | POSTMODERN HISTORICISM | BEYOND HISTORICISM |
|---|---|---|---|---|---|---|---|
| Eclectic based on historic styles. | Team effort. Inclusivism based on pragmatism, technology, and the arts. | | In the broadest and most inclusivist sense, where the tangible and the intangible receive their wildest interpretations and where the "intangible" touches the spheres of the divine.<br><br>Tangible        Intangible | Focus on selected issues of the problem. Intentional neglect of issues that are not central to the solution according to the discretion of the artist. | "Problem solving." Based on the exploration of the wildest variety of tangibles, including focus on social issues, based on research and the "scientific." Bias towards the tangible, felt neglect of the "intangible."<br><br>Christopher Alexander | Eclectic based on historic precedents as sources of stylistic and formal resolutions. Substantial "rhetorical" concern for the "intangible." | Apparently concerned with tangible and intangible, historic precedent and technology, all with strong concern for non-Euclidean geometry. |

**Fig. 1-2.** *Evolution of attitudes toward architectural design, oscillating from the broad to the narrow, including the inclusivism of Jean Labatut.*

Labatut's main argument was that "things are not as they are, but as we are." Through his extraordinary essay, perhaps the best ever published on aspects of architectural creativity and the act of creation by architects through composition, he addressed the issue of relativity of judgment. He also further qualified the meaning of function to include its physical, intellectual, and emotional components. Labatut cried out for a human architecture, and dug deep into history to find his arguments. He chose first the Charioteer of Delphi, a universally admired work of art, in order to test the possibility of unanimity. But "a listener disagreed and declared it a poor piece of sculpture, even not sculpture at all!" would be Labatut's conclusion. And so Labatut gave us freedom to disagree! Gone is the supremacy of the "star" architect's judgment. For the first time in twentieth-century America, the client enters the picture; and he enters through academia. "Things are not as they are but as we are," Labatut would repeat; "it is that fact which leads the client to that supreme judgement when he pronounces those fateful words, 'I like it,' or 'I do not like it.' His judgement is based on needs and desires." And finally, he blasted the teacher to shake his students and disciples: "A good difficult client can make a better architect, while a too easy client can make an architect creatively lazy" (Labatut, 1956).

Labatut argued in favor of the indivisibility of design and construction, the need for a clear understanding of the problem and an endorsement of the Lao-tzu sequence of events, *experience, assimilation, forgetfulness,* and *composition,* as the steps for creative design. This method, transmitted to him from his master of architectural composition, Victor Laloux, was the one found in the philosophy of Lao-tzu. Labatut also gave us his secret: "The way to learn is to assimilate; the way to know is to forget."

Other students of creativity have endorsed this promising, tactical, and very difficult lifelong process of creative abstraction. Gaston Bachelard, in his *Poetics of Space,* quoted Jean Lescure in support of similar arguments on the topic of "creative forgetfulness": the state of affairs when—because of a lifetime of assimilated input from education, reading, and experience—you reach the state of knowledge (wisdom) using what you have learned, digested, and transformed through your inner being and brain, without necessarily remembering when and where you heard it. Your own creation comes out as a new composition, heard once upon a time, in some place, on some remote occasion. A song from your past, your song.

But for this to happen, one needs to use the proper means, to subject oneself to appropriate limitations, with the use of tangible and intangible elements. All of these are needed to create an architectural composition and its inherent architectural form. Jean Labatut thus introduced the elements of "tangible" and "intangible," the known and quantifiable versus all those unknown and inexplicable things that cannot be rationalized that if there, will make a total, unique, and complete design. They will make the project "to be what it wants to be," as Louis Kahn had said; they will make it the building for the intended client—the shelter for people's physical, intellectual, and emotional needs. The tangible things are learned and should be taken into consideration; the intangibles are not visible; they have to be searched for. The architect has to find them in the client's makeup. He must search for all human, spiritual, metaphysical factors, the symbols, and the meaning of the terms, the language, the beliefs and superstitions of the client. No, Labatut would not agree with the narrow focus of some of his students. He would certainly disagree with Post-modern historicism and the stylistic histrionics of the 1970s and mid-1980s.

The attitude of the Ecole des Beaux-Arts was the first "narrow" one. The attitude of *parti* or the "big idea" (always in terms of form) was the basis of everything that was to follow. The *parti* as a rule was a formal statement of classical or neoclassical origin. It represented the framework of limitations. All efforts were supposed to respect its constraints and tolerate problems so as not to violate the "elegance" of the *parti* preconception. The Beaux-Arts idea has been criticized repeatedly on many levels, not the least of which has been for its stifling of the creative achievement.

The first broad interpretation of architecture as a creative act was officially established by the Bauhaus after World War I. The creative product was to be pragmatic, responsive to manifold needs—physical, social, technological, artistic. This was an inclusivism of the tangible and scientific. Yet simultaneously with the Bauhaus, several individual architects were practicing (and believing) what was later to be preached by Labatut: an all-inclusivist architecture based on both tangible and intangible concerns. Gunnar Asplund was the foremost of these architects. Some obscure characters such as Rudolph Steiner and several German architects of the time (like Hugo Häring), concentrated mostly on explorations of the intangible. Le Corbusier, Frank Lloyd Wright, and Mies van der Rohe would occupy the successive peaks of the narrow interpretation of creativity. Despite the writings of the first two, their attitude toward creativity largely depended upon a "style"; their styles were, of course, original and constantly changing or evolving (the three major styles of Le Corbusier, the six styles developed by Frank Lloyd Wright), but they were decisive preconceptions in the development of their projects.

Jean Labatut's creativity model occupies the second peak of the broad interpretation of architectural creativity. To the right of Labatut's pivotal "broad" peak we encounter another narrow interpretation; it was narrow in that it tolerated unequal emphasis on the various parts of the design, accepting concentration on one aspect of the design to the deemphasis of others. This attitude was represented by Paul Rudolph. While dean at Yale in the early 1960s, he had stated at the 1963 AIA Convention at Miami Beach: "The artist ignores certain problems, addressing himself to a selected few. He proceeds to solve these so eloquently that everyone understands the statement and its truly glorious solution. . . . It is axiomatic that certain problems be ignored if a great work of art is to be created, and if in the hands of the artist this is justifiable, indeed necessary." We could call this the creativity of artistic license; Rudolph's attitude set the tone, yet further on it raised concerns about the issue of quality as related to the concept of creativity.

Lawrence Garwin, architectural educator and supporter of the problem-solving process of architectural design, articulated the debate on the issue. Is a "creative" design necessarily a good design? He pointed to Rudolph and to the group of supporters who held that if a building is to demonstrate creativity, it should excel in some aspects of design not similarly demonstrated by its contemporaries. That it should excel in all design aspects was not seriously considered. Garwin observed that in these circles, a "creative," in some respects excellent, building was considered to be a "great" building. Buildings that solved more than one problem were simply "good" buildings. The continuation of this debate saw the split of architects into two distinct camps: "artists" and "professionals." We regard this situation with some skepticism. In retrospect, and based on a personal conviction that architecture is certainly an art as well as a profession, we view distinctions of this sort as unfortunate indications of the confusion of the times. Buildings can be "creative" whether they excel in one or more respects or whether they "excel" in total, as an average of their components. There is "creativity" in totality, as well as in the parts and the detail. There is creativity with regard to the concept, and there is creativity with regard to all the components of architecture. It is certainly an extraordinary task to create a building that is "excellent" and at the same time "creative" in all respects, yet it is possible. Many people have tried to do it, and it has happened.

The next peak of our curve is occupied by the "broad" interpretation of architectural creativity that came about as a result of a combination of concerns of several individual educators, the collective body of architectural educators (ACSA), and a number of schools of architecture. Through a series of events, committee appointments, and quantitative studies on the subject, they came up with the endorsement and implementation through curriculum changes of what became known as the "problem-solving-oriented" design process. This attitude, heavily influenced by social overtones and uniformity in education, called for avoidance of "design excesses" and "integration of more design criteria into a rational system which can be instrumental in creating an optimum design solution." It was expected that "the most creative architects would find their search for expression strengthened, not inhibited."

Despite the breadth of the concerns, the problem-solving-based efforts were heavily biased in favor of tangible facts. Later on, the attitude became identified with bureaucratic processes, "professionalism," statistical analysis, and techniques of programming and cost-benefit evaluation. The attitude was destined to doom, with only one survivor, Christopher Alexander. Alexander, an individual without precedent in recent architectural history, equipped as a mathematician (and therefore deeply cognizant of the quantitative techniques architects were trying to master in an amateurish manner) stayed on his feet all the time, constantly "learning" and broadening his concern about creativity. Early enough, Alexander saw the need for the inclusion and consideration of intangibles as a prerequisite to human architecture. His "star" shines brilliantly still today.

In the course of the events presented thus far, Postmodernism (especially Postmodern historicism) is an insignificant event, at least from the perspective of architectural creativity, because all Postmodern historicism did was to revive the Beaux-Arts attitude of the *parti* as the catalyst for creativity. Postmodern historicism is the final peak of the curve of prevailing ideas with regard to architectural creativity.

Jean Labatut was totally misinterpreted by most of his Princeton graduates, who turned into Postmodern historicists during the mid-seventies. But we do not argue that we have not come a long way from where we were. Architecture always gets richer, with every "stone," every challenge, every possible angle of looking at something. Postmodernism, broadly considered and carefully distinguished from Postmodern historicism, had inclusivist intentions to start with. It favored the reappearance and institutionalized exploration of possibilities that had not been touched before. Instructors of the late 1970s and early 1980s opened up their horizons, and although there was a very clear bias and emphasis on history, several instructors explored obscure and metaphysical issues, having developed by now a series of distinctive channels that have helped and can further help to enhance architectural imagination and creativity through rigorous instruction.

Today we are at the beginning of perhaps the richest period of a broad understanding of the concept of architectural creativity through intangible and tangible means. In fact, we believe in the supremacy of the "intangible," while we have broadened our horizons to explore new tangibles. We are looking for new horizons to explore new tangibles. We are looking for new associations, new stimulation, studying other arts and artists we had never studied, or in ways we had never approached them before. Not only that, but we approach architecture as a creative act in a very balanced way. Our work does not negate our professional destination, while our professional goal does not assume supremacy over our intellectual goals. In doing so, we advocate that it is important to pursue our lives and to take the attitude that creativity will largely depend on the balance between the primordial prerequisites to creativity—that is, the balance between the "carefree" and "play" elements versus the "serious" element. This broad context is the context for this book.

## PREREQUISITES FOR ARCHITECTURAL CREATIVITY

### Some Widespread Misconceptions

There is a tendency among many people, lay and educated alike, to be impressed by and consider as architecturally creative works of unusual, unique, extravagant, startling, or bizarre configuration. Works that may possess none of these attributes, that may exist calmly and in harmony with their surroundings, serving the purpose they were intended to, may not be considered by many as worthy achievements. We can safely say that an architectural project has more of a chance to be considered by public and peers alike as a "creative statement" if it possesses visual characteristics of the "weird" and "never before seen." A project that may appear at first glance to be a restatement of what has been seen before, no matter how serious or sincere, may be passed over as deserving no further attention and critical scrutiny.

This can be easily verified by any one who has participated in architectural competitions as contestant or judge. It is often the "unique looking" and "new," and certainly the design which is exquisitely presented, that attracts the attention of jurors. One has to be extremely strong not to be charmed by the sirens of "flashiness" and sleekness of presentation. Between the circumstance of "appearing creative" with tricky strategies, a mastery of communication techniques, renderings, and other forms of depiction, and the circumstance of being "serious," thoughtful, deep, and at the same time authentic and innovative, lies much of the dilemma of architectural educators today, at least in the United States, and many architectural creators, including creative professionals.

Another widespread notion is that of the "creative" artist as a carefree, play-loving, fun-loving individual, who can create "under the influence," or any other "influence," and whose life style is a prerequisite to creative endeavor. There is also a widespread contrary notion of the "professional" as a serious person, a member of the Establishment, usually a mediocrity. To be creative, you are certainly expected to be an "artist." We are talking, therefore, about two stereotypical, yet widespread notions, two extremes that are well established in the prevailing attitudes of many students and educators.

### The Carefree

"Carefree" is certainly different from "careless." To be carefree is to be free of worries, anxieties, distress. It is a state that permits undivided attention to tasks, helps you be cautious, protects you and helps you be in control of your time and your creative effort. Being carefree, burning with desire to create and being uniquely useful to society is a blessing for those who enjoy such a state and can devote themselves totally to creative tasks. Not being carefree is often a great handicap to creativity, although there are legendary and well-known examples of creative individuals and inventors who worked in the midst of misery and adversity. Tadao Ando, criticizing his compatriots for "producing architecture demonstrating lack of independence," was quick to point out in their defense that the reason for this state of affairs was the burden imposed upon them ". . . to think of architecture as no more than an economics-related act . . . swept up into a social organization, demanding the production of no more than mistake-free architecture."

Picasso was free throughout his life and carefree for most of it. He did not have to work an eight-hour day because he was working all the time; his life was play, his play was his work, his work was his creations, his creations were his life; in a never-ending process that lasted ninety years. The same has been the case with some architects, although not many; they became, in fact, more creative with the arrival of a carefree stage of life, a state that coincided with the passing of years and the gaining of experience. The carefree state, along with their attitude toward play and some doses of fun, allowed them to give themselves license to explore architecture from angles they would have never dared earlier—for example, Philip Johnson becoming highly eclectic and Gunnar Birkets permitting his inclusivity to accommodate historicism when he thought it appropriate. Yet can anyone argue that the not so carefree (for most of his life) and certainly not so playful Mies van der Rohe, the very serious and concerned "professional" architect, was not one of the most creative architects of this century?

When the design instructor today poses such questions to himself regarding the personalities, creative status, and creative prerequisites of some of his more glamorous predecessors, he is confronted with a complicated dilemma regarding which side to take. American architectural academia allows a certain degree of the carefree status to architectural design instructors at a relatively young age. There is a general tendency to be carelessly carefree when one is young, especially when one is just entering life, and to consider play most significant, both in life style and in the instruction process. One frequently sees posters announcing "gang-band," "ad-hoc," "laissez-faire," "instant city," or "let it happen" creative events, usually promoted by the younger among us. The attitude changes drastically with more experience, professional involvement, personal awareness of the constraints of architecture in the real world, or evaluation and critical scrutiny of studio design projects done in the past. There are, of course, instructors who never progress to any other attitude toward creativity in the studio. Some never explore the difficult proposition of being creative, while at the same time dead serious about the task and the destination of architecture.

Such ideas will bring us face to face with what is perceived here as one of the major current handicaps of meaningful architectural creativity in the studio: the harmfulness of a careless, play-oriented disposition versus a disposition characterized by the element of being serious.

## The Play Element and the Serious Element

The Dutch historian Johan Huizinga repeatedly addressed the importance of the "play element in life" in his two famous books, *Homo Ludens* and *The Waning of the Middle Ages*. He offered us a convincing interpretation of Western European culture and civilization from antiquity to recent times through the lens of play: the ceremonials, the city as theater, politics as a nobleman's game, the play element of war, and so on. Plato, on the other hand, who had repeatedly concerned himself with the fine arts and creativity, provided us with the clearest distinction between the various forms of fine arts, arguing through a series of dialogues that arts such as music, theater, painting, and sculpture are largely dependent on "play," while the art of architecture is totally based on the serious element. Both Huizinga and Plato help us to set up a healthy framework for a well-conceived notion of the play and the serious elements in architecture.

According to Huizinga's analysis, those periods in the history of civilization that were clearly distinguished for the acceptance and regular performance of ceremonials, rituals, and festivities following the "noble" rules of "play" were more creative in many senses, particularly in the arts (ancient Greece, twelfth-century medieval Europe, eighteenth-century England), as opposed to periods during which the "play" element was absent or existed only in the form of war games or more pretentious ceremonies like mock trials. When the "play" element was atrophied or absent, as in Roman times, we see civilizations characterized by austerity, sterility, and oppression. Their works of art and their buildings are perhaps distinguished more for bulk and size than for quality and spiritual aspects.

To a great extent, Huizinga repeated, but in a more precise, condensed, and yet very creative way, many of Plato's notions and beliefs regarding "play" and "creativity." From both writers, we gain the insight that the advantage of "play" (or a life style characterized by a well-established play element), is twofold: Individuals gain personal and spiritual satisfaction both through achieving and through the admiration bestowed upon them by society. They followed "the rules of the game," but in "noble" and "unique" ways, and those who, whether artists or politicians, were admired and respected most, were those who played the game the best. "Gentlemen" were those who recognized the same rules for a particular game. One had to be attentive to the rules and serious regarding their application. At the same time, one had to know the rules well to follow them correctly and in ways one's opponent had not thought of. This was necessary in order to win. In the absence of rules (or in ignorance of their existence), the outcome was obvious: miscommunication, an inability to play, dependence on referees, and finally defeat (for both sides, as there is no point in a bad game), chaos, disapproval by the observers (society), and perhaps eventual war.

The analogies are rather obvious for the "game" of architecture: The element of creativity in this art can be seen as the unique way of dealing with and handling each situation, each building as a complex "match" of unimaginable and often unmanageable sets of rules and circumstances. When we view architecture from such a perspective and also consider the rewards society bestows upon architects for having won a clear and good game, we can start to appreciate the importance of the serious element in the whole endeavor. Good and creative architecture comes from a balance between carefree, "fun," "play," on one hand, and "serious" on the other. It is this delicate balance that is missing from many "games of architecture" when victory is seen only as getting the commission or maximizing the monetary rewards. It is at this point that the Platonic conception of architecture as a "serious" act alone may offer some illumination regarding the meaning of the serious element. As Manolis Andronicos, the renowned Greek archeologist, has noted, Plato did not characterize architecture as involving play (παιδια). According to him, "Plato considers architectural works to be creations of a serious need and very serious disposition of man, that are realized, of course, through the most worthy methods that man possesses." Andronicos also observes that Plato regarded the practice of architecture only as the preoccupation of architects with construction (οικοδομικο εργο), while he did not consider as part of the architect's tasks all the nonmaterial decisions, those that express the human spirit and elevate architecture to levels of higher spirituality.

Because of the absence of this distinction, Andronicos finds no essential difference in the Platonic concept between buildings, whether the building is a simple hut or a sophisticated temple. The difference was one of quantity not quality, and it was from this perspective that Plato viewed all the creations of man, calling the activity devoted to their realization "the human art of building houses or more generally, settlements." Plato later contrasts the importance of the art of building (οικοδομικη) with other utilitarian arts such as farming, and places the work of the builder on a higher plane as a noble and distinctive occupation. It is of great significance for us here to point out that Plato distinguished the dependence of the art of building on public opinion and on society at large, pointing out the inseparable relationship of building and architecture to the meaning of politics.

Yet a partial exposure to Platonic thought may leave the student with an incomplete picture of the philosopher's evolutionary and eventually all-inclusive perception of architecture. If Plato had stopped at his earlier notions, he would have left us with an austere notion of architecture as a profession, a building activity, totally controlled by construction technology and utilitarian needs, an architecture based solely on the serious element. Yet Plato also sought to expand his understanding and the notion of architecture, and he finally introduced into his argument a concern for building structures that were not strictly utilitarian. His means for doing it were the dream, the fantasy, the visionary proposal, the unreal world where "even construction could become a wonderful game, just to please the eye." Plato placed such wonderful buildings in the imaginary city of Atlantis, "where next to the usual and simple buildings were others with carefully selected stones, white, black and red, that made you think of beautiful weavings, deriving from this game exceptional pleasure (ηδονη) rooted in the game's own nature." In a sense, Plato attempts to make the buildings of Atlantis expressive and reflective of divine attributes. Plato gave himself license to be imaginative and all-inclusive, to go beyond the "serious" and the narrowly pragmatic. Yet he did this in his mind only; for all practical purposes, he never changed his attitude toward the "serious" with regard to reality. But summing up all the dimensions of Platonic thought, we have a fully rounded notion of the architect as a person who does not have all the answers, who is the noble guide of the workers, who conceives the project and who supervises its realization. It is true that Plato never accepted anything else but seriousness for realistic architecture, nothing of the playfulness of other arts. He was dead serious, but dead serious for an all-inclusive resolution: utilitarian, visual, and spiritual.

## THE ALL-INCLUSIVE SYNTHESIS

Let's now attempt a synthesis of the best of Plato and Huizinga to arrive at a better-balanced view of creativity in architecture. First, do this exercise. Substitute the word "architecture" for the word "civilization" in the following quotation from Huizinga:

> "Real civilization" [architecture] cannot exist in the absence of a certain play-element, for civilization [architecture] presupposes limitation and mastery of the self, the ability not to confuse its own tendencies with the ultimate and highest goal, but to understand that it is enclosed within certain bounds freely accepted. Civilization [architecture] will, in a sense, always be played according to certain rules, and true civilization [architecture] will always demand fair play. Fair play is nothing else than good faith expressed in play terms. Hence, the cheat or the spoil-sport shatters civilization [architecture] itself. To be a sound culture-creating force this play-element must be pure. It must not consist in the darkening or debasing of standards set up by reason, faith, or humanity. It must not be a false seeming, a masking of political purposes behind the illusion of genuine play-forms. True play knows no propaganda; its aim is in itself, and its familiar spirit is happy inspiration. (Based on Huizinga, 1950)

You could also rewrite it by substituting the word "building" for the word "play" and even perhaps attempt other exercises with different substitutions. But it must be obvious by now where we stand: *It would be a blessing to be able to consider architecture as play; to derive personal joy by doing it; never to become careless and always to retain a serious attitude toward its technical, scientific, and social responsibility dimensions without ever giving in to a narrow one-sided or monodimensional focus on any one of the components. What we aim for ultimately is to have a work of utility become a statement of beauty as well as a cause for spiritual satisfaction.*

Easier said than done. Yet in order to achieve all this, one should be prepared to widen one's horizons, to challenge oneself, to accept the need for creative exploration, to rid oneself of "creative laziness" and to dwell on the challenges presented by the intangible as well as the tangible factors that affect the practice of architecture.

Now we have come full circle. It is the time for students, architects of the future, to express themselves. When asked to write their own, uninhibited understanding of "creativity" as related to architecture and hand it in prior to a lecture on creativity, students came up with the following definitions:

- It is the urge a person has to be creative—to be a doer.
- It is the constant search for the unique.
- It is the dissatisfaction with the predictable, the trivial and mundane.
- It is the thought (action) process which conceives, perceives, and searches for the optimum statement of a work that has not been seen or done before, even though it may have existed as a type.
- It is the search for improvement for something else.
- It is anxiety and dissatisfaction with the widely accepted status quo.
- It is the day and night preoccupation, mental and physical, of a person who constantly searches for new ways of doing things and new ideas.
- It is the state of existence of a person in constant effort for "improvement."
- It is the reason for existence of the doers.
- It is the source of happiness for those who create.

Thoughtful and provocative as these concepts were, none addressed directly creativity in the studio, although most of the students in this group were at the time deeply immersed in it through several channels of creativity in their respective studios. Some were content; others were trying hard; some were frustrated.

In the chapters that follow we will do our best to explain some of the most important channels, starting with the intangible ones.

## References

Aalto, Alvar. *Sketches*, ed. Göran Schildt. Cambridge, MA: MIT Press, 1979, pp. 76, 160.

ACSA. "Creativity in Architectural Design: The ACSA Committee Reports." *Journal of Architectural Education*, 19, 2 (September 1964).

ACSA West Central Regional Meeting. *Fostering Creativity in Architectural Education*, ed. James P. Warfield. Champaign: University of Illinois Press, 1986.

Anderson, Harold. "Creativity in Perspective." In *Creativity and Its Cultivation*, ed. Harold Anderson. New York: Harper & Row, 1959.

Ando Tadao. "Wombless Insemination—or the Age of Mediocrity and Good Sense." *Japan Architect*, no. 347 (March 1986).

Andronicos Manolis. *O Platon ke e Techni* (Plato and Art). Thessaloniki, 1952, pp. 113, 114, 119, 122.

Antoniades, Anthony C. "The 'Care-free' and 'Play' Elements vs. the Element of 'Serious' in Architectural Creativity."In *Fostering Creativity in Architectural Education*, ed. James P. Warfield.

Aristotle. *Metaphysics*, VII.7(1032 B 15). Trans. Richard Hope, with an analytical index of technical terms. Ann Arbor: University of Michigan Press, 1963.

Bachelard, Gaston. *Poetics of Space*. Boston: Beacon Press, 1969.

Barron, Frank. *Creative Person and Creative Process*. New York: Holt Rinehart & Winston, Inc. 1969.

Baruch, Givoni. "Creativity and Testing in Research." *Journal of Architectural Education*, 32, 4 (May 1979).

Blundell, Peter Jones. *Hans Scharoun*. London: Gordon Fraser, 1978.

Broadbent, G. H. *The Design Method*, ed. S. Gregory. London: Butterworth, 1966.

———. *Design Method in Architecture*. New York: Wiley, 1973.

Butcher, S. H. *Aristotle's Theory of Poetry and Fine Art*. New York: Dover Publications, 1951.

Cassirer, Ernst. *The Problem of Knowledge*. New Haven, CT: Yale University Press, 1950, p. 49.

Chang, Amos Ih Tiao. *The Tao of Architecture*. Princeton, NJ: Princeton University Press, 1956, p. 59.

Dow, Alden B. "An Architect's View on Creativity." In *Creativity and Its Cultivation*, ed. Harold Anderson.

Garvin, Lawrence W. "Creativity and Design Process." *Journal of Architectural Education*, 19, 1 (June 1964), pp. 3,4.

Ghiselin, B. *The Creative Process*. New York: New American Library, 1952.

Ghyka, Matila C. *The Geometry of Art and Life*. New York: Sheed and Ward, 1946.

Götz, Ignacio L. *Creativity: Theoretical and Socio-Cosmic Reflections*. Washington, DC: University Press of America, 1978, p. 25.

Huizinga, Johan. *Homo Ludens: A Study of the Play Element of Culture*. Boston: Beacon Press, 1950, p. 211.

———. *The Waning of the Middle Ages*. Garden City, NY: Doubleday, Anchor Books, 1954.

Kepes, Gyorgy. *Language of Vision*. Chicago: Paul Theobald and Company, 1969, p. 23.

Koberg, Don, and Bagnall, Jim. *The Universal Traveller*. Los Altos, CA: William Kaufman, Inc., 1972.

Labatut, Jean. "An Approach to Architectural Composition." *Journal of Architectural Education*, 11, 2 (Summer 1956), pp. 33, 34.

Le Corbusier. *Creation Is a Patient Search*. New York: Praeger, 1950.

———. *Towards a New Architecture*. New York: Praeger, 1960, pp. 197, 219.

Lyndon, Donlyn. "Design: Inquiry and Implication." *Journal of Architectural Education, 35, 3 (Spring 1982)*.

Maritain, Jacques. *Creative Intuition in Art and Poetry*. New York: Meridian Books, 1958.

Moore, T. Gary. "Creativity and Success in Architecture." *Journal of Architectural Education*, 24, 2/3 (April 1970).

Pauly, Daniele. "The Chapel of Ronchamp as an Example of Le Corbusier's Creative Process." In *Le Corbusier: Ronchamp, Maisons Jaoul and Other Building Projects, 1951–1952*. Trans. Stephen Sartarellik, ed. Alexander Tzonis. New York and London: Garland, 1983, p. xviii.

Plato. Politia, Gorgias, Protagoras, Kritias.

Robinson, Julia Williams, and Weeks, Stephen J. "Programming as Design." *Journal of Architectural Education*, 37, 2 (Winter 1983), pp. 5–11.

Scolari, Massimo. *Hypnos*. New York: Rizzoli, 1986, p. 16.

Smith, Paul, ed. *Creativity: An Examination of the Creative Process*. New York: Hastings House, 1959.

Sontag, Susan. *Styles of Radical Will*. New York: Dell, 1966, pp. 3–34.

Stanislavski, Constantin. *An Actor Prepares*. New York: Theatre Arts Books, 1984, pp. 51, 52, 62.

Stravinsky, Igor. *Poetics of Music*. Cambridge, MA: Harvard University Press, 1970.

Sullivan, Louis H. *Kindergarten Chats and Other Writings*. New York: Wittinborn, 1947; Dover Publications, 1979.

Taylor, Irving A., and Getzels, J. W., eds. *Perspectives in Creativity*. Chicago: Aldine, 1975.

Tigerman, Stanley. "JAE Interview: Stanley Tigerman." Interview by JAE editor Peter Papademetriou. *Journal of Architectural Education*, Fall 1982.

Valèry, Paul. "Four Fragments from Eupalinos, or the Architect." *Selected Writings*. New York: New Directions, 1950, pp. 162–183.

Van Eyck, Aldo. "R.P.P. (Rats, Posts and Other Pests)." *The 1981 RIBA Annual Discourse*. Royal Institute of British Architects, London.

Venturi, Robert. *Complexity and Contradiction in Architecture*. New York: Museum of Modern Art, 1966, pp. 46, 89.

Wolin, Judith. "In the Canyon." *Journal of Architectural Education*, 36, 1 (Fall 1982), pp. 8, 10–13.

Wrede, Stuart. *The Architecture of Erik Gunnar Asplund*. Cambridge, MA: MIT Press, 1979.

Wright, Frank Lloyd. *In the Cause of Architecture*, ed. Frederick Gutheim. New York: Architectural Record Publishers, 1975, p. 145.

Wurman, Saul Richard. *The Words of Louis L. Kahn*. New York: Access Press and Rizzoli, 1986.

# Chapter 2 Metaphor

*". . . for if a City, according to
the opinion of philosophers be
no more than a great House,
and on the other Hand the
House be a little City. . . ."*

Leone Battista Alberti

Alberti clearly felt the need to suggest that his readers conceive of the City as ". . . no more than a House . . ." while he also suggested that they conceive of the House as "a little City." He asks his readers to conceive of one thing as if it were something else. He asks them to displace their attention and to think of the house as a city and vice versa. In other words, he asks them to employ a metaphor so that they can acquire a better understanding of the topic under discussion (in this particular case he was discussing the origin of building).

We all perform metaphoric acts whenever we

- Attempt to transfer references from one subject (concept or object) to another.
- Attempt to "see" a subject (concept or object) as if it were something else.
- Displace the focus of our scrutiny from one area of concentration or from one inquiry into another (in the hope that by comparison or through extension we can illuminate our contemplated subject in a new way).

Figure 2-1 shows these concepts in diagram form.

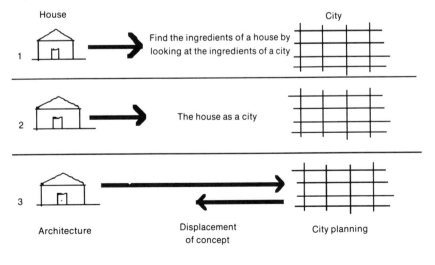

**Fig. 2-1.** *Metaphor: transfer, "as if," displacement.*

29

The use of metaphor as a channel to architectural creativity has been popular among architects throughout this century. It has been found to be a very powerful channel, more useful to the creator than to users or critics. In fact, the best metaphors and their best uses are those that cannot be detected by users or critics. In these cases metaphors are the "little secrets" of the creators. The metaphor is also useful to the architecture instructor. Many instructors have used them, especially in recent years. Through design exercises that depend on metaphoric departures, it is possible to test and to develop students' fantasy and imagination. Those who are already imaginative will not have any trouble with the "metaphor," and it will be an additional ingredient that broadens and deepens their capacity for fantasy and imagination (see Figure 1-1).

The power of metaphor has been appreciated by respected architectural educators, who have even considered it to be the bedrock of imagination. In broader terms, the metaphoric channel can be useful and beneficial to any creator. It will offer opportunities to see a contemplated work in another light; it will force the creator to probe new sets of questions and come up with new interpretations; it will send the mind into previously unknown territories. The purpose of metaphor therefore can be universal, although this does not mean that everybody will find it easy and profitable to operate via this particular channel. Some may find it very difficult at the beginning. Many, especially students who already have some practical experience with reality, may not even want to hear about the possibility of looking at buildings as "something else." These are the people who need metaphor the most; an instructor has to be very persuasive and inspire trust in order to motivate such students. Some will eventually become the most sincere devotees of this particular channel, and be grateful for the horizons it opened to them. Metaphor can be helpful in achieving the "new" at many points in the building and the design/conceptual process. The shape of the building may be seen in a new light. The overall organization may become more expressive of the content. The architect's communication of the "feeling" of a particular building type may become more explicit. Finally, metaphor may help enormously to generate substantial new concepts with regard to the *authenticity* of a building. (Authenticity is the generic identity of a particular building, which every architect should understand and follow in designing the building.)

Through metaphor, especially when it is approached with the technique of displacement of concepts (Schon 1963, 1967), one may apply the knowledge and interpretations already understood for the case of the named item of displacement (which may be a subject, an object, a situation, or even another art—i.e., to consider "architecture as dance" and to attempt to interpret symmetry versus asymmetry in terms of classical ballet versus modern dance) in one's own work.

## CATEGORIES OF METAPHOR

We can identify three broad categories of metaphor: intangible, tangible, and combined.

1. *Intangible Metaphors.* Those in which the metaphorical departure for the creation is a *concept,* an *idea,* a *human condition,* or a *particular quality* (individuality, naturalness, community, tradition, culture).
2. *Tangible Metaphors.* Those in which the metaphorical departure stems strictly from some visual or material character (a house as a castle, the roof of a temple as the sky).
3. *Combined Metaphors.* Those in which the conceptual and the visual overlap as ingredients of the point of departure, and the visual is

excuse to detect the virtues, the qualities, and the fundamentals of the particular visual container (the computer, the beehive, both being "boxes" of relevant proportions, yet having the qualities of discipline, organization, cooperation).

Most architects have a tendency to avoid intangible metaphors as starting points, and many can be easily inspired by tangible metaphors, with various degrees of success.

The strength of any particular use will depend on the degree of detectability of the visual characteristics of the tangible metaphor. Instances of such detectability are called literal interpretations of the metaphor. Literality is not appreciated as a good thing, since it takes away from both the metaphorical departure and the final creation; neither of the two will be what each one "wants to be." The new creation must always transcend its visual resemblance to the metaphorical departure. Obviously, the most difficult, demanding, and at the same time promising category is the combined one. This is especially true when the newly created work, while eliminating the visual and objective memories of the departure point, has retained or even upgraded the essential qualities possessed by the initial model.

All three categories of metaphor can be further distinguished as to their strength for the purpose of critical evaluation or setting design goals. Figure 2-2 illustrates these distinctions very well.

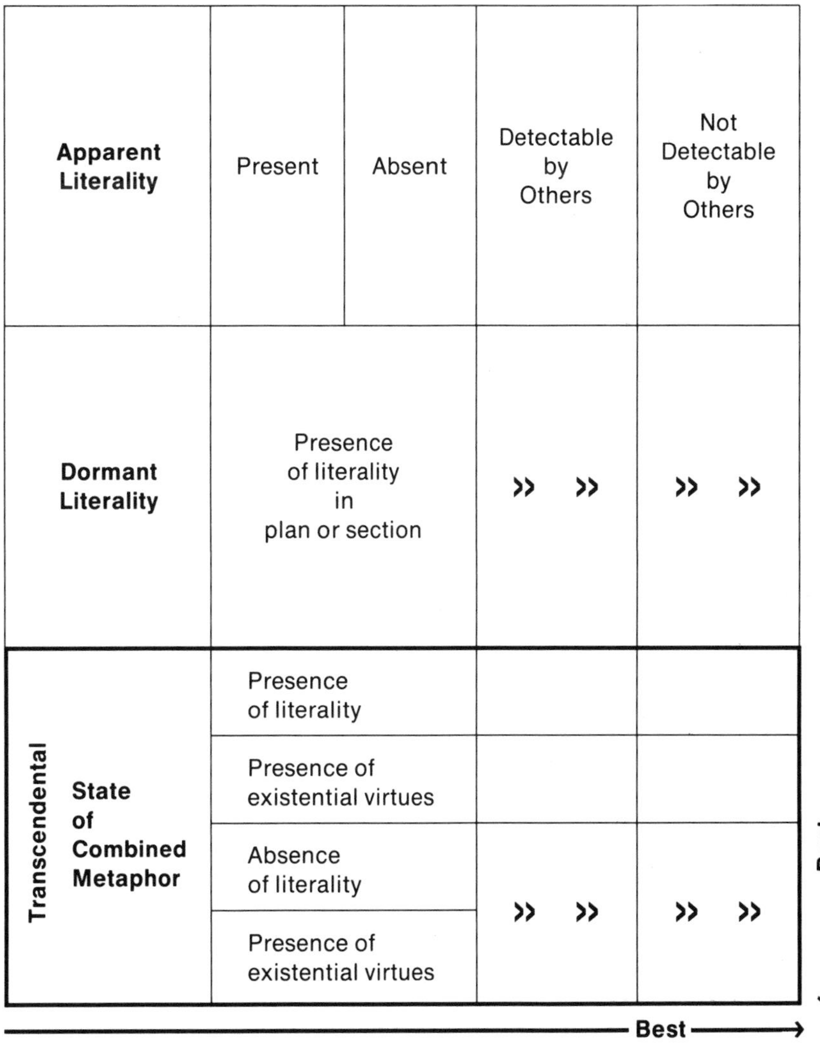

| | | Present | Absent | Detectable by Others | Not Detectable by Others |
|---|---|---|---|---|---|
| **Apparent Literality** | | Present | Absent | Detectable by Others | Not Detectable by Others |
| **Dormant Literality** | Presence of literality in plan or section | | | >> >> | >> >> |
| **State of Combined Metaphor** (Transcendental) | Presence of literality | | | | |
| | Presence of existential virtues | | | | |
| | Absence of literality | | | >> >> | >> >> |
| | Presence of existential virtues | | | | |

Best →  
Best ↓

**Fig. 2-2.** *The hierarchical significance of metaphor for critical and design purposes.*

## HISTORICAL OVERVIEW

All three categories of metaphor have been employed by architects with varying degrees of success. In the historic overview that follows, we will elaborate and clarify this theoretical framework while we survey and categorize some examples of recent applications of metaphor.

### The Nietzschean Origins

Architects have been at home with metaphor in the twentieth century. In fact, some of the major movements in architecture during this century have been labeled by the metaphors they employed. *The machine* was the metaphor of the Modern movement; *the ruin* has been attributed as the metaphor of the Postmodern movement. Other branches or refinements of these movements also employed metaphors as their basis for inspirational departure. Technology or vigor of the new society were among the metaphors of the Russian Constructivists. Anthropomorphy and vertebration (the house with a core and heart) were the metaphors of the Postmodern Historicists, whereas the nonvertebrate (no core, no heart, void) was the metaphor of other branches of the same movement, such as those pursued by Peter Eisenman and Frank Gehry. Some of the most important building types of this century were initially advocated in metaphoric terms. The glass skyscraper, for instance, was conceived as a brilliant, free-standing crystal on the landscape.

The beginning of the use of metaphor in this century goes back to the early German Expressionist architects and had Nietzschean origins. Architects such as Bruno Taut and Josef Emanuel Margold used to keep notes in their sketchbooks from Friedrich Nietzsche's *Thus Spake Zarathustra*, a philosophical work filled with architectural metaphors. In spite of the antisocial attitude of this work, early Expressionist architects in Germany accepted the text as a source for their creative efforts. Nietzsche described the creative act in terms of ecstatic revelation. This certainly appealed to the Expressionists and to many other German and Central European archi-

**Fig. 2-3.** *Building influenced by the Nietzschean conception of the Zarathustra. Schönbrunn Hofpavilion, railway station pavilion for the emperor's use, Vienna, ca. 1896; Otto Wagner, architect. (Courtesy Professor Jay Henry)*

tects of the time; the result was a series of projects evoking mountain images because, according to Pehnt: "Zarathustra lives in the perilous solitude of the mountains."

Many well-known Central European architects, such as Joseph Maria Olbrich and Otto Wagner, created architecture using the metaphor of the mountain. They were among the first to impose on the world a superhuman vision, to remind the viewer of the greatness of the universe in contrast to the "smallness" of humanity. It was perhaps this superhuman attitude and the antisocial nature of Zarathustra that made architects of other cultures look at metaphors with skepticism; and it was perhaps Nietzsche and his appeal to the German intellectuals that made for the widespread acceptance of metaphor among German architects.

## An Array of Attitudes

Porphyrios, who observed the use and the abuse of the metaphor in the architecture of this century, focused on its use by Alvar Aalto, the foremost Finnish architect of the century, as one who made buildings out of intangible metaphors. Aalto's buildings developed as metaphoric acts based on the concepts of *individuality, naturalness, community,* and so on. The critical acclaim given Aalto is nothing but an acceptance of the idea that we can produce buildings based on the intangible metaphor of *humanity,* perhaps the greatest of all metaphors.

The Berlin Philharmonic building designed by Hans Scharoun (1956–63) was conceived through a metaphoric vision that he had regarding a tangible condition, hills covered with vineyards. The interior of the building is a reminder of this visionary landscape. People are the grapes, while the platforms are the slopes of hills, and the ceiling is a tent (see Figure 2-4). This landscape is like a "skyscape." Scharoun, a utopian and a believer in socialism, referred to public buildings metaphorically, as "town crowns" (*stadtkrone*) or "people's halls" (*Volkshaus*):

> The community building was seen as the principal element in a town, a physical representation of the people and their aspirations, and the living evidence of unity between art and people. It was to be the crown of the town. (Blundell Jones, 1978, p. 76)

The Germanic tradition of architectural greatness as man in opposition to nature continued, and came to the United States via the teaching of Oswald Mathias Ungers. As an admirer of the Expressionists, Ungers became one of the foremost advocates of the power of metaphoric reference as a means to architectural creativity. Ungers was the author of theoretical essays and exhibitions as well as the designer of a good number of theoretical projects based on metaphorical departure. He considered the city as a metaphor, while his designs for houses are characteristic examples of his idea that a house is not only the result of a metaphorical conception, but with the change of the metaphor, can be transformed in time, especially through the manipulation of landscaping elements. The season of the year became the metaphor, giving the house its appropriate "dress" (another metaphor) and its corresponding architectural expression.

Ungers had a great influence on some of his colleagues in the United States. John Shaw, an architecture teacher at Cornell, developed a theoretical course on metaphors. His students were called upon to come up with metaphoric interpretations and make metaphoric statements of various building types, such as a School of Architecture metaphorically conceived as a beehive, or a house conceived as "one's castle." A large urban condominium might be conceived as a "tree full of birds' nests."

There is a certain romanticism in approaching architectural creativity through metaphor. In fact, the whole architecture of Frank Lloyd Wright has been presented by Thomas Beeby as being deeply rooted in metaphor. Wright's buildings, according to Beeby, were products of his effort to reconstruct images based on the departure of the mythic Taliesin, while the American house was to be a Usonian house, something for Usonia, which was Wright's intellectual and visual conception of America.

We occasionally encounter a certain grandeur and megalomania in the employment of metaphor. One example is Bofill's low-cost housing projects in France in St. Quentin-en-Yvellin and in Paris, which employed an imperial morphology and the scale of Versailles. Many projects conceived as metaphors often exhibit problems of scale. This is perhaps due to the fact that metaphors tend to produce aphoristic, utopian, universalized results, in spite of the initial good intentions of the artist. To create a building for a school of architecture that can be interpreted metaphorically as a beehive, for example, leaves no room for the individualistic or talented and shy student who may not want to work as a bee, within regimented routines of cooperation, collaboration, and hard work expected from all the other bees.

It comes as no surprise, then, to learn that metaphor has been favored by architects who have domineering personalities and who perhaps find inspiration and justification for their dreams in superhuman and often "out of scale" metaphors. Yet as an architect grows, he or she also "graduates" to a more correct use of metaphor.

Ricardo Bofill is a case in point. After producing an aesthetically simplistic and weak case of the literal interpretation, as in the Muraja Roja, a housing project painted red, a "wall-like" building on the crest of a hillside in Calpe, Spain, he "graduated" to higher levels of metaphor with varying degrees of success. He named his subsequent projects after the metaphors that generated them. Walden Seven in Barcelona is based on the utopian metaphor of Thoreau's Walden, while visually it resembles two huge Mediterranean rocks with pigeonholes on their sides. The rock-pigeonhole metaphoric interpretation is attributed to the critic Broadbent, not to the architect. This points to the possibility that a multilayered metaphorical interpretation may exist for any given project, and that such a possibility is not a bad thing.

Two of the major initial metaphors used by Bofill in the early stages of his creative efforts were the arena and the cathedral. Every one of his public spaces has been conceived as an arena for public interaction. His early attempts to articulate such public spaces were the Walden Seven and Kafka's Castle projects. Walden Seven does not look like the naturally forested, calm landscape Thoreau had conceived. Kafka's Castle may indeed remind one of dreams someone might have after reading Kafka.

This brings us to the important point of the relationship between the metaphoric departure and the final visual result. In the case where a creator starts from a metaphor, analyzes its content and essentials, and then creates a project on the basis of the content and the essentials, we have one possibility for creativity. The result may not look at all like the metaphorical analogue, but it has the attributes and the virtues of the metaphoric condition. Walden Seven is a case in point. Waldens were environments of serenity, concentration, nature, green leaves, and water. Walden Seven has most of these characteristics, yet it in no way looks like a forest surrounding a pond. In this sense the project is very strong from critical point of view on the basis of the theoretical weighting of metaphor, as outlined in Figure 2-2. The case is equally strong in many of the buildings of the late Greek architect Takis Zenetos. His metaphors, the "sunglasses" of a building and "the building as an umbrella," have produced buildings extremely sensitive

SKETCHES FROM PROPOSALS FOR ALPINE ARCHITECTURE, BRUNO TAUT ARCHITECT.
AFTER "ALPINE ARCHITECTURE" HAGEN 1919, AFTER PEHNT.

ARCHITECTURAL FANTASIES FROM LANDSCAPES INSPIRED BY THE READING OF ZARATHUSTRA; WENZEL AUGUST HABLIK.
(AFTER ETCHING IN THE SERIES SCHAFFENDE KRÄFTE, 1909 AND AFTER WOLFGANG PEHNT).

"ARCHITECTURAL FANTASY" BY HERMANN BILLING (FROM "STADBAUNKUNST ALTER UND NEUER ZEIT" I, NO. II, 1920, AND AFTER WOLFGANG PEHNT).

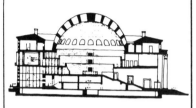

THE FIRST STUDY FOR THE STOCKHOLM PUBLIC LIBRARY BY GUNNAR ASPLUND BASED ON THE METAPHOR OF THE HUMAN SKULL

THE INTERIOR OF THE BERLIN PHILHARMONIC BASED ON THE METAPHOR OF HILLS COVERED WITH VINEYARDS. HANS SCHAROUN, ARCHIT.

A HOUSE FOR ALL SEASONS. OSWALD MATHIAS UNGERS ARCHITECT
(AFTER "HOUSES FOR SALE" BY EMILIO AMBASZ).

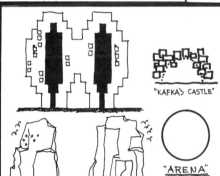

FRANK LLOYD WRIGHT, "USONIAN" STYLE. AFTER PERSPECTIVES OF "USONIA, No. I".

"KAFKA'S CASTLE"

"ARENA"

"THE LITTLE CATHEDRAL"

WALDEN SEVEN (ABOVE) MEDITERRANEAN ROCKS (BELOW).
THE METAPHORS EMPLOYED BY THE TALLER DE ARQUITECTURA (AFTER TEXTS AND AFTER SKETCHES BY RICARDO BOFILL).

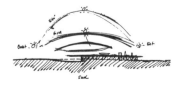

NAUTICAL MUSEUM AT BREMERHAVEN
1969 - 75.
HANS SCHAROUN - ARCHITECT.

"HOUSE FOR A COSMOPOLITAN" SHAPED AFTER THE GLOBE
ANTOINE-LAURENT-THOMAS VAUDOYER (1756-1846). AFTER VAUDOYER AFTER C. NORMAND 1785 AND AFTER "VISIONARY ARCHITECTS" LEMAGNY, J.C. 1968.

SKETCHES BY TAKIS ZENETOS: "THE GLASSES OF THE BUILDING (ABOVE) AND "THE BUILDING'S UMBRELLA" (BELOW). THE METAPHOR DOES NOT EFFECT THE RESULT LITERALLY.

**Fig. 2-4.** *Summary of metaphor in the twentieth century.*

to the sun and the local climatic conditions, without any need for visual imitation as in Bofill's Kafka's Castle.

The German Maritime Museum in Bremerhaven (1969–75), by Hans Scharoun, looks very much like a boat. It is a case of a literal interpretation of the visual characteristics of a battleship, and as such it is an inferior case of the use of the particular metaphor; it would certainly have been much better if the architect had concentrated on the conceptual ingredients of the metaphoric battleship (strength, perfection), rather than being content with the romantic appeal of the visual characteristics of a boat. As we have already pointed out, there is general agreement among teachers, critics, and even creators that literal interpretations of metaphors do not have the strength of the creative results based on metaphoric interpretations that focus on essentials. They are, however, easier to achieve and are therefore frequently attempted, especially by students.

Among the many architects of the past who used metaphors in their literal states were the visionary architects of the eighteenth century, of whom Boullée and Ledoux were the most prominent. Several among them, especially the last two, were favored by early Post-modernist instructors who used them as source metaphors when exploring design projects through the channel of metaphor. The literality of these originals, along with the "historicist" predisposition of Post-modernism, did not produce the best results one could expect of the metaphor.

## Paradigms of Essentiality: The Japanese Example

Japanese architects have been among the most recent devotees of the metaphoric channel. In fact, it has been said that the Japanese have long favored metaphor. Some of the best among recent Japanese architects, such as Arata Isozaki, Kazuhiro Ishii, Minoru Takeyama, Kazuo Shinohara, and Kisho Kurokawa, resort constantly to metaphors for inspiration.

Of course, we should point out the influence on many of these architects of the educational institutions of the East Coast of the United States. Many were educated as graduate students or taught as instructors in these schools and had a chance to come in contact with places such as Cornell, where Ungers and the occasional others from Europe, such as the Krier brothers, used to teach and visit.

Arata Isozaki, a most poetic and prolific architect and writer of theoretical essays, has given priority to metaphors as a means of architectural creations; although many of his buildings come across as literal interpretations (the country clubhouse building that looks like a question mark), the departure for his creative endeavors is usually metaphoric. His critical sense of the architecture of his peers is also at its best when he uses metaphoric screening. The essay he wrote on Le Corbusier on the concept of the erotic relationship of Corbu with the sea and the Mediterranean, in particular, is perhaps one of the greatest written hymns of metaphoric critical interpretation.

Kazuhiro Ishii did substantial research at the beginning of each of his projects. He traveled to the United States, in order to sharpen his East-West references. The Rockettes of Radio City Music Hall gave him the vision for his "dancing colonnade" in the Naoshima Gym. Research into the typology of windows produced his thesis project at Yale, subsequently built on the metaphor of Mondrian's "Boogie Woogie" paintings, creating in this case a Tokyo Boogie Woogie. Minoru Takeyama also used metaphors, but seldom stayed within the essentials. Rather, his projects were cases of shallow literal interpretation.

Kazuo Shinohara, on the other hand, is perhaps the most powerful of all recent Japanese architects, one who could be called the Luis Barragán

A

**Fig. 2-5.** *The influence of the Mediterranean on Le Corbusier as argued by Arata Isozaki: a love affair with the sea world, the rocks, the caves, and the light of the sun through the water as seen through interiors. **A.** The Monastery of Ste. Marie de la Tourette. **B.** Interior space, Ronchamp Chapel.*

B

of the Far East. Shinohara has achieved the three-dimensional articulation of the literary appreciation of Japanese qualities of silence, laquer textures, and rustication versus glitter, much like those we find in Tanizaki's writing on the aesthetics of silence. Shinohara's houses are the result of efforts to create in the poetic tradition of the haiku. In this sense his architecture comes across as an attempt to create using the broadest metaphor of the haiku. We might even suggest that he attempts through this metaphor the creation of a national architecture, since the haiku is an original Japanese invention and national treasure. Furthermore, concepts such as silence, texture, and light are of equal significance to the Japanese, as Tanizaki pointed out in his *In Praise of Shadows*. To be able to build a house around the theme of silence is a most demanding metaphorical endeavor, more difficult perhaps than Aalto's efforts to produce architecture using the metaphors of individuality, anti-authoritarianism (the "home feeling" of the Säynätsalo Town Hall), improvement of nature (as is the case with the "new Finnish landscape" generated through the roof line of the Lapia house in Rovaniemi, and the "everlasting daylight" achieved via numerous artificially lit skylights).

To go beyond that and to build a house using the metaphor of silence and the metaphor of the haiku is further evidence of the unique Japanese approach. Shinohara's architecture, like Barragàn's and Aalto's, belongs to the level of the spiritual, where the regional and the national merge, producing eventually an expression of the universal. The initial metaphor disappears or goes absolutely undetected, producing instead a new spatial and spiritual ambience, a new synthesis.

## Other Examples

Many distinguished architects have resorted to metaphors for inspiration. Jörn Utzon's Bagsvaerd Church near Copenhagen was conceived as a space for humans under the clouds that defines a spiritual finite between us and Heaven, or the infinite. His early sketches clearly suggest the relationship to the verbal concept, while the finished project clearly demonstrates that he went far beyond the original conception. The Finnish architect Reima Pietilä has also sought inspiration in metaphors. His student union building Dipoli in Otaniemi was conceived as "an assembly for primitive men living in a cave," while the Kaleva Church (from The Kalevala, the epic of the Finnish people) in Tampere was conceived, among other things, as a structure based on the fish, the sign of the early Christians which in its Greek spelling meant *Jesus Christ Son* of *God, Savior*. Fish are also vital actors in The Kalevala who sustain and feed the people of Finland. The plan of the church is a case of literal interpretation, carefully hidden from the perception of the viewer, a secret between architect and God. Pietilä's undetected literality, similar to that of Gunnard Asplund in the Stockholm Public Library (where the cross section of the main library hall was initially conceived as the cross section of the skull that houses the brain, the "library as the brain of the community"), is certainly superior in its charm to the obvious literalities of the past (a house for a geographer that looks like the globe, or a house for an archeologist that looks like an ancient column) or of the present.

Yet there may be cases where some literal resemblance to the metaphoric departure may be desirable. In these instances, where the essentials of the metaphoric content have been satisfied as well as the literal formal resemblance achieved, the result may be powerful and unique projects, distinguished for their concepts as well as their charm. One such project is the Petal House in Los Angeles by Eric Owen Moss, an extraordinary, charming, landscape- and neighborhood-respecting project, which opens

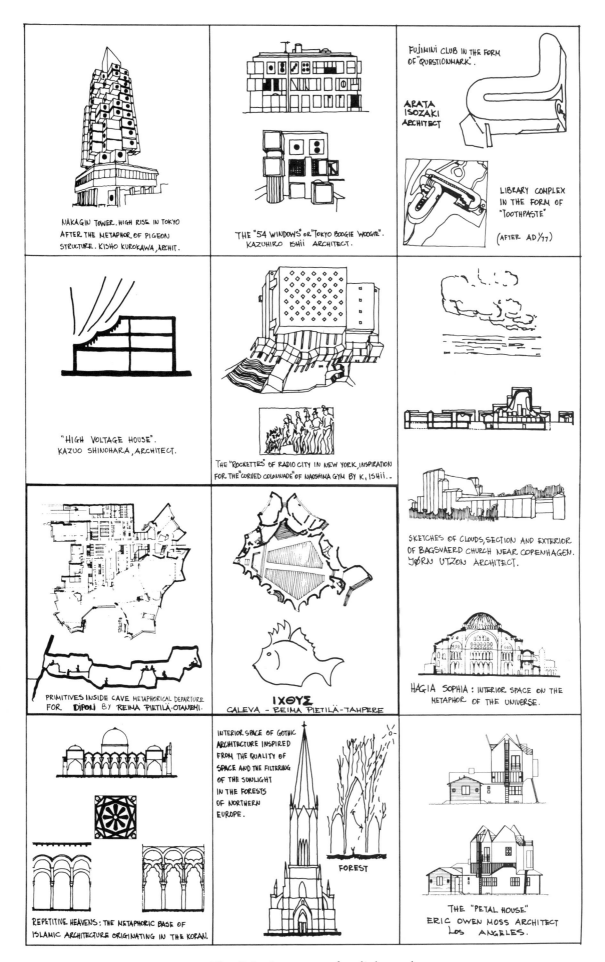

**Fig. 2-6.** *A summary of applied metaphors.*

its petals to the sky, like a flower about to bloom, like the young couple that will bloom and create a family, and add its fruits to the society. This project is clear evidence that metaphors need not be employed only for large-scale projects. Individuals can have an equal voice, and it can be expressed through metaphors in small- or medium-scale projects.

Antoine Predock has proved to be the master of the medium scale, with extraordinary success. Among his numerous metaphorically conceived projects, two are significant for our purposes: the New Mexico Heart Clinic and the Albuquerque Blood Bank. The first announces its destination through the literal iconography of a "beating heart" achieved via stones and mortar. The second building is a case of the multilayered application of metaphor, perhaps the strongest such application we have seen so far. The striking blood-red building, facing the equally striking red sunsets of the Rio Grande Valley to the west, not only signifies blood, the vital ingredient of life, but further on, with its "red on red" against the sunset background, points back to life. The sun that is about to set (like the person who has lost blood) will rise again. The sun cycle is the metaphor for human life.

Architects may not necessarily have had these metaphors in mind; it is after all we who interpret them, and we who use these metaphoric interpretations for our own future creative design purposes. Figure 2-12 is a summary weighting of the significant metaphorically conceived buildings of our time. Further reading, study, and contemplation are necessary to understand the suggested paradigms and to draw our own personal conclusions. Yet we should be receptive to the widely accepted metaphoric interpretations that have come to us through history, tradition or myth, because only through their acceptance will we be able to build for and within the intellectual context of a particular community or people. All people feel comfortable with and proud of the monuments of civilization. They appreciate them and tell stories to their children about the myths that surround their existence. Many such stories or myths are metaphors. Our communal spirituality has been served through the use of metaphors for centuries of history. Most Christian churches were conceived as "the house of God on

**Fig. 2-7.** *The extraordinary Basgvaerd Church near Copenhagen; the metaphor of the heavens is to be discovered in the interior space. Jörn Utzon, architect. (Courtesy Martin Price)*

*A*

*B*

**Fig. 2-8.** *The Kaleva Church by Reima Pietilä; a house of religion for the people of The Kalevala, the Finnish epic, based on a plan with the form of the fish, the early Christian symbol.*

**Fig. 2-9.** *The Stockholm Public Library: a building conceived through the metaphor of the skull, inside which one finds the brain-library, the intellect of the community. Gunnar Asplund, architect.*

**Fig. 2-10.** *New Mexico Heart Clinic. Antoine Predock, architect. A pulsing heart appears on the highway elevation of the building (not visible here). (Photo by Robert Reck, courtesy of the architect)*

**Fig. 2-11.** *Blood Bank, New Mexico: a blood-red building.*

| Architect | Building | Literality | Detectable | Not Detectable | Architect's Secret | Substantial Literality | Detectable | Not Detectable | Architect's Secret | Authentically Substantive Wholesome use of Metaphor |
|---|---|---|---|---|---|---|---|---|---|---|
| Bofill | Red Wall | ● | ● | | | | | | | |
| | Kafka's Castle | ● | ● | | | | | | | |
| | Walden Seven | | | | | | | | | ● |
| Predock | Blood Bank | ● | ● | | | | | | | ● |
| | New Mexico heart clinic | ● | ● | | | | | | | |
| Kurokawa | Nakagin towers | | | | | ● | ● | | | |
| Isozaki | Club | ● | ● | | | | | | | |
| | Library | ● | ● | | | | | | | |
| Ishii | 54 Windows or Tokyo Boogie-Woogie | ● | ● | | | | | | | |
| | Naoshima Gym | | | | | ● | | ● | | |
| Shinohara | House under high voltage line | ● | ● | | | | | | | ● |
| | House in Itoshima | | | | | | | | | ● |
| Zenetos | Amalias | | | | | ● | | ● | | |
| | Glyfada | | | | | ● | ● | | | |
| Scharoun | Berlin Philharmonic | | | | | ● | | ● | | |
| Pietilä | Dipoli | | | | | ● | | ● | | |
| | Kaleva Church | ● | | | | ● | | ● | ● | |
| Asplund | Stockholm Public Library | ● | | | | ● | | | ● | |
| Utzon | Bagsvaerd Church | | | | | ● | | ● | | |
| Aalto | Säynätsalo City Hall | | | | | ● | ● | | | ● |
| | Lapia House | | | | | ● | | | | |
| | Skylights | | | | | | | | | ● |
| Moss | Petal house | | | | | ● | | ● | | ● |

**Fig. 2-12.** *Categorizing and weighting of metaphorically conceived buildings.*

earth''; the dome of Hagia Sophia in Istanbul was conceived as the sky, and
the multiplicity and constellation-like quality of the many domes of Muslim
mosques can been conceived as the constellations of the seven skies about
which the Koran has been so specific. The same can be said of the Gothic
architects who created their miracles through efforts to stimulate the sublime on the metaphor of "light filtering through the leaves of the great trees
of the green forest." (No better reference can be suggested on the topic of
sacred and the spiritual metaphors than *The Sacred and the Profane* by Mircea
Eliade.) Any attempt to combine metaphors with the spiritual, the exotic,
and the multicultural, in geographic and cultural settings that are unfamiliar
to the student or to the architect, using alien stories and myths, may also
result in cases of extraordinary creativity and produce projects and experiences that are invaluable to students. Many of the most pleasing projects
developed and designed by my students had all of these ingredients in their
problem statements.

## APPLIED AND DIDACTIC DIMENSIONS

Metaphor has been used and treated repeatedly throughout the history of
civilization, in language and literature as well as in philosophy and the
creative fields. It has been also used in the teaching of creative architectural
design. Some of the best recent metaphoric conceptions of our world have
been conceived and written about by contemporary philosophers. Allan
Bloom's metaphor of the university for instance, which relates the meaning
and essence of the university to its physical containers and their architecture, the architecture of its fake Gothic buildings, which in spite of their
falsity generate an image of unity and a physical environment suggesting
the unity of the approach to the pursuit of knowledge, should be read by
every design student. Philosophy gave us our first comprehensive focus on

**Fig. 2-13.** *The Ronchamp Chapel by Le Corbusier.*

**Fig. 2-14.** *Dipoli, Student Union Building in Otaniemi; Reima Pietilä, architect.*

the metaphor through Aristotle; now it updates the inquiry for our contemporary purposes through Allan Bloom. Another modern philosopher, Donald Schon of MIT, explored the metaphor theoretically from the standpoint of design and studio instruction needs. After his endorsement of Aristotle, the first teacher on the subject (as he was in so many others), Schon elaborated on Cassirer's concept of the radical metaphor and on its basis he developed the theory of "displacement of concepts." He argued that the metaphor's role in the emergence of new concepts is fundamental. Among other things, Schon pointed out the strength of shifting one's attention from one inquiry into another, of treating "the new as old."

Displacement of concepts occurs whenever we say "architecture as." In each case we make a metaphor: "architecture as music," "architecture as theater," even "architecture as dance." Such metaphorical applications, in spite of their great promise, are very difficult to implement except in a superficial way. Designers who attempt them must be possessed by the extraordinary discipline that is needed to immerse oneself in another field (music, literature). Successful metaphoric involvement of this kind demands a great portion of a person's creative life, and it takes place at critical turning points in the creator's life (such as when an architect turns musician in order to become a better architect, or vice versa, as was the case with Iannis Xenakis, who was Le Corbusier's collaborator before he became a musician.) Because of the extraordinary significance of "large-scale" metaphors like these, we will examine them in separate chapters. Also signifi-

cant for the architect who decides to explore the metaphoric channel is the study of how metaphors are employed in literature and poetry. For the same reasons given above, we will examine these cases separately in other chapters.

**Fig. 2-15.** *Outdoor reading areas, "flowers of concrete." Main library, University of Stockholm; Ralph Erskine, architect.*

## APPROACHING THE METAPHOR

The metaphoric channel has its pluses; it also has minuses. Everything depends on the way we approach it. I believe extreme "esotericity" (an attitude of appearing different and sophisticated), accompanied by attempts to over-intellectualize and create a new language and new terms for metaphors, is not helpful to the creative person. It can create gaps in communication between creatively inclined people, be they instructors, students, architects, or ordinary people. Such attitudes alienate people. This has happened with semiotics, linguistics, and the historicist license of architects in the recent past. It was the esotericity and the overall attitude of the proponents of the various groups that had an adverse effect on communication between creators, rather than the promise of what they were proposing.

Students need not be introduced to intellectual endeavors through intellectual gymnastics; on the contrary, one should start as simply and comprehensibly as possible, and hope that in time one may graduate, through effort and experience, into a truly sophisticated and deeper thinker—what the Greeks call a "stochastic thinker," one who cares for the essentials. Louis Kahn was one of these. His question, "What does the building want to be?" is much simpler and more straightforward than saying, for instance, "What should the coding of this building be?"

The metaphor may be poetic, but the concept that may be generated through it should be meaningful and substantial; this should come about through simple probing and understanding, rather than mental gymnastics. Very simple metaphors, such as the house as a computer or the residence for the single-parent life style conceived in the metaphor of an airplane trip and the related modulated catering would produce much more immediate and imaginative results than metaphors out of a Brechtian drama. Simple metaphors applied after the fact in order to describe human artifacts, such as the metropolis, the cathedral, the head village, or national, geographic, or cultural metaphors such as "the land of the rising sun," the "Red Sea" or the "Black Sea", and the "Silk Road," respectively, have not been looked upon with creative scrutiny in architecture, although some of them have produced great works of art in music, as well as in perfume, fashion, and car design (Chloe, the "smoking" evening costume, the Ford Mustang).

Because Postmodernism, especially Historicist Postmodernism, resorted to metaphor and linguistics for so much of its theoretical and critical interpretations, it produced very little in the way of a welcoming climate for the use of the metaphor as a path to architectural creativity. It put off, frightened, and alienated many architects, instructors, and students. One factor in promoting this adverse reaction was the incomprehensibility of the language and the esoteric "lingo" employed by its theoreticians.

Metaphor has always been with us; and as great minds are simple minds, we should follow the attitudes and paradigms of the great architect-doers, who were also stochastic thinkers, like Aalto, Kahn, Scharoun, Utzon, Pietilä, and Shinohara. Such a route might lead us to a great beginning, rather than attempting to plunge into "the metaphor" by delving into the paradigms of Postmodern historicism or the incomprehensibility of linguistics.

**Fig. 2-16.** *Architect's residence and studio in Albuquerque, New Mexico; Bart Prince, architect.*

## Summary

The metaphoric channel to architectural creativity that views buildings and concepts as if they were something else about which the designer has a more concrete knowledge is treated here in an elementary and systematic way. The channel has been one of the most popular during recent years, and it receives its due theoretical treatment here by casting clarity in the definitions, categorizing and weighting the various metaphors for design purposes, addressing and discussing the use of metaphor by individual architects in the twentieth century, beginning with the origin of the metaphor. Further elucidation is made using metaphorically conceived buildings. Attention also focused on the issues of literality vs. metaphoric essentiality which I consider fundamental for the proper use of the metaphor under any creative circumstances. This chapter ends with suggestions for correct use of metaphor for teaching purposes.

## References

ACSA West Central Regional Meeting. *Fostering Creativity in Architectural Education*, ed. James P. Warfield. Champaign: University of Illinois Press, 1986.

Alberti, Leone Battista. *Ten Books on Architecture*. London: Alec Tiranti Publishers, 1965. Book L, Chap. IX, p. 13.

Ambasz, Emilio. *Houses for Sale*. New York: Rizzoli, 1980, pp. 4–16, 102–114.

Antoniades, Anthony C. "Evolution of the Red." *A + U Architecture and Urbanism*, September 1983, p. 393.

———. "Antoine Predock: un caso d' 'inclusivita syntetica' " with English translation, "Antoine Predock: A Case of Synthetic Inclusivity." *L'architettura*, no. 401 (March 1989), pp. 178–198.

Beeby, Thomas. Lecture series. University of Texas at Arlington, 1983.

Blundell, Peter Jones. *Hans Scharoun*. London: Gordon Fraser, 1978, p. 36.

Bloom, Allan. *The Closing of the American Mind*. New York: Simon and Schuster, 1987.

Bognar, Botond. *Contemporary Japanese Architecture*. New York: Van Nostrand Reinhold, 1985.

Broadbent, G. H. "Bofill." *Progressive Architecture*, September 1975.

Cassirer, Ernst. *The Problem of Knowledge*. New Haven, CT: Yale University Press, 1950.

Conrads, Ulrich, and Hans G. Sperlich. *The Architecture of Fantasy*. New York: Praeger, 1962.

Eliade, Mircea. *The Sacred and the Profane*. New York: Harcourt, Brace and World, 1959.

Greene, Herb. *Mind and Image*. Lexington, KY: The University of Kentucky Press, 1976, p. 109.

Isozaki, Arata. "Eros or the Sea." In *GA11, Couvent Sainte-Marie de la Tourette*, ed. Yukio Fukagawa. Tokyo, 1971.

Lemagny, J. C. *Visionary Architects: Boullee, Ledoux, Lequeu*. Houston: Gulf Print Company, 1968.

Machado, Rodolfo. "Images." *VIA 8*, 1986.

Pehnt, Wolfgang. *Expressionist Architecture*. London: Thames & Hudson, 1973, pp. 41–42.

Porphyrios, Demetri. *Sources of Modern Eclecticism*. London: St. Martin's Press, 1981, pp. 113–115.

Sanderson, Warren. "Kazuo Shinohara's 'Savage Machine' and the Place of Tradition in Modern Japanese Architecture." *Journal of the Society of Architectural Historians,* 43, 2 (May 1984), pp. 109–118.

Schon, Donald A. *Displacement of Concepts*. London: Tavistock Publications, 1963, pp. 42, 37, 34, xii.

———. *Technology and Change*. New York: Delacorte Press, 1967.

———. "The Architecture Studio as an Exemplar of Education for Reflection in Action." *Journal of Architectural Education*, 38, 1 (Fall 1984), pp. 2, 5, 9.

Sontag, Susan. *Illness as a Metaphor*. New York: Farrar, Strauss, 1977, pp. 32, 33.

Tanizaki, Jun'ichiro. *In Praise of Shadows*. Leete's Island Books, 1977, pp. 7, 9, 15.

Wolin, Judith. "The Rhetorical Question." *VIA 8, Journal of the Graduate School of Fine Arts, University of Pennsylvania,* 1986, pp. 24, 30.

Wurman, Saul Richard. *The Words of Louis L. Kahn*. New York: Access Press and Rizzoli, 1986.

# Chapter 3 Paradoxes and Metaphysics

*Channels to Creativity*

*And May God deny you peace
but give you glory.*

Don Miguel de Unamuno

## THE BROADEST PARADOX

Within the context of the generally accepted attitude that the role of the architect is to build, it sounds unreasonable to expect architects to occupy themselves with the question of buildings that cannot be built, no matter how imaginative their design. The logical conclusion is that the "unbuildable" building should not be any concern of the architect, who, after all, is focused on building actual structures. Yet much of the evolution of the discipline of architecture is the result of a paradox: The progress of the "buildable" depends in fact on explorations into the "unbuildable." In order to build better in the future, you must not build in the present. To put it in a more abstract and direct way: "In order to build you must not build." Architects through the ages have understood and embraced this dilemma. Others (including architects) have classified these people as visionaries or scholars, rather than builders. As a rule public opinion rewards those who build, even though they may build badly. But the quality and evolution of architecture depends on an insistence among architects that they contemplate this paradox and consider choices such as these: today vs. tomorrow, bad vs. potentially excellent, here and now on earth vs. in heaven.

John Hejduk, the very influential design instructor and chairman at Cooper Union in New York, wrote in praise of the efforts of Daniel Libeskind years before he won the international award for the Jewish Museum in Berlin: "He has plunged his hand up into heavens and has caught some stars and at the moment of his contact the stars have turned to metal and have achieved weight and our universe has turned to the density of a pewter reflecting a light unseen before" (Hejduk, in Libeskind, 1981). Even if Libeskind had never intended to build (and his award-winning project for the expansion of the Jewish Museum in Berlin was the proof that he wanted to build all along), his effort to "grasp the stars" would have been worthwhile, even if it resulted just in inspiring Hejduk. And even if he and Hejduk, or Eisenman and Aldo Rossi, were never to attempt to build their visions, the rest of us would certainly have gained. Someone would probably have eventually made their visions reality. Their loss would have made for a poorer world, and a poorer architecture.

The paradoxical as well as the metaphysical can form a very powerful channel for architectural creativity, provided we realize that the concepts of "today" and "tomorrow" are not mutually exclusive. On the contrary, they are complementary. Architects in order to build on the earth today should look to the stars and to tomorrow. To do this of course requires a lot more work, something we expect from those who approach their profession as a vocation. Paradox originates from a Greek verb that refers to the understanding (or the concept) a person has of a particular entity (idea or object). What is logical is understood to be the conclusion at which most people arrive with regard to a particular issue, based on assumptions generally accepted by the majority. Yet what is often accepted as "logical" may not necessarily be true, if the assumptions on which it is based are wrong. A paradox is also called antinomy (*antinomia*), which means against the law when "law" is understood as the commonly accepted truth. Historically, the paradox has been employed by philosophers, social critics, scientists, and politicians as a means to criticize and to illustrate a critical point, while suggesting alternate ways of doing things. It required erudite receptors, it was vested with certain degree of irony, it had in it the ingredient of humor, and while its subject matter was secular, it often sought the divine. Nobody would criticize an architect who has built if he were to say: Architects don't know how to build. The paradoxical, in other words, affords one the license to criticize from within.

Paradoxical statements often bring together whole sets of ideas with regard to existing "knowledge" and "truth" as seen by the one who makes the statement. Paradox is apparently a sound proof of an unacceptable conclusion. It is a statement that appears to be contradictory and seemingly says two different things which may even sound absurd, but which is nevertheless true and often sublime.

Another view of the term is related to the idea of the obscure (that which is there, hibernating, yet nobody looks for it); yet the paradox as a channel to architectural creativity is tactically different from the "obscure" (which is another channel to creativity) because it constitutes a disciplined confrontation with society and widely accepted ways of doing things. The obscure represents a search into corners where society would not bother to look (or invest money). In this sense, the paradoxical route to creativity has in it the element of confrontation. It stirs up public opinion, objections, and heated debate. One could therefore say that paradox is not only suited to democratic societies, but also necessary for the evolution of their architecture. The most common tension between society and those who create through paradox is condemnation of the latter. Those who use the channel of the obscure find no such tensions, as people generally take the attitude that those who search in obscure corners are best left to themselves.

So the paradox is a very demanding route to creativity; the tensions and the dangers of a personal and psychological nature require the investment of extra discipline, extra articulateness, and greater knowledge in order to defend one's position. These creators are the advocates for a New World. They should therefore know all the practices and prejudices of the old. They must rise from David to Goliath in order to confront and defeat him. The weapon of such an architect is education, hard work, talent, and persistence. Such an architect's life can be seen metaphorically in biblical terms, since he must take the attitude that weakness is strength (his weakness is his strength), that their gain is his loss, that in order to build you must not build.

In purely architectural terms, he may have to operate with similarly paradoxical statements such as these:

The presence of absence
The absence of presence
To construct is to de-construct
To compose is to de-compose
A city of life for the city of the dead

An inherent paradox of the paradoxical route as practiced by its follow-ers is that despite its goal of rectifying things, it is totally incomprehensible to those who need to make the change; so instead of helping to solve problems, it creates more problems and enlarges the gap between society and creators. There is a need for simplification and communication. The architect must make an extra effort, if his other real goal is to help improve things and come up with relevant and improved designs. So this architect should talk about the paradoxical route in non-paradoxical terms. First and foremost, he should declare his regard for the people he is designing for; he should try to understand them, to enter their minds and hearts and see things as they do. His primary task would be to discover their primordial roots, to study the framework of their metaphysics. After all, if he is one of them, it should be his metaphysics as well.

## THE METAPHYSICAL INQUIRY

Metaphysics deals with the unknown. It contemplates whatever lies beyond the physical—everything that lies beyond the grasp of science and the boundaries of logic. Its overall focus is the concepts of "infinity" and "God."

Metaphysics has been pursued historically by two major groups of people: philosophers, who for our purposes will represent what we call the "conventional wisdom group," and an array of others, such as magicians, alchemists, members of secret orders, theosophists, parapsychologists, and representatives of the (secret) sciences of the past. These two groups have approached metaphysics in two fundamentally different ways, and in the difference lies the key to the proper appreciation and the use of metaphysics for architectural purposes.

The second group claimed they knew what "was there," what awaited humans after death, for instance; they knew but kept it "secret," to reveal it only to their equals, the other magicians, the other alchemists, the mem-bers of the secret order, the Cabala or the clan. There has obviously been tension between them and the main body of society, which embraces as a whole and has been guided in general by the views of the prevailing philo-sophical system, whatever it may be. Those who hold to the prevailing ideas, and more often the authorities, will denigrate metaphysics and the "secret sciences" in general as difficult to comprehend, unclear, enigmatic, unduly mysterious. As we will see, the same two groups of metaphysicians also exist in architecture.

The goal of metaphysics, whether through philosophy or through the other inquiries, is to grasp and interpret the unknown; the main position of philosophy, however (and in consequence its fundamental difference from the metaphysics of the other group), is that metaphysics by definition can never "grasp" anything because *it is always in the process of a beginning* (Kanellopoulos, 1956). According to its students, metaphysics is always at the stage of introduction. It never becomes sure about its probes, and it is never conclusive because it never finds what it is after. It exists only as an overlap between philosophy and theology; the central concern of meta-physics is "reaching God," the understanding and explanation of the divine essence.

Major philosophers and theologians since Plato, Pythagoras, and Aristotle have all been concerned with metaphysics. Aristotle attempted to explain everything, even the "inexplicable," via the use of logic. Plato and the Pythagoreans, although they used logic, gave priority to "*intuition*" as opposed to what they called "*cold logic.*" The Pythagoreans in a sense started the debate between feeling and logic, something that was to occupy architects repeatedly during this century.

For all metaphysicians, the contemplation of the ideas of space and time is a central topic of the metaphysical inquiry. Space, of course, is also a key concern in architecture. In fact, it has been held that "architecture is born in man when he becomes conscious of the infinity of space and the inevitability of death" (Kanellopoulos, 1956). Contemplating architectural space, therefore, its qualities, its finite versus its infinite states, as well as probing the absolute, or its eternal qualities, in relationship to the central preoccupation of life, which is death, is the central topic of the metaphysics of architecture. We could therefore suggest that metaphysics is the eternal state of introduction, the ongoing invigorating struggle of architectural aesthetics to find what perhaps is there, what is perhaps the ultimate architectural space, the thus far "unknown" state of architectural excellence, the divine in architecture. Much of the struggle of truly creative architects, the waiting, the sacrifices, and the dedication, goes into the search for the "unknown."

In the broader context, the metaphysical inquiry plays the role of catalyst in terms of the paradoxical channel to creativity, for it deals with the scrutiny of the validity of our suppositions about the "unknown" ingredients of space and architecture as they relate to other great unknowns, such as life and death. It compares our suggestions to the generally accepted wisdom; it probes spheres beyond the physical and eventually develops a theory of its own "new world," the new reality of the imagination.

- What do people think about things?
- What are the prevailing concepts?
- How would our suggestions affect the real and the unreal, physical versus the nonphysical, life versus death?

It is obvious that questions of this kind require philosophical probing and higher degrees of debate. From our own point of view, the final probe will have to do with the implementability of the suggestions, while the *ultimate critical test* will have to take place after the realization of the design, if such a design can be physically built with our current resources.

Probing ideas through the catalyst of metaphysics may therefore have a dual outcome, a realistic conclusion or an impossibility. The critical evaluation of the realized work will have to do with the degree to which the solutions celebrate life as opposed to the paradoxical departure from the opposite, say, death. In this sense the paradoxical route to architectural creativity is a minuet between opposites, and paradoxically enough, not a paradox. The paradoxical channel plays a dominant role in the fantasy-imagination process and is perhaps one of the more promising means for new discoveries, even though these discoveries may have to wait to be implemented (see Figure 3-1).

Assuming the inconclusivity of metaphysics, and assuming a relationship between metaphysics in general and architectural metaphysics, we can safely say that "metaphysical architecture" can never be built. Its physical ideas will be only approximations, introductions to a new direction. Because if it is built, it becomes part of the science, the history, and the practice of architecture; it becomes known, and thus is no longer metaphysics.

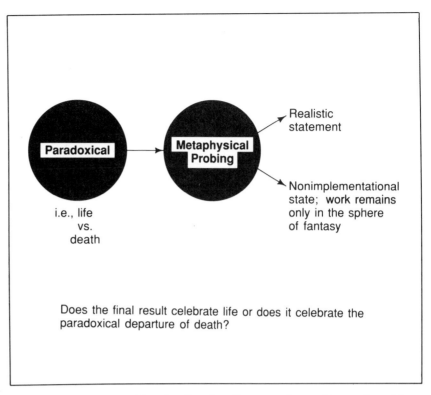

Realistic
statement

Paradoxical

Metaphysical
Probing

Nonimplementational
state; **work remains
only in the sphere
of fantasy**

i.e., life
vs.
death

Does the final result celebrate life or does it celebrate the
paradoxical departure of death?

**Fig. 3-1.** *The paradoxical and the meta-physical: possibilities and attitudes.*

Some architects, like the Russian Supremacist architects Leonidov, Malevitch, and Feodorov, either through personal inclination or because of outside circumstances, remained at the philosophical level, and always qualified as true explorers into the realm of the metaphysical and the ideal. There was nothing more moving and aesthetically pleasing for me in the Malevitch exhibition at the Staedelijk Museum in Amsterdam in the summer of 1989, than the large black and white photograph showing the body of Malevitch lying in state, covered by a white sheet, in eternal serenity, surrounded by his art work in his studio. It was an image he had conceived while alive. More recent architects such as Peter Eisenman and Aldo Rossi, who also invested long periods of their lives in exploring and discovering the form of their world views of infinite vs. finite space in relationship to life and death, went beyond the stage of contemplation and began to build. When they started building, they stopped qualifying as metaphysicians in the philosophically accepted sense. If John Hejduk, Daniel Libeskind, Massimo Scolari, or Zaha Hadid start to build, they will stop being considered metaphysicians as well. The truly metaphysical architects are those who devote themselves to contemplation of the "unknown," who probe and suggest designs based on its imagery and do not make buildings out of them. And here is one of the major paradoxes of architecture, a paradox within a paradox: We advocate the need for a channel of the "impossible," while we also take the position that architecture means to build. If it is so, then why do we want metaphysics, since we know it cannot be grasped, it is inconclusive, it has no end, it is always in the state of beginning?

The answer is simple: We do not want the architect to become a metaphysician; we want him always to be an architect, a builder-architect, that is. We want someone who will probe into metaphysics—as well as into everything else—yet who will always stop, contrast the suppositions of his probing to the constraints of reality, and convert his learning into a building. We want the architect to be an *adjuster,* a person who will see the impossibilities of the absolute and be satisfied by the mere effort to reach it. At the same time he will be able to perform thoughtful compromises that will permit an implementation of this "absolute conception." In this sense, his projects will always be a point of departure for another "compromise" via a new search into the sphere of the unknown, and the revised statement of another new building.

Architects of this metaphysical-paradoxical channel are creators who could perhaps be compared to the alchemists, who claimed that they had found the truth, only they had really found very little—perhaps nothing. The point is that *they had dared* to consider something others would not even attempt. Yet civilization, as we know, has advanced through the contributions of alchemists. Conventional wisdom is occasionally wrong (as it was so for so many centuries about the universe), while the ideas of the alchemist are eventually proved right (as was the case with the explanation offered by Galileo). We could suggest that architectural metaphysics is the touchstone of architectural progress, for as the art advances step by step, each step becomes a new reality, a new beginning.

It is the training in the speculative, the drawing and the making of models of unbuildable projects, that sharpens the brain to understand the virtually and eternally inexplicable. The discipline that will turn the thinker into an architect is the conventional wisdom, everything that has been proved to be buildable, the approved way of doing things. Kahn, Eisenman, Rossi, and Gehry are architects. Some go back and forth, (Rossi, Eisenman) spending more time in contemplation than others. They build less. Those who build more have less time for exploration.

Paradox and metaphysics represent, in a sense, the test of the strength and ambition of the architect with regard to quantity vs. quality. The architect thinks and waits for his time. Reima Pietilä waited twenty years for his time to come; so did a score of others, such as Aldo Rossi, Peter Eisenman, and Feodorov and Frank Lloyd Wright in earlier times. It requires extraordinary strength to be able to operate outside the existing framework, to be in constant conflict with the prevailing notions. It takes extraordinary courage, self-denial, and personal sacrifice to spend more time on thought than on practice. Thought also "costs" the creator time and money. If the architect, who should build, thinks more and builds less, the world will become a much better place. More creative architects will have an opportunity to take more part in its construction. The world, after all, is the best we can do at any given point in time; it is the compromise between the vulgar and the divine.

## PARADOX AND METAPHYSICS IN ACTUALITY

The paradox is indeed a channel to immortality. And we have already admitted that it is good to be ambitious, to want to become immortal. There is no better precedent in this respect than the example offered by the late Spanish philosopher Don Miguel de Unamuno. He devoted his life to the questioning and exploration of paradoxes concerning issues of everyday life as well as eternity. In addition to the major body of his philosophical work, he produced a series of extremely well-crafted stories, case studies on the possibilities of the paradox. The heroes of these stories are not generally accepted by society; on the contrary, society ignores the possibility of their potential as human beings. As created by Unamuno, they are even fresher, more human, and superior to most of the other members of society. Unamuno's characters are "men," real men of flesh and bones who die and who struggle against death. As Anthony Kerrigan said (1956, p. xv) "The madness of busy imaginative man attracted Unamuno's sympathy. . . . He always considered Don Quixote more real than Cervantes . . . closer to immortality." Unamuno's effort revolved around the idea of creation; his heroes, results of his own imagination and creativity, suddenly stop the action and confront the author, demanding to know which of the two is more "real"! The character, the creation, or the author, the creator? "So I have to die as a fictitious being? All right, my Lord creator, Don Miguel de Unamuno. You too will die and return to the nothing whence you come. God will cease to dream you" (Kerrigan, 1956, p. xvi).

## UNAMUNO AND DON QUIXOTISM

Unamuno has a unique significance for creativity and creative people. For him, to defy death is to become immortal, and immortality can be achieved only through the deeds of man, even through the ridiculous. This ridicule is not accepted by the masses; it is hidden, undiscovered, obscure; it is extremely paradoxical to create heroes out of the "ridiculous."

Don Quixote achieved immortality through this ridicule. Don Quixotism, a theory developed by Unamuno after the study of Cervantes' major hero, represents in a way the best precedent any creative person may have regarding the possibility of a search through channels unacceptable to the masses and conventional society. Unamuno should be considered one of the most important personalities of our century because he suggested a concrete path to unique and previously unexplored territories. He searched for new situations in life. It is indeed a new situation for a conventional ear to hear the philosopher's ultimate belief regarding a disciplined life style and life process: He wishes all people this: "And may God deny you peace but give you glory."

## CONTEMPORARY QUIXOTISM IN ARCHITECTURE

It is certain that one may not have peace when attempting to explore ideas and concepts outside the usual. The status quo is threatened, and so is the construction industry and the building codes. One should have courage in order to create. To attempt explorations through disciplined exercises that might be described by others as ridiculous may certainly produce discoveries, by the mere fact that nobody else has dared to approach a problem in these terms. There is a chance to perhaps find what was already there. The paradoxical and the ridiculous, which is often a by-product of the former, can be among the most promising means to creativity. History, especially recent history, provides us with a whole stock of examples (see Fig. 3-2).

Isn't it paradoxical that the visions of the Constructivists, the visions and forms created by a young group of architects who had embraced the Communist ideology and were creating in early postrevolutionary Russia, became reality many years later through some other young architects, the members of Arquitectonica, a successful architectural partnership operating within the capitalist system? The paradox lies in the proposition that the creation of a luxurious capitalist office building can be realized through reference to formal and synthetic models of another era and of another system totally outside what is generally accepted as appropriate by capitalist clients. Now is this the paradox, or is it perhaps the mere discovery that the profit-oriented goal of the capitalist developer could be best met through models of systematically ordered and technologically efficient architecture like those invented by the Constructivists? Whatever the case may be, we would not have the recent large-scale projects of Arquitectonica if we did not have the paradoxical reference to the work of the Russian Constructivists. Nor would we have the two projects of Ricardo Bofill in St. Quentin-Yvellin (The Arcades of the Lake and the Aqueduct) if Bofill had not attempted to offer low-income residents a collective habitation that would resemble in concept and "style" the palace of Versailles. It is paradoxical to make a house for the poor that resembles the palace of a king,

"THE PARADOXICAL" WILL NOT BE ENCOUNTERED IN THE "MAIN TRAFFIC". IT HIBERNATES "HIDDEN" IN THE ALLEY.

"DON-QUIXOTISM" BY MIGUEL DE-UNAMUNO: POSSIBILITY FOR A CREATIVITY CHANNEL.

PROPOSAL FOR THE MONUMENT OF "SOVIET" INDUSTRY (ABOVE). PROPOSAL FOR "CAPITALIST" OFFICE BUILDING (BELOW).

LAKE

"THE ARCADES OF THE LAKE" BY RICARDO BOFILL.

THE TERRACE OF THE "CASA MILA" BY GAUDI.

AFTER GIORGIO DE CHIRICO "THE ENIGMA OF A DAY IN 1914"

U.S.A. PAVILION IN THE EXPO OF MONTREAL R. BUCKMINSTER FULLER, ARCHITECT.

EXERCISES IN OPTIMISM THROUGH PARADOXICAL AND OBSCURE SUGGESTIONS: FULLER'S SUGGESTIONS REGARDING THE POPULATION OF THE EARTH AND THE "NINE CHAINS TO THE MOON"

"GLOBAL THEATER" BY ALDO ROSSI (AFTER PHOTOGRAPH OF THE WORK).

SOCIAL CENTER BY LEO KRIER IN ST. PETER'S SQUARE. (AFTER LEO KRIER'S PROPOSALS IN "ROMA INTERROTTA".

FREE OPEN SPACE/PUBLIC BUILDING. FROM PROPOSALS BY LEO KRIER IN "ROMA INTERROTTA".

PROPOSAL FOR A BRANCH BUILDING OF THE "BEST" PRODUCTS. IS THE "BEST" THE ILLOGICAL? CREATION BY SITE

"SLEEPING SONATA" FROM "THE SLEEPING LABORATORY" OF THE "GREEN CITY" PROPOSAL BY SOVIET ARCHITECT CONSTANTIN MELNIKOV. THE SLOPE OF THE BUILDING WOULD HELP ECONOMIZE PILLOWS!

**Fig. 3-2.** *Some paradoxico-metaphysical cases.*

yet it is always a good idea to sharpen one's mind and sketching abilities around the proposition of creating such a collective palace.

It is paradoxical to encounter noble and great deeds, deeds of noblemen and knights, performed by a person of folk stock. Yet Don Quixote is the proof that this can happen, at least as Cervantes imagined it. We would not have Don Quixote if Cervantes had not let his imagination loose on the paradoxical. Unamuno argues that all Spaniards, like Don Quixote, would attempt to immortalize themselves. But Don Quixote does not ensure the continuation of his name by making ten legitimate children, as the Catholic Church may have wanted him to do; he does it through his battles with windmills and other similarly unexpected "deeds."

Don Quixotism, a theory of the progress to immortality through a questioning of issues to do with life and death, is Unamuno's metaphysics. It is certainly metaphysics because it confronts questions beyond the physical existence. Questioning death is one of the major preoccupations of metaphysics. It is paradoxical that while one probes death, one makes discoveries about life and takes positions on its quality and character.

Some of the major minds of our century, great contributors to art and to science, struggled with metaphysical questions and developed their creative positions through such probing. Giorgio De Chirico did this through his preoccupation with antiquity and the human conditions of departure and the eternal return. Buckminster Fuller did it in numerous fields, such as mathematics, architecture, and poetry. Fuller, an applied inventor and abstract philosopher, frequently resorted to metaphysics, to the paradoxical and sometimes the macabre. Much of his contribution had to do with his ability to communicate complex and complicated issues to the ordinary person. He made use of obscure paradigms no other person had thought of before. "Nine chains to the moon," for example, was a new way of telling people that the distance between the earth and the moon would be equal to nine chains, each one equal to the length of the whole population of the earth when one individual sits on the shoulders of another. The immensity of the distance can easily be visualized through creative explanations that use obscure (and intuitive) means for their articulation. In certain instances, Fuller used the macabre to serve his purpose. In order to convince us that, after all, we are not so many on this planet, despite the claims of others, he said that one could cram the whole population of the earth into 114 Empire State Buildings; but if we were to take the water out of human bodies and compress what remained, all we would need would be one Empire State Building. It is paradoxical to care about life and yet to talk about it through macabre examples. Herein lies Buckminster Fuller's creative genius, his ability to communicate. His life was a continuous exercise in the task of creation. And it is clear that constant preoccupation with ideas, doubts, and mental travels in corners others would not think to search, along with a continuous dialogue with oneself, are absolutely necessary for creative work. Fuller's sketches on synergetics go back to 1948, whereas the publication of his landmark book on the topic did not take place until 1976. Buckminster Fuller certainly had peace with himself throughout these years; he certainly has glory now.

Closer at home are architects such as Aldo Rossi, Massimo Scolari, Daniel Libeskind, John Hejduk, Peter Eisenman, Frank Gehry, and Zaha Hadid. All have employed the paradox in its most "architecturally alchemical" expression. Their degree of metaphysical involvement varies: some pay more attention to words, to literature, and fiction (Hejduk, Libeskind, Rossi); others such as Scolari focus on the seductive power of drawing. Gehry focuses mostly on materials and geometry. Hadid has been totally devoted to geometry and the oblique. Eisenman, perhaps the exemplar, and at the same time more of a pragmatist than the others, has created through the paradox in an inarticulate and difficult to comprehend manner.

This whole route to architectural creativity was given to us through the work and writings of these architects. They referred to each other, creating an inner circle that could hardly be encroached upon by others, their audience included. One of the earliest references in recent literature to the paradox was made by Daniel Libeskind in his critical essay on Aldo Rossi's "Theater of the World." Libeskind observed: "In a world bereft of transcendence, the practice of architecture, like the culture it embodies, is irremediably caught between the paradoxical alternatives of unreason and the ardent faith in a salvation through knowledge" (Libeskind, 1981, p. 3). Yet Rossi's paradoxical beginnings first appeared in his competition entry for the Modena Cemetery, where he approached death through the concept of life. The whole design was based on the concept of an abandoned house, desolate and deserted. The reversal of concepts of the roles of life as death and death as life, yet at the same time a life devoid of life, is paradoxical indeed.

Unlike Rossi, Scolari's overall paradox is that he seeks life through *hypnos,* the concept of oblivion and sleep, a concept contrary to the perception of the status quo and society at large that conceives of creation as the product of sleepless energy, action, and work. Wasn't it equally paradoxical when Constantine Melnikov proposed a "sleeping laboratory" for a society (the Communist in the USSR) whose emphasis was on work. Indeed, it was a paradox within a paradox: Melnikov's project was the creation of his work, which was supposed to be what Russian society wanted—work.

All these examples bring us finally to Libeskind's "sticks and pikes," the nails and chaos, all of which, if nothing else, disturb the pragmatic framework of spatial conditioning. Libeskind's sticks and pikes, metaphorical pricks to pragmatist sensibility, are "heavenly constellations" in the Hejduk interpretation. And Peter Eisenman wrote: "Few ideas have been built. Few buildings are anything than the latest mode of shape making." How then can we avoid the predicament of shape making, avoid the Libeskind or the Hadid morphology, and do buildings that display the richness and the originality of the paradoxical, while at the same time achieve the pragmatic goal of "buildability"? We've already answered this question. Now we will go a little further by suggesting two possible ways of doing it.

## BEYOND ALCHEMY

It is easy to copy Libeskind, Hadid, or Hejduk. Yet it is difficult to adhere to the principles and be essentially original as these creators were, without being simply a shape maker, essentially phony, or even a lighthearted plagiarist. Direct, literal efforts to develop projects derivative of the iconographic identity of the projects of those one admires will not make original works. The next possibility is literally to depict through form the contention of the paradox, the "pikes," for instance. Although this may be fine symbolically, since the pikes or the nails have a very strong symbolic meaning, it is nothing more than the expression of an abstraction. Even in the Libeskind project, one would have to wonder how all this is to become "building" as opposed to staying an illegible, chaotic garden, to be seen only by planes taking off from Berlin.

The answer is communicated only through projects conceived via the "paradoxico-metaphysical" route taken by Eisenman, Gaudi, Bofill, and Gehry, interpreted through drawings and conventional building practices. Of course one has to be very cautious in this endorsement, as it does not represent a critical evaluation on my part; I just illustrate an attitude. In this respect I believe Gehry to have been so far the most convincing, because if we accept the definition of the paradox as something that was always there, then Gehry's architecture is the best application of this concept. Take, for instance, his own personal house in Santa Monica—or any other frame house for that matter. Such houses have always "been there," but people took no time to "see" them. Gehry peels off the skin, tears the house apart to see what is inside. He searches it as if it were a child's toy; he actually "de-constructs" it. Deconstructivism here is as understood and performed by an architect, and not as initially conceived as a philosophical system of organization, systematization, and restructuring by the French philosopher Jacques Derrida in the late 1960s.

It is all certainly paradoxical, and it is certainly the place where conventional criticism comes into the picture. Because if "creativity" is joy, then to destruct is, in the Gehry (and also in the Eisenman) case, creative. Here is one of the critical liabilities of these particular efforts, all of which gave rise to architectural Deconstructivism. Destruction can easily lead to decapitation, choking. To what extent could an instrument of death such as a knife produce life? Gehry, along with Claes Oldenburg, proposed, among other things, a "knife"-looking building for their Venice Biennale project. To what extent could one produce nobility and comfort through the paradox? To what extent could concepts such as death, crime, and sadism, be useful for the creation of works aimed at the opposite? Jean Genet proved that it could be done. He brought poetry out of trash, sainthood out of crime.

**Fig. 3-3.** *Resting place for Bishop Atesis: an exotic and multicultural project of paradoxical foundation and metaphysical intentions. Design by Ernest Millican; the author's second-year design studio, 1984.*

It is the intellectual interpretation of concepts such as these and the mental struggle of the creator that will eventually produce each individual answer. It is the strength and the basic architectural discipline that must eventually channel all the mental searching from the oceans of the paradox and the metaphysics into the harbor of implementable reality: structure,

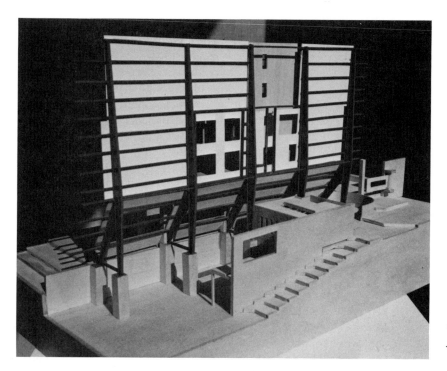

**Fig. 3-4.** *What more paradoxical than asking someone to design a house along the lines of an outdoor movie theater, to reconcile the antithetical concepts of "loud" and "quiet." Yet the inventive student will discover abandoned outdoor theaters and will learn from the forms and the rhythms of these extraordinary structures, creating in the process unique functional "infills" to enrich with life an otherwise decaying outdoors. Model of project by David Caves, from the third-year design class of George Gintole, UT Arlington, 1987.*

order, rhythm, proportion, scale, and all the other elements of the discipline. It is because of this complexity that the channel of the paradoxical and metaphysical is considered one into which one "graduates" as one grows more "design mature" and experienced, as one gets older. One should not want to be left out of architecture if one wants to become an architect.

Both paradoxical exploration and metaphysical contemplation are integral ingredients of a channel of architectural creativity that brings us closer to the divine. Yet both are difficult, and exceptionally dangerous; their waters are filled with Sirens and treacherous shoals. Lucky are the students who will find a truly "metaphysical" teacher. Lucky is the city whose architects have been trained in this channel.

Isn't it perhaps paradoxical that Berlin, a divided city for over twenty years, and all that it implies (oppression, memories of death and persecution) became, by the late twentieth century, the laboratory for the liberation of architectural ideas and the testing of the architecture of the obscure? One certainly does not want any more divided Berlins, but one would certainly hope for more such architectural laboratories.

## Summary

In this chapter, two intangible and fluid concepts, paradox and metaphysics, are defined for their application in architecture in the broader context of philosophy and other fields. Both are considered to be complementary ingredients of a highly promising, but also easily misapplied, channel to architectural creativity. The paradoxico-metaphysical theory of Don Quixotism proposed by the Spanish philosopher Miguel de Unamuno is one inspiration and challenge for architects. Those who have created works using this channel are also discussed in this chapter, which closes with some warnings about the need for maturity and a belief in the role of the architect as a builder as prerequisites to using this particular channel.

# References

Arnold, John. "Creativity in Engineering," in *Creativity*, ed. Paul Smith, New York: Hastings House, 1959, p. 44.

Bofill, Ricardo. *L'Architecture d'un homme*. Interviews with François Hebert-Stevens. Paris: Arthaud, 1978.

De Chirico, Giorgio. *Amamneses apo ten Joe mou* (Memories of My Life). Milan: Rizzoli, 1962; Greek edition, Ypsilon, 1985, p. 89.

Fuller, Buckminster. *Nine Chains to the Moon*. Carbondale: Southern Illinois University Press, Arcturus Books Division, ca. 1963.

Eisenman, Peter. "Yellow Brick Road, It May Not Lead to Golders Green." *Oppositions*, no. 1 (September 1973), p. 28.

―――. *House X*. New York: Rizzoli, 1982.

Esslin, Martin. *Antonin Artaud*. Middlesex, Eng.: Penguin Modern Masters, 1976, p. 131.

Flanagan, Owen J., Jr. *The Science of the Mind*. Cambridge, MA: MIT Press, 1984, pp. 77–81.

Hofstadter, Douglas R., and Dennett, Daniel C. *The Mind's I*. New York: Bantam Books, 1981.

Hejduk, John. Preface. In Libeskind, Daniel, *Between Zero and Infinity*. New York: Rizzoli, 1981.

―――. "Vier Entwurfe: Theatre Masque, Berlin Masque, Lancaster/Lanover Masque, Devil's Bridge." Publication in Rahmen der Ausstellung an der eth. Zurich, 1983.

Ingraham, Catherine. "Slow Dancing: Architecture in the Embrace of Poststructuralism." *Inland Architect*, September–October 1987.

―――. "Milking Deconstruction or Cow Was the Show?" *Inland Architect*, September–October 1988.

Juha, Ilonen. Avoimen taivaan Berlini: Daniel Libeskind Lavistaa ilmakehan. *Arkkitehti*, 1, 1988, pp. 24–33.

Kanellopoulos, Pan. *Metaphysikes Prolegomena: o Anthropos-o Kosmos-o Theos* (Introduction to Metaphysics: Man-Cosmos-God). Athens, 1956.

Kerrigan, Anthony. Introduction. In Unamuno, Miguel de, *Tragic Sense of Life*. New York: Dover Publications, 1954.

Libeskind, Daniel. "Deus ex Machina/Machina ex Deo: Aldo Rossi's Theater of the World." *Oppositions* No. 21, MIT Press, Summer, 1981, p. 3.

―――. *Between Zero and Infinity*. New York: Rizzoli, 1981, p.7.

Lissitzky, El. *Russia: An Architecture for World Revolution*. Trans. Eric Dluhosch. London: Lund Humphries, 1970, p.67.

Mackie, J. L. *Truth, Probability and Paradox: Studies in Philosophical Logic*. Oxford: Clarendon Press, 1973, pp. 23, 25, 27, 296, 297.

Maddi, Salvatore R. "The Strenuousness of the Creative Life." In *Perspectives in Creativity*, ed. Taylor and Getzels. Chicago: Aldine, 1975, pp. 173–187.

Marvel, Bill. "The Architecture of Frank Gehry." *The Dallas Morning News*, February 16, 1987, p. 6C.

May, Rollo. *The Courage to Create*. New York: W. W. Norton, 1975, pp. 14, 30.

Rella, Franco. In Massimo Scolari, *Hypnos*. New York: Rizzoli, 1986.

Rossi, Aldo. "The Blue of the Sky: Modena Cemetery, 1971 and 1977." In *Free Style Classicism*, 1982.

Sassaki, Hiroshi. "The Best of the Constructivists: Tchernykhov and His Design." *Process Architecture*, No. 26, Tokyo, 1981, p. 14.

Scolari, Massimo. *Hypnos*. New York: Rizzoli, 1986.

Starr, Frederick. *Melnikov: Solo Architect in a Mass Society*. Princeton, NJ: Princeton University Press, 1978.

Tchernykhov, Jacob. "Architectural Fantasies." *Process Architecture*, No. 26, Tokyo, 1981.

Tigerman, Stanley. "California: A Pregnant Architecture." LaJolla Museum of Art, 1983, p. 28.

Unamuno, Miguel de. *Tragic Sense of Life*. New York: Dover Publications, 1954.

———. *Abel Sanchez and Other Stories*. Chicago: Gateway edition, 1956, p. xv.

Wright, Frank Lloyd. *A Testament*. New York: Bramhall House, 1957.

# Chapter 4 The Channel of Transformations

One of the major themes of the modern movement in architecture was "Form follows function." This dogma came under direct attack by critics of modern architecture in the mid-1970s. They dismissed the whole modern movement. The literature of the 1980s is full of references for or against functionalism. Although we believe in the importance of function in its broadest possible interpretation (where everything is considered to be part of function—including the spiritual destination of the building) and although we think that the condemnation of an architecture on the grounds of function alone is not fair, we will bypass this debate here. It will suffice to call attention to the fact that Postmodernism liberated architecture from its dogmatic functionalist attachment (which was generally utilitarian) in favor of other concerns neglected since the Renaissance, (such as the reintroduction of humanism, an emphasis on history and historic memory, and an overall "romantic license" encouraging a variety of stylistic approaches). The idea that form can be manipulated ("massaged") without regard to functional requirements gave impetus to a reconsideration of form in evolving new design techniques.

One of the positive and meritorious by-products of Postmodernism has been its contribution to the further evolution of the channel of transformation, the central method of form manipulation from classical times to today. Both practicing architects as well as design instructors and students of the 1980s became seriously involved with this channel of architectural creativity. We are in a position today to draw a very clear picture of its possible directions and to make a judgment on the merits and liabilities of each of them.

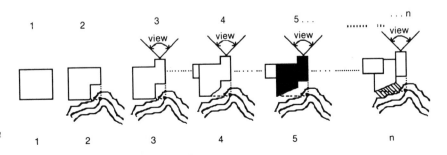

**Fig. 4-1.** *The traditional transformation process.*

Our working broad definition for the time being will be that *transformation* is a process of change of form whereby the form reaches its ultimate stage by responding to a multiplicity of external and internal dynamics.

## MAJOR STRATEGIES

We distinguish three major transformational strategies:

1. *The traditional strategy:* progressive evolution of form through step-by-step adjustability to "constraints" such as external (site, view, orientation, prevailing winds, environmental criteria), internal (functional, programmatic, structural criteria), and artistic (the ability, will, and attitude of the architect to manipulate form, along with the attitude toward budgets and other pragmatic criteria).
2. *Borrowing:* the license of borrowing formal departures from painting, sculpture, objects, other artifacts, and learning from their two- or three-dimensional properties while constantly probing interpretations with regard to their applicability and validity. Transformational borrowing is a case of "pictorial transferring" and can also qualify as a "pictorial metaphor." When a garden becomes the basis for a transformation process in the making of a house, then the garden is the metaphor of this particular house.
3. *De-construction or De-composition:* suggests a process whereby one takes a given whole apart in order to find new ways to combine the parts and to evolve possibilities of new wholes and new orders under different structural and compositional strategies.

The traditional strategy implies that the architect has already decided on an overall three-dimensional formal container which has evolved out of basic programmatic considerations and compositional needs. This in itself supplies a restraint in an otherwise limitless range of options. This particular strategy, although it refines, articulates, and massages the overall external configuration of the building, narrows down the expectations of the visual outcome. If an overall formal container is taken for granted, say a cube, and given an overall permitted number of transformation moves in response to certain optimum constraints, the final result will be predictable. If the designer is a computer with a built-in ability to evaluate the occasional outcome move, it will always produce the same ultimate transformation result. This is what happens with traditional architectural environments or with architectural practice where codes are very restrictive and practitioners are of similar ability. The range of ultimate solutions will be virtually predictable, with only some subtle differences. This basic model of architectural transformation, on which we elaborate in greater detail later, came under scrutiny by many Postmodern architects and instructors, who developed what we identified above as strategies 2 and 3.

It is obvious that strategies of the second category accept the license of transformation via "unrelated" forms (a painting is not a house), something totally unacceptable from the point of view of conventional transformation theory encountered in science, biology, mathematics, and the theory of knowledge. The last category, de-construction/de-composition, has been considered different from transformation, a notion we obviously do not endorse. As we are going to see, they are nothing more than cases of noncanonical transformation. No matter how ill-conceived or misunderstood they may be, they constitute transformations and should be embraced under the umbrella of transformation.

## THE THEORY OF TRANSFORMATION

To acquire a common base for the further understanding and evaluation of the various transformation strategies, we should first look at what is already available via the sciences that have already studied transformation. We begin with the biologist D'Arcy Thompson and his major work, *On Growth and Form*. Thompson used mathematical and analytical concepts and *related forms* compared through scientific methodology. According to him, "Transformation is a process and a phenomenon of the change of form under altering circumstances." He assumes that there is a dual possibility for describing form at any given time:

1. Descriptive—through the use of words
2. Analytical—through the use of numbers, mathematics, and the Cartesian coordinates

One can immediately point out the direct link to architectural form, in that it can be described through words, what has been recently referred to as "narrative," and through "drawing," which is the ultimate depiction of architectural form. Thompson has argued in favor of the mathematical definition of form, because it has "a quality of precision that cannot be found in mere "descriptive" description; as he put it: "Common words are simply vested with ambiguity and very often mean different things to different people." It is not surprising, considering the architectural analogy of narrative/drawing that many design instructors press for the production of more drawings. The drawing, no matter how inconclusive or unrefined it may be, possesses the qualities of specificity and clarity along with endless freedom for evolution. We can say that transformation is, after all, a visual act.

In abstract terms, a form can be "petrified" at any stage of its evolution and described through a system of Cartesian coordinates. Later on it can be translated into numbers and then into words. Every time Thompson studied an animal, he would inscribe it into a net of rectangular coordinates, then translate them into a table of numbers, from which, as he argued, one could get the pleasure of reconstructing the animal.

This first step of Cartesian "petrification" of the form along with its analytical description is fundamental. If the system of coordinates is about to suffer "alteration" or "deformation" for any reason, then all the points of the outlined surface of the form move analogously, governed by the mathematical formula of their description, producing a new form, a "trans-

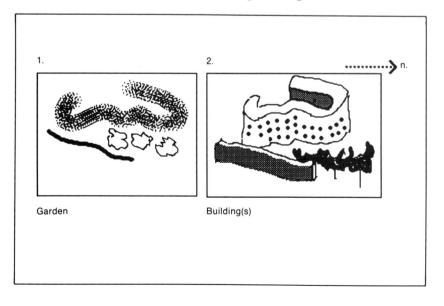

Garden                    Building(s)

**Fig. 4-2.** *Transformational "borrowing."*

formed" depiction of the initial form. Thus transformation, in the biological sense, is a predictable change of form under altered conditions, those that dictate the new position of the initial coordinates. According to Thompson: ". . . we obtain a new figure which represents the old figure under a more or less homogeneous *strain,* and is a function of the new coordinates in precisely the same *way* as the old figure was of the original coordinates x and y."

The idea of deformation corresponds to the change of alteration of the coordinates, something that in architecture should be understood as the alteration of the system of assumptions under which architectural decisions are made or the end design is evaluated. The biological inquiry would certainly consider "unhealthy" the conditions that make for a deformed leg, let alone a broken leg. If architectural assumptions are prepared to tolerate "broken" buildings of choked or frustrated parts, then the accepted result will still be the product of transformation, one whose coordinative assumptions only psychiatry could be able to analyze and understand.

In the Thompsonian sense, one should not attempt to study *unrelated* forms; only related forms can offer the biologist the acquisition of knowledge and the accumulation of comparative and critical experience on the basis of which he can predict form during the stages of evolution of an organism, when new conditions such as time, change of locality, change of seasons, call for the evolution and the growth through life. Isn't that good enough as an analogue for an architectural beginning—transformation of related forms as opposed to unrelated forms, with emphasis on drawing as opposed to narrative. But it is a fact that everything changes, and architects (good architects) also "grow"; they "graduate" into higher spheres in their perception of the world and in design competence. We do not deny that it is possible to operate successfully even when breaking all conventions, provided there is judgment and design ability.

The preceding discussion is summarized in Fig. 4-3. As all the items and possibilities contained in it belong to the realm of transformation, we can attempt all the possibilities. We should be cautious in the challenging situations of the "forced" or "weak" columns and invest more energy in them. Concentrate on the "natural" and the "strong" whenever you are in doubt or not absolutely certain as to the social validity of your contentions.

| Transformation | | | | | |
|---|---|---|---|---|---|
| Biology | Architecture | Natural | Forced | Strong | Weak |
| Related forms | A building into a building | ● | | | |
| Unrelated forms | A painting into a building | | ● | | |
| Descriptive | Narrative | | | | ● |
| Analytic | Drawing | | | ● | |
| "Normal" coordinates | Accepted practices | ● | | ● | |
| Altered coordinates | Imposing new frameworks | | ● | | ● |

**Fig. 4-3.** *The biology/architecture analogue.*

## THE THEORY OF KNOWLEDGE

The theory of knowledge now comes in handy to help us understand the aspects of the broader framework that affects transformation. Should we always accept whatever is considered to be "the way of doing things"? Or is it possible to challenge and alter frameworks of operations, to find new ways of seeing the world and doing things? *Assumptions* are central topics in the theory of knowledge. The goal of this field is simply to find *truth*. In our analogy between the theory of knowledge and architecture, we equate assumptions to architectural assumptions and truth to form.

Truth, which is what philosophers and people seek, is the result of a particular set of assumptions affected by many forces, such as the values of society, prevailing ideas, and the concept of freedom, as well as the state of mind of the person who seeks to explain or understand a situation. A great example for the exploration of the broad transformations of society is the university. Descartes devoted much of his time to the extraordinary problem of resolving which set of assumptions to follow and how to go about knowing what is truth. Not knowing which set of assumptions is the right one, he develops the theory of doubt, a set of radical theses and hypotheses that accept that the senses are fallible and can always deceive us, and that there is what he called a *deceitful demon* who "unfailingly misleads us into accepting error for knowledge." Descartes used his own experiences and admitted that all he had accepted or possessed of the highest truth up to that moment he had received from or through the senses. Further experience and self-evaluation convinced him, however, that the senses had sometimes misled him, and that therefore it was part of prudence "not to place complete confidence in that by which we have even once been deceived."

This led him to the hypothesis of the *poisoned well,* in which he assumed that the prudent man will avoid drinking from a well that once gave him indigestion. Yet one is never safe because one is never absolutely sure that no other well is contaminated. We can easily follow the path of Cartesian desperation; there must be, after all, a single item of authentic knowledge. If one finds it, then one might discover through it the universal truth. That single item of truth is the Cartesian *cogito.* If one finds it, it is enough to validate a general source of knowledge—"the clear and distinct perception of the mind." That clear and distinct perception lies within the domain of the cognitive activity of a mind. This is fundamentally a psychological and personal process; thus we are always "stuck" because our own personal perception of our own *cogito* may be consistently wrong. We are stuck, as Descartes was stuck.

Today we believe that we can very well obtain actual knowledge from the poisoned well. As Rescher states: "The cold and cruel fact is simply this, that imperfect sources are the only ones there are. If we can not make do with them, we must retire and leave the sceptic in possession of the field." (Reschez 1980, p. 182)

We are constantly participating in a process of transformation, the transformation of our own mental attitudes, the making of our inner beings in time. Our selves, our intellectual makeup, are the result of an ever-changing process of transformations whose coordinative assumptions are the circumstances of our time, as we see and perceive them.

Jorge Silvetti has best described all of this with regard to architecture, looking at it not only as a two-dimensional description as Thompson did, but including notions of what appear to be an appreciation of the process of transformation in mankind. He defined transformation as:

> . . . those operations performed on the elements of a given existent code
> which depart from the original, normal, or canonical usage of the code,

by distorting, regrouping, reassembling, or in general altering it in such a way that it maintains its references to the original while tending to produce a new meaning. (Silvetti, 1977, p. 48)

We embrace the definition of Silvetti as an advanced model for architectural transformations. It not only starts with an "existing code" of things, but it seeks to evolve it, always retaining the references to the original, which will always make architecture part of the society, the place, or the region that produced it. Silvetti calls for changing the usage of the code, not for the eradication of the code itself. Silvetti viewed the Renaissance as a transformation of antiquity, Mannerism of quattrocento architecture, Neoclassicism of Classicism, ecclecticism of the past as a whole, and so on (Silvetti, 1977, p. 43).

While the transformational evolution of architecture as interpreted by Silvetti occurred naturally, in time, through the evolution of civilization, several recent architects have attempted to alter the assumptions of every known conceivable rational system of coordinates. Foremost among them is Peter Eisenman, whose sole justification for doing what he has been doing has been "Nobody else had done it before" or "because it was there." He has been exploring just the opposite of the canonical way, practicing intentional arbitrariness, avoidance of the logical conclusion of what had come in the previous transformational move, and an overall strategy of deconstruction or de-composition, terms that originated from Deconstructivism, the philosophical system of Jacques Derrida. He has baptized his methodology of design, which he has insisted is not transformation (a notion with which we have disagreed) with these terms. Yet we are open to Peter Eisenman and to any serious artist who will take the time and explore for our sake anything that nobody has seen before. This is the way through which we learn and collectively evaluate our basic wisdom and our history.

The first Deconstructivist projects that were built by the late 1980s, the Amsterdam North housing project by Rem Koolhaas and the Parc de la Villette by Bernard Tschumi, left me with a choking feeling, made me feel "squeezed" by the shifts of the planes and "re-oppressed" by making me move under the pilotis or away from the ground when in La Villette. We have reservations, but we still applaud the efforts of Zaha Hadid and her students to challenge the notions of tranquillity and gravity. Yet in this case the self-evaluative commentary of her students has produced what we think are the best results from the lessons of such radical explorations. Alex Wall wrote about the efforts of the Hadid studio: "The goal of transforming architecture requires a literacy and analytical capacity that is rarely found in fourth or fifth year students, and it is only through the suggestive power of drawings that these aims can be approached. The danger is that the drawing can become too fluent, skating over the real issues and, in a breathless whir of brush and pen, create startling images which have no authority."

It is exactly at this point that we are compelled to contemplate critically several recent transformational efforts. Many architects produce scaleless, deformed, choked, and ultimately uncomfortable projects. Peter Eisenman's overemphasis on otherwise imaginative "narratives" provides tangible expression of the weakness of the narrative for reliable transformation results. The transformation of Verona based on a narrative of Romeo and Juliet and a whole set of plays on words is a case in point: the result is an arbitrary entity, a "stub" in the old city and everything it stood for in our memory.

The most frequent violation has to do with the Thompsonian principle of related forms. When a garden or a painting, for instance, is taken as a departure for transformation in the design of a house, we are about to encounter once again the ever-present problem of literality. An egg cannot be transformed into an apple, unless one is extremely hungry, in which case one eats everything. Yet both eggs and apples are edibles, as much as gardens or paintings and architecture are arts. Of course one can learn from any art; yet one will learn a lot more from transformation by being selective and avoiding the pitfalls of literality. Buildings as gardens are metaphors, in the same way as buildings out of the didactics of a painting belong in the broader inquiry of cross-fertilization, which we will address later.

The architect who attempts the channel of transformation should spend more time posing the right questions, rather than torturing himself or herself with other issues. Exercises such as "What will happen to the civic area of Chandigargh under additional population and use requirements, under altered political circumstances and economic pressures, with labor and materials such and such?" would constitute a valid and constructive exploration within the context of the orthodox understanding of the theory of transformation. This exercise would constitute an exercise of related forms in urban design. We could develop a score of problems on other scales: "What will happen, for instance, if the house you have designed for yourselves is going to be transformed into a much larger building, say a hotel, since the zoning ordinance has changed and you would like to take the economic advantage while at the same time avoiding having your view cut by the new building designed for the lot in front of you. At the same time would you want to retain some of the "house" qualities of your house design?" What will happen to the relationships between size and scale? What will happen to the ordering of the structure? How will the textures of the house be interpreted (perceived) in the larger building? Is there enough site to accommodate a new and larger building, or do we need to forget about the idea, since the courtyards and the open spaces of the house will have well-like proportions if we are in the same lot. Are we finally to conclude that a totally different solution is needed if our lot is to remain the same?

There is extraordinary complexity even within the traditional category of transformation. We propose to stay with this, to elaborate on its ingredients, to argue its complexities and leave the more complex approximations for later, for the architectural "graduation" that will come from within one's own experiences and later attitudes in life.

## STUDYING THIS CHANNEL

Recent instructors and architects offer an extraordinary list of possibilities for the study of transformation. Here are some of the more frequently encountered ones:

1. Exercises where the departing prototype is an existing precedent, a meritorious historic building, or an admired work of another architect. Among such cases were the projects given with the French Hôtel, the villas of Palladio and several houses by Le Corbusier as precedents.
2. Exercises where the departure was based on the precedent of a garden or a town (especially Renaissance gardens and Italian towns).
3. Departures from works of art (especially painting and sculpture), objects of the environment, or preselected shapes (even letters of the alphabet).
4. Departures from one's own previously designed or built buildings.

Much of these experiences focused on unrelated rather than related forms, total absence of program, and frequent use of irony, nonsense, and arbitrary scenarios. The main cause of this was probably the negative attitude of many recent architects and instructors toward function and their effort to distance themselves from the Modern movement.

## Problems and Liabilities

Problems were at a minimum in cases where the departing precedent was a building. In fact, this is a very fruitful method, as the well-resolved building of the past, a "related form" to the building we are about to come up with after several transformational moves, has addressed all the problems one addresses in buildings that can be instructive to start with. One must be cautious in going beyond the basic "mimetic" stage and reinterpreting the last suggestion so as to constitute a new entity with a right to existence on its own merits.

If the departure building is one designed before by the student or the architect, the eventual project would also be original in the broadest sense. Nobody would accuse the creator of copying or plagiarizing, while the creator would have extra satisfaction of having transformed one of his own projects and thus having transcended himself in the best possible sense. The buildings James Stirling proposed for the Nole Plan in the Roma Interrotta were transformations of earlier buildings he had built. In our own studios we have paid extra attention to this category of projects and have even stressed not only the precedental route with neglected but highly meritorious building types out of the Greek vernacular architecture, but asked students to transform their previously designed projects into buildings of higher scales and other destinations.

The garden, town, or other environmental precedent as starting points for the making of a building have the basic liability of unrelated forms. An egg cannot teach the botanist how to make better apples. This route is further burdened with dangers for eventual literality, where the axes or the heights of tree formations literally become the axes and the heights of buildings. We suggest in these instances being more careful, so as to discover the hidden secrets of a garden, its general mood, the degree of mystery, the quality of its textures, the degree to which it involves the senses, and with these observations on our palette to proceed to our transformation. The town can offer its perspectives, its limited vistas, the resolution of time/space/experience constraints. We should certainly focus on these aspects in order to go beyond literality. The only guarantee of avoiding literality is to focus on the essentials—the characteristics that offer uniqueness and authenticity to an object—rather than its visual characteristics alone.

Similar observations can be made for the case where the point of departure is a work of art or an object of the environment. In these instances students are usually asked to select a specific painting, relief, sculpture, or object. Functional requirements are usually nonexistent, or if given, are abstract and unrelated to the form. In this case one attempts to understand the underlying principles of the work under scrutiny, its compositional components, the relationship of axes, the solids vs. voids, the textural relationships of the painting, the importance and hierarchies of shapes and colors, the shadows and gradations, the planes and depth, and finally the overall aura of the work. These are documented through a series of sketches and often include models. The constructive part consists of a "jump" in scale, a three-dimensional adjustment and series of transformation depictions in which the effort is to bring architectural character to the whole.

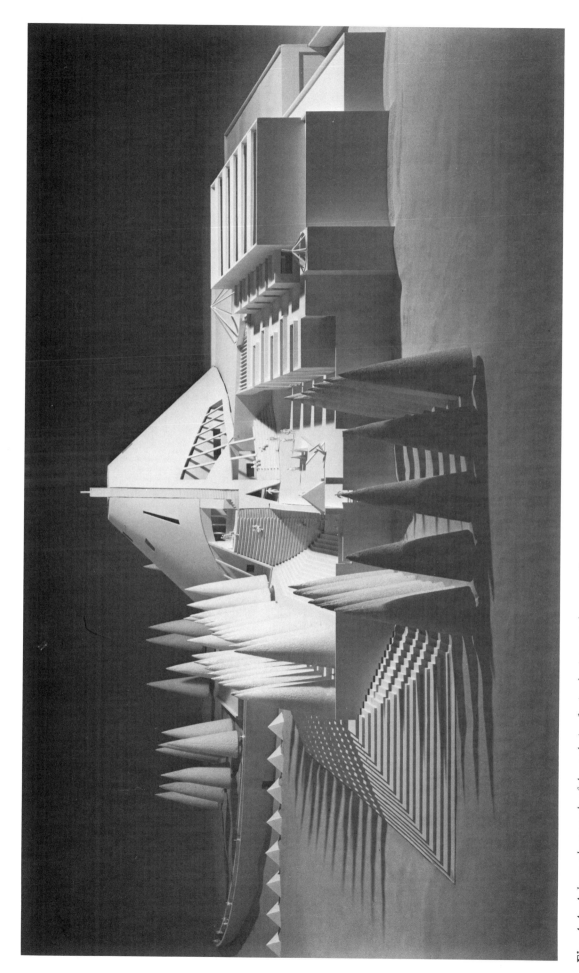

**Fig. 4-4.** *A large photograph of the cockpit of a jumbo jet pasted on a wall next to the drawing table of one of Antoine Predock's associates who was working on the University of Wyoming American Heritage Center and Art Museum may very well have suggested the transformational origins and the symbolic metaphorical departure for the project. (Photo copyright Robert Reck, 1986; courtesy of Antoine Predock, architect)*

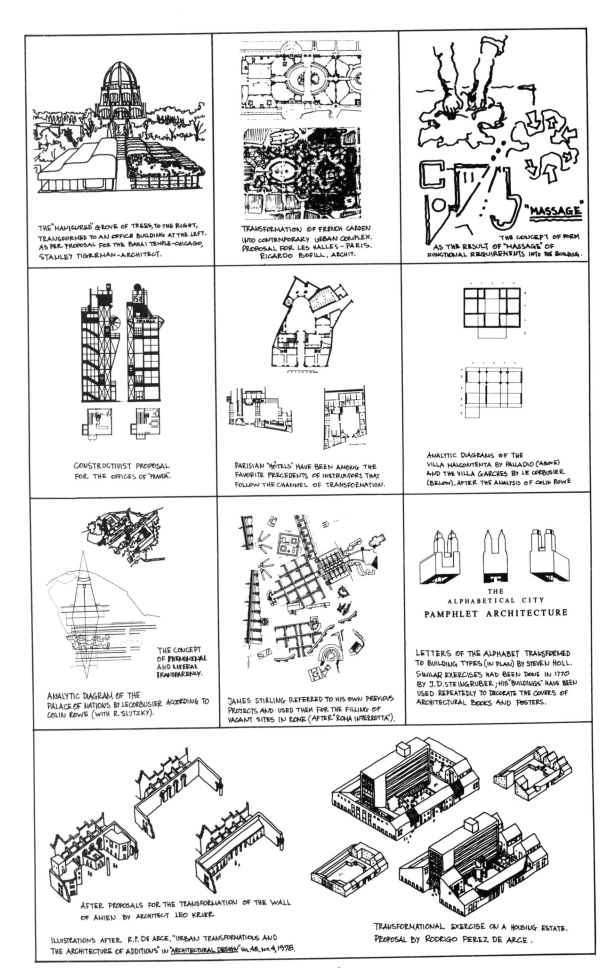

THE "MANICURED" GROVE OF TREES, TO THE RIGHT, TRANSFORMED TO AN OFFICE BUILDING AT THE LEFT. AS PER PROPOSAL FOR THE BAHAI TEMPLE-CHICAGO, STANLEY TIGERMAN-ARCHITECT.

TRANSFORMATION OF FRENCH GARDEN INTO CONTEMPORARY URBAN COMPLEX. PROPOSAL FOR LES HALLES - PARIS. RICARDO BOFILL, ARCHIT.

"MASSAGE" THE CONCEPT OF FORM AS THE RESULT OF "MASSAGE" OF FUNCTIONAL REQUIREMENTS INTO THE BUILDING.

CONSTRUCTIVIST PROPOSAL FOR THE OFFICES OF "PRAVDA".

PARISIAN "HÔTELS" HAVE BEEN AMONG THE FAVORITE PRECEDENTS OF INSTRUCTORS THAT FOLLOW THE CHANNEL OF TRANSFORMATION.

ANALYTIC DIAGRAMS OF THE VILLA MALCONTENTA BY PALLADIO (ABOVE) AND THE VILLA GARCHES BY LE CORBUSIER (BELOW), AFTER THE ANALYSIS OF COLIN ROWE

THE CONCEPT OF PHENOMENAL AND LITERAL TRANSPARENCY.

ANALYTIC DIAGRAM OF THE PALACE OF NATIONS BY LECORBUSIER ACCORDING TO COLIN ROWE (WITH R. SLUTZKY).

JAMES STIRLING REFERRED TO HIS OWN PREVIOUS PROJECTS AND USED THEM FOR THE FILLING OF VACANT SITES IN ROME (AFTER "ROMA INTERROTTA").

THE ALPHABETICAL CITY PAMPHLET ARCHITECTURE

LETTERS OF THE ALPHABET TRANSFORMED TO BUILDING TYPES (IN PLAN) BY STEVEN HOLL. SIMILAR EXERCISES HAD BEEN DONE IN 1770 BY J.D.STEINGRUBER; HIS "BUILDINGS" HAVE BEEN USED REPEATEDLY TO DECORATE THE COVERS OF ARCHITECTURAL BOOKS AND POSTERS.

AFTER PROPOSALS FOR THE TRANSFORMATION OF THE WALL OF AMIEN BY ARCHITECT LEO KRIER

ILLUSTRATIONS AFTER R.P. DE ARCE, "URBAN TRANSFORMATIONS AND THE ARCHITECTURE OF ADDITIONS" IN "ARCHITECTURAL DESIGN" Vol. 48, No. 4, 1978.

TRANSFORMATIONAL EXERCISE ON A HOUSING ESTATE. PROPOSAL BY RODRIGO PEREZ DE ARCE.

**Fig. 4-5.** *Selective visual overview of transformation examples.*

The "solids" and "voids" of the painting, for instance, read as streets and buildings, the axes as circulation, the "texture" as "density," intensity of activities or the "overall social interaction grain" of an urban or building proposal. The color stimulates suggestions for materials and color combinations. The broad assumption is that function will eventually find its place through appropriate "massaging." The pioneering historical precedent of this particular case of transformation was achieved in the studios of the Russian Constructivists.

The advantages of the channel of transformation are as many as its potential disadvantages. When the transformation departures touch the boundaries of the extreme, the effect on students may be negative unless the instructor is exceptionally experienced and alert so as to coach and warn them throughout the creative process.

## Some Cautions

*Scale.* The most frequent problem encountered in transformation exercises has to do with scale. The enlargement or reduction of a form that was correct at a certain concrete stage of its evolution loses its scale if transformed only proportionally, without the necessary formal and proportional changes of its parts, so that they may be able to respond correctly for the new size (statically and visually). If the deer, for instance, were to acquire the size of an elephant, and if it were to keep the deer silhouette, it would be out of scale. The new deer would be exceedingly heavy and the weight acquired through the new volume could not be supported by the "deer" legs. The surface of the cross section of the legs will eventually have to change to carry the new weight, eventually taking on the proportions of the legs of an elephant. Thus the elephant-sized deer will not look like a deer any more, but like an elephant. A living room of a small house transformed into a hotel cannot be turned into the lobby of a large hotel by "blowing up" its size; it will be out of scale if its new structural requirements are not met, if the column grid is not intensified, if the depths of beams and trusses are not appropriate. The problem of scale can be avoided in actual cases of transformation through careful attention to the relationships that exist between size and structure and their appropriate resolution.

*Whole vs. Parts.* The second and very serious problem has to do with the application of transformation to the component parts. In general they are not scrutinized in depth (except in the case of de-construction/de-composition, where one is not concerned about the unity of the whole). As a result the transformation is incomplete. The parts play a superficial role, and carry with them attributes of a previous stage that may not be desirable in the new one. If, for instance, a particular staircase of the same house transformed into a large hotel does not find its appropriate new role, formally as well as functionally, and still insists on being a staircase, nobody will be able to ascend it: its steps will be out of scale and useless. If the result of transformation is to be correct, it has to happen organically, from within, where all the constituent parts play analogous and harmonious roles.

*Forced Externalities.* An act of architectural design based on transformation can be seen as analogous to the transformation of a business, an institution, or a political organization. Abrupt changes in business or political establishments, in a political party or the composition of a government cabinet, may create tensions, and sometime very destructive tensions. Discontent and revolution may occasionally be the result. In similar terms externally imposed transformational forces presented as "design strategies" may result in the formal unhappiness of "transfiguration"—a reality which

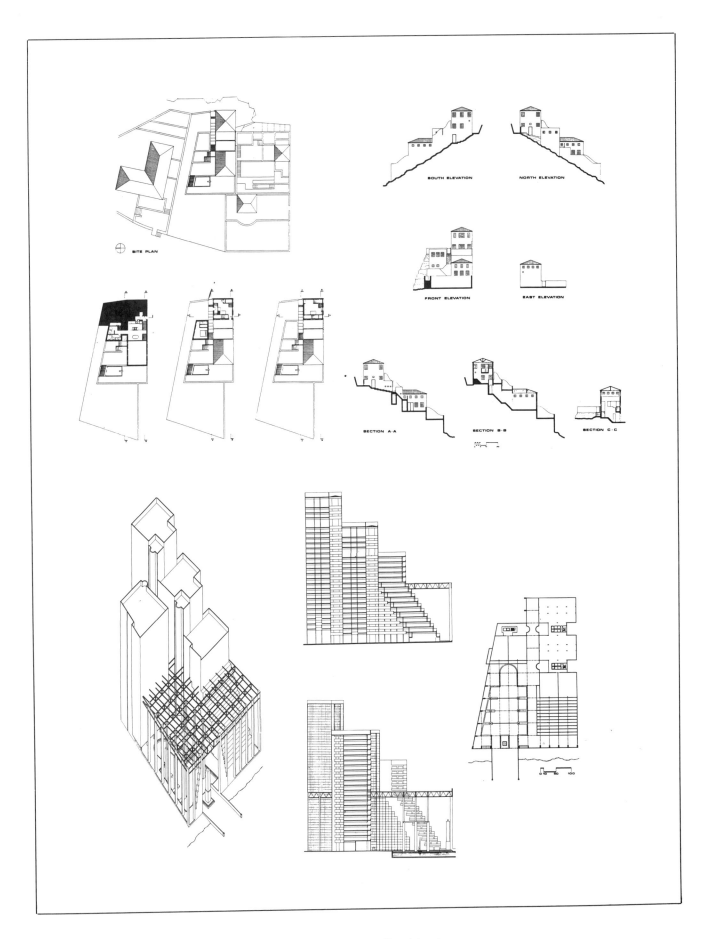

**Fig. 4-6.** *Challenging the concepts of scale, size, and structure as affected by the transformation process. Student project, transformation of a house into a hotel. Mike Smith, author's fourth-year design studio, UT Arlington.*

is the result of an act exerted violently and abruptly from the outside. The designer's personal whim is often the cause of this malaise, and it is frequent among designers and students who believe they "know" or "feel" what the final outcome wants to be without the need for the discipline of the inquiring step-by-step process.

*The Problem of Semantics.* The last and very essential problem of the transformation channel has to do with semantics. The term "transformation" is burdened by connotations of visual significance (because of form). It is closely associated (and related and often confused) with two broad groups of words: (1) form, shape, type, figure, outline, silhouette, kind, which describe visual conditions, and (2) formation, plastic accommodation, crystallization, deformation, disfiguration, distortion. The last three describe negative conditions of form or have negative connotations.

Because of the plethora of terms and the dubious meaning of each one of them, students may easily get confused, often get trapped into semantics and even accept some as legitimate acts of form manipulation that under normal circumstances should be avoided as undesirable. The design instructor has to be careful with choice of words when attempting this channel of creativity. We also believe that de-composition or de-construction are unnatural and forced transformation practices of the highest conceivable degree of arbitrariness and with the highest potential for misinterpretation and misconception not only for the practices themselves, but for the broader inquiry of which they are a part. They should be dealt with, if they are to be dealt with at all, with the highest degree of caution.

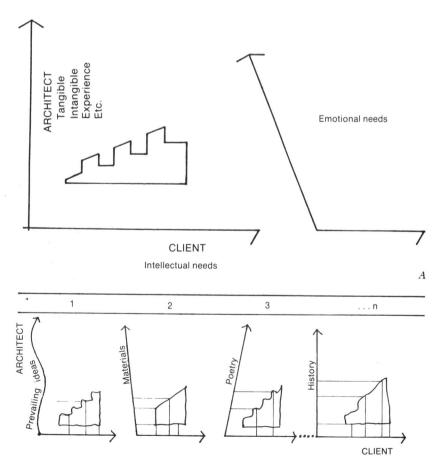

**Fig. 4-7.** *Concepts of architect/client coordinates.* **A.** *The various design concerns can be plotted along two axes of coordinates, one representing the architect and the other representing the client.* **B.** *Innumerable possibilities of axes.*

## AN INCLUSIVIST ATTITUDE FOR TRANSFORMATION

Transformation has been used by most people as a visual proposition. Dimensions of a social, functional, and engineering nature have yet to enter the transformational inquiry. We suggest a need for broadening the concept of transformation. A new attitude is necessary for inclusivist design, where both tangible as well as intangible constraints are taken into consideration.

Figures 4-7, 4-8, and 4-9 abstract the architectural project as a result of a transformational process whereby the occasional transformational move is always affected by the nature of the two coordinates, *architect* and *client*. If we assume complexity and dynamism in the correct analytical depiction of each one of these coordinates, none of which is eventually a straight line ("architect" is affected by many factors, such as education, experience, overall attitude and "client" has long vs. short range goals, profit orientation vs. absolute quality), we can see the exponential complexity of the factors that affect the coordinates and therefore the transformation process. The "inclusive" architectural project developed through transformation is a virtual impossibility, since it is virtually impossible to come up with a result that will satisfy every conceivable parameter. Yet if the project is to be in harmony with itself and the world, it will have at least to be at peace with its own world, its architect and the particular client.

The facility that is introduced in the process when one takes as many of these considerations out and focuses on much fewer—say style or exter-

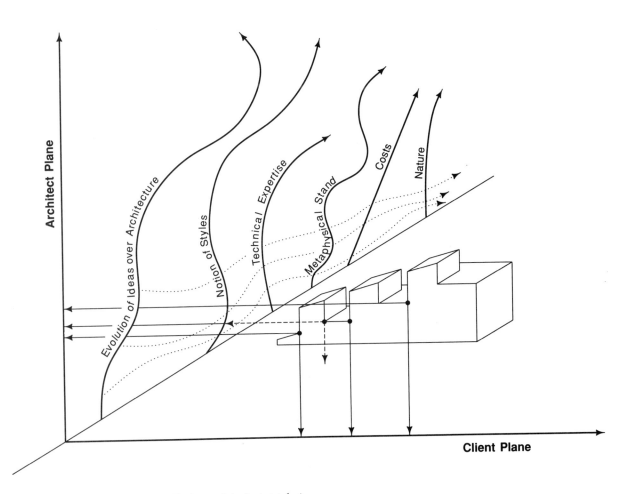

**Fig. 4-8.** *The exponential difficulties of inclusivist design.*

**Fig. 4-9.** *A project by the author: a condominium in Saronis.*

nal looks only—does not produce good architecture. Architecture, in order to have meaning, has to be a reflection of life, which after all is a most complex affair. At the same time we do not endorse the incorporation of unnecessary complexities for the sake of complexity only, such as the Eisenman de-construction/de-composition. My personal belief is that the traditional category of logical, sequential, overall and "inclusivist" transformation process is the most fruitful and promising. Any adjustment to the plan has a *simultaneous* effect on all the other aspects of the form. Any transformational move must be seen with simultaneity in mind, always checked through plans, sections, and elevations (though the elevations are not so important to start with, they become so only inasmuch as they address the aspect of final appeal to the public domain and the aspects of scale and contextuality). This methodological suggestion, posed as the transformational methodology of "simultaneity," is summarized graphically in Figure 4-10. It calls for four major steps of transformational involvement:

1. The visual statement of a variety of conceptual ("big idea") approaches to the problem, through all the documents of their three-dimensional depiction (plans—sections—elevations—and axono-metric sketches and models). Each one of these varying "big ideas" is conceived as an intellectual transformation of the potential essence of the uniqueness of the project ("What does the building want to be?").

2. Evaluation of the ideas and selection of the biggest, the one which in our judgment satisfies the problem in the best possible way and is in harmony with the two major coordinates of Fig. 4-11. This "biggest" idea is called "the optimum alternative" and constitutes a base for further formal transformational explorations. At this stage it is clear that the departing base was generated by the designer through the inner dynamics of the project and without the need for precedent. If precedents are used, we enter the transformation process suggested here through step 3 below, thus depriving ourselves of a wholly original contribution.

3. In this stage we develop further through transformations of the whole and of its parts the optimum alternative so that the final retains the initially accepted overall concept of the "biggest idea." We are always careful not to violate or lose this idea. On the contrary, the goal through each transformational move should be to strengthen it in every possible sense, in the most inclusivist possible way, to the best of our ability. As we make these moves we constantly bombard the evolved product with input from as many channels of creative consideration as we may be proficient at, thus enriching the resolution of the design. In this sense the transforma-

| variations of optimum alternative | $2$ | $2_1$ | $2_2$ | $2_3$. . . . | . . . . . . | $2_N$ |
|---|---|---|---|---|---|---|
| Site Plan | | | | | | |
| Plans | | | | | | |
| Sections | | | | | | |
| Elevations | | | | | | |
| Axonometrics | | | | | | |
| Models | Foam core board helps | | | | | |

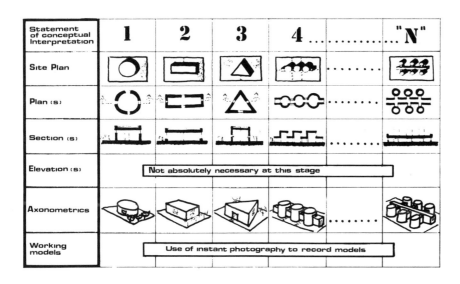

| Statement of conceptual Interpretation | $1$ | $2$ | $3$ | $4$. . . . . . | . . . . | "N" |
|---|---|---|---|---|---|---|
| Site Plan | | | | | | |
| Plan (s) | | | | | | |
| Section (s) | | | | | | |
| Elevation (s) | Not absolutely necessary at this stage | | | | | |
| Axonometrics | | | | | | |
| Working models | Use of instant photography to record models | | | | | |

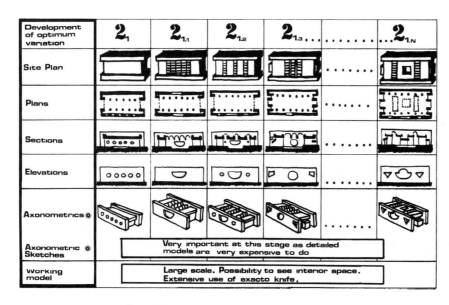

| Development of optimum variation | $2_1$ | $2_{1.1}$ | $2_{1.2}$ | $2_{1.3}$. . . | . . . . . . | $2_{1.N}$ |
|---|---|---|---|---|---|---|
| Site Plan | | | | | | |
| Plans | | | | | | |
| Sections | | | | | | |
| Elevations | | | | | | |
| Axonometrics ◉ | | | | | | |
| Axonometric ◉ Sketches | Very important at this stage as detailed models are very expensive to do | | | | | |
| Working model | Large scale. Possibility to see interior space. Extensive use of exacto knife. | | | | | |

**Fig. 4-10.** *Simultaneity in the design process, as taught by the author.*

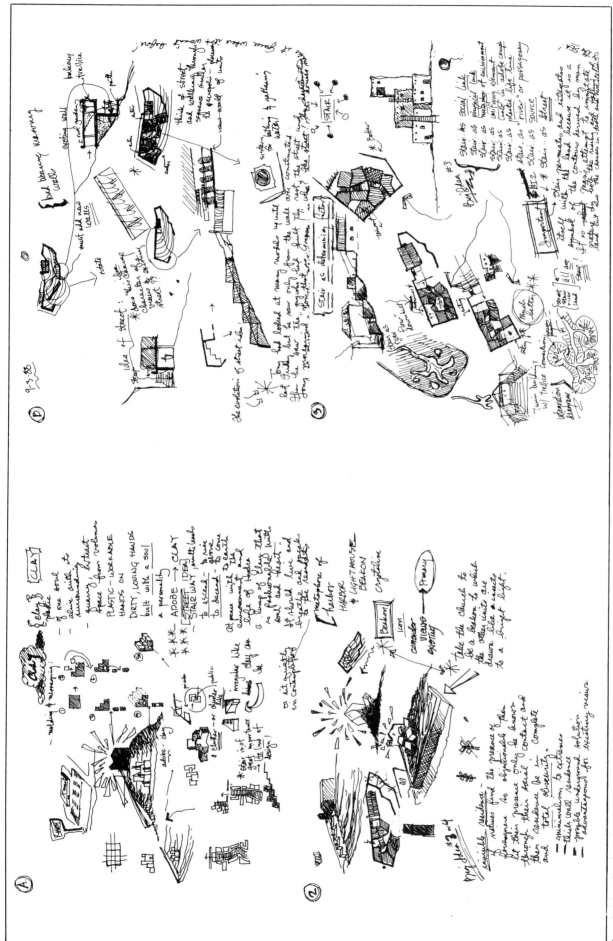

**Fig. 4-11.** *Sketches for a "Big Idea": the first step in the process of simultaneity. Sketches by Joe Riley, from the author's fourth-year design studio, UT Arlington, 1987.*

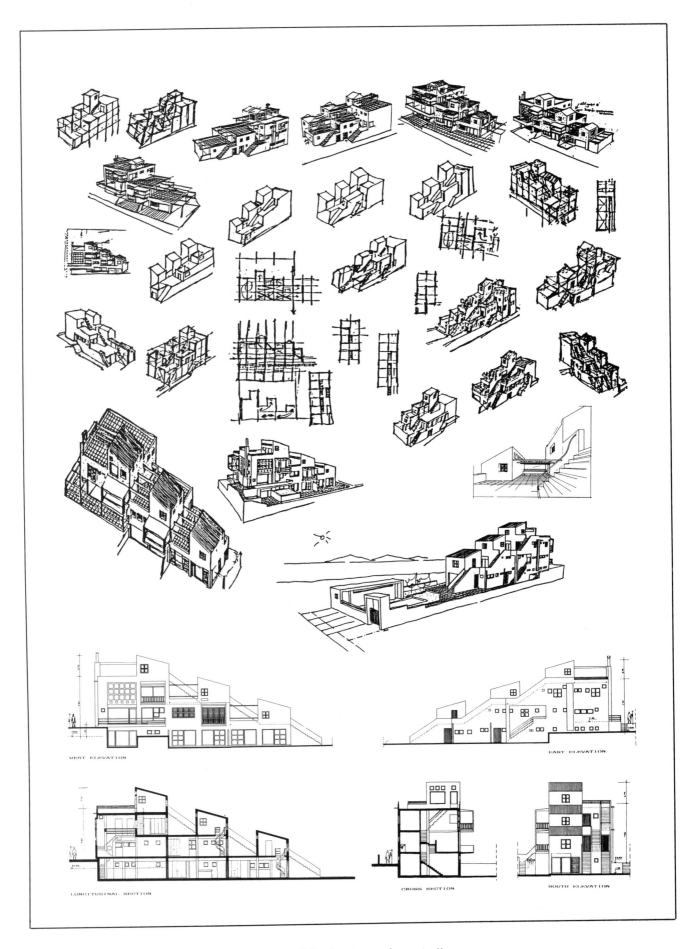

**Fig. 4-12.** *Author's sketches from the exploration of the "optimum alternative" stage of his condominium project at Saronis.*

tional methodology suggested here becomes a vehicle through which the designer accommodates many passengers that can embark for the final destination, all contributing to the long, difficult, but eventually rewarding trip.

4. The easiest step of the process is the last one: communication of the final transformational result so that others can "read" and understand it, react to it, and debate with the hope that they will accept and build it.

Transformation in architecture will have meaning only when it is considered as a complex inclusivist act, devoid of the visual and formal handicaps of the past. Our position is that the transformationally derived form via the methodology of "simultaneity," will be correct from an inclusivist standpoint only if it is the summation of inclusivist transformational acts. The composer must be strong and constantly alert to the sirens of easy abstraction or to the advocates of "monodimensional" transformation.

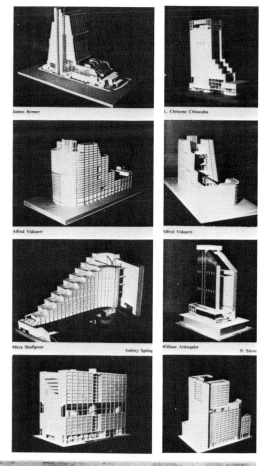

**Fig. 4-13.** *Simultaneity in the design process. Convention hotel in Dallas, Texas. From the author's fourth-year design studio, UT Arlington, 1977, 1979.*

The educational merit of the channel of transformation lies with the very fact of the great number of problems one may encounter and the extraordinary discipline that is necessary in order to avoid them. It provides a good opportunity for the experienced teacher who can help students navigate its waters. Transformation is not just a channel, but a sea of creativity. Each act of design through its waters should be like the Odyssey, a sincere and truthful fight with the elements, worth the risks, the discipline, and the effort. It is the ultimate "transformation" each of us should seek, and it is my strong suspicion that the "channel of transformation" can very well help us achieve this goal.

**Fig. 4-14.** *The Villa Savoye at Poissy, France (1930) by Le Corbusier is the transformation of an earlier symmetrical design.*

## Summary

This chapter is a short introduction to the concept of *transformation*. It summarizes the findings on transformation in biology and the theory of knowledge and suggests an architectural analogue. It suggests the validity of the biological requisite of "related forms" drawn from D'Arcy Thompson, while from the inquiry of Descartes it equates the whole notion of the context of assumptions that affect transformation with the context of assumptions in architecture. An outline of the broad categories of exercises in architectural transformation is accompanied by a discussion of advantages and commonly encountered problems. The chapter concludes with a suggestion for a transformational attitude via the methodology of simultaneity.

# References

Anderson, Stanford. "The Fiction of Function." Lecture, Texas A&M School of Architecture, March 29, 1985.

Antoniades, Anthony C. "Simultaneity in the Design Process and Product Results." *Technodomica*, Athens, June 1979.

Argan, Giulio Carlo. "Roma Interrotta." *Architectural Design*, Michael Graves, guest editor, 49, 3-4 (1979), pp. 43–49.

Bofill, Ricardo. *L'architecture d'un homme*. Interviews with François Hebert-Stevens. Paris: Arthaud, 1979, p. 118.

Carpenter, Edward. *The Act of Creation: Essay on the Self and Its Powers*. London: Allen and Unwin, 1904, p. 29.

Dennis, Michael. *French Hotel Plans*. Ithaca, NY: Cornell University Press, 1977, p. 14.

Eisenman, Peter. *House X*. New York: Rizzoli, 1982.

Holl, Steven. "The Alphabetical City." *Pamphlet Architecture* No. 5, New York, 1980.

Morgan, Cheryl. "The Garbage Model." *Association of Collegiate Schools of Architecture*, 1986, p. 138.

Peterson, Steven. "Space and Anti-space." *Harvard Architectural Review*. MIT Press, 1980, p. 89.

Rescher, Nicholas. *Scepticism: A Critical Reappraisal*. Totowa, NJ: Rowman and Littlefield, 1980, pp. 177, 181, 182.

Rowe, Colin. *Mathematics of the Ideal Villa*. Cambridge, MA: MIT Press, 1978.

Silvetti, Jorge. "The Beauty of Shadows." *Oppositions*, No. 9, MIT Press, Summer 1977, p. 48.

Stirling, James. "Roma Interrotta." *Architectural Design*, 49, 3-4, (1979).

Thompson, D'Arcy. *On Growth and Form*. Cambridge, Eng.: Cambridge University Press, 1942, 1966, p. 269.

van Bruggen, Goosje. "Waiting for Dr. Coltello." *Artforum International*, September 1984, p. 90.

Wall, Alex. "Transforming Architecture." *AA Files* II, Spring 1986.

Zygas, Paul Kestutis. "Constructivist Ammo for Dada's Revenge." *SAED Lecture Series*, February 16, 1984.

# Chapter 5 The Obscure

*Primordial and Untouched*

The power of the obscure has been proved repeatedly. Other arts have used it; some of the best of film, television, writing, and music have been inspired by it. Antonioni, Monty Python, Charles Kuralt, and scores of others have created through the obscure. Writers certainly know that "the more obscure their subject, the more chances they will have to be original." But one must get into the habit of looking at things from "obscure" angles. This requires discipline and persistence. In my essay "The Matrix of Athens," published in Greece a few years back, I attempted to present and comment critically on the history, the qualities, and the grain of the city of Athens through one hundred verses, all of which had five lines, each one starting with one of the five letters that composed the word ΑΘΗΝΑ (Athens). We cannot draw universal conclusions out of exercises such as this, nor would we guarantee that everything pertinent to Athens could be said even in one hundred verses. Yet one constantly makes discoveries in the process, realizing possibilities that may not have been contemplated before. Perhaps the most extraordinary gain of my explorations into the matrix of ΑΘΗΝΑ (Athens) was the unique verse contributed by my nine-year-old niece, who upon inquiry as to the efforts of her uncle, returned a minute or two later with a piece of paper on which she had inscribed:

| | | | |
|---|---|---|---|
| A | Αθανατη | A | She |
| Θ | Θεα | T | Started |
| H | Ηταν | H | As |
| N | Νωριτερα | E | An |
| A | Αυτη | N | Immortal |
| | | S | Goddess |

There was immediate proof of the relationships between myth, perpetuation of the race, and primordial beginnings. Two broad categories of the obscure can be useful to the creative process in architecture: (1) The obscure of the "primordial"; (2) The obscure of the "hibernating untouched." The first category is highly personal, covered by layers of years, and the history, tradition, and subconscious collective practices of a people. The second is

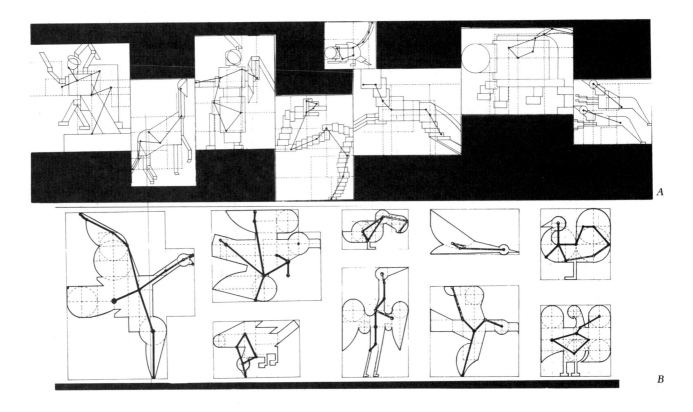

**Fig. 5-1.** *Stimulating the imagination through abstraction and geometric analysis of the constellations.* **A.** *Huyhn Kim-Hang,* **B.** *Randy Brown,* **C.** *Tim Johnson. From the third-year design class of George Gintole, UT Arlington, 1988.*

objective; it has physical characteristics, but it has not been seen or paid attention to yet. It can be a source of inspiration in the creative process.

Both categories of the "obscure" possess a quality of extraordinary dynamism, since through them we give birth to something whose seeds have existed since primordial time. Let us look more closely at each category.

## THE PRIMORDIALLY OBSCURE

We have frequently used the expression "design constraints" to describe parameters or variables that affect design. And we have preferred the term "constraint" because it better describes the "strain" often imposed by a parameter or a variable. Any form is always the result of this "strain." Among the constraints that affect design are some intangible factors that are exceedingly difficult to understand. The primordial obscure is one such constraint. Primordial factors are "obscure" because they are hidden deep in the "primordial" part of each person. Often such constraints cannot be explained, even by the people whose lives and personalities have been shaped by them. Most people are simply unaware of the subconscious influence of such constraints. Myths, religious beliefs, customs and superstitions, rites and ceremonies, use and appreciation of color, the appreciation of the landscape, overall concepts with regard to space, and the language and its use are key constraints of this nature.

The awareness of such issues diminishes as people become more sophisticated, as they become more involved with current values. The evidence of the obscure (how each people first perceived the world) exists in the memories of the very few, and hibernates in the oblivion of rarely used books kept in libraries and museums.

The cross-cultural differences of today's plural society have magnified exponentially the bulk or volume of the obscure. The large number of the cross-cultural differences (including differences in perception) that have been proved to exist and the increased number of obscure aspects have made the task of the architect extremely difficult, and they have added extra work to the design process. Architects must try harder than ever to under-

**Fig. 5-2.** *The aesthetics and dynamism of the "ruin," an obsession of Postmodernism, a reality in Greece. "From the ruin I created my adobe," says a Greek verse by Odysseus Elytis.*

stand clients and come up with appropriate solutions. Architects who do not pay attention to the obscure are not rendering due service to their clients, and are also depriving themselves of an oppotunity to come up with creative answers to design problems. The effort to use the obscure is rewarding and can produce exceedingly creative results, particularly within a plural environment. We do not advocate architects trying to understand the various cultural peculiarities of peoples in a Freudian or any other analytical sense; this is the job of psychoanalysts, students of culture, medical people. The architect should only observe, respect, and take for granted whatever others have found; he should then design with that in mind. It is too risky to try to do the job of other professionals and to do more than what one has been trained for.

Some of the contstraints that have been studied by those who specialize in environmental psychology definitely should be included in any inquiry into the obscure. These are territoriality (the need to define and defend one's own space) and topophilia (love for place). Other issues, such as rituals, ceremonials related to building practices, and other customs of broader significance can also be tackled directly and even provide hints for conceptual interpretations of a project. If architecture is indeed a cultural index, as we believe it is, an architect should delve into the foundations of the specific culture, group, or client he is designing for. It will be helpful to the young designer to be exposed to as many customs as possible and to debate their significance for designs of the past. For instance, what would be today's equivalent of the sacrifices that took place on the foundation stones of buildings in many cultures in the past? How would one go about today taking care of a particular client's superstitious need for assurances with regard to the "solidity" of his building? What myths are found in a particular client's origins? Is the client perceived to be "pagan," or is he or she a "religious" person in the more contemporary sense?

Questions such as these are not difficult to find; one has only to ask them, and to look for answers through research on a project-by-project, client-by-client basis. As we study such issues, we may begin to realize the significance assigned by the client to each particular item and design accordingly, because, for instance, it would be irrelevant to design small openings for the house of a contemporary Greek who has been brought up to view open horizons, the vastness of the sea, and to "embrace" the outside with his eyes.

One good way to cover the issues of the primordially obscure is to tackle them in a systematic way, beginning with those that have broader significance. The suggested order of investigation therefore should be as follows:

1. Myths
2. Customs
3. Rituals and ceremonies (with a particular eye for those related to building practices)
4. Religious factors
5. Linguistic hints and origins of words that describe a specific project
6. Miscellaneous topics of unique emphasis and significance (such as color, attitudes toward certain textures)
7. Whether the particular client has any preference for any "obscure" items enumerated above

## Myths

Some cultures are blessed by rich and fascinating mythologies. Students should be encouraged to read about myths, regardless of their own cultural

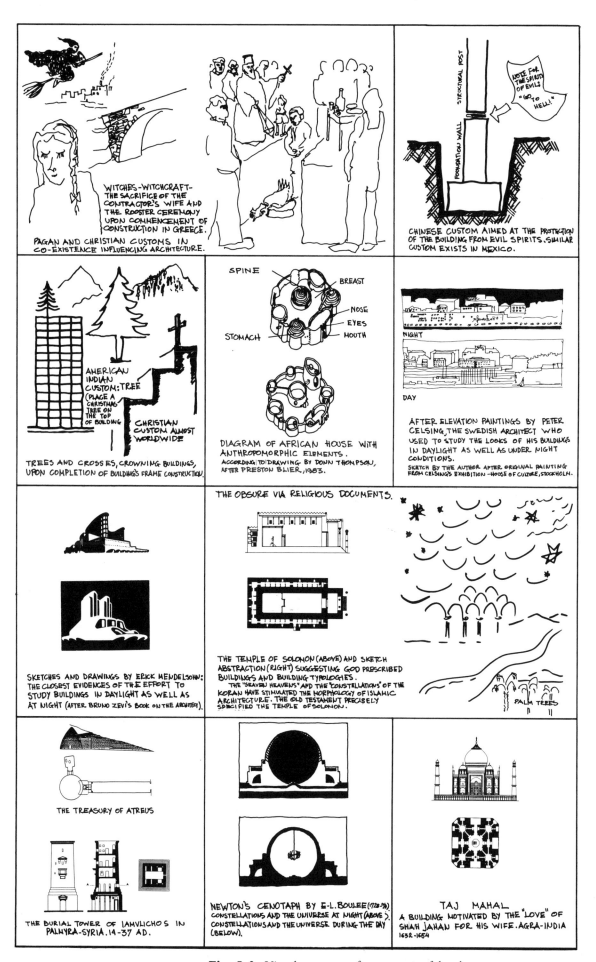

**Fig. 5-3.** *Visual summary of components of the obscure.*

origin, because all mythology is a source for the development of imagination according to Vico.

A myth is a fairy tale, a story heard in childhood that we believe to be true. It is the way our ancestors explained the inexplicable, the origin of things; myths are the explanations they gave for phenomena, for the adversities or the enemies they had to overcome in order to survive. Myth is the first interpretation of the cosmos, usually scientifically wrong, but always real because it was our first interpretation of the reason for the universe. Myth is in direct contradiction to today's emphasis on the utilitarian. The Mahabharata, Gilgamesh, Hercules, Achilles and Ulysses, Aeneas, the Valkyries, Wainamoinen and the heroes of the Kalevala, the sun and the moon, Buddhist and Christian myths, brother sun and sister moon, Merlin and the birth of the British people. . . . Hydras, dragons, warriors, plagues and floods, disaster and adversity, death of the samurai are just some of our store of human mythology. But we will not discuss any of them here. It would be unfair to take away from the original narrators of such myths—Homer, Virgil, Goethe, Murasaki Shikibu, the unknown singers of Finland, Edith Hamilton, Mircea Eliade—students should read the originals.

## Customs

In a search for customs, we will inevitably encounter ritual and ceremony. In our search, we even found customs directly related to architecture, design and construction practices. Virgil in his *Aeneid* and Joseph Rykwert in his extraordinary book *The Idea of a Town,* where he discusses rite and ritual as related to Rome, will give you a lot more. Geography and cultural anthropology are the best sources for the study of customs. Should an architect also happen to speak the particular language of his client's origin, he would find an extraordinary repository of references in the local literature; there is hardly a place on earth, no matter how small and unknown, that does not have its indigenous local scholar (usually a schoolteacher, a retired civil servant, or a religious elder) who has a book on the customs of the place. Such books are usually the first that were written, treasures of information on local cultures. We have found six broad categories of customs to be of help to the designer: sacrificial customs, exorcism customs, offering customs, good deeds, celebration, and social customs.

*Sacrificial Customs.* These customs are directly related to the act of creation. We take one life (i.e., the lamb) in the hope that life will be transferred to another (e.g., the field will have a good crop). Sacrificial customs related to building include the sacrifice of animals on foundation stones (Greece), or under the central post of round houses (Mexico, the Philippines). Human sacrifice was common in antiquity. (The most recent recorded one was the sacrifice of the builder's wife in the foundation ground-breaking ceremony for a bridge in Greece, during the eighteenth century.)

*Customs of Exorcism.* These are often found in China, Japan, Africa, Mexico, and the Philippines. Notes may be placed at critical points of the building (under the posts, in the foundation, at the turning of stairs and bridges) telling evil spirits to beware. Such devices were supposed to protect the building from fire, wind, and other disasters.

A variation of this custom had a direct effect on architectural form: the Chinese and Japanese made it a habit to turn bridges by 90 degrees in order to confuse the spirits with the abrupt turn.

*Customs of Offering.* At critical points during the construction (laying the foundation, placement of the first beam, pouring of the first slab), wine, food, or sweets would be offered in order to strengthen and "sweeten" the house and its "spirits," the ancestors, and the construction workers. Alcohol from palm trees has been a favorite treat for the foundations of many tribal village buildings in Africa.

*Warnings and Good Deeds.* Do not kill the house snake, or disaster will befall you (such snakes are usually in the basement, protecting the space from mice and insects and keeping the provisions and the upper floors clean). Do not cut the birch tree Wainamoinen is told in the Kalevala; the cuckoo will nest there to sing, the eagle will rest on it, and even you may relax under its branches. It will be a good omen if you are visited by an owl (she devours the garden snakes, as well as the mice). Thus it will be good to plant a cypress tree from which she can survey your garden and protect your house. The household whose chimney is selected by a stork to build its nest considers this an honor. The annual arrival of the storks suggests the coming of spring, while their presence will guarantee a field without snakes for that particular farmer (in Greece, the Balkans, the Soviet Union).

These customs have direct and visible effects on the architecture of the regions; they are visible in the size of the gardens, the placement of particular landscape elements, and the provision for excess fireplaces to accommodate the storks while not losing too much heat inside.

*Celebration.* These customs are often timed to take place at the end of the construction process, and are often accompanied by food, dance, and wine. The end of construction is demonstrated by symbols such as trees, crosses, or flags. Crosses and flags have obvious religious and nationalistic connotations. The tree is a remnant; the high steel workers in the Chicago area once were Indians, and the tree that they place today on top of completed construction represents for them the green forests of their native lands, something they had lost when they came to the city to find work. The tree is also a symbol of the union for Americans and for many other people.

A recent celebration custom is the open house held by developers, real estate people, architects and owners; it is the opportunity to show the house to the world, to prospective buyers, to clients, to magazine editors, and to friends. It is an occasion for a display of community pride by the various patrons of public and communal buildings who were influential in the building process.

*Social and Regional Dynamics.* These customs often had a cruel ending in antiquity—human sacrifice. The annual offering of young men and women from the Athenian republic to the king of Crete to be devoured by the Minotaur, or the sacrifice of young girls to the waters and the pacification of the Nile in ancient Egypt, were typical of these customs. Other communal customs had happy endings and are still practiced in many lands. Unless they are taken into consideration, there will be no public space for square dancing, outdoor celebrations during various holidays (Christmas, Epiphany, Santa Lucia's Day, May first, May fifth). Without consideration of the requirements for regional and communal customs, of which all cultures have plenty, urban design and the architecture of the outdoors will become poorer.

## Rituals and Ceremonies

Rituals and ceremonies are often integrally related to customs. They have been with us since ancient time, and have been used in an effort to enrich our lives with experiences different from the ordinary. They are used by both nonreligious as well as religious and urban people, often as a means to establish a hierarchy. In a historic context they were part of the theater of life.

Rituals are often associated with the process of entering buildings, and behavior when in certain spaces. They called for appropriate articulation of various elements of a building. The threshold, the entrance, the public fountain, the throne room, the house shrine, the altar, were spaces of tangential rituals that united the external world and the users. Certain behavior was expected as well as encouraged by the mere existence, the shape, and the proportions of such spaces. Ritual could be found in small-scale buildings as well as in large-scale and urban complexes. The public bath, the clubhouse, the hotel, and the resort are among the better known, while the ritual of life in them has been best described by literature and the cinema. Other spaces are devoted to rituals of domestic and absolutely private nature; the dining room, the bedroom, the private study, were conceived as spaces for the rituals of food, sex, and work, vital human acitivities whose sacred origins have been argued by Mircea Eliade. In Figure 5-4 we provide a visual summary of the items (scale, building type, behavior) involved in the ritual-space reciprocity.

We could not conceive of the correct architecture for certain building types, such as the church, the synagogue, or the shrine, without a knowledge of the ritual and ceremonial requirements of the functions to be performed in them. One extraordinary precedent for a large building type whose overall architectural articulation as well as the architecture of its parts was largely dictated by the ritual(s) of everyday life was the monastery. In many parts of the world, the university campus still retains its ritual foundation. It is, we believe, the most "wholesome" modern example of large-scale architecture where ritual and overall architectural form are tightly interrelated. The frequency of ritual, however, is not as dense in the university as it is in the monastery; in the latter, ritual occurs daily (various liturgies, calling monks to dinner, daily activities). Both building types should be studied with an eye for the "ritual-ceremonial" impact on the overall architectural form.

We believe these two types of buildings deserve more attention than has been paid to them by literature; they can be useful to the goal of inclusivity through the tolerance, plurality, and democracy that can be found in them, as opposed to the palace (symbol of authority), the large-scale building type singled out by scholars and design instructors alike as the favorite precedent for the ritual-form interrelationship.

Small-scale architecture has its own champions in the ritualistic sense. It would be inconceivable to think of a Japanese house without an awareness of the unique ceremonial of life that takes place in it (wearing the appropriate kimono, taking off the shoes, making all bend for their entrance into the space through the low entrance) or to think of a tea ceremony pavilion without a deep knowledge of the tea ceremony and its associations.

Pavilions, gazebos, the lawn, the garden, the overall exterior and the interior circulation of buildings are architectural components that can enhance the rituals and ceremonials of life. If we pay attention and contemplate these components, we will have covered a good part of an otherwise neglected territory. Yet responding to such requirements in a tactical way is not a difficult task. The difficulty starts when the architect searches for ceremonial codes that are not obvious, that would be desirable, or that

|  |  |  | Space | Ritual—Activity |
|---|---|---|---|---|
| Historic | Small Scale | Traditional Often Forgotten | "Threshold" | Bow upon entering. Pay respects. Pray |
| | | | Gate —building / city | Identify, pay respects, receive keys of the city |
| | | | Propylaea | Protect city or precinct. Guards territory, can be friendly and welcoming to hostile. |
| | | | Fountain | Drink water, refresh, relax, wash. Baptism, catharsis, rebirth. |
| | Large Scale | Building and Urban Types | Circulation | Rhythm of movement. Pace, expected hierarchy in the procession. Horizontal-vertical. Visitors-inhabitants. |
| | | | Public baths | Roman, Japanese, Muslim. |
| | | | Clubhouses | Men, academicians, business, entertainment. |
| | | | Resort towns | Hotel ritual, casino ritual, mineral baths ritual. Time scheduling, dress code. |
| | Unique Scale | | Tearoom | "Threshold" ritual, bow, very low entrance, overall ritualistic behavior. |
| Contemporary | Domestic | | Dining Sleeping Work Entertaining Guests Outdoors | Elaborate variations pending architectural period, style, economy, and relationships with external world. Such activities were often influenced by imported rituals of exotic nature observed abroad. |
| | Workplace | | Reception Work station Coffee break | Identification, magazines, sound, "image ambiance," individualization, territorial communal work ritual. |
| | Eternal Precedents | | Monastery University | Large-scale examples of "ritually" derived wholes. |

**Fig. 5-4.** *Items of ritual space reciprocity.*

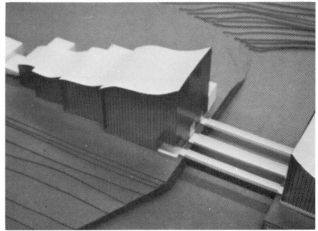

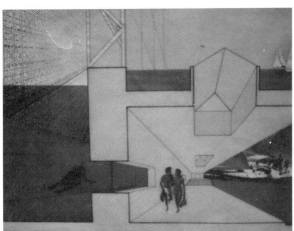

**Fig. 5–5.** *The poetics of "night," "the sky," "water," and "the breeze." Pavilions for sailboat exhibitions in Dallas, Texas. From the author's studios at UT Arlington. Left column: Eric Jakimier; right column: H. Suleimani.*

would be acceptable if they were to be "uncovered" and introduced. There is unfortunate reluctance on the part of many people with regard to anything that might make for a more aesthetic, and literally healthier, way of life, as rituals and ceremonies always do. The architect has to be particularly alert to uncover and introduce the right amount, the "right excess steps of circulation," the "right amount of stairs in the interior space," "the right provision for lighting and acoustical possibilities of a ceremonial nature."

The major difficulty in the incorporation of ritual as a design-enriching vehicle is the attitude of modern people to anything nonutilitarian; they consider it a waste of time and money. This attitude is obviously widespread among large segments of the population. Of course, architects cannot impose other ways of living on people, no matter how beneficial these ways may be. As architects, however, we should always try, in the hope that sometimes the circumstances will be right.

The architect may not always be able to connect his suggestions with familiar ceremonial behavior, and some of his ideas may sound strange. Not everybody, for example, is prepared to accept a tea ceremony metaphor or a celebrational atmosphere for their house, but most people will listen much more easily to explanations based on the ceremonials of eating, listening to music, entertaining friends, offering parties for children, or performing annual rites within the religious or social codes of the cultural or business group to which they belong. The good architect, who genuinely cares about improving his clients' lives, should also employ the ritual of good diplomacy. Catharsis, rejuvenation, rebirth, new life, prosperity, joy, connection with the historic memory and the past are often the by-products of rituals and ceremonial practices. The creative architect must look rigorously for ceremonial behavior, make a careful list of its requirements, and try to incorporate it into his architecture. Inclusion will upgrade the life of any building, the modest adobe as well as the palatial residence, the public building or the entire urban space.

## Religious Factors

If a client is religious and comes to the architect with a commission for a building with particular religious requirements, the religious factor would be obvious. Yet the broader issue is more complicated in the everyday practice of architecture in our modern plural and democratic society; "religious preference" is not usually discussed at the awarding of commissions. The creative architect must be tactful, careful, and alert to latent religious feelings that are often not openly expressed. To be able to uncover and design for such latent requirements would make the life of the client a great deal richer. The author has particular experience with Greek orthodox clients who, though will not state their deep devotion to their beliefs, will feel much happier if the architect provides for an iconostasis and a nook for the candle in a secret place that only they themselves will know exists.

In the much broader sense, religion takes many more forms today than it used to have in the past. For many people, religion is their work, or sports; for many single parents, their religion is their children, and for far too many people, religion is their money. The good architect must uncover all these preferences, be open-minded, and produce designs that reflect a client's particular set of needs.

## Linguistic Hints

Most words hide their own meaning. One of the first steps for the architect should be to search the etymology of the type of project, to look at the key

words. He or she will probably find hints of what the project really ought to be. Take, for instance, the word "etymology." It is a composite word of Greek origin, from two parts: the word "etimos," which means ready, and the word "logia," from the word "logos," suggesting the science of words. Thus etymology means: the ready meaning of the word. It promises to take us to the meanings of words, most often through the words themselves.

Good dictionaries are as indispensable to the architect as a good brain. Should a particular word provide difficulty, the architect should be prepared to say it through other words, or even through a sentence of explanation. Step-by-step etymological analysis of words, often moving from one language to another, will help the architect reach the origin of the word, the primordial, primitive application, the basic meaning and connotation. In most instances, words of the age we live in are direct descendants of earlier eras of humanity.

Once again, we do not advocate the architect or designer becoming a linguist. Architecture, in fact, has suffered enough from the incomprehensibility of its self-proclaimed exponents. We propose a very simple thing: that the designer look at a good dictionary and take the linguistic hints into consideration when working on a project. This linguistic search can be most rewarding, and it is the first step, the key to the realm of the obscure and the primordial.

**Fig. 5-6.** *Uniting religion with concepts on the origin of man. The darkness of the cave and the hope of light; the celebration and glory of the sky. Taivallahti Church in Helsinki. Timo and Tuomo Suomalainen, architects.*

## Miscellaneous Topics

It is extraordinary what effect the landscape exerts on people. The color of the earth, the filtering of the sunlight through trees, the suggestion of the openness of the horizon, the finite versus the infinite perception of the sky, the "smell" of the earth and the auditory dimensions of the surroundings, the sounds and colors of the birds, tranquillity or its absence, and finally the prevailing temperatures, which make some people prefer living outside and others inside. All of these have a definite effect on the attitude of people toward specific items of architectural design. Largely because of the effect the primordial landscape (the landscape of their ancestral origin) has on people, they appreciate differently the following:

color (Mexican–American Indians)
texture (Japanese, North Americans)
sound (Greeks, French, Germans)
vistas (Greeks, New Mexicans)
indoors vs. outdoors (Mediterranean vs. Scandinavian people)
ample vs. limited space (Americans vs. the Japanese)
inland sites vs. sea or lake sites (mainlanders vs. islanders)
up vs. down (Greek islanders prefer flat interiors because of the hilly terrain)

The architect must look carefully into all these subjects, and ask questions of the client. Ask clients to recall their childhood memories, where they used to play, the colors they used to wear, to describe color memories from the past, childhood games, expeditions, and excursions during the school years, positive or negative memories from the childhood house, the terrain, and impressions of important buildings in the community. There is a literature on these subjects, but it is scattered, and requires good research and often original effort to locate it. In the last section of this chapter, we include suggestions for research into several such topics.

## Affiliative Tendencies

How many times have we admired other peoples' houses, buildings we have seen, countries we have visited? Some people are open about it, becoming active and joining clubs such as the Friends of the Orient. Latent affiliative preferences can be extraordinary clues for the architect; they can often suggest qualities that will personalize and authenticate a design. It would be easy to incorporate an Aalto principle in a design for a "Finnophile." It would be equally easy to propose a minimal atmosphere in something designed for a lover of Japan.

But the architect has to be careful; people are not always open about their affiliative tendencies because they know their peers do not often approve of external influences. Further, they do not have a clear idea of what they want from the other culture, and are often content with the visual signs and solutions they saw in the other country—a tatami mat, a Mexican sombrero, a Greek blanket. The architect can elaborate upon the "discovery" of such tendencies, lead clients into discussions of essentials, rediscover with them the meaning and the principles at work in the making of the artifact or the architecture. The architect should then be open and willing to elaborate on the various themes and offer them to the client through the design in which they are *re-created* for the clients' own needs. This would be an instance of incorporating the exotic and multicultural into an actual design. The creative architect should look carefully for an opening in this direction, discover the latent affiliative tendencies of clients, and through a process of avoiding direct copying and literal analogies, create orginally from it.

## THE "HIBERNATING UNTOUCHED"

Many situations, physical or not (mood, feeling) have not been explored for architectural design purposes. The design instructor must urge students to identify and tackle such subjects for design departures. Such obscure angles have already produced extraordinary masterpieces in other arts, in poetry, literature, music, and film. The attitude of Edgar Allan Poe, as an explorer of "atmosphere" and mood and the environment at night, or the fact of the supremacy of night in certain parts of the world (say Scandinavia) during large periods of the year can stimulate design explorations. To challenge students to think of the night or of the crucial few moments of the transition from sunlight to night (or artificial light) while sitting on a porch, or to think of the abstract dynamism of the night under different sky and atmospheric conditions, may be more revealing than any textbook references on lighting and illumination.

One student had written in his sketchbook:

> . . . I was seated on the porch, drinking beer and listening to my compact disc playing "Antarctica." It must have been eight-fifteen, eight-twenty, sometime around there, April 18, spring. All of a sudden, as the sun was going down, I sensed another sun coming up gradually from the room behind my back to the left of my cheek, through the door and the mosquito screen. The one light—the daylight—was going off, another light—the forgotten light in the room inside—was smoothing up the lighting atmosphere of the house inside. This didn't last long, just a few minutes. When I realized that I had never experienced such a situation before, everything was gone. It had become all dark outside. The light of the lightbulb inside. Mosquitoes came out and I got inside.

The student was asked to treasure this experience and to try to pursue it in one of his designs. His next condominium project had a series of articulated porches so that others could experience the momentary unique transition of another "Antarctica" and the lighting minuet.

Design theory seminars provide the best opportunity for explorations into the hibernating obscure. There is plenty of time for research; ideas can be discussed with other members of the class, and more ideas may emerge. Such findings can be incorporated into design projects at later time, in school or in life. The studio, unless it is a thesis studio with plenty of time for research, is not the best platform for such explorations. Among the topics we have occasionally suggested for such research, the most successful were those that addressed the relationships of extremely well known human conditions to architecture:

Love and architecture
Departure and architecture
Waiting and architecture
Architecture and the sound of birds, waves, rain
Architecture and the olfactory sense: flowers, gardens, perfumes
The poetics of night, the sky, the water, the breeze
Fear and architecture; anti-fear environments
Architecture of the animals: nests, lagoons, caves
Settlements on tiny rocks
Architecture and landscape based on the prescriptions of religious documents

All these topics address constants that have been with humans since primordial times (love, habitation, fear, satisfaction of the senses). Strange as it may sound, very little about them is widely known in the applied architectonic sense, although there have been buildings directly inspired by these topics. Figure 5-7 summarizes buildings through history that would have never been generated were it not for the motivating force of love. It provides a taste of the available wealth, and suggests that if the critical concern over architecture takes the angle of focus on the human condition, it can become constructive and stimulating in the future for "human" architecture.

We do not elaborate further on the suggested topics because we do not want to intrude on the dynamism of the process of students discovering them through original research. They must make it on their own through a course focusing on these issues. Equally important is their own reading of mythology, as opposed to hearing about it from others.

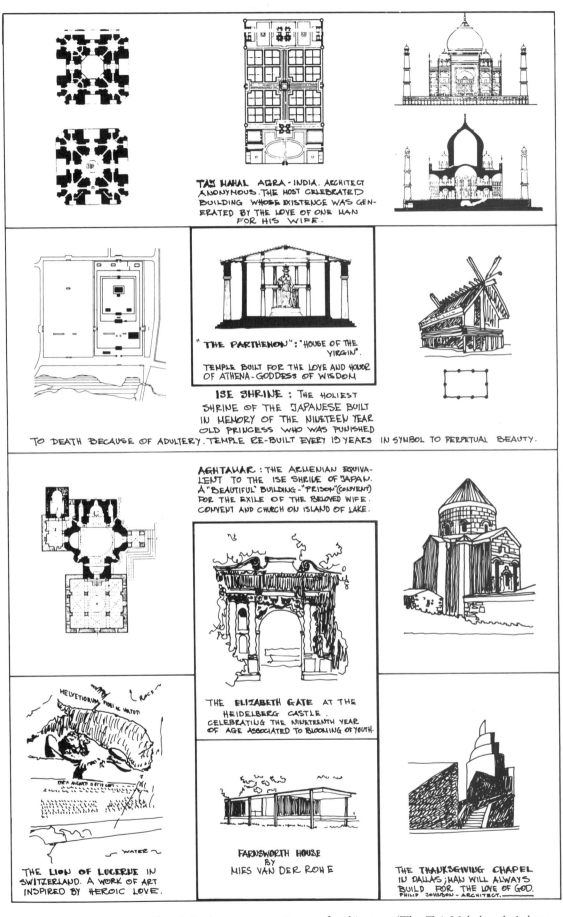

TAJ MAHAL AGRA - INDIA. ARCHITECT ANONYMOUS. THE MOST CELEBRATED BUILDING WHOSE EXISTENCE WAS GENERATED BY THE LOVE OF ONE MAN FOR HIS WIFE.

"THE PARTHENON": "HOUSE OF THE VIRGIN".

TEMPLE BUILT FOR THE LOVE AND HONOR OF ATHENA - GODDESS OF WISDOM

ISE SHRINE : THE HOLIEST SHRINE OF THE JAPANESE BUILT IN MEMORY OF THE NINETEEN YEAR OLD PRINCESS WHO WAS PUNISHED TO DEATH BECAUSE OF ADULTERY. TEMPLE RE-BUILT EVERY 19 YEARS IN SYMBOL TO PERPETUAL BEAUTY.

AGHTAMAR : THE ARMENIAN EQUIVALENT TO THE ISE SHRINE OF JAPAN. A "BEAUTIFUL" BUILDING - "PRISON" (CONVENT) FOR THE EXILE OF THE BELOVED WIFE. CONVENT AND CHURCH ON ISLAND OF LAKE.

THE ELIZABETH GATE AT THE HEIDELBERG CASTLE. CELEBRATING THE NINETEENTH YEAR OF AGE ASSOCIATED TO BLOOMING OF YOUTH.

THE LION OF LUCERNE IN SWITZERLAND. A WORK OF ART INSPIRED BY HEROIC LOVE.

FARNSWORTH HOUSE BY MIES VAN DER ROHE

THE THANKSGIVING CHAPEL IN DALLAS ; MAN WILL ALWAYS BUILD FOR THE LOVE OF GOD. PHILIP JOHNSON - ARCHITECT.

**Fig. 5-7.** *Love as a motivator of architecture.(The Taj Mahal and Aghtamar drawings, adapted from Henri Stierline,* Encyclopedia of World Architecture. *New York: Van Nostrand Reinhold, 1983)*

## Summary

Age-old attitudes toward the cosmos have disappeared from attention, "obscured" by other values and the "modern" way of life. In this chapter we examine our primordial beliefs and propose their rediscovery and inclusion in the design process. Myth, custom, ritual, and language form the basis of the "primordially obscure." But any other angle from which architecture has not yet been seen is also considered to belong to a separate category of the obscure. We strengthen this channel through intensive efforts to see architecture from "obscure" vantage points, such as "night and architecture" and "love and architecture."

## References

Antoniades, Anthony C. "Evolution of the Red." *A + U Architecture and Urbanism,* May 1986, p. 29.

————. "Humor in Architecture." *Technodomica,* August 1979.

————. "Athenas Mitra" (Matrix of Athens). *Sygchrona Themata,* 27 (June 1986).

Blier, Suzanne Preston. "Houses Are Human: Architectural Self-images of Africa's Tamberma." *Journal of the Society of Architectural Historians,* 42,4 (December 1983).

Candilis, George. *Batir la vie.* Paris: Stock, 1977.

Eliade, Mircea. *The Myth of the Eternal Return.* Trans. Willard R. Trask. New York: Pantheon, 1954.

————. *The Sacred and the Profane.* New York: Harcourt, Brace and World, 1959.

————. *Ordeal by Labyrinth: Conversations with Claude-Henri Rocquet.* Trans. Derek Coltman. Chicago: University of Chicago Press, 1982.

Hamilton, Edith. *Mythology: Timeless Tales of Gods and Heroes.* New York: Mentor, 1940.

Ishii, Kazuhiro. "Intentional Regression." *Kenchinku Bunka,* July 1975.

Mead, Margaret. "Creativity in Cross-Cultural Perspective." In *Creativity and Its Cultivation,* ed. Harold Anderson. New York: Harper & Row, 1959.

Oates, Joyce Carol. *On Boxing.* Garden City, NY: Doubleday, 1987.

Oliver, Paul. *Shelter, Sign and Symbol.* Woodstock, NY: The Overlook Press, 1977.

Porphyrios, Demetri. *Sources of Modern Eclecticism.* New York: St. Martin's Press, 1982.

Rykwert, Joseph. *On Adam's House in Paradise.* Cambridge, MA: MIT Press, 1981.

————. *The Idea of a Town.* Princeton, NJ: Princeton University Press, 1976.

Vico, Gianbattista. *The Autobiography of Gianbattista Vico.* Ithaca and London: Cornell University Press, 1944.

Whitehead, Alfred North. *Symbolism: Its Meaning and Effect.* Barbour-Page Lectures, University of Virginia, 1927. New York: Capricorn Books, 1959.

# Chapter 6 Poetry and Literature

Some of the best descriptions of urban environments were those made of Paris by Henry Miller. If Paris had never been built, an urban designer of talent could have perhaps created it just by following Miller's descriptions. Dickens did the same for a bygone industrial London; for character and feeling of sophisticated multicultural recent America, one would seek the work of Richard Brautigan. Writers are unquestionably good sources for inspiration on many aspects of life, for the best among them describe life itself as they have seen it and experienced it, in spite of the many attempts to cover up the autobiographical changes of name and efforts to make one believe the situation is fictitious. Literature and classics are an indispensable tool for the intuitively inclined architect and architectural instructor. Yet literature is sometimes so utterly explicit that not much is left for the student to interpret. Let's look at some of the uses of poetry and literature in architecture.

## USES OF POETRY AND LITERATURE

Poetry and literature can be very useful to the designer in both didactic and inspirational terms. They are useful in a didactic sense in the following ways:

1. Through the observation of the governing rules for the structure of a particular work of literature or of a poem.
2. Through observations of the way writers and poets go about revealing the essentials of the plot, the central message.
3. Through the way writers deal with "mystery" and "surprise."
4. The overall economy of means and the amount of discipline on the part of the creator.
5. The meaning assigned to the various terms and situations used.
6. The particular use of language, the texture in the use of words and the overall texture of the literary tapestry.
7. The rhythm and the rhyme, and the overall tenor of the work with regard to the rhythmic rigor vs. the lack of it or the existence of other means for the treatment of the element of time (i.e., the classical vs. the modern).
8. The emphasis on form vs. the emphasis on meaning.
9. The overall tone of the piece (poem or novel) as a critical commentary on its time and place, a crafted piece expressing the conventional wisdom and the overall attitude of a people toward the issues contemplated.

10. The invaluable contribution of the commentary of writers and poets on their craft, as well as the contribution of literary criticism, a highly developed body of aesthetics that has a very strong relationship to the aesthetics of architecture.

Ralph Waldo Emerson, through his essays on the poet and literature, was among the first to address the reciprocal effects of poetry and literature on the human need for creative expression and stimulation of the imagination. In recent times Margaret MacDonald, in her landmark essay "The Language of Fiction," reinforced the suggestions we made above on the overall positive and didactic effects of poetry and literature. MacDonald provides the most convincing recent evidence for the attitude that literary works should have the ingredient of "convincing plausibility" as opposed to being totally out of the context of the reality of the place and "people" who generated them.

The idea of "convincing plausibility" rather than "unconvincingly possible" has immediate applicability to architecture, while it also suggests that literature as well as architecture largely depends on the receptivity of its audience, the "people" for whom they were generated. Without appropriate "receptors," poetry and literature do not exist. Novels and poems in which readers do not find themselves leave them untouched. Yet obviously not all people are the same. The world is composed of many different groups. The appreciation of things and concepts varies from group to group, from culture to culture; the mental images, the collective memory, and attitudes toward objective vs. subjective differ. And the objective vs. subjective disposition of the receptor greatly affects the usefulness of poetry or literature as a means for stimulation of architectural ideas.

There are elaborate discussions on the topics outlined above in books of literary criticism, and design students should be aware of these works and encouraged to make their own observations as they study poems or novels if they happen to go through this particular channel of creativity. Here we will focus on the broader issues through which architecture can benefit from poetry and literature.

## Inspirational Benefits

Poetry and literature can be inspirational for architects in two broad ways, the direct and the composite.

*Direct Inspiration.* The direct channel occurs through literal interpretations of the environments described in the literary work. There is static literal interpretation, when one makes a direct visual interpretation of the form and space elements of the environment as described in the literary work. There is also dynamic interpretation, when the architectural product is free of the direct depiction and focuses instead on the abstract communication of the "aura," the "spatial ambiance," and the overall "essence" of the literary piece.

These ideas can be understood by looking at set designs for the theater: a set design in which one can see balconies and streets as spelled out by the *Romeo and Juliet* script would constitute a direct literal interpretation of the play. An abstract set design in which we cannot see recognizable physical elements, but where we have no doubt whatsoever that Romeo and Juliet are about to have an encounter, would belong to the category of the direct/dynamic. In order to achieve the direct/dynamic, one must uncover and try to understand the "aura," the "mood," the "feeling" of the poem or of the literary piece.

Discovering (understanding, becoming cognizant of the particular discipline), for instance, T. S. Eliot or Edgar Allan Poe would be an invaluable gain for the architect. Take Poe, a poet of particular significance for our purposes, because he also wrote on aesthetics, and the synthesis of poetry, in ways that could be of great help to architects. Poe has been presented, among other things, as the writer of the "Poetic sense of the night"; he has repeatedly described night, especially the moments of the dusk, as part of his way of creating the atmosphere of a place. Architects who might be inspired to evoke such situations through space and architectonic language would be creating dynamic rather than static works.

*The Composite.* The final possibility of the use of poetry and literature we have called the composite. This is the case of inspiration in which the architect is influenced by what he or she reads (or has read) and is motivated to write. He writes notes to himself, scribbles down ideas, or becomes more systematic by writing fiction, writing poems, recording aphoristic statements, and writing essays about projects, before or after he has designed them, for personal or publication purposes.

If he is an architectural instructor, he writes design "problem statements" for the student design projects. Any one of these methods can be used before or after the design, yet it is in the predesign process that writing by the architect can be most beneficial. Of course, writing cannot and should not substitute for a simultaneous emphasis on drawing.

All the subcategories of the composite have been used occasionally as vehicles to creative architectural design. Contrary to the notion that architects do not write, or that architects are inarticulate, the fact is that the majority of the distinguished architects throughout history did indeed write, and a good number were prolific and accomplished writers (Frank Lloyd Wright, Le Corbusier, Alvar Aalto, Eric Mendelsohn). Several of them even wrote poetry, often incorporating poems in their theoretical essays, or publishing it for its own sake. Le Corbusier and John Hejduk are two well-known examples.

## Literary Influences on Recent Architecture

The architectural "problem statement" as a literary piece became very popular from the mid-1970s to the late 1980s. Teacher-architects such as John Hejduk, Rodolfo Machado, Jorge Silvetti, and Peter Waldman were the pioneers. They produced an anthology of programmatic narratives that could stand as literary pieces on their own merit; beyond the precision in the use of language, their writing is provocative and open ended, encouraging diversity of interpretation. *Provocation* and *open-endedness* are, in fact, key qualities of writing whose goal is not only the challenge of imagination, but also the development of critical thinking on issues of the individual versus the society.

The programs written by Peter Waldman for his students exemplify the genre. Literary minuets of sorts, they convey the mood of time and place, while they progressively introduce the reader to the secrets, the likes, and the personalities of the fictitious clients, Sigismundo and Lady Malcontenta Malatesta. One person's mental fixation about a period or a group of people can easily seduce others into the same channel of fantasy if it is presented in a vivid and suggestive literary manner. Waldman's characters possessed "plausibility," a fundamental requisite for being accepted by others (especially students).

John Hejduk's writing has been enigmatic, highly provocative and stimulating. His problem statements are appropriately labeled "masks." To uncover the mystery of the mask will reveal the real face, the being, the road to the architectural Xanadu. Giorgio De Chirico once said: "What shall I love unless it be the enigma?" John Hejduk has become the sphinx of architectural writing of our time—a sphinx of delightful charm. One wonders how many of Hejduk's students have managed to untie the enigmatic knots. One certainly wonders whether the intoxicating power of a Hejduk narrative, with its enigmatic and exponential open-endedness and the occasional insertion of poetry, is the answer for a universal formula for problem statement writing. I believe that although it can challenge the student's imagination, it removes us so completely from the sphere of reality—that challenging arena of architecture—that it requires careful attention on the part of the student, the instructor, or the school so that other scenarios and other studios can gain the students' attention for their applicability and reality.

To our knowledge, Rodolfo Machado has produced the best essays of the kind we are asking for, where "Heaven meets Earth." His sensitive and highly emotional attitude is balanced by a serious inclination toward pragmatism, something many Postmodern instructors lacked. Machado's attitude has been a combination of subjectivity balanced by a high degree of self-discipline. Machado, moved by his own designs, accompanies them through the hidden spheres of his imagination with fiction or literary essays as original as the designs themselves. He gives life to his works; taking the position that they were built and are alive, he assumes the role of critic or historian of the future, looking back at his projects, describing them, evaluating them, or even lamenting their future.

Machado's literary triptych in *Architecture and Literature* is perhaps the best evidence of the power of the architecture/literature reciprocity. His postscript from this work perhaps summarizes it best:

> Fictions are the testimony of a longing for another reality, a reality that is different from most of the built reality; the rhetoric is there to make the reader desire that which has been imagined. . . .
>   Don't we want the as-of-yet nonexistent to exist?"

Much of what Machado strives for will depend on the tone of the fiction, the "plausible impossibility" of Aristotle. If the fiction is to lead the architect to "implausible impossibilities," then we are confronted with a case of the absolutely impossible, the improbable, and perhaps ultimate despair. Such a route would not be helpful, and works of this type, in spite of the publicity they have been given, should be viewed with great skepticism. In our view, typical of this "implausible impossibility" is the whole architecture based on the Eisenman fiction, best exemplified by his proposal "Moving Arrows, Eros and Other Errors," based on his fictitious theoretical construct (deconstruction-reconstruction) of the Romeo and Juliet town of Verona.

Considering the quality of the student projects we have seen by students of these instructors, we would say that the fictional narratives struck home and produced very positive results. We can therefore suggest that the architectural "fiction" or "narrative," in order to be beneficial, has to fulfill the following conditions:

1. Be really able to stand alone as fiction
2. Be pleasing on its own merit
3. Be personal as well as universal
4. Be expressive of an inner need for self-criticism
5. Be original and thoughtful
6. Be provocative and open-ended, as well as obscure enough to involve the active participation of the reader.

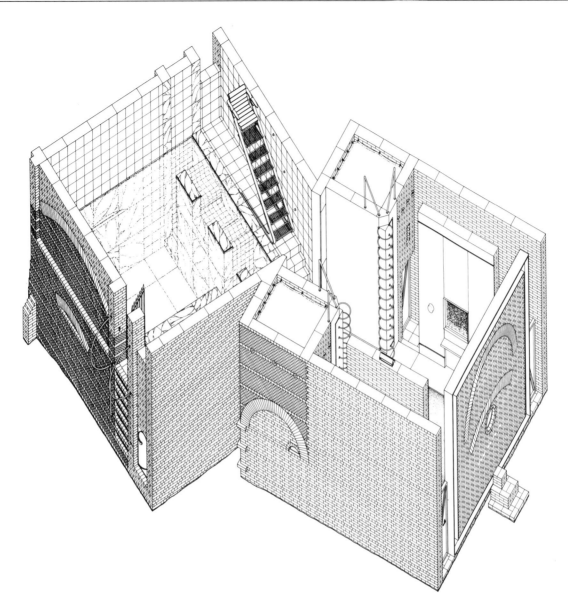

**Fig. 6-1.** *"Taberna ancipitis Formae Architectorum Machadus Silvettusque Mirabile Inventio MCMLXXXIII."* *(Courtesy Rodolfo Machado)*

The question then arises: Which of the various literary forms is more powerful as a vehicle for the stimulation of the designer—fiction, essays, or poetry?

## THE SUPREMACY OF POETRY OVER LITERATURE

We have already argued for the supremacy of drawing over narrative in our discussion of the channel of transformation. Yet at this stage we do not deny the pleasure as well as the benefit that can be derived if one feels at home with the narrative or the writing of scenarios. We should be open, contemplate them, and always encourage dynamic interpretations of such scenarios in drawing. The best scenario is to do the narratives first and then project them into drawings. We do not argue this. What we argue is the studious and deliberate effort on the part of every designer to expose him or herself to literature and even more to poetry in general, while focusing on the poetry of their own land, as well as the poetry of the people they design for.

It would be inconceivable to ask an architect who has not studied the Homeric epics to design for the Greek life style and the Greek landscape. It would be equally absurd not to ask every architect, city planner, urban

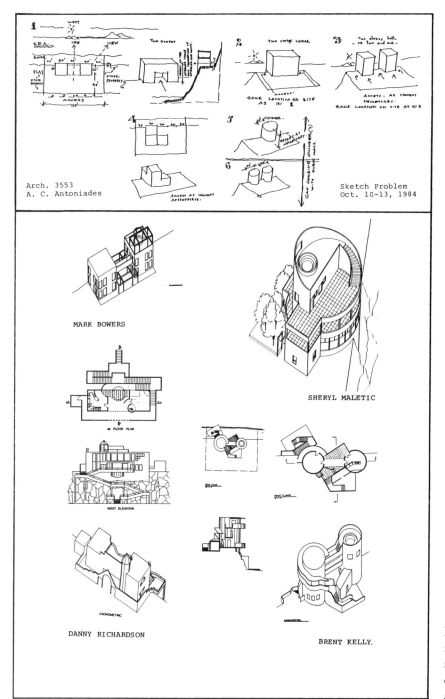

**Fig. 6-2.** *Sketch problems for a weekend retreat for a writer based on the "weekend reading" of the work of the assigned writers. (From the author's third-year design studio at UT Arlington)*

designer, interior designer and landscape architect to read Virgil's *Aeneid*. The epic of any land offers the architectonic foundations of the primordial, and a deep study of such works makes one realize that not much has really changed from what these poets described in their epics. It would be more appropriate to the Greek climate and culture to go on adopting the simplicity and richness of the Ulyssean palace (with its spaces and antispaces, courtyards and upper quarters, with the olive tree holding and being part of the bed, symbolizing the eternity of fidelity), rather than looking at examples from other customs alien to the place.

Pikionis and Aris Konstantinides, two of the most thoughtful and influential architects in modern Greece, were extremely well versed in the two epics, and many of the critical sugestions Pikionis made to his students were offered directly out of the Homeric verse. Alvar Aalto would never perhaps have done the architecture he did for Finland if it had not developed from, among other ingredients, the feelings of national and regional pride he acquired through the reading of the Kalevala, the national epic of his own country. Furthermore, one could argue, he would have never been challenged in the overall literary sense had it not been for the subsequent relationship and friendship with the literary critic Göran Schildt, his biographer. The same was true for Frank Lloyd Wright, whose exchanges with his cousin, the great American poet Carl Sandburg, left a lasting and challenging mark on him.

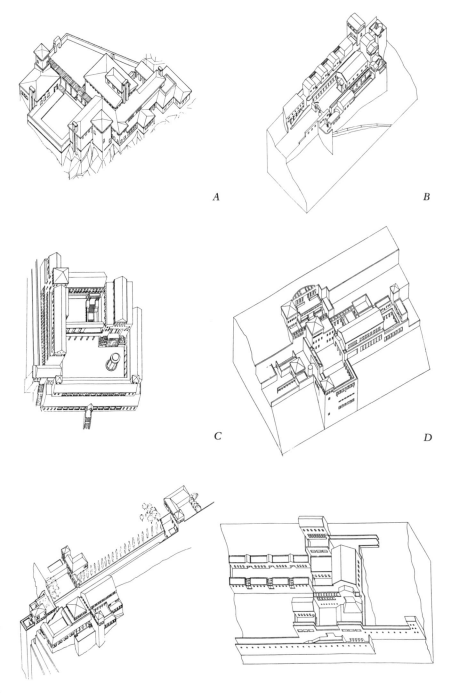

*A*

*B*

*C*

*D*

*E*

*F*

**Fig. 6-3.** *Palace of Odysseus. Student proposals after reading the* Odyssey. *A. Guy Chipman. B. Hsin-Joy Wong. C. Shin Jung-Seoh. D. Amran Abdul-Salam. E. Jimmy Craig Miyoshi. F. Ro-haida Brahim.*

Contrary to what we believe, the supremacy of poetry over other forms of literary expression, recent architectural literature has focused more on the literature of fiction, the essay, the narrative and the novel. Its limited attention to poetry has been concentrated on selected works of an "epic" nature, such as Milton's *Paradise Lost,* a favorite reference of the Postmodern period and the wrong example, I believe. This particular poem has been criticized by poets; Edgar Allan Poe found the economy of its means out of proportion and was very critical of its length, finding it a work composed of many smaller poems of inner measure and substance, much stronger in their separate existence than the lengthy whole. It can also be criticized by non-poets, particularly in architectural terms, in that it provides a precedent of "not knowing where to stop the composition" and of sacrificing the impact and the "delight" of the occasional delightful parts to an unnecessarily lengthy whole. Yet despite our disagreement over the nature of the literary and poetic precedents selected, the editors of *VIA 8,* the Journal of the Graduate School of Fine Arts of the University of Pennsylvania, brought the literature-poetry-architecture argument into focus, setting the stage for discussion, debate, reference, and precedent on the subject. This journal issue that focused on key literary figures of metaphorical, obscure, and metaphysical inclinations (Poe, Borges, Eco) will be the best introduction to the literature-architecture relationship for some time to come.

## POETRY: THE POETIC PALETTE

Students and architects should study the poets of their land or of the land of the people for whom they are attempting to build. Of course, they should be careful and selective. Romantic, sentimental poets, whose approach is descriptive, verbose, and narrative, can be avoided, as their work is already too "static" a source to start with. Poets who searched deep into their environment, their people, and themselves, who are brief and precise, can be outstanding sources for illuminating understanding and providing dynamic inspiration. The poetry of the best among the Greek poets sprang from the secrets and the apocrypha of the land, the people, the art and architecture that flourished in it, the language and the collective existence of the country. Poets such as Dionysios Solomos, Kostis Palamas, Angelos Sikelianos, Constantinos Cavafy, George Seferis, Odysseus Elytis, Costas Varnalis, and Yannis Ritsos became in a collective sense the "genius loci" of the Greek landscape, architecturally conceived.

The poetry of Greece has distilled popular notions and understandings regarding space that are fundamental in architecture. Aspects of the "significant" and the "signified," meaning as related to architecture, human scale, the relativity of environmental impact, aspects of environmental change and human engineering, become crystal clear through reference to certain poems of George Seferis. The same poet made extraordinary conceptual references to Greek places and the Greek house, and he eventually made us understand the complexities, temperament, and incomprehensibility of both "country" and "house," these personal and primordial archetypes.

Other poets addressed other aspects of the Greek space before Seferis. Kostis Palamas frequently referred to landscape and architectural creations, and he employed architectural allegory on many occasions in his poetry. He spoke about Greece, its greatness, its art, and its past glamour through buildings ("the Temple," the Parthenon, "the rock," the Acropolis). Cavafy became the poet of the "broader Greek space," the poet of the Hellenic Diaspora, a Diaspora that owes its existence to the constant attraction exerted on it by the motherland, the meaning of Greece which recognizes no boundaries, no geographic or historic limitations.

Yet other poets, such as Varnalis and Ritsos, gave us other details of the Helladic space: the gathering places of the working people, the taverns, the evening bars, the cafés, the cemeteries, the places of political exile—in other words, they pointed out and expressed the places of everyday life, places and spaces of gloom and grief, thus completing the portfolio of Greek space. It is difficult to single out a body of poetry that dealt with the physical world and architecture in a more metaphysical way than the poetry of twentieth-century Greece. And since the architect is the poet of space par excellence, it is inevitable that he seeks in poetry relief and companionship in the struggle of the creative process, inspiration and stimulation, and even a point of departure for his own work.

Many of the routes to creativity that are argued here exist in poetry. Metaphors and allegories are present in most of the works of Greek poets. Cavafian poetry is based on metaphors; this poet frequently employs elements of the environmental space, the city, the house, the windows, the walls, the streets, in order to express through them the psychological and existential condition of his concern. In Cavafy's poetry and especially in the whole process of evolution of his famous poem, "The City," one encounters extraordinary alliance of the concerns of the literal, the metaphoric, and the sensual/experiential. These are aspects of reality which should also concern the architect creator.

The architect searches for the authenticity of the cities or for the uniqueness, the intellectual essence, the meaning of "house," "window," "door," "wall," "nooks," "corners," or other details of the project under construction; good architects should not accept recipes and standard solutions. Creation in the poetic sense, and as Jean Lescure has argued, must be based on pure beginnings and be "an exercise in freedom" (see Lescure in Bachelard 1969; also Chang 1956). The knowledge of the discipline, the knowledge of history, the knowledge from the study of precedents must "be accompanied by an equal capacity to forget knowing. Not knowing is not a form of ignorance, but a difficult transcendence of knowledge." And as an artist in his effort to achieve the "possibility of a fresh impact must not create the way he lives," he must "live the way he creates"; poetic architects—that is, creative, fresh architects, do research, but also search inside themselves. They try to see all the parameters of the problem; the tangible and the intangible aspects of architecture. They understand what must be mastered and forgotten, if the result is to transcend expedient triviality and become a true poetic creation, a unique creation, or statement of freedom.

The anonymous Greek architects who produced the architecture of the islands, the architects who were equated by Aris Konstantinides with the "people" and the people of Alexandria, not Alexander the Great and his city planners, were the main shapers of the life and character, the urban uniqueness of Alexandria, a city that is a summary of the Greek spirit, the beliefs and the life style of the race. When we refer to the works of the poets that express such a people, it is as if we refer to the body of architectural criticism as stated by the people themselves. Poets represent the collective psyche of the people; they are the voices of the collective spirit. Greek poetry therefore represents a treasure of such criticism; when the poets speak, it is as if one finds there the commentary and the thoughts of the whole people. The "Basement Tavern" of Varnalis, for example, represents an archetype of the social life of Greece of a period gone by.

Poetry as well as literature (but we believe poetry more than literature), can be extraordinary channels for architectural creativity only under appropriate circumstances. Readers may already have experienced some difficulty with the discussion based on the example of contemporary Greek poetry. Yet this was necessary for me personally, as it represents part of

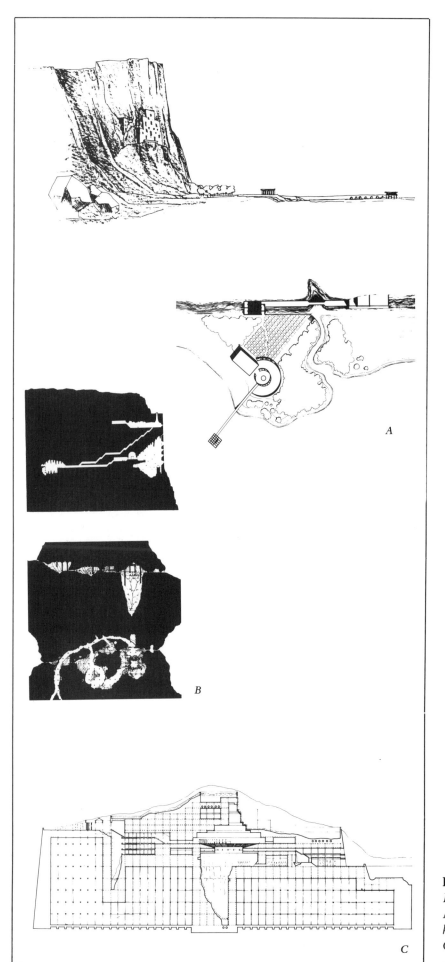

**Fig. 6-4.** *Sibyl's Cave and the Infernal Regions: designs inspired by reading the Aeneid of Virgil.* **A.** *Sibyl's Cave: Rohaida Brahim.* **B.** *Infernal Regions: Jimmy Craig Miyoshi.* **C.** *Infernal Regions: Amran Abdul-Salam.*

**Fig. 6-5.** *Visual depiction of Homeric passages that inspired the Elpenorean architecture, an architecture of stairs and terraces, at the cutting edge between celestial sublimity and freedom, handicapped nowadays by restrictive building codes. From the* Odyssey, *Papsody L.* **B, E.** *Architect, the author.* **D.** *Project by author's student, Christine Page.*

my own effort to construct a personal "poetic palette" for my own architectural design references (Fig. 6-5). It is natural that non-Greek readers may have difficulty with the poets presented; yet it is my belief that if a poem is carefully selected to address universal values and concepts familiar to most people, then that poem can easily be accepted by everyone, as it will excite the emotions and the spirit. It is that kind of excitement that the instructor should seek to stimulate, and it will come only through carefully selected examples that will help students produce results.

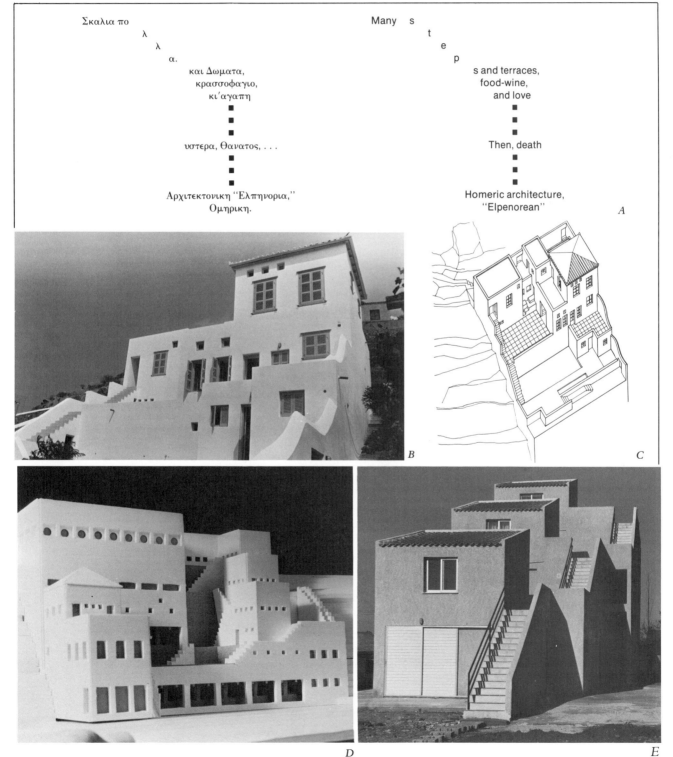

If in a cross-cultural situation instructors encourage students to select poets representative of their own cultures, it will be like helping them to produce works that will be in tune with the intellectual and spiritual life of the place they come from or the particular place for which they design, because poetry is the power of the collective emotion of a people, the collective critical attitude of a place, the birth of life from within.

It is not difficult for the architect versed in poetry to take some time to produce a list of the poets of his or her own country and the significance of their particular contributions. There are, of course, instances where such research is already available. The American architect is rather lucky in this respect, especially because of the extraordinary Wallace Stevens. One could call him "the poet of architects," for he wrote with direct architectonic metaphors, often naming architecture in his poems or even using it as the title for his creations. Stevens was strong enough to give credit to physical space and to the landscape-supplied forms for the lessons he derived about order, which he used subsequently in order to construct a landscape of the mind.

In the absence of literary studies such as those available in the case of Stevens, the architect must do the search completely on his or her own. He or she may perhaps not be absolutely right in strictly literary terms—after all, architects are not literary critics—but he or she will have done him or herself a great favor by collecting a palette of his or her own poetic framework of awareness. This palette will come in handy for future architectural projects, or when he or she is in doubt about the general appreciation of things and the meaning assigned to things and ideas by other people. Such a "poetic palette" can be developed by each student individually; it can begin through a design studio or a theory course on the poetry/literature—architectural design inquiry.

## UNIVERSALS OF POETIC VIRTUE

If the poetic palette is seen as an individual responsibility for a nationally and regionally relevant architecture, then the study of what one could call the *universals* of poetry could help achieve a much better architecture over-all, in total peace with the eternal values shared and appreciated by most of humankind. We must understand the basic wisdom of the poets themselves with regard to their craft, as well as the typical universal cases that exemplify the best of poetic virtue. Each architect should contemplate them as well, and should do mental as well as actual design exercises, setting as the goal the same rules and restrictions observed in poetry.

We have found these universals to be the following:

1. Form vs. content aspects of the poem
2. Rhythm as a technique of poetic structure
3. Relationship of poetry to music
4. Pure vs. enriched (or burdened) by social content
5. Economy of means (long vs. short) and desired aesthetic impact
6. Nonconformism to any one of the above and attitudes on "uniqueness" as advantage or handicap

The design instructor can guide the discussion on each of these topics, while pointing out specific references for the opinions of both poets and architects on the relevant subjects. We have not found a more comprehensive discussion on all of these items than the essay "Attitudes on Poetry and Aesthetics" by Edgar Allan Poe. Equally fundamental is his other essay, "The Philosophy of Composition."

It is also my belief that we cannot afford to miss the significance and importance of the Japanese haiku as a model not only for architectural design philosophy and the philosophy of the essence, but as an overall prototype for a discussion of the relationship between a work of art, the discipline of the art, and the economy of means. The haiku, this seventeen-syllable poem, I consider to be of much greater significance for poetry/architecture design didactic than the epic that is favored by several architectural writers and architectural instructors at the present.

## Actual and Metaphoric Significance of Haiku

Our emphasis on haiku is based on the fact that these poems manage to say as a rule whatever they were set to say with no more words than necessary, while they almost always open up numerous avenues for further interpretation and the imagination of the reader. Haiku, after all, is as open-ended as Zen itself. It has to be taken for what it is and for whatever the reader can do with it. Its power is exponential. Whole designs can be worked out on the basis of one brief haiku; a haiku could be conceived in return as the greatest statement any critic could render in an effort to sum up the essence and dynamism of a design. Smart designers, like smart people, will understand; one does not need many words in order to be convincing about the essence of things.

> The old pond
> A frog jumps in
> Plop!

The work of the Zen poet Basho, creator of this haiku (perhaps the most famous of all haiku) should become mandatory reading for the creative design student. For Basho has captured the essence of nature, the concept of space and infinity, the temporal and the universal, the essence of life and art. His haiku will teach, inspire, and excite; they will make the designer think twice and make him confident about the importance of *knowing when to stop*, a discipline which, of course, will take him the greater part of a lifetime to acquire.

In purely metaphoric terms, architects may eventually develop the ambition to create their own "architectural haiku" in stones and mortar, and set such edifices as the goal of their architectural creations. And like the Zen monks, such architects may not want to talk about their designs, pretending ignorance and hopefully having reached the state of creative Nirvana. We believe that Luis Barragán, Ricardo Legorreta, Kazuo Shinohara, and the (small-scale) Tadao Ando to have been such haiku architects. Mies Van der Rohe was perhaps the most glamorous, the only difference being that he spelled out the "less is more" instead of leaving us with the memory of his Barcelona Pavilion.

Haiku or any other form of art that might set in motion the development of the imagination and encourage the designer to exercise his or her mental and critical faculties is an appropriate "metaphoric" vehicle for architecture. Whenever poetry reaches its highest level of excellence, and whenever an architect manages to achieve a building based on the principles and means of such poetry, we are confronted with the highest form of resonance, the achievement of art. We believe that poetry can lend its haiku to architecture as the metaphoric goal for architectural excellence.

## Some Suggestions

We certainly cannot prove scientifically the universality of our contentions in this chapter. But we have become personally convinced of their validity through the design results experienced with the projects given to students when we followed the poetry/literature channel to architectural creativity.

*A*

Fig. 6-6. *Architectural haiku by the late Luis Barragán and Ricardo Legorreta. A. Luis Barragán, the Egerstrom House, Mexico City, 1967–68. B. Ricardo Legorreta, IBM Building, Guadalajara, Mexico.*

*B*

Fig. 6-7. *"Three Villages" shopping center in Westlake, Texas. Ricardo Legorreta, architect.*

We followed the arguments presented above, talked about the various issues, discussed and analyzed poets and specific poems, encouraged students to start working on their own "poetic palette," and placed particular emphasis on haiku. I believe strongly that it would be very beneficial to others, especially those who deal with cross-cultural studios, to share these experiences and personal beliefs and attempt the poetry/literature channel in their own studios.

If in a cross-cultural situation instructors encourage students to select poets representative of their own cultures, they will be helping them to design in tune with the intellectual and spiritual context of the place of their origins. And if the same students are also exposed to the universally held notion of the poets with regard to discipline and the inherent rules of poetry, they will eventually produce architectural designs possessing the power to raise collective emotions.

**Fig. 6-8.** *Entrance court, Camino Real Hotel, Mexico City. Ricardo Legorreta, architect.*

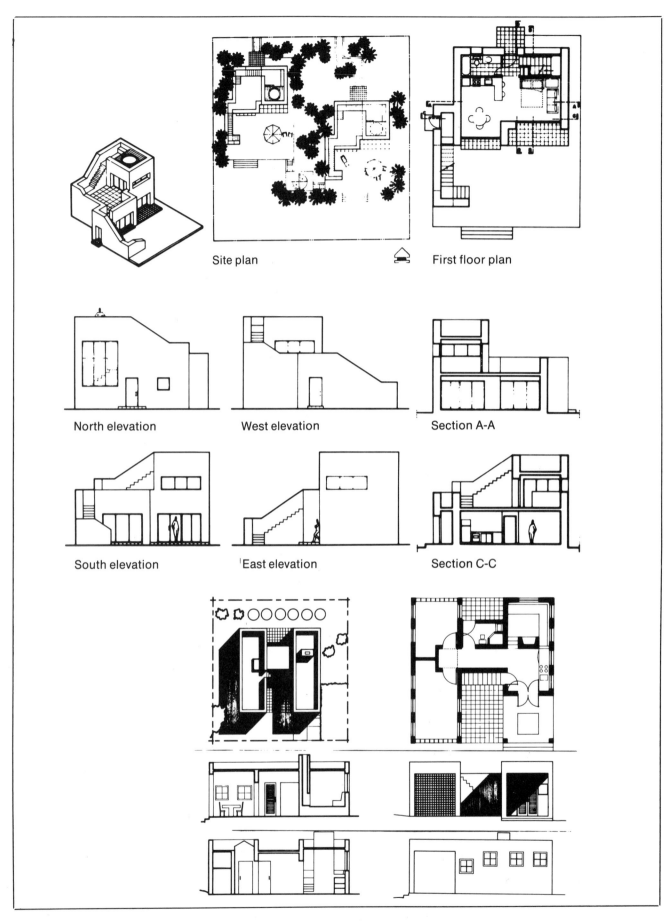

Site plan       First floor plan

North elevation     West elevation     Section A-A

South elevation     East elevation     Section C-C

**Fig. 6-9.** *Samples of architectural haiku from the studio. Design for a vacation bungalow in Mexico, Cliff Welch (above) and Eric Jakimier (below). From the author's second-year design studio, UT Arlington, 1984.*

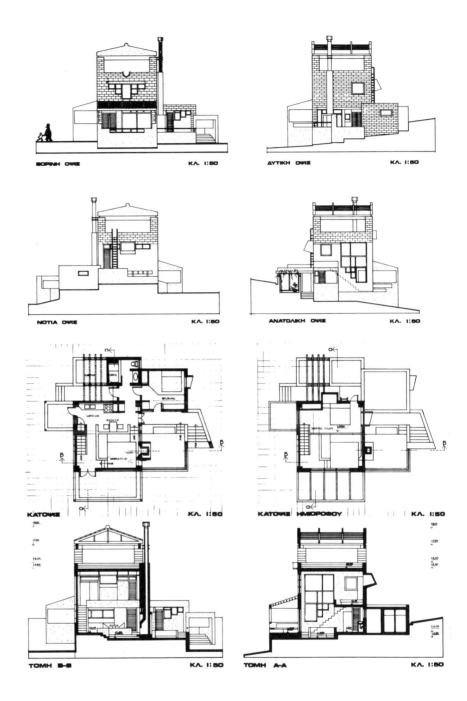

**Fig. 6-10.** *Villa Natassa. Proposal for a vacation bungalow in Corfu. Unbuilt project, 1978. Exercise on a T. S. Eliot–Odysseus Elytis theme. Architect, the author.*

## Summary

Poetry and literature are two powerful vehicles to architectural design. Literary methods are particularly useful and we propose the hypothesis that poetry is superior to literature for creative design purposes. Poetry is presented as the body of written word that summarizes collective attitudes of people, and is the requisite for national, regional, and local design, expressive of the particular uniqueness of place. A designer should have a "poetic palette" that includes local as well as universal ingredients. We use Japanese Haiku poetry as the metaphor for the ultimate goal of architectural poetry.

# References

"Art and Literature." *VIA 8, Journal of the Graduate School of Fine Arts, University of Pennsylvania*, 1986.

Bachelard, Gaston. *Poetics of Space*. Boston: Beacon Press, 1969.

Bard, James. *The Dome and the Rock: Structure in the Poetry of Wallace Stevens*. Baltimore: Johns Hopkins Press. 1968.

Chang, Amos Ih Tiao. *The Tao of Architecture*. Princeton, NJ: Princeton University Press, 1956, pp. 70, 71, 72.

Eliot, T. S. Introduction. In *The Art of Poetry*, by Paul Valéry. Bollingen Series XLV.7. Princeton, NJ: Princeton University Press, 1958.

Emerson, Ralph Waldo. "The Poet" and "Literature." In *The Complete Essays and Other Writings by Ralph Waldo Emerson*, ed. Brooks Atkinson. New York: Random House, Modern Library, 1940.

Homer. *The Iliad. The Odyssey.*

Leatherbarrow, David. "The Poetics of the Architectural Setting: A Study of the Writings of Edgar Allan Poe." *VIA 8, Journal of the Graduate School of Fine Arts, University of Pennsylvania*, 1986, p. 9.

Lerup, Lars. "Research for Appearance." *Journal of Architectural Education*, 32, 4 (May 1979), p. 22.

Machado, Rodolfo. "Fictions on Fictions: A Postscript." *VIA 8, Journal of the Graduate School of Fine Arts, University of Pennsylvania*, 1986, p. 83.

———. "Images." *VIA 8, Journal of the Graduate School of Fine Arts, University of Pennsylvania*, 1986.

MacDonald, Margaret. "The Language of Fiction." In Kennick, *Art and Philosophy: Readings in Aesthetics*. New York: St. Martin's Press, 1964, p. 307.

Poe, Edgar Allan. *Poese ke fantasia* (Poetry and imagination). Athens, 1988, pp. 103–110.

Stevens, Wallace. *The Necessary Angel: Essays on Reality and the Imagination*. New York: Knopf, 1951.

Trypanis, C. A. *A Medieval and Modern Greek Poetry*. New York: Oxford University Press, 1951.

Valéry, Paul. *The Art of Poetry*. Bollingen Series XLV.7. Princeton, NJ: Princeton University Press, 1958.

Virgil. *The Aeneid.*

Waldman, Peter. "A Primer of Easy Pieces: Teaching Through Typological Narrative." *Journal of Architectural Education*, 2 (Winter 1982), pp. 10–13.

Whiterman, John. "Site Unscene: Peter Eisenmann: Moving Arrows, Eros, and Other Errors." *AA Files #2*, Summer 1986, pp. 78, 79.

# Chapter 7 The Exotic and Multicultural

*One learns the language
through translating; I do not
mean the one he translates from,
but his own.*

George Seferis

*Each of us is a kind of
crossroads, where things
happen.*

Claude Lévi-Strauss

There are two photographs of Freud taken inside his study, a few hours before he left his home forever. They show the dolls and paraphernalia he had collected during trips to various parts of the world. To him they represented the summary of the world cultures, constant symbolic reminders of a broader framework of which he was only a part.

When people in earlier times crossed Asia in pursuit of the silk trade, going with their caravans through canyons and inaccessible mountains, they carefully selected rest places to tell their stories, exchange information about the road, visit the temples they built for their gods, and live in harmony and peace for as long as they were together. Whenever different peoples came face to face for a common cause, trade or knowledge, humankind experienced instances of harmonious equilibrium and peace. Ideas flourished along with the advancement of material wealth and prosperity of all sorts.

Architecture has been of particular significance as an agent of peace, of cross-cultural and intellectual evolution. It can enhance multicultural harmony and coexistence, while it can benefit from multiculturalism. Evidence of the multicultural universalism of architecture is the love with which architects have studied their history over the evolution of their discipline, along with their love for nature, wherever they may have found it. History is the flesh, bones and intellect of humankind. Nature is the source of the stones, mortar, and materials used by architects. History and nature are the tangible and primordial universals that have brought mutual respect and fraternal association among architects, while they have generated the tolerance and excitement for everything foreign and exotic.

The idea of the exotic has long fascinated writers and philosophers. Aristotle referred to it occasionally, while the whole inquiry of history as well as the inquiry of geography would have never been written were it not for the thirst for the exotic. This thirst made writers such as Herodotus and Stravon visit remote lands, and record and report their findings.

Much of the subsequent advancement of humankind is due to similar attractions to the exotic. Recent fields such as cultural anthropology developed out of visits and research by scientists to exotic lands. Claude Lévi-Strauss and Margaret Mead are among the better-known pioneers in these endeavors.

As we will see, the exotic has a dual nature that can render it beneficial to those who involve themselves with it; they can learn from it directly, or they can sharpen the understanding they have of their own culture. On the other hand, they will come to an eventual state of creativity, full and content with what they have seen and absorbed, ready to start their own lives and to produce their own creations for their own people and place. We suggest that a serious wandering with the exotic in the pursuit of knowledge can help us reach the eventual state of really knowing ourselves and the context of our own culture and the culture of our people, thus affording us the luxury of a psychological nirvana for really creative and original endeavors.

## THE DUAL NATURE OF THE EXOTIC

The exotic, a word of Greek origin, has a dual meaning: the one is physical, the other metaphysical.

The physical refers to items that exist in other places, outside the boundaries of the pivotal point of reference. It has a geographic connotation. The more remote the place of the origin of the person who seeks the exotic, the stronger the power of the attraction seems to be. We consider exotic places that are remote from our own. Sometimes people go to extraordinary extremes to see exotic places and study exotic cultures for themselves. The pursuit of the exotic may occasionally become an obsession.

The metaphysical concept of the exotic has negative connotations. The exotic in this sense is conceived as the mysterious, metaphysical power to keep someone far away, to charm, distract, disorient, and often deceive, while eventually destroying a person. The negative associations have been presented metaphorically through the transformation of the anthropomorphic into the bestial. Homer was the first to articulate this view of the exotic. The Sirens, his particular poetic creatures, with the intoxicating sound of their songs had the power to arouse the imagination of navigators, who would fantasize them as beautiful women, worth the detour to see, only to discover, when it was too late, that these were not beautiful women but man-eating beasts. The Homeric parable is still true today and summarizes all the pluses and minuses of the spell of the exotic.

In architecture, the exotic can be didactic and a source of stimulation for the imagination; it can also deceive, disorient, and distract if not approached with forethought; one should do as Ulysses did, tie oneself to the mast; pass by the sirens, see for yourself, take with you whatever you may consider worthwhile, and leave. Continue toward your original destination. This destination in architecture, as we have so often stressed, is to design and build. Now we are going to suggest further to *build in the place where you know you belong,* where the people, their culture, the area and the materials, are those of the land you were destined to serve.

Many who were obviously devoured by the sirens of the architecturally exotic were not tightly disciplined in the field of architecture. Some were even well-known architects, who eventually became notorious for having failed in their efforts to build in exotic lands. Le Corbusier's buildings in Chandigarh in India, Louis Kahn's effort with the government buildings in Pakistan, Walter Gropius's effort with the American Embassy in Athens, along with the score of the secondary architects and foreign

architectural firms who built in the Arab countries, have long been evaluated by those who have lived in them as failures. These architects never
took the time to genuinely understand the people, the climate, the materials, the methods of construction, and the techniques of foreign places.
The overall record of architects who have built in exotic lands is simply
failure.

The cause of that failure was the architects' superficiality and arrogance
in believing that the mere desire to build in a place without investing the
necessary time in the study and digestion of everything that has to do with
the place, would be enough for success. There is obviously an inherent
conflict between "business timing" and the time it takes to digest and make
an exotic culture part of you. It takes a very strong personal decision to
settle and make a career in an exotic place. For one person to become
"another people" in culture and in spirit is a very difficult, lifelong process
that only a very few can manage successfully. Some positive examples are
Ralph Erskine, an Englishman who made his career in Sweden, Antoine
Predock and I. M. Pei, French and Chinese born, respectively, who remained in America after their studies and developed meteoric careers there;
Jörn Utzon and Henning Larsen, both from Denmark, who did some of
their best projects in remote areas such as Australia and the Arab world.
Walter Gropius was apparently well aware of this fact, perhaps through
personal experience. When Ricardo Legorreta asked him once where to go
in order to do graduate studies in architecture, Gropius asked him, "Where
do you want to practice?" Legorreta replied, "Mexico." "Then go to Mexico" was Gropius's advice.

Now that we have placed the cart before the horse and warned of the
dangers of the Sirens, we will focus on the positive aspects of the exotic
and the multicultural experience which we have found to be exponentially
beneficial if confronted within a studio context and with constant care and
discipline.

In the first place, if we were to pay attention to the findings of the
anthropological explorers, we would discover a wealth of information
about the ancestors of all humankind and our primordial beginnings. Many
of our primordial requirements, such as emotion and mystique, or the
desire to understand the world around us, along with a preference for
"nonfunctionalist" architecture, can certainly be helpful for a discourse on
the current architectural debate. Much of the exotic that exists even today,
both in place and in time (most of us claim to live in the twentieth century,
yet there are others who live in conditions characteristic of previous eras),
can be brought into focus, addressed and generate a channel of architectural
creativity. The exotic and multicultural can be of extraordinary instructive
and practical as well as creative significance.

## THE MULTICULTURAL ENVIRONMENT

The advent of Third World countries, the availability of government grants
and programs, and the widespread desire among many students in the
world to educate themselves while traveling or to study in foreign countries
has brought a unique multicultural grain in the composition of the student
population of many universities, especially in Europe and North America.
This situation has been particularly evident in architectural studios. It has
brought an "internationalism of cultural content," which in return has
stimulated the generation of the exotic and multicultural channel to architectural creativity in a way unprecedented in previous generations.

Tolerance of and a predilection for the investigation and exploration
of problems and projects existing in remote countries, other than the ones

in which the schools of architecture are located, are the key to furthering this creative channel. Projects of an exotic and multicultural nature are favored and encouraged by many creative instructors and administrators alike. Certain schools have made their name exactly because they have followed the route of openness toward problems of a multicultural and exotic nature. A design project for a house for Giorgio De Chirico on a site in Greece, a passive solar energy tourist village in Crete, or a house for the "poor man" in Pakistan are welcomed as studio or theses projects by the Architectural Association in wet and affluent London. This school is probably the leader today in this particular mode of creativity enterprise; its annual student exhibitions, along with the catalogues that accompany them, are stimulating and delightful testimonials to the effort and to the uniqueness of the results. One could hardly find any opposition in most schools of architecture in North America today to studying any project, no matter how exotic, remote, and multicultural it may sound. Housing in Hong Kong, or in Teheran, intellectual retreats and building projects in Italy, along with an abundance of efforts to restore and re-work Rome and other Italian towns, are testimonials to the endeavors in many schools today.

Foreign students studying in America find no opposition to their doing theses projects in their countries of origin. Through such projects the student learns by being exposed to the instructor's philosophy, research methodology, and design process; the receptive instructor learns from the student by being exposed to a civilization and a way of thinking about problems and design issues otherwise unfamiliar to him. Such theses often find their way to lower-level design studios in the form of abstract problem statements. Freshmen and sophomores are thus introduced to issues and points of view otherwise unfamiliar to them.

Many instructors turn to the route of the exotic and multicultural immediately after their first visit abroad, often to the countries of their students. Many of the local instructors become, upon return, strong supporters for the hiring and invitation of foreign colleagues. The cycle of multicultural effect frequently expands, when the foreign instructor takes his students for trips to the country of his origin, making sketches, measurements on the site, design proposals, or preparing studio programs for the semester ahead.

The multicultural spirit in design education began in the United States with the advent of Gropius, Mies van der Rohe, and Eliel Saarinen. Harvard, MIT, and the Granbrook Academy of Art were the first schools to adopt the multicultural path to architectural creativity we advocate here.

## GAINS FROM THE MULTICULTURAL EXPERIENCE

The multicultural experience can greatly enhance design education through two distinctive sets of benefits that cannot be found in studios with homogeneous student populations. The first includes behavioral gains; the second is composed of imagination-enhancing ingredients. Here are the behavioral gains:

1. The overall class environment has a different behavioral aura. There is usually more tolerance and civility, in the effort of the locals to make a good impression on their guests.
2. There is extra effort on the part of everybody to use the language of sketching and drawing more, as the foreign tongue doesn't come easily to foreign students, especially during the first months of study abroad.

3. There is constant reference on the part of foreign students to places, names, and ways of doing things never heard of before.

4. There is an extra effort at cooperation between the members of the multicultural group that strengthens ties for team projects which may be undertaken later in the semester.

5. There is a latent atmosphere of well-conceived competitiveness in the effort to excel and give a good impression to the colleagues of the host country.

6. There are always the first weeks of every foreign student's study in the exotic country during which he demonstrates the best of whatever he learned from his studies home (the first project always carries with it the lessons from the student's past). This is beneficial to the other students, as they can see what happens elsewhere.

## The Imagination-Enhancing Benefit

Projects of an "exotic" and multicultural nature have the power to enhance the imagination, for a variety of reasons:

1. They release imagination from timetables and the constraints of reality.

2. In the absence of relative ignorance, any discoveries or solutions to particular problems are far more important than similar gains derived through solutions to problems with a known set of constraints, within the home culture.

3. The selective process of the brain is not bound by the behavioral constraints of the exotic culture, so it acts "lightheartedly," picking up whatever suits its purposes. One can be more intuitive within a culture which is not one's own, freed from the constraints of one's own culture and discipline.

4. The excellent opportunity provided for the combination of several creativity channels, both intangible and tangible. These can be tested through one channel, the exotic and multicultural channel.

The behavioral gains are self-evident; we focus instead on the imagination-enhancing benefits, in the order listed above.

Over time, several exotic environments have developed their own unique constraints; the regulations that nowadays control many exotic settlements in Greece are such constraints; they have reduced the development of architecture on several occasions to set design exercises. The designer who is not bound by such restrictions, yet who is genuinely concerned about building within the substantial constraints of this exotic land (scale, topography, climate), may provide more imaginative solutions to the problems of today, including contextual and iconographic ones, than the reality-bound professional who operates in these places, for whom restrictions bore instead of stimulate and retard further evolution.

Local architects become easy victims of what we could call the disease of "explorational inertia." They soon find themselves easily satisfied by the thought-free solutions that are available to them through the suggested "traditional prototypes"; this is a noncreative and at the same time a profitable proposition. The further paradox is that foreign designers find it easier to accept such restrictions, without wasting time on the mental torture the few concerned locals experience when they try to "break" and improve the codes. Immediate acceptance of the codes (the occasional set of constraints) sets the designer free, affording more time for design exploration within the selected idiom. I have been astonished at the discipline and respect displayed by my American students towards codes and zoning ordinances that control the historic settlements of Greece. The multicultural experience, then, enhances the freedom to reject, but further it enhances the discipline to accept and conform on the surface while being more creative in substance.

The degree of the gain from multicultural design experiences is easy to accept. When alien, exotic programs are integrated with programs that call for values other than our own, the project can present an extraordinary beginning for intuitive and fresh results. Although the students' interpretations may not be as definitive or refined as those who know the actual conditions and are part of this culture, the gains may be relatively enormous compared to what would have been gained if they were asked to operate on a project of a known culture. In the latter case the result would constitute only a refinement of something already known, while in the former case the whole process and the creative result is totally fresh and new. Each student becomes a "little Archimedes," with his own little discoveries, as opposed to have them handed to him via tradition or instruction. Everything new we find or improvise within the unknown set of the exotic constraints is like discovering the world on our own, and we do not forget our own discoveries.

The selective editing process that is afforded to the designer via the exotic is an extremely beneficial factor. The designer acts in exotic situations like the creative poet who opens a history book not like a historian, but like one who seeks in it the fancies of his imagination, the historic moment or the personality that will tickle his poetic creative impulses. The poet who keeps arbitrarily whatever suits his imagination gives food to the visions of his heart and crafts his own poem out of the landscape of civilization.

The wider the multicultural experience in the studio, the more projects or references offered, or the greater the number of cultural points of view, the greater the chances for scanning through cultural landscapes. It would be wrong to take the painter and place him in front of a particular landscape and tell him, "Paint it . . . now!" The painter must look at it day and night, over time, during a variety of seasons, under different lighting and atmospheric conditions. He or she will then select when and under what circumstances to do it, and if he or she will even need to look at it in order to do it. It is the same with the poet, the novelist, the photographer, and the filmmaker. Multiculturalism and the exotic, when performed from a distance, require absolute freedom in order to produce results.

The combinatorial benefits that may be derived through exotic and multicultural exercises in the studio can be broad or small in scale, ranging from site and topographic awareness, the use of materials and attitudes toward detail all the way to dealing with issues of urban, regional, and societal significance. I will elaborate on these particular benefits, for I believe they represent the major core of benefits that can be derived through this particular channel.

## Inclusivity via the Exotic

*Site.* It is extraordinary to ask somebody who has never seen the sea or a hilly, rocky site to try to imagine the sea, to simulate through contour models the rocky terrain, or to attempt to draw images alien to their own environment and experiences. Exotic sites in exotic lands—that is, sites and places totally unfamiliar, call for surprises and raise questions, while they send the imagination on exceptional trips into the unknown. Although slides and films of the exotic place can help, it is the written word, the well-selected poem, the literary essay or the sociological finding that can have the best effect on the imagination. It is the nonconcrete and descriptive that calls for the greater participation by the students and asks them to picture through the mind's eye environments unseen before.

*Materials.* The path of multiculturalism can also be beneficial in the exploration of materials. Naturally derived materials, masonry, and native substances may be as unfamiliar to the student of a technologically advanced country as plastics and high tech may be to a student from the Third World. It is beneficial and creatively stimulating when a student realizes that not all walls have to be six or eight inches thick and that other thicknesses, due to other materials, may bring plasticity, light, and shadow effects along with energy savings, visual appeal, and textures that would have never been explored if one were to stay with what is already available in the native region and what the local traditions and building trades already know. Such explorations may result in new interpretations, refinements, or other ways of looking at subsequent projects of the local culture or of established design practices.

*Details.* No instructor or studio manual can communicate the significance of detail in architecture unless one experiences life in exotic places. Under such circumstances, the student will come to appreciate the detailing conquests of the twentieth century. Only through living in exotic places can one understand what it really means to have window assemblies without mosquito screens, what it means to have no perfect fit of door or window sill and to be constantly invaded by ants and other crawling creatures, and to face the upkeep of a house on an ongoing, full-time basis, constantly fighting the elements and the decay process. The area of detail is therefore an area for appreciation of what the technologically advanced cultures have achieved in opposition to the exotic, which can be admired only for its craftsmanship and the persistence of the builder in solving problems. Yet these are no match for the high degree of resolution achieved by machines and contemporary building technology. Exotic detailing, studied with a critical eye, will reveal the high cost of the proposition for today's applications, and will further suggest that the new fit is far superior to it as a problem-solving proposition. It is in the area of detailing that contemporary architecture has the best to offer its exotic and traditional counterparts.

*History.* When the exotic and multicultural is combined with efforts to understand history or in an applied involvement with environments of historic significance, the project may be additionally enhanced and produce multiple results. There is no way to define the character of the exotic project. It depends totally on the intuitiveness and the creative imagination of the instructor. One could integrate site with culture, with history and civilization, with situations of the obscure and paradoxical. The program could be manipulated to sound exotic and obscure, for real sites or for exotic lands and exotic functions of the instructor's imagination. A Polish legation in Venice for the visit of Pope John Paul II, could be as beneficial as a pavilion for the ashes of a holy bishop on a rocky island in Greece, as good and stimulating as a project in an architectural competition given in Mexico a hundred years back, or a resort settlement on the steep rocks of some Mediterranean coast or an inactive Hawaiian volcanic crater.

Scanning the list of projects given by various instructors in some of the more imaginative programs of architectural education in the United States suggests the richness and imaginative crafting of studio programs. It is unfortunate that the merits of the channel have not been accepted universally, and that there are still many programs based on the idea that design institutions must serve only the immediate locality. Such parochialism may, of course, produce students who may be able to construct and detail certain building types within the realistic constraints of their locality, but who may add very little to the creative evolution of architecture.

## Case Experiences

The exotic and multicultural channel to architectural creativity can be greatly enhanced through courses on meritorious vernacular architecture; the information and the stimulation gained through the visual resources of such courses can be invaluable.

The exotic and multicultural has been an occasional preoccupation of mine, given the appropriate opportunity in studio situations. In fact, there was a semester where the mix at my school was exceptionally multicultural, both in the faculty and in the student body. The availability of colleagues from Austria, Denmark, Germany, Greece, Israel, Italy, and Poland made that semester most rewarding in the teaching of design. A multicultural group of faculty in a strong collegial relationship among themselves, and a multicultural group of competent, eager students can be a wonderful experience.

**Fig. 7-1.** *Kindergarten in Naoshima and Naoshima Gym.* **A.** *William Lashbaugh.* **B.** *C. Sauvel.* **C.** *Randy Hughes.* **D.** *Aubrey Springer.* **E.** *Hunter Collins.* **F.** *Abdul Doulch.* **G.** *Gary Murphy.* **H.** *Jim Bernett.* **I.** *Martha Welch.* **J.** *Paul Solon.* **K.** *Randy Hood.*

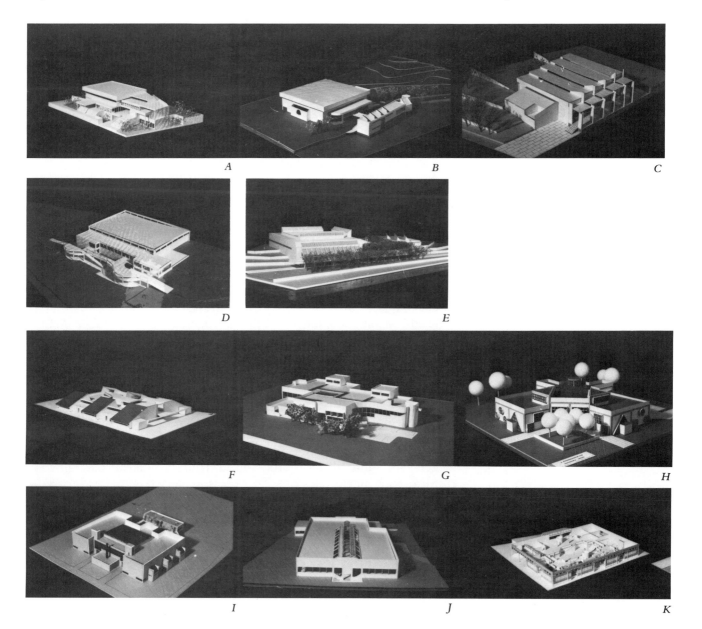

To illustrate the possibilities of this route to creativity, I will present and discuss here a series of projects from my personal studios, in the hope that they may be illuminating to others. The goal is not to reach those who may be already doing such projects or who may perhaps have made similar efforts within the particular channel, but to reach the many others who have emphasized other channels (historic precedent, metaphor, transformation) without realizing the combinatorial possibilities and the instructive dynamism of the exotic and multicultural channel.

*The Naoshima School Projects.* Exceptional among such studio experiences was the case of two projects for a Naoshima gym and a kindergarten (Fig. 7-1). The project was well coordinated and Kazuhiro Ishii, the actual architect (at that time running his own studio as a visiting professor at UCLA), participated in the jury. Everything was delivered to the students in doses, through an orchestrated process. The project was presented as an "abstract exotic" exercise in the first place, as if the buildings had not been built. As it progressed, it became known that they were working on a real project whose architect would visit to critique them upon completion. The whole affair evolved into a most rewarding experience which lasted for months beyond the studio completion date. After his verbal remarks at the jury session, Kazuhiro Ishii sent written comments to each student, and in a most surprising gesture on his part, included some of the projects in one of the presentations of his own work, suggesting the radius of influence of his Naoshima projects. His overall participation and his final generous gesture were gifts of pride to the participating students, treats to remember for the rest of their lives.

*New Museum of the Acropolis.* The project for the new Museum of Acropolis was submitted as an entry in the competition for the prestigious project. It received a purchase award, but it also stimulated the students, two of whom visited Greece and Europe after their experience with the competition (Fig. 7-2).

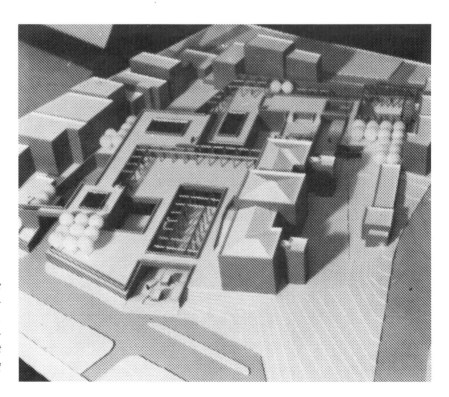

**Fig. 7-2.** *Panhellenic competition for the New Museum of the Acropolis. A. C. Antoniades, architect. David Browning, Aaron Farmer, Daron Tapscott, collaborators. Purchase award. Fourth-year/eight weeks project. UT Arlington, spring 1977.*

*American Embassy in Peking.* The trip of President Nixon to China stimulated a design studio project for the American Embassy in Peking (Fig. 7-3). Yet it was the Dallas City Hall, at that time under construction, which inspired discussion and perhaps influenced most the character of the presented entry. The case of I. M. Pei, architect of the City Hall, emerged in the discussions. It gave students the chance to contemplate the significance of one man's dedication to another culture. Students went to hear him talk about his personal transformation at a public lecture at the Dallas Museum of Fine Arts. In that particular instance, both students and instructor were clarifying for themselves their personal attitudes with regard to the international practice of architecture that was going on through the opportunities afforded architects during the early seventies, especially in Saudi Arabia and other Arab nations. Discussions regarding architecture as a vocation and profession, with the architect as an agent for peace and international cooperation, superseded concerns over the technical matters involved in the design of the embassy building type. Everyone was surprised to hear from two of the guest critics on the jury, one of whom was a prominent Dallas architect who had participated in the design of an American embassy in Europe, that it wouldn't matter anyhow, because the design would be reviewed eventually by the security people without the architect ever learning the final decisions.

**Fig. 7-3.** *American embassy in Peking, China. Steve Eberley and Steve Swicker. Fourth-year/five weeks project. UT Arlington, spring 1975.*

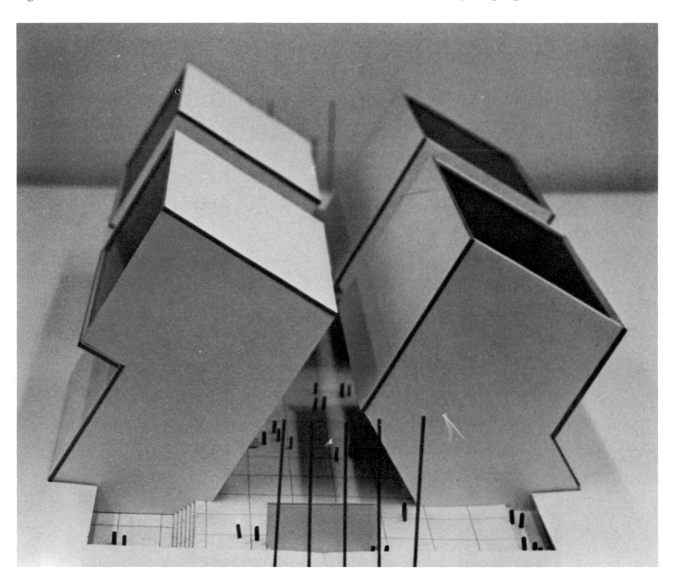

*The Ronchamp Compound.* The scale of the exotic and multicultural project plays a decisive role in the success of the exercise. We have found that small-scale projects of shorter duration afford greater benefits than large-scale projects of longer duration. The small-scale project, if given in an advanced studio where the basic design issues have (hopefully) struck home, can provide a good excuse for more reading, more involvement in the search for the essentials of the culture under study. One can even talk about sketching problems of an exotic and multicultural nature. Discussions can continue in a cyclical fashion as more research material comes in from reading in the weeks that follow. It is, of course, the intuitiveness of the sketch problem that will make it bloom or wither.

What architectural student would not like to have a project next to one of Le Corbusier's? Who would not consider it a challenge to do something in Greece, in Italy, or in one of the mythical places read about in history books? The sketch problem for a visitors' center by the entrance of the compound of Ronchamp (Fig. 7-4) and two sketch problems for tourist bungalows in Corfu, Killini, in Greece and in Baja California-Mexico proved to me once again that remote contexts represent unique challenges that are welcomed by students (Fig. 6-2).

*Mixed-Use Center on Leros.* Projects in foreign lands that have a touch of history and are at the same time related to issues that trouble us globally today, both intellectually and pragmatically, are very good candidates for the success of multicultural design projects. Problems common to all are in a sense the common unifying denominators of humankind, independent of culture or locational origin. The common denominator of such a project has to be well researched by the instructor; if it does not exist, the project may fail. Every student was concerned in the mid-1970s about the debate on styles, history, the due morphology. When they were told that these were concerns not unique to a particular period, but that every period had its own anxieties, and when they were presented with the little known case of the Italian architects of the thirties who had created a score of buildings

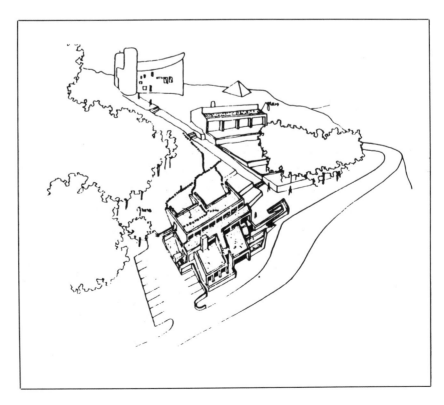

**Fig. 7-4.** *Visitors Center at the entrance of the Ronchamp compound. Barry Read, nine-hour sketch problem. Fourth year, UT Arlington, fall 1981.*

in their effort to understand the debate of their time (rationalism-modern movement) in the Dodecanese Islands, they enthusiastically got involved with design projects for mixed-use buildings on the island of Leros, next to some heavily loaded Italian architecture of the 1930s. The design project in this sense can become a vehicle for the lasting understanding of history, while at the same time it can become a vehicle for the continuation of a historical trend, not historical imitation.

*The Contemplation Pavilion and the Bishop's Tomb.* The multiculturally exotic projects that had the highest and most creative results, however, were those that combined the physically exotic with the intellectual. One could define as "intellectually exotic" a project that addresses itself to values and mental connotations alien and exotic in comparison to one's own. The project for a contemplation pavilion in a private garden in Andros, Greece for the well-traveled, well-educated couple (Fig. 7-5), as well as the project for the resting place for Bishop Atesis (Fig. 7-6), a holy man, a humanist and spiritual leader, on the island of Skyros, were among the most intriguing and stimulating experiences of this nature. The young designers became totally committed; they were absorbed with the uniqueness of the sites and the open horizons of intellectual and value possibilities, and they tried to respond as best and comprehensively as they could. It was very hard to distinguish the projects qualitatively; most of them were unique and fresh, reaching in fact the sphere of the "poetic."

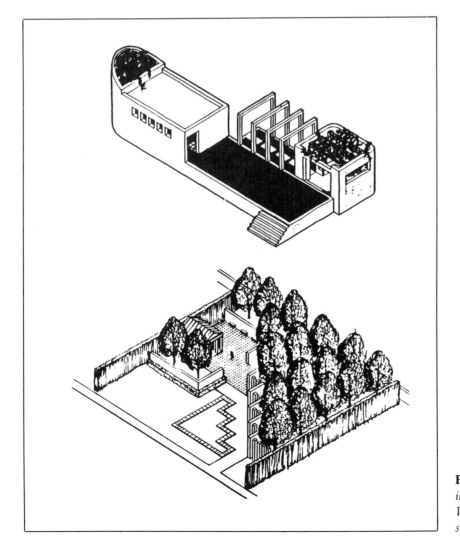

**Fig. 7-5.** *Chapel-contemplation pavilion in private garden, Andros, Greece. Cliff Welch, Ignacio Rodriguez. The author's second-year design studio, UT Arlington.*

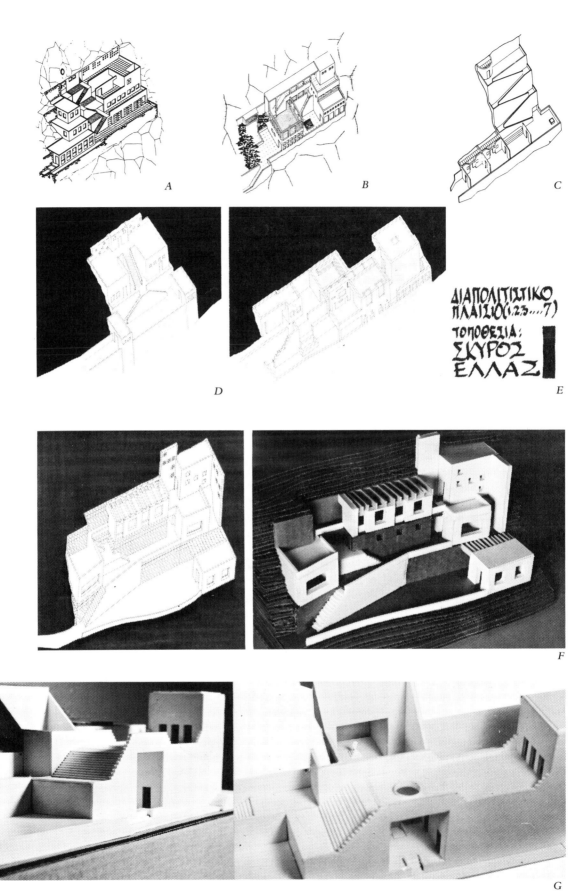

**Fig. 7-6.** *Space-spirit-light: a resting place for Bishop Atesis, Skyros, Greece. Student designers from Lebanon, Mexico, USA, Finland, China (Fig. 7-7) and instructor (the author) from Greece.* **A.** *Isam Khatib (Lebanon).* **B.** *Samuel Pena (Mexico).* **C.** *Lance Fuller (USA).* **D.** *Jussi Hyppöla (Finland).* **E.** *Felipe Flores (Mexico).* **F.** *Allan Reagan (USA).* **G.** *Ernest Millican (USA).*

## Project Options: Exotic vs. Real Ingredients

The exotic and multicultural project can take an extraordinary variety of forms, with some ingredients of the project being highly exotic while others are highly pragmatic and universal. A semester of a design studio can become a minuet between the exotic and the realistic. Here are some options:

1. We can have absolutely exotic sites with totally familiar functional requirements (tourist settlements in unfamiliar sites, with unfamiliar materials).
2. We can have absolutely familiar sites with totally exotic functional and intellectual frameworks (alien cultures, unknown customs).
3. We can have a combination of both.
4. We can have totally exotic sites and totally exotic functional requirements, based on real sites, or on sites from the instructor's imagination.
5. We can have the exotic and multicultural right around the corner, which is the case with large metropolitan areas of plural and democratic countries with immigrants from many ethnic, cultural, and minority groups other than the dominant one(s).

The advantages of the options vary depending on the coaching and the goal of the instructor. The positive effects of each one of these possibilities have to do with the degree of sharpening of the imagination in the visual and physical sense, in the opening of the intellectual and cultural horizons of the students, in the exposure to a variety of social problems, in the involvement and solution of real and frequently neglected problems. I personally believe in the good balanced dose of the combination: The exotic and multicultural project where the exotic is balanced with real and comprehensively pressing problems of building, of urban and regional significance.

One of the best exercises I have given in this respect was a resort/ second home/intellectual and relaxation retreat to facilitate the decentralization of Athens, attracting the "have not" urbanites (currently trapped in the big and polluted metropolis) to settlements that were to be built on inaccessible steep rocky sites of various island coasts. The exercise attempted to bring together issues of urban dynamics of environmental and territorial significance, while calling for improvisation and ingenuity with regard to construction methods, and architectural solutions. The exercise emphasized prototypes, made use of metaphor, and considered utilitarian aspects in the most realistic sense. Samples of Aegean architecture were analyzed (see Figs. 7-8, 7-9), while the poetry of Odysseus Elytis and George Seferis was brought in. Relevant texts were studied for the aura of the sought-after environments. This exercise proved that a very small architectonic module can give an opportunity for a most "inclusivist" exploration, where a good number of creative channels can be combined under the umbrella of the exotic.

The category of exotic and multicultural projects around the corner from the school is also significant, because it involves everybody in the process, including the traditional relationship of the school to its immediate locality. It is rather easy to locate such projects in the United States. The "around the corner exotic" is ever present in its broadest (and often wildest) sense. Many theses projects in community-oriented schools are of this nature. Several such projects frequently find their way into regular design curricula, especially in advanced studios.

One personal experience in this respect was a project for a religious community center for the Greek community in Dallas, Texas (Fig. 7-10).

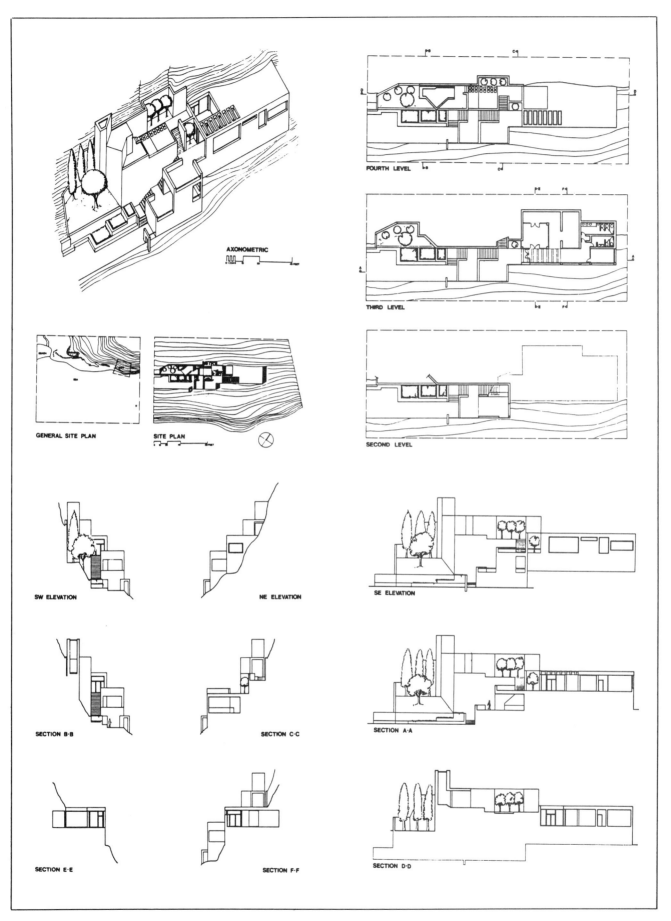

AXONOMETRIC

FOURTH LEVEL

THIRD LEVEL

SECOND LEVEL

GENERAL SITE PLAN

SITE PLAN

SW ELEVATION

NE ELEVATION

SE ELEVATION

SECTION B·B

SECTION C·C

SECTION A·A

SECTION E·E

SECTION F·F

SECTION D·D

**Fig. 7-7.** *Project by N. G. R. Fai (China). Resting place for Bishop Atesis, Skyros, Greece. (The author's second-year design studio, UT Arlington, spring 1984)*

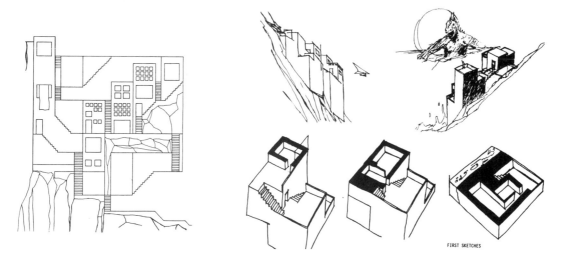

FIRST SKETCHES

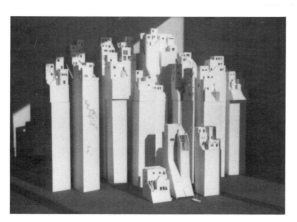

**Fig. 7-8.** *Poetics of inclusivity: a demonstration. "Exodus" to the rocks of the Aegean from Athens.*

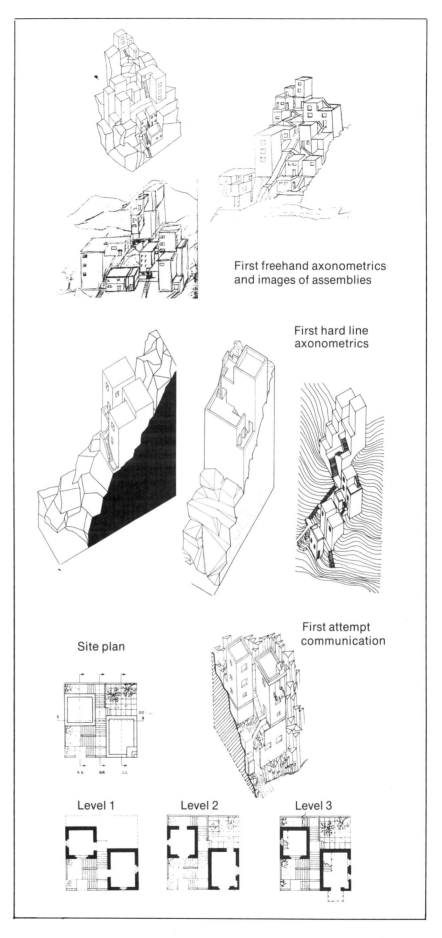

First freehand axonometrics
and images of assemblies

First hard line
axonometrics

First attempt
communication

Site plan

Level 1      Level 2      Level 3

**Fig. 7-9.** *From the design process of the "exodus" from Athens to the Aegean rocks.*

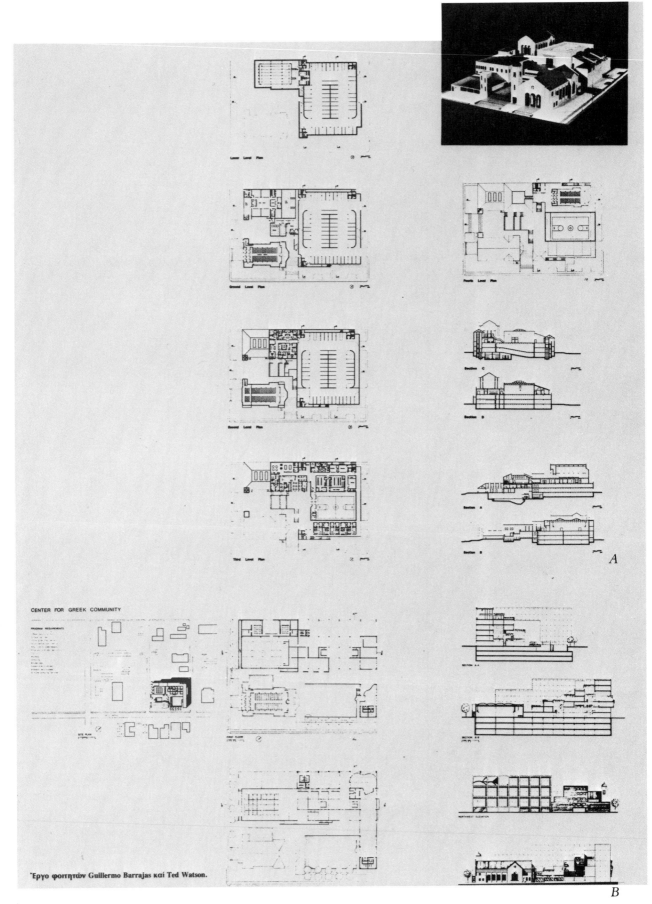

**Fig. 7-10.** *The exotic "around the corner": religious center in Dallas, Texas.*
**A.** *David Peckar and Dean Smith.* **B.** *Guillermo Barrajas and Ted Watson.*
*(Fourth-year/eight weeks project. UT Arlington, spring 1979)*

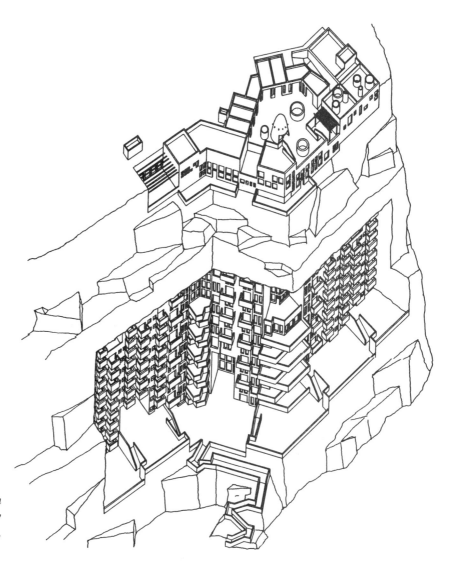

**Fig. 7-11.** *Hotel-intellectual retreat in Chaco Canyon, American Southwest by M. Mitler. (Fourth-year design studio, UT Arlington, 1983)*

This project investigated the opportunity to integrate in one architectural complex a microcosm of Greek culture and civilization, including, among other things, expansion of the existing church, housing for the senior citizens, a school, a day care center, library, gym, health care facilities, and a typical Greek café. The students were introduced to Greece through lectures, readings in selected Greek literature, and Greek music. The historical precedents analyzed were taken from Greek vernacular architecture, the typology of the Greek hill town, and the monasteries of Mount Athos. The international and multicultural dimension of the project can best be shown by the fact that this Greek Orthodox community was designed by a group of students who included, besides the Americans, one student from Turkey, and three Muslim girls from Lebanon, Jordan, and Bahrain. These students not only produced a series of challenging and fresh projects and involved themselves with cultural issues and questions contrary to their own, but they had the chance to expose themselves to the problems and issues of a particular ethnic group in their host country.

## THE NEED FOR RIGOROUS INVOLVEMENT WITH EXOTIC PROJECTS

We claim that there is need for a good dose of involvement with exotic and multicultural projects in every architect's career. In spite of the problems of multiculturalism, the occasional romantic misunderstanding and the occasional undigested imitation of form as opposed to substance, one will always learn one's own culture, one's own architecture, if one attempts to understand the architecture of others. We strongly believe in the saying of George Seferis that the one who translates other tongues learns his own language better in the process. We even welcome the physical "exile" in an exotic culture, in countries whose Sirens attract us. Tightly roped on our "Odyssean mast," our strong desire to practice architecture in our own land, we will have the opportunity to appreciate our own architecture better, since the distance and the new input of the exotic architecture and culture will permit us to evaluate our own architecture better. This is certainly not a new idea; it has happened in almost every art. Some of the best criticism on one's country as well as some of the best novels were written by writers away from their home countries, living within foreign contexts (Gertrude Stein, Henry Miller, Ernest Hemingway). We do not therefore completely endorse the advice Walter Gropius gave to Ricardo Legorreta. We believe instead that there is a need for rigorous but measured exposure and in-depth study within a multicultural context and on a number of fronts: (1) through design studio projects while in school; (2) through participation in international competitions (they offer the best opportunity a young architect can have to sharpen his or her design abilities); and (3) through actually living and working in exotic places for moderate periods of time and with the sole goal the return to one's own country to practice architecture.

These suggestions are not my theoretical whim; they have been observed in many cases of architects distinguished for their creative designs. With the exceptions of those who have dedicated themselves for one reason or another to the embrace of cultures other than those they were born in, the majority of the others had a substantial record of multicultural and exotic exposure. After all, it is not accidental, I believe, that some of the most poetic and creative architects today are products of multicultural architectural education, evolved through exotic international competitions, or spent a good number of years in foreign countries.

## Summary

In this chapter, the exotic is viewed from the positive angle of cross-cultural fertilization, although there is the possibility of "sirenic" encounters that might cause irreversible problems for the designer. We address the "physical" and "metaphysical" nature of the exotic. We also discuss the multicultural nature of recent educational trends that have brought the element of the exotic into the design studio. The multicultural environment is an asset. It has behavioral and design-enhancing benefits. Several design constraints (site, materials, details) are particularly clarified if viewed through an exotic lens. The categories of exotic design exercises are presented, along with projects from the author's personal experience. The chapter concludes with a call for rigorous involvement with design projects of an exotic and multicultural nature.

## References

There is no specific bibliography for architecture on this particular topic other than the brochures published occasionally by the various schools of architecture. Another source is the annual Project Review publications of the Architectural Association in London. For related readings on cross-cultural issues, see:

A

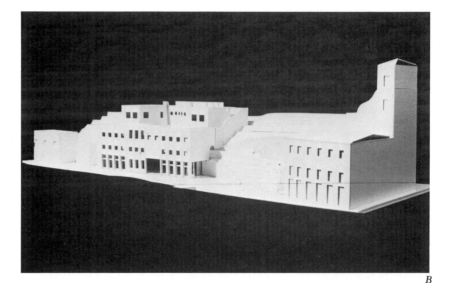

B

**Fig. 7-12.** *Cultural Center, Hydra, Greece.* **A.** *Student designer, Tom Wilkins.* **B.** *Student designer, Stephen Brookover.* **C.** *Student designer, Christine Page Taylor.*

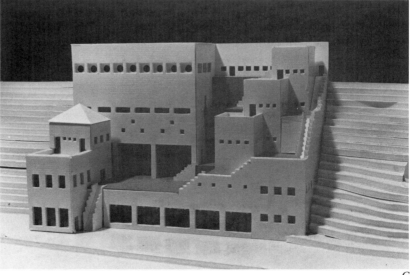

C

**Fig. 7-13.** *Housing project on property with existing church. Fall 1988.* **A.** *Student designer, Paul Mayeux.* **B.** *Student designer, Patrick Goodwin.* **C.** *Student designer, Johnnie Morgan.*

Deregowski, Jan B. "Some Aspects of Perceptual Organization in the Light of Cross-Cultural Evidence." *Studies in Cross-Cultural Psychology,* vol. 2, ed. Neil Warren. London: Academic Press, 1980.

Lévi-Strauss, Claude. *Myth and Meaning.* New York: Schocken Books, 1978. pp. 4, 16.

Okonji, Ogbolu M. "Cognitive Styles Across Cultures." *Studies in Cross-Cultural Psychology,* ed. Neil Warren.

Warren, Neil, ed. *Studies in Cross-Cultural Psychology.* Vol. 2. London: Academic Press, 1980.

# Part 2 TANGIBLE CHANNELS TO ARCHITECTURAL CREATIVITY

# Chapter 8   History, Historicism, and the Study of Precedents

*Architects today are too educated to be either primitive or totally spontaneous, and architecture is too complex to be approached with carefully maintained ignorance.*

Robert Venturi

There is no doubt that the study of precedents enriches the stock of images in one's mind. Historical precedents, precedents from similar projects done by other architects, along with mental images of prototypes of environments or buildings one may have seen through travel, represent undeniable input into the mind of each creator. Inasmuch as creativity is a process largely due to the workings and complicated operations of the unconscious, the stockpiling of information, images, and lessons from precedents may be a very conscious act to feed the mind in the hope of fruitful stimulation of the imagination when the mind may be called to create something similar. Through an extraordinary process of human "editing," the brain of the creator selects and organizes all the relevant information and all the stockpiled images and brings them out as digested sets of possible visual, image, or meaning combinations. This process which is widely accepted by students of psychology, can be easily proved through one's personal experiences. It has been verified in the cases of successful creators who have offered feedback after their own experiences. There is no doubt that study enriches the "knowledge" of one person, while the quality and formal study of a subject, or subjects, differentiates the various individuals between the "more" from the "less" educated. Value-oriented societies often rank individuals according to degree of education and frequently offer them more creative roles in the affairs of the community. The general population respects and admires the genuinely educated members of the society and considers them its advisors, sages, and creative problem solvers.

The specialized study of precedents, be they historic or real and contemporary, may perform a similar role for prospective creators and generate the "educated" among them, those who may eventually become leading innovators. Inasmuch as there is general agreement that the possibility for distinctive creativity may be enhanced through systematic stockpiling of images through periods of systematic study or travel during one's life, there is substantial debate as to the merits of specialized and systematic stockpiling of specific visual information and precedents upon the call for the creation of a specific project. Those involved with the teaching of architectural design are divided into a number of camps. There are those who support the idea of the study and research of historical and applied precedents relevant to the project at hand; those who reject the merit of such a process and who may even consider it a means to biased and unintuitive solutions; and those who may find a good and moderate dose of precedental reference helpful and stimulating.

If one considers that not everybody has been blessed with equal talent in regard to creativity, one may understand the relativity of any one of the above positions. An absolutely unique and talented creator may indeed have no need for references, while it is possible that forced input of precedents, be they historical or other, may handicap or retard genuine creativity. Other individuals, however, may benefit from the endeavor. It is therefore a case of individual needs that determine when the precedent path may be helpful and to what degree.

## THE RECENT EMPHASIS ON PRECEDENTS

Architectural education today, especially in the United States, emphasizes a path to creativity through the study of history and through specialized research on precedents. Historical research constitutes the beginning for many design projects. Leading institutions of architectural training, such as Princeton, Cornell, and Harvard, and official architectural publications, such as *The Journal of Architectural Education*, have played a pioneering role in the emphasis on history and the study of precedents in design education. Leading teacher-architects are strong advocates and consistent users of the precedent channel. It is not accidental that the strong wave of history-based design education that prevails in the United States is not so evident in Europe and elsewhere. The general argument is that the United States, young and new, had no strong historical and identifiable cultural origins and that through the lack of study of history during the early twentieth century, when the fathers of the modern movement "negated" history, the country found itself at a disadvantage and is now in the process of catching up. This was also probably true for many young architectural creators of the 1970s who also tried to catch up on an individual basis.

In response to this need, American architectural programs tried to associate themselves with the historically rooted architectural heritage of other countries. It is of interest that Italy, and especially Rome, have been singled out by most American schools as the referential source, continuing a tradition of love for Italy that has been institutionalized in the American architectural world since the founding of the Rome prize in the late nineteenth century. Although the love for Italy is an interesting topic of study in itself, the truth of the matter is that Rome and Italian architecture constitute at this moment the favorite source for the historical stimulation of most American designers to the exclusion of other equally deserving and meritorious sources. There are scores of contemporary design projects located on historic sites and in the cities of Italy. A great number of these projects call for contemporary building programs, and their formal expressions are derived or inspired through disciplined study of Italian prototypes of buildings or urban designs. It is true that not all design instructors are genuinely versed in history, but it is also true that a great number of design instructors today, especially those who were educated in the mid-seventies in schools of the East Coast of the United States, follow the historical route to teaching architecture and stimulating creativity. A whole new language was generated, and terms used during the 1950s and late 1960s received new names (i.e., "footprint," often confused with "site plan"). Competitions and prominent magazines became advocates and carried the message of the history-based route to creativity. The discourse on, and knowledge, and interpretations of historical examples became unprecedented, and the period of Postmodern architecture became an era of a love affair with history, Rome, the Renaissance, Mannerism, and the Baroque. We believe this positive state of affairs can be further improved by a more balanced and cross-cultural attention to historical precedents, such as rigorous study of classical Greek, Byzantine, Muslim and Far Eastern architecture, and of African, South and North American Indian work.

## HISTORY VS. HISTORICISM

There is no doubt that an understanding of history can offer invaluable insights to the serious architect. Through the historical framing of a project, he or she can acquire knowledge of the cultural, technological, and philosophical parameters that were in place during the creation of the building. These explanations make the building qualify as an index of the civilization of its time. Attention to history that does not consider the interrelationships and repercussions of these parameters is superficial and can bring adverse results for any new creation derived from history. If it is only formal details or visual historical clichés that influence the designer, the result may be unreal, out of scale, an exercise in set design.

"Historicism" is differentiated from "history" in that it pays one-sided attention to history, often looking only at form, and frequently becoming

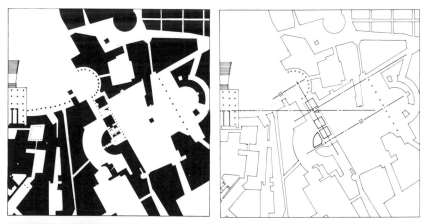

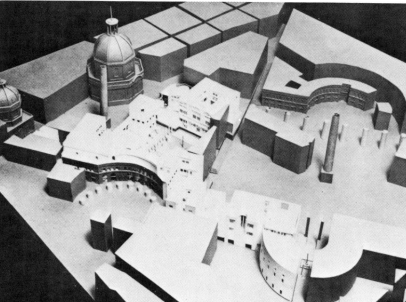

**Fig. 8-1.** *The Italian Connection II or the missing link: project from the studio of Bill Boswell by Barbara Mahan, Dwight Jones, and David Swaim. (Courtesy of Bill Boswell)*

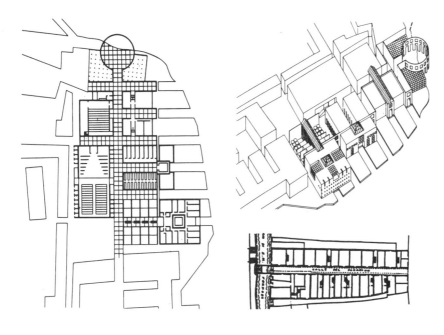

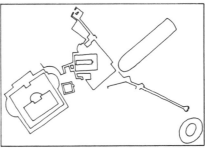

Fig. 8-2. *Transformation of a historical precedent: Calle de Paradiso, a medieval street in Venice. (From the studio of Martin Harms, after* Journal of Architectural Education, *winter 1982)*

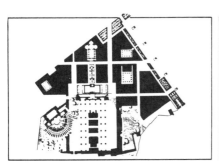

Fig. 8-3. *Urban design strategies by Steven Peterson; cases where the proposals are the result of a combination of historical environments with recent prototypes. From Peterson's proposal for "Roma Interrotta," where the transformational result included the mixing of a Roman theater with fragments from Fifth Avenue and Rockefeller Center in New York City. (After Steven Peterson in "Roma Interrotta,"* Architectural Design, *49, 3–4 (1979))*

dangerously eclectic. It addresses architecture at a less comprehensive and shallow level than real historical investigation.

Although many historicist architects and especially many historicist critics attempt to present historicist and contemporary eclecticism as a polysemantic affair, the argument usually falls to pieces with experience, a visit to, and in-depth scrutiny of the projects, especially from the scale/technology point of view. Among the very few on record to have spoken of "history" and "historicism" in terms of their effect on creativity was Bruno Zevi. Based on long experience in teaching and writing, he charged that history as taught by the Beaux-Arts was a process aimed at the reduction of (historical) phenomena to "styles . . . the death of history and the death of original creativity." According to Zevi, the stylistic interpretation of historical forms, along with the canons of symmetry, dynamic composition, rhythm, and so on, as codified by the Beaux-Arts, generated "mannerist" as opposed to "creative" architecture. He argued that " . . . the great creative geniuses were anti-classical, seeking resolutions of their architectural problems through asymmetry," which according to his argument " . . . pushes you to abandon your laziness, compels you to think and not apply formal, abstract solutions to social and human questions."

Frank Lloyd Wright, Le Corbusier, and Alvar Aalto are among Zevi's anticlassical heroes. They are considered models whose work exemplifies the non-Mannerist, the creative and unique. Zevi has also suggested that the teaching of history should employ the means and media of design rather than lecturing and essay writing, and it should create a clear language

**Fig. 8-4.** *Historicism can produce highly unsuccessful results, especially when the adopted styles are manipulated by profit-oriented interests. Instant ancient columns and pediments are not sufficient to offset the scale problems of thoughtless applications. From the gargantuan case of defunct historicist Chelsea Harbor in the Chelsea area of London.*

**Fig. 8-5.** *Historicist morphology will always subject the client to extra costs, even in the most careful applications and exploitation of appropriate building technology and sensitive design: detail from the United Airlines Terminal, O'Hare Airport, Chicago. Helmut Jan, architect.*

understood by all architects. He was very critical of the confusion generated by the predicament of semiotics, and charged that it was responsible for the creation of a "comic breed" of architects in a human zoo.

Zevi was the most serious critic of the direction of architectural history and the associated concepts of historicism, Beaux-Arts history based methods of design, and the historicist revivalism of the 1970s. His was a criticism from within, as he spoke with the license and authority of the historian. Inasmuch as I am compelled to agree with the arguments of Bruno Zevi, I must realize the polarity of his polemic. I certainly side in principle with his main contentions, yet I want to go beyond the bounds of his polarity. I am not willing to give up the element of time, because it is time that renders it very difficult to acquire an "inclusivist" appreciation of history. It takes time to have at hand the complete range of factors that affected the creation of the historical works. Our occasional appreciation of architectural history is at best fragmentary (as it is also about to be evolutionary), due to new information that may emerge in time, that casts light on the inclusivist environment of an era. This general discussion leads us to the need for elaboration of what we should understand as inclusivist appreciation of architectural history and based on that to make further proposals about the "correct" use of history for the architectural designer.

## THE INCLUSIVIST APPRECIATION OF ARCHITECTURAL HISTORY

The architectural designer appreciates historic artifacts, but he also "investigates" them for design purposes. Whether appreciating or investigating the goal should be the same: inclusivity. Historical inclusivity is the study of history that combines analytic and synthetic tasks, while it attempts to gain a total overview of the tangible as well as the intangible parameters that were at work in the making of the artifact. The designer's investigation should include the following:

### Analytical Endeavors

1. Study of existing descriptive documents of the precedent (plans, sections, elevations) available through archeological research, or architecturally measured drawings.

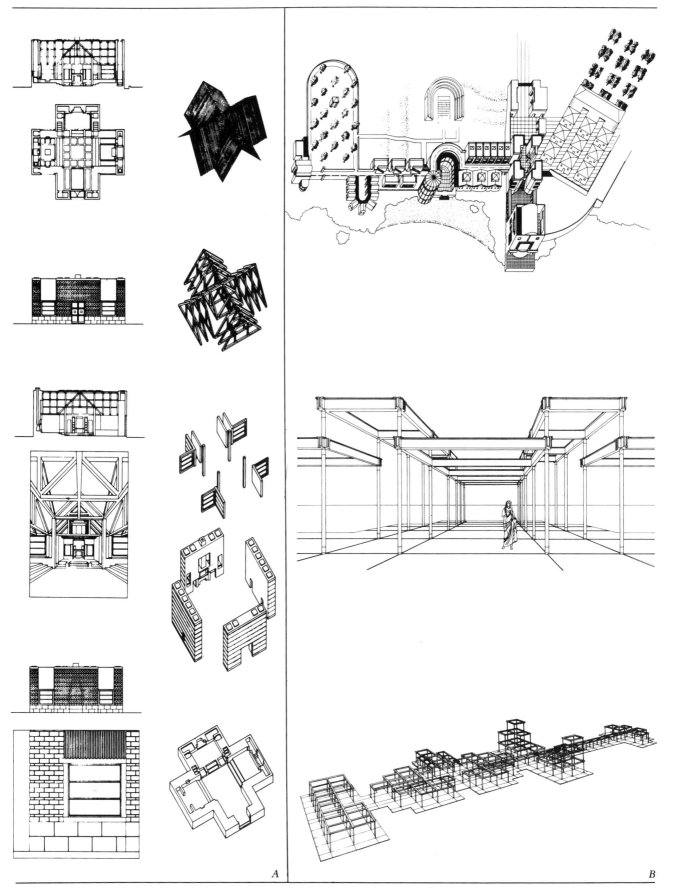

**Fig. 8-6. A.** *A house for Thoreau. Project by Eric Maltam.* **B.** *Pliny's Villa. Project by Chris Walsh. Design exercises from the studio of Judith Wolin combining historical precedent with the reading of literature and poetry. (After* Journal of Architectural Education)

A

B

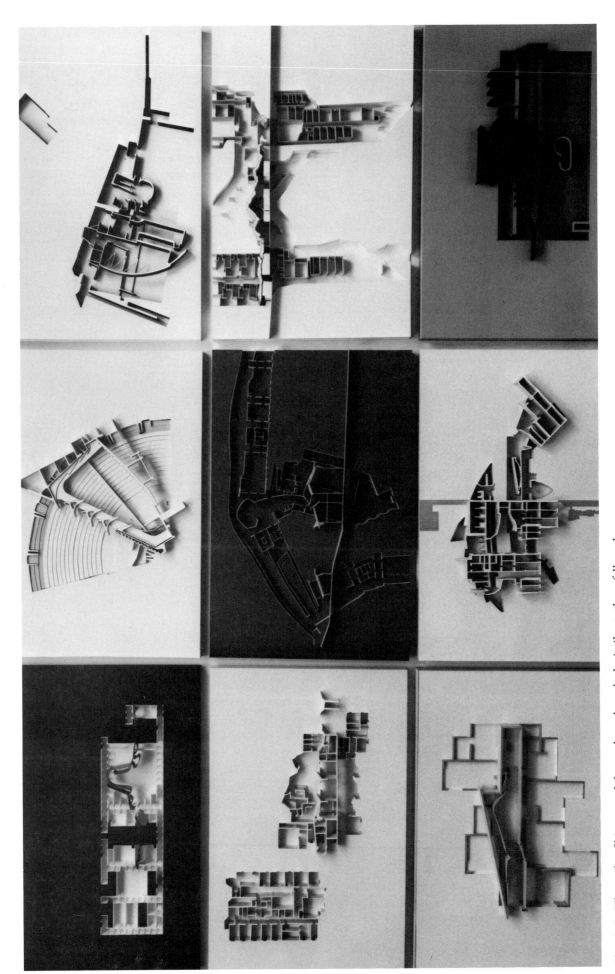

**Fig. 8-7.** *The study of history and theory through methods similar to those followed in the design studio, as advocated by Bruno Zevi. The use of a spatial model as a tool for understanding precedents. From the theory classes of Martin Price. Photos courtesy of Martin Price and Craig Kuhner.*

2. Study of the regional characteristics (climate, materials, regional peculiarities).
3. Study of structural and constructural methods.
4. Sociocultural "framing" of the studied work (history of the culture, lifestyle, and civilization during the period and comparison to similar artifacts of other areas and periods.)
5. Search for the obscure, the mythic, and the symbolic, along with a concern for the intangible values of the era that perhaps were at work during the making of the particular precedent (monument or vernacular example).
6. Concept of space, both interior and exterior.

**Synthetic Endeavors**

7. Interpretation of the studied precedent with regard to similar precedents of its time, and similar or analogous buildings of today.
8. Hypothetical suggestions about the extent of the similarities or analogies between the studied period and today.
9. Thesis suggesting the validity of the adoption of the studied precedent as an extension of history for the solution of today's needs.

These tasks may sound "monumental," yet they are not necessarily so if one focuses on one particular building type; the task can even become easy through historical precedent "banks"—computer programs to which architectural designers may have access.

**Fig. 8-8.** *Precedents of "inclusivist significance": The Monastery of Megisti Lavra, Mount Athos, Greece. At a glance, through one photograph, one encounters a multiplicity of architectonic concerns: The urban (monastery as a complex), the metaphysical (tombs of three Byzantine emperors), and the detailed (embroidery-like decoration through brick construction) are vividly apparent.*

At present, the analytical part is pretty well covered by research available through historical scholarship. The designer must work harder on the synthetic part of the precedent appreciation, and it will be his or her personal interpretation that will eventually help him or her to come up with "fresh" design solutions, not interpretations of others' work, no matter how documented that work is. Designers must always bear in mind that they are not historians or archeologists; their role should be interpretive, like that of writers, not philologists or literary scholars. It is the designer's personal interpretation of the actual facts we are after, not the scholar's dry, factual knowledge.

## The Correct Use of History

A substantiated, and at the same time imaginative, interpretation of architectural history is as much a creative task as any other activity, including design. Time is the heart of both history and historicist phenomena. The "correct use" of history is the prerequisite to architectural design that is genuinely evolutionary.

The correct use of history on the part of the designer should include references to one's own history, as well as references to history on a cross-cultural basis. This is very significant today because of the plural reality and the universality of the problems facing various societies. A commercial building in Tokyo or Hong Kong is as much subject to a cross-cultural appreciation of history as it would have been if the building were built in London.

The "inclusivist" and "correct" use of history by today's creative designers should include the following broad areas of concern:

1. Reference to local historical prototypes
2. Reference to global prototypes
3. Reference to "remote" as well as "closer" historic times
4. Rounded exploration of the historic precedent
5. Critical judgment in the selection and the kind of precedent

It is obvious that one-sided historical references would be "exclusionary" and thus should be avoided.

I believe it would be incorrect to disregard the local precedents in favor of global prototypes or projects from abroad. Such cases would promote eclecticism and produce irrelevant buildings, at least from the cultural and the users' perspective. Local as well as global prototypes should be studied simultaneously, interrelatedly, not in isolation.

Basic to the use of history are the elements of remote and close with reference to time. Precedents from the distant past may be totally irrelevant for some recent cultures, and relevant for others. Each culture must decide upon its own remote vs. close time frame. Nevertheless, avoiding precedents of the recent past may deprive the design process of the chance for genuine evolution. Periods of revival give a chance for further explorations of the promises and liabilities of art movements of the relatively recent past that were not given sufficient time to mature, for one reason or another. (This was the case with Russian Constructivism or with the Greek regionalism in the twentieth century.)

The designer must exercise disciplined judgment in selecting the time frame of historical references. While learning as much as possible about the building through history, he should focus carefully on the appropriate time frame, and explore the recent past as deeply as possible. It will be more sequential and evolutionary to create works on the basis of the immediate "yesterday" rather than to seek answers in the very distant past. The recent revival of Russian constructivism by Kristian Gullichsen and the Deconstructivists is more relevant than the Palladian revival of Postmodern historicism, because the former is at least an effort within the technology of this century that remained substantially unexplored.

The last item of significance that will guarantee the correct and beneficial use of history for creative design purposes is the kinds of precedents one selects.

## Partial vs. Inclusive Precedents

Like any new building we do, some buildings of the past were partial architectonic acts (putting emphasis on style or form alone), while others were inclusive. Furthermore, some important precedents have been studied by historians or other scholars only "partially" (architectural historians have been notorious for emphasizing façades to the exclusion of the section and the interior of buildings), while only a very few have been studied inclusively. I stand unequivocally in favor of the inclusivist precedent and suggest it as the right kind of precedent for a designer to seek.

In the absence of original inclusivist research, the designer should undertake it on his own or avoid the precedent. Otherwise his awareness of it will be only superficial, with superficial repercussions on the contemplated design. Textbooks of architectural history have very little to offer in terms of inclusivist precedent. The designer must seek the right kind of precedent in archeological references or in historical treatises, in the lifelong research projects of noted historians.

Historical research has bequeathed to us both partial and inclusivist precedents. The Parthenon is usually presented as a partial precedent; the "epitome of classical beauty," "rationality of form," "proportional perfection," and so on. Very little is ever said about the overall significance of this project for the weakening of the national defense of the various Greek states. In fact, the Periclean diversion of defense funds from the Treasury in Delos for construction of this project had adverse effects in the long run for all the Greek alliances. Partial precedents would also be those included in the catalogues prepared by Durand of the Ecole des Beaux-Arts and other students of building typologies because they relied on graphic communication only. The recent Postmodern period saw the revival of the partial precedent when catalogues of historic buildings were indiscriminately used as "form givers" by young designers and historicist instructors alike. It is obvious that such manuals, although valuable for the thoughtful and sincere explorer, should be approached with great caution. Instructors should encourage students to undertake further study on the precedents they may select to follow. One should try to go beyond the superficiality experienced during the decade of Postmodernism. Precedents and the old should be dressed with meaning. One effort to debate such superficialities was the book *Classical Architecture: The Poetics of Order* by Alexander Tzonis and Liane Lefaivre. The writers tactfully opposed several Postmodern theoreticians and through systematic analysis and critical argument explained the rules and the essence of classical architecture.

The Palace of Knossos, on the other hand, would be a precedent that has been occasionally dissected and presented through the inclusivist perspective argued in terms of tangible and intangible constraints. The inclusivist instructor should seek the inclusivist precedent, and students perform the inclusivist framing of the precedents they study prior to using them for design didactics. Precedents with no possibility of research evidence that would permit inclusivist framing should be avoided as superficial and counterproductive. It is more important to have the whole story, even of an unknown modest building (the storehouse in Japan, the "cruck frame" English medieval house, the pigeon structures in Tenos) than employ a

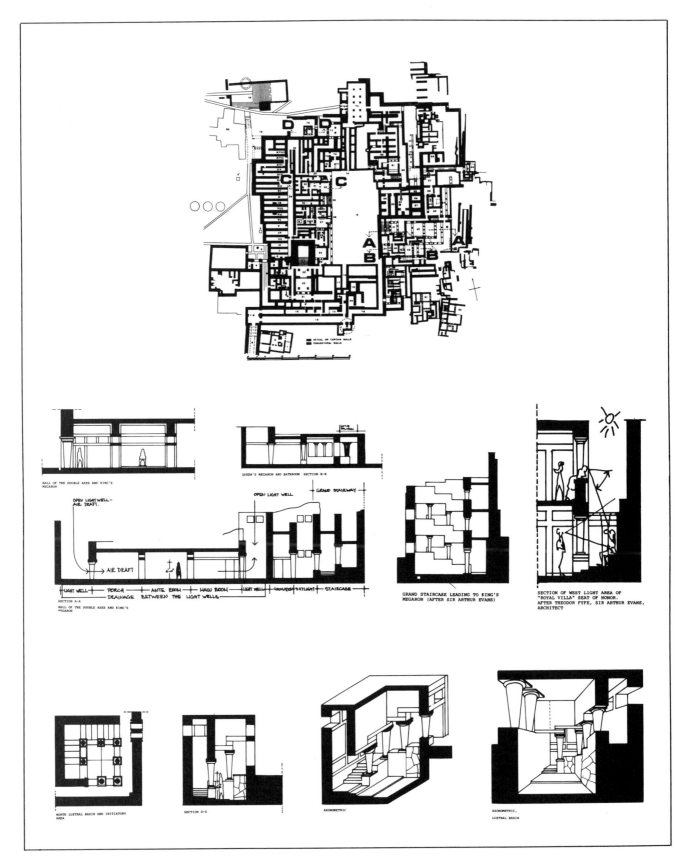

**Fig. 8-9.** *The Palace at Knossos, Crete, an "inclusivist" historical precedent adopted by the author and studied on a continuous basis since his student days. (From A. Antoniades, "Cretan Space,"* A + U Architecture and Urbanism, *October 1984.)*

famous monument of partial precedental validity.

Among the historical precedents that have enjoyed the best inclusivist treatment by researchers we have found very useful and recommend the following: The Palace of Knossos, the monasteries of the order of Cluny, the Alhambra and Generalife in Granada, and the *kura* (storehouses) of Japan.

## The Need for Tolerance

Based on these ground rules for the inclusivist and correct appreciation of history as well as our suggestions for the right kind of precedents and the qualitative distinction we assigned between history and historicism, we now call attention to the need for genuine personal introspection as a means of enforcing each designer's attitude toward the two.

It is very significant that the designer view his own architectural evolution within the framework of his own life. One has no better historical evidence than one's own experience; it would be detrimental not to pause and reflect sincerely on one's own projects and values. As Panagiotis Michelis has argued:

> Time is the greatest judge of values, because with increasing distance, judgment becomes clearer, the spectator penetrates the essence of the work more easily, and by removing himself from time, confronts this essence candidly and sincerely. At the same time, however, art touches its own times, and should in fact tread firmly to express those times, so long as it knows how to place the ideas of art beyond time itself. (Michelis, 1977)

In consequence, personal introspection within the broader framework of real and in-depth historical understanding can be a very positive path to architectural creativity. Such introspection may even transform the designer's historicist tendencies of youth into a real historical disposition and help him or her produce the mature projects of a career. Because of this possible transformation, we believe that historicism may perform the role of preparing one to enter the road of real history and that even the shallow architectural creations of early life are prerequisites and historicism even acceptable for didactic purposes. Personal introspection, critical scrutiny, and time will take their turn and both projects, genuine and shallow, will be evaluated, and will eventually constitute the basis for new beginnings in the future, in the mature years of the architect.

We do not therefore flatly deny "historicism" as a possible path to creativity, because we would eliminate the chances for substantial comparisons and the evolution that is expected to take place throughout a designer's life. Historicism and referential derivation of any sort should be given the benefit of the doubt, conceived as paths to creativity.

## Massage and Manipulation

One may not believe in historicism, nor in referential formal derivation, yet one might be able to produce meaningful and intuitive results through a series of formal and intellectual transformations, should one introduce into the process candid, critical scrutiny and keep in mind the multilayered nature of the architectural artifact. In a process of design where the doctrine of form follows function has been replaced by an understanding that both can be "massaged" and "manipulated" for their mutual benefit, historicism and referential derivation can be of extraordinary significance.

It is a question of how one goes about utilizing the potential of each path to creativity, not whether some paths are valid while others are not. It does not mean that history and historicism should produce buildings with "pediments" and visual signs of the past. The iconography and formal resemblance to the precedents of the past currently exhibited by many projects in the United States is evidence of a shallow appreciation of history. One would expect to break one's fingers if one were to knock on the massive walls and the interior colonnades of many historicist buildings, rather than leaving with the memory of sounds similar to a child's toy drum upon knocking on such walls. The library in San Juan Capistrano by Michael Graves is a good example. A deceiving building in several respects, its function, scale, texture, sound, lighting, and general disposition demonstrate none of the lessons one could have learned from the study of the neighboring mission. The earlier architects were honest in terms of the correct use of materials, the use of light, the expression of textures; if we are going to refer to the past, why is it that we do not pay attention to the honesty they possessed and try to make it a part of our own creation?

## A Caution

The personal dialog of the designer for his own introspection or for the occasional critique of his own projects must take very seriously into consideration the aspect of honesty touched on above. It is perhaps the most important aspect confronting historicism today. In some instances, it has reached levels that were (and still are among many people) unacceptable. Forgery and stealing, acts condemned by law, are in some ways tolerated, or even unhesitantly performed by many. Philip Johnson, notorious for his deep knowledge of history, but also notorious for his spirited intellectual arrogance, stated in one of the publications in which he defended "new classicism" the following: "I could not not copy." Should a law of "architectural copyright" exist, much of the current copying and frequently shallow historicist practices would be avoided, or at least the architects perhaps would have to put a plaque on the walls of their buildings, offering footnotes (it would have been appropriate to offer visual footnotes) to the references they used.

In contrast, and in a warning against the plagiaristic and copying mentality, one could speak of the positive possibilities of a well-conceived historicism, which indeed could be nothing else but the eclectic and inclusivist study of history. Projects of well-conceived historicism, especially when attempted in studios where one would try to integrate the study of history with the training in design, demonstrate that student work can be serious as well as inventive, daring as well as realistic, original as well as primordial, diverse as well as contextual, contemporary as well as a continuation of a sequential past.

The primordial is absolutely fundamental in creativity, and the study of history can help here because it takes the creator back to the sources of his or her origin, to the primitive stages of humankind. In this sense, and as much as one believes like Vico, Cassirer, and Mircea Eliade that the origins of imagination and creativity are in the "primitive with the mythic," history can be of invaluable help.

The concepts of myth and primordiality bring to the surface a series of topics that must be resolved when in the channel of history (even historicism-eclecticism) or in the path of precedents. What strategy should one use for the selection of precedents? What considerations should be taken into account? What should be a "healthy" (truthful) attitude toward the lessons of history with regard to their applied use in the design studio? What should be the general guiding principles for instructors, students, and architects alike? My personal belief is that the precedent strategy, beyond the narrow architectonic criteria for the selection of kinds of precedents

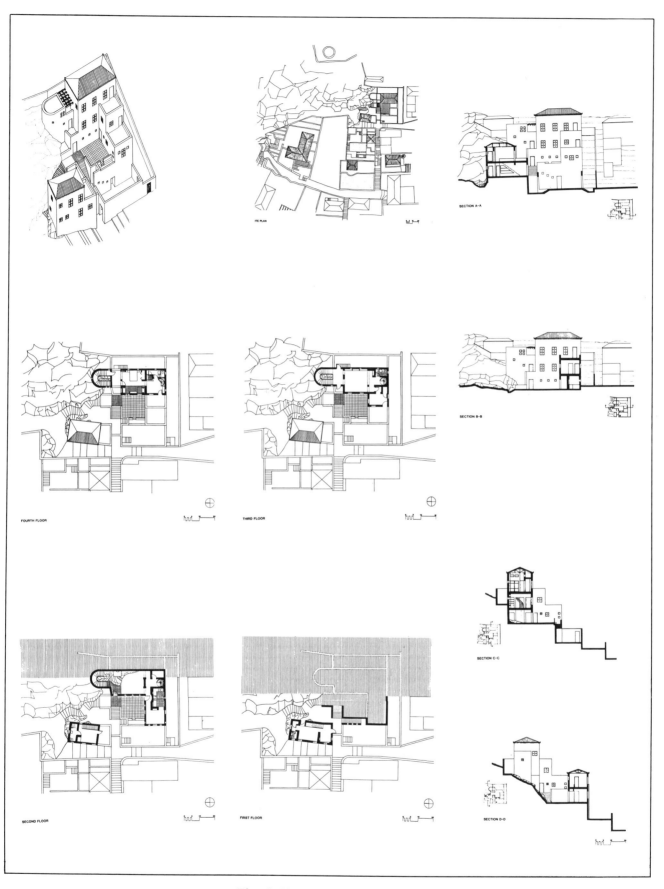

**Fig. 8-10.** *Design projects in places controlled by historic zoning ordinances (Santa Fe, New Mexico; Hydra, Greece) afford the opportunity for contemplation of the "presence of the past" and produce buildings that appear as if they have been there forever. Final presentation drawings by Tom Maxwell for architect's home office, Hydra, Greece, from the author's fourth-year design studio, UT Arlington, 1988.*

discussed above, should also take into account the sociocultural nature and the cross-cultural setting of today's architect.

The selection of precedents from the sociocultural perspective should consider the following:

1. The plurality of the student groups and their cross-cultural differences.
2. The inherent difficulties in the use of precedents arising from the proliferation of slides, the proliferation of publications, and the deceptive power of photography, requiring from the instructor a demanding and editorially inclusivist role.
3. The early statement of positions without regard to the due understanding of the meaning of terms such as "history," "historicism," "styles," and eventually "classical" vs. "contemporary," since the architecture we do is for the period we happen to live (and the future), not for the past.
4. The clarity of the instructor's own position with regard to the broader framework (and the past), along with substantiative critical argument as to why one aligns oneself with a particular period, a particular line of architectural thought, a particular style, or a particular bias.

In the discussion that follows we elaborate on these beliefs in the hope that our conclusions may become clear.

## THE CROSS-CULTURAL PREDICAMENT

I was genuinely perplexed when, as a young design instructor in the United States (University of New Mexico), I discovered that there were no measured drawings of the Indian pueblos and that students in this country did not view the native architecture of this land as a prerequisite to any further study in terms of their architectural history. This perplexity was subsequently furthered when I discovered that school administrators were working hard to organize trips to Europe and other places abroad, leaving their students virtually blind with regard to the architectural riches of this land. Memories of time spent in island towns, sketching and measuring churches, houses, and old monasteries as a young architectural student in Greece, in the stimulating warmth of architectural collegiality, further infuriated me. My own students would be the poorer because of this.

As it is inconceivable that an architect should not study his own roots and his own culture, it is equally perplexing and inconceivable to practice what one could call "precedental straitjacketing," forcing students to accept precedents from one and only one country.

## On the Concept of Bias

Michael Graves, an architect highly dependent on the use of history and precedents, and one who has written occasionally and candidly about these topics, has accepted the idea that "There is a bias or a point of view through which an architect looks at his precedents." His whole approach to the use of precedents is based on that bias. Graves, in a sense, reinforces the notion of the cross-cultural differences in people (something which psychologists have proved with regard to perception to a substantial degree).

It is therefore important to realize that the lessons of a particular building will be different for different people. It will depend on their particular bias. Such biases are affected to a great extent by the school, the curriculum, and the liberal arts grounding (or not) of the architect. An African student will interpret Rome differently than an American or a Scandinavian, even though his sketches may be better than the others. It will not hurt if the design instructor refreshes his concerns through reference to studies on cross-cultural differences: There should be special effort to include examples from the cultures of the student group. Man is in the foundation of every culture, and architecture serves man. The instructor who goes to the roots of design in every precedent will find the "good" in precedents of every culture.

Under the circumstance of a cross-culturally balanced use of precedents, students will realize that there is more than one way to solve well a particular problem and that they should put their own minds to work to decide which one should be their own way and why. In this way students will create rather than just passively receive and follow.

If one accepts the premise of architectural inclusivity, then one should accept the cross-cultural selection of precedents and the cross-cultural teaching of history as prerequisites to inclusivist instruction. Yet these beliefs bring us face to face with some very peculiar problems of the era vis-à-vis the proliferation of precedent resources. Only as early as the early 1960s, architects were learning their precedents through instructors' sketches on the blackboard. There was an "economy of principle" in this case. The student had enough time to absorb, store, and transform the relatively few, yet well selected, samples that were offered to him by the instructor. Subsequently a few architects began to travel, to rely on their own eyes and sketches, following the route suggested by Le Corbusier. Today, however, all this has changed. You can hardly find a school that does not have a constantly improving and updated slide library.

Although this is an event of extraordinary significance, particularly unique for students of advanced countries, it is both blessing and handicap. The abundance of slides and the availability of projection equipment requires extraordinary discipline on the part of the instructor (especially the architectural historian, and the theory and design instructors); this also generates extraordinary problems for the student who is constantly struggling to absorb. It is hard to reach the discipline previously imposed by the blackboard (size of area, ability and quickness in sketching) and the chalk dust on the instructor's fingers. Additional handicaps arise with the ease of creating false images due to the inherent property of the medium; photography can easily deceive.

*Slides have introduced the deceit dimension of the magazine into the classroom:* excellent slides (of buildings that have not been experienced personally by the instructor) may easily help perpetuate myths about certain buildings, or create impressions that may be easily reversed upon encounter with the real thing. I experienced an extraordinary feeling of "letdown'" upon personal visits to several glamorized, "photogenic" buildings of the mid-1970s. Perhaps the greatest feeling of wonder and discontent came at a visit to the Ichi-ban-kan building in Shinjuku, Tokyo, which made the covers of the two first editions of the very influential *The Language of Post-Modern Architecture* by Charles Jencks. I have had many other similar experiences.

All this points to the particular issue of slides as a means for "precedental" education and the potentially inherent handicap. The positive aspects are many, especially the possibility of stimulation and the personal myth or interpretation an imaginative student may offer to a slide. It is possible to create just through the encounter with a single appealing image (in spite of the content of what is seen), immediately or in the future, when the brain will release this image as circumstances require. Arata Isozaki has written about his fixation with Ledoux: he had in his mind some images of projects by Ledoux he had seen during his student days in the 1950s.

Slides enrich the quality of the visual subconscious depository of the mind. It is the responsibility of the instructor to exercise extraordinary discipline, to present the precedents inclusively (showing plans, sections, and interiors, not just exterior shots of elevations), and to explain them as clearly as earlier instructors did. They had to take their time, time to enjoy in the process their beautiful sketches on the blackboard.

## THE ROLE OF THE DESIGN INSTRUCTOR

The most important aspect, however, with which instructors of design have to come to grips, is the issue of their broad personal perceptions and beliefs with regard to history. Uncontemplated alignment with one group or another, or endorsement of a particular fashion or style are not guarantees that the instruction will be beneficial. One must deal with these subjects and deal very seriously on a self-searching level. In this respect, one would have to ask oneself questions regarding one's own roots, and one's personal position and relationship to the past, the present, and the future.

Design instructors should be very critical of the occasional qualitative judgments on architectural periods rendered by historians, theoreticians, and aesthetes, especially when such judgments are based on partial information and nonscholastic evidence. Because there were times when whole periods of architecture were unjustifiably condemned as unworthy, when some periods were vested with supremacy over others, and the literature was characterized by bigotry and parochial one-sidedness. The design instructor will have to be a presence in all of these issues, demonstrate the inclusivist case, and express his or her own positions very clearly with regard to the questions of style, exemplary architects, eclecticism vs. inclusivism, perfect vs. imperfect, understanding of the classical and the contemporary, overall attitude toward moderation and restraint as opposed to an undisciplined disposition, attitude toward research, and research work habits.

What follows are my personal positions on these issues, which may act as a foundation for adoption or debate for other instructors and students.

## On the Question of Style

It appears from a distance that the occasional debates on style and the various classifications of architecture dance around the pivotal concept of the classical. Much ink has been spent on this subject by historians, aesthetes, and critics. Some students of the architecture of the late seventies and early eighties pointed out the confusion in the minds of many people regarding the "classical revival" in the third quarter of the twentieth century, a by-product concern of the occasional debate between classical Greek architecture and the architecture of the Italian Renaissance. These two notorious examples were occasionally viewed by scholars (and their followers) in very fanatical terms, some favoring one period while downgrading the merits of the other. The decade of Postmodernism was biased toward the Renaissance. The proliferation of pro–Renaissance literature, often generalized and esoteric, would only parenthetically point to the merits of classical Greek architecture. Further on, this literature took for granted the lessons of architects it admired (Vitruvius, Palladio, Alberti), none of whom had seen a real classical Greek building. On the other hand, statements such as those of Victor Hugo that "from the truthful ancient Art the Renaissance created a false Art," or similar statements by Frank Lloyd Wright, who often quoted Hugo, could be very harmful if taken at face value and believed unquestioningly.

## Exemplary Architects and Scholars

The inclusivist historical probing of the wholesome designer should go beyond such attitudes. Both sides should be heard, and with equal rigor: Vitruvius, Palladio, and Alberti should be eternally enhanced by Matila Ghyka, Fletcher, and architects such as Le Corbusier.

The best architects of this century were in fact graduates of both cultures, highly versed in both classical Greece and the Renaissance. They were also able to include in their best projects the best of the lessons of both. Alvar Aalto is, in my opinion, the premier example in this respect.

## On the Perfect vs. the Imperfect

Eclecticism looks only at one culture, whereas inclusivism looks at the whole depository of knowledge in the entire spectrum of human civilization. Every peak, everything which humankind produced at its best, is the property of the whole human race. It does not mean that everything produced by any particular era was perfect and meritorious as a precedent. One should look for the unique, the qualitative subtleties; the exceptions rather than the rules may have a lasting effect on the design student. For instance, one could not easily forget that the "perfection" of classical Greek architecture owed much to a series of conscious and consistently applied human imperfections which guaranteed the existence of a constantly present hidden source of life in the work, known today as the "latent movement" of a work of art. Such "imperfections" were the divergence of the columns, their entasis or bulging, the curvature of the Parthenon, the deviations from canonical ornamentation and pictorial representation, the various irregularities in the arrangement of the building complexes, the slight turning of the lion heads of the water spouts, and the slight slanting of the ridge tiles, among others.

All of these have been found to contribute to what K. A. Romaios, a Greek academician, described as the "latent movement," a quality and a theory regarding the works of ancient Greece similar to William Henry Goodyear's theory of the "latent picturesque," on the basis of which Panagiotis Michelis argued that "In Greek Art the plasticity and picturesqueness coincide" and that "through dialectical contrasts, a union is born. . . ." In other words, they observed that the source of the life distinguishing the classical buildings of Greece was the planned and strategically distributed touches of "imperfection," those elements of humanly imposed tension, as opposed to the canonically observed rules of order and the diagrammatic geometricity of the Renaissance.

## The Discipline and Work Habits Issue

The act of design requires not only theoretical knowlege and a culturally comprehensive disposition, but work habits and practical tasks such as sketching, drawing, and model making. History has much to offer on this subject. We should constantly refresh our memories about the artistic inclusivity and the extraordinary professional ingenuity of Brunelleschi; the model-making habits of Michelangelo; the fact that Palladio as well as Mies van der Rohe started as a stone carver and a bricklayer, respectively; and that a healthy sense of how to get the commission is fundamental to the process of the making and the quality of the designer.

Because of these facts, inclusivity is most important when we address the subject of architectural history. Classical Greece and the Renaissance, for instance, can produce a richer synthesis if they are considered together. It would be an extraordinary source of fulfillment to be able to produce buildings, as the ancient Greeks did, that possess a quality of unseen har-

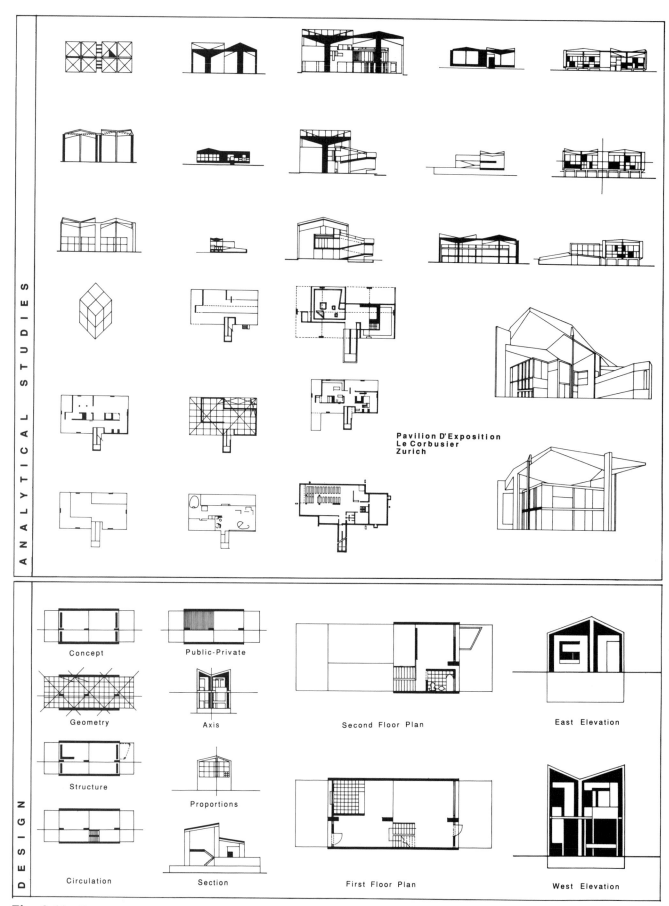

Pavilion D'Exposition
Le Corbusier
Zurich

**ANALYTICAL STUDIES**

**DESIGN**

Concept

Public-Private

Second Floor Plan

East Elevation

Geometry

Axis

Structure

Proportions

First Floor Plan

Circulation

Section

West Elevation

**Fig. 8-11.** *Contemporary precedents and design projects "in the manner of the masters." Student project based on analysis of the Pavilion d'Exposition of Le Corbusier in Zurich. Hanieh Waichek, from the third-year design class of Andrzej Pinno, UT Arlington, 1987.*

mony as opposed to the immediately and visually detectable, while at the same time being able to animate them spatially and make them modularly and proportionally appealing, as was the case with the Renaissance. Yet such a result is easier said than done. It requires study and devoted application, both in theory and in actual design training. Furthermore, it requires a strong understanding of the element of relativity that affects the act of inclusivity. This can be illustrated with the inclusivist appreciation of the term "classical," a concept often assumed to be self-evident, yet really complex, circumstantially dependent, subtle and dynamic, and finally a requisite for the understanding of the concept of the "contemporary."

## The Concepts of the Classical and the Contemporary

While recognizing the significance of several academic studies on the subject, especially John Summerson's *The Classical Language of Architecture* (MIT Press 1963) and Alexander Tzonis-Lefaivre's *Classical Architecture: The Poetics of Order* (MIT Press 1987), and after careful consideration of the material we have surveyed, I have decided to "displace" myself once again and accept help from philosophy and aesthetics, with particular attention to the work of the noted Polish philosopher Tatarkiewicz. His analysis provides a model that is considered more inclusive and therefore will have greater validity as a point of departure.

In the Tatarkiewicz arguments, a creation would be understood as "classical" if it is characterized by a twofold understanding of the term: the general understanding and the qualified understanding. Under the general understanding, "classical" should mean something that is the more mature, the most excellent product of a culture. The work of Pericles in the fifth century, known as the Golden Age of Greece, has been considered the most excellent expression of the culture of antiquity, its values and all it aspired, the state of its technology, a qualitative summary of the arts, the pinnacle of the intellect of the time. Similarly, the Gothic cathedral of thirteenth-century Europe, a product of the mature expression of the Middle Ages, is also "classical" (Gothic architecture had been regarded by many in the past as inferior). The qualified understanding of "classical" (applied to all the arts) denotes culture, art, and poetry, with certain characteristics, such as moderation, restraint, harmony, and balance between parts. The "language of classical architecture" (Greek, or Roman of the period of Augustus, or Gothic) would refer to the discourse that attempts to find the visible elements that would make explicit these elements.

Several students have detected the rules that were followed in achieving moderation, restraint, harmony, and balance between parts, along with whatever was hidden or "latent," especially with regard to the classical architecture of Greece. The elements of moderation and restraint have been proved without doubt, while the element of harmony and balance have been examined at several levels of investigation and proved as well.

If one accepts that in order to call something "classical," it should qualify under both interpretations of the term, then it may become easier to examine and classify a work accordingly. Herein lies the merit of definitions, because without them we cannot embark on aesthetic and critical arguments, both of which are necessary for the process of evolution. It is not so important that there may be disagreements as it is that there be well-conceived argument and the desire to improve, recycle, or conclude that for one reason or another, the defended work does not have to be "classical" but is whatever it is, for these reasons. Under the qualified interpretation of classical, the Gothic is not classical because it does not demonstrate restraint and moderation. According to Tatarkiewicz, periods that would qualify under the two-part understanding of the classical are Roman times under Augustus, France under Charlemagne, and Florence under the Medicis.

It becomes very clear that twentieth-century architecture is not "classical" in any sense, while one could suggest that the arts of aerospace engineering and computer design have met the conditions of the first interpretation of the classical. The culture of the times has produced spacecraft and computers that are the pinnacles of the values and technology of the time and demonstrate the excellence of human achievement in this respect. Yet one could not speak about the second layer of interpretation; we are far from going into space with moderation and restraint, while what our spacecraft leave behind is not beneficial for human life.

It will be helpful now if we conceive of "classical" as a condition occupying the top of the curve of the evolution and refinement of art, to call everything before it "primitive" or "archaic" (accepting the names of the terms as initially used in art history), and to call everything after it "decadent" (with reservations). It is important to qualify the "decadent," to give it the benfit of the doubt, thus leaving the absolute qualitative interpretation to future critics.

These terms should be used only under the assumption of a common culture; another interpretation might apply when the culture changes. When the cultural framework changes, and yet the images produced are equated or criticized on the basis of images produced by other cultures in the past, one is apt to get confusion. In cases where a civilization or an artist, instead of seeking original forms that would be expressive of his or her own cultural traits, borrows forms out of the classical periods of other cultures, we generate pseudoclassical, classicist, or neoclassical artifacts which are always inferior to the classical.

## CONCLUSIONS

The study of history or of particular precedents will permit one to make sound judgments about the relative merit of the work under scrutiny, to learn lessons that may be helpful in one's own creativity. It will eventually be the individual's own morality that will dictate the final word and permit him or her to create with the goal of "originality within one's own cultural framework," or to borrow. Clearly the period of the early 1980s was one of personal moral judgment as to what should be the pinnacle of the expression of the era. Architects such as Philip Johnson admitted to copying; critics such as Helen Searing and later Charles Jencks institutionalized their own understanding of what classicism should be. In spite of the efforts of both writers to clarify their conception of classicism, neither addressed the fundamental issue of the negative connotation of classicism, so well understood in the nineteenth century. In the absence of debate on the validity of classicism as a worthwhile attitude to accept, we seem to have elaborated on an argument based purely on the negative condition of "pseudo," the lie. Is our era one of global "liars"? Do we want to be one of the liars? Some will say that a lie admitted is not a lie. The answer should obviously rest with each creator separately.

The current emphasis on history can have positive effects. The issue should not be one of history or not, but rather of deep, honest, and comprehensive referential understanding, rather than shallow, dishonest, formal and superficial review. Although there has been some exceptional writing regarding what one could suggest as a well-conceived appreciation of history, many of those who claim history as the basis of creative activity, both instructors and architects, tend, in our judgment, to be shallow and superficial. T. S. Eliot has provided us with an exceptional account of the

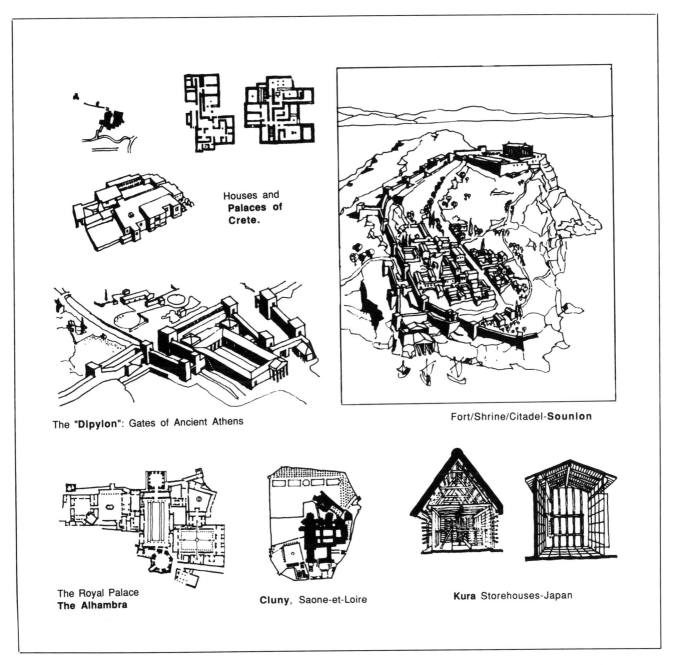

The "Dipylon": Gates of Ancient Athens

Houses and
**Palaces of
Crete.**

Fort/Shrine/Citadel-**Sounion**

The Royal Palace
**The Alhambra**

**Cluny**, Saone-et-Loire

**Kura** Storehouses-Japan

**Fig. 8-12.** *Tracings of "meritorious historic precedents" by students after archeological measurements or proposed reconstructions by scholars, reveal plan, massing and compositional secrets that can not even be detected through actual visits to the projects.*

sane and creative appreciation of history. Through the study of history one can develop a historical sense which, according to Eliot, "is indispensable for anyone who would continue to be a poet beyond his twenty-fifth year; and a historical sense involves a perception not only of the pastness of the past, but of its presence."

Eliot speaks of poetry and we speak of architecture. Both are poetic acts. Historical sense can make an architect more acutely aware of his place in time, of his own contemporaneousness. History and historicism are two paths to creativity that could be considered metaphorically as two peculiar narrow paths on a steep cliff leading to new, undiscovered territories and taken by two different kinds of explorers. The careful and sure explorer will use all his or her past experience to stay alert and on course in pursuit of the promised Shangri-La. The overexcited and inattentive person who may constantly have Shangri-La perceptions on his or her mind may miss the path, fall off the cliff, and never make it. Both paths go to the top, but only the explorer will reach it.

## Summary

Architectural history is considered to be the qualitative differential that distinguishes architects among themselves. Architectural precedents from the remote as well as from the recent past can be didactic and can enhance the design process. In this chapter we discuss the differences between history and historicism, and present arguments for the right use of both. We define the "inclusivist" appreciation of history as opposed to the "partiality" of historicism, address the concept of the correct use of history, and make suggestions for selecting the right kind of precedents. Further emphasis is given to the need for personal retrospection on the part of each designer as a means of moving from historicism to history. The chapter closes with a discussion of the key questions that have affected designers' appreciation of history, such as style, and concludes with the need to raise the architect's "historical sense."

## References

Antoniades, Anthony C. "Mount Athos: Historic Precedent to Arcological Post-Modernism." *A + U Architecture and Urbanism*, September 1979.

———. "Cretan Space." *A + U Architecture and Urbanism*, October 1984.

Bouras, Charalambos. *Mathemata Istorias tis Architectonikes* (Lessons of Architectural History). 3 volumes. Athens. Vol. I, 1975; Vol. II, 1975/1980/1984.

Cassirer, Ernst. *The Problem of Knowledge*. New Haven and London: Yale University Press, 1950, pp. 217–225.

Curtis, William J. R. *Modern Architecture since 1900*. Englewood Cliffs, NJ: Prentice-Hall, 1987.

———. "Toward an Authentic Regionalism." *Mimar 19*, Spring 1986.

Dean, Andrea O. *Bruno Zevi on Modern Architecture*. New York: Rizzoli, 1983, pp. 44, 48, 62.

Eliot, T. S. "Tradition and the Individual Talent" in *Perspecta 19, The Yale Architectural Journal*, 1982, p. 37.

Evans, Joan. *The Romanesque Architecture of the Order of Cluny*. Cambridge, Eng.: University Press, 1938.

Fanelli, Giovani. *Brunelleschi*. Scala Books, 1980, p.32.

Frampton, Kenneth. *Modern Architecture: A Critical History*. London: Thames and Hudson, 1980, 1985.

Grabar, Oleg. *The Alhambra*. Printed in the USA, Oleg Grabar, 1978.

Graham, James Walter. *The Palaces of Crete*. Princeton, NJ: Princeton University Press, 1962.

Graves, Michael. "Referential Drawings." *Journal of Architectural Education*, 32, 1 (September 1978), p. 24.

Ghyka, Matila C. *The Geometry of Art and Life*. New York: Sheed and Ward, 1946.

Isozaki, Arata. "The Ledoux Connection." In Jencks, *Free Style Classicism,* p. 28.

Harms, Martin. "Historic Precedent in the Studio: Projects for Venice." *Journal of Architectural Education*, 35, 2 (Winter 1982), p. 29.

Jencks, Charles. *The Language of Post-Modern Architecture.* Academy Editions, 1978.

————. "Free Style Classicism." *Architectural Design.* London, 1982.

Kahn, Louis. "The Invisible City." *Design Quarterly*, No. 86/87 (1972), p. 61.

Le Corbusier. *Towards a New Architecture.* New York: Praeger, 1960, pp. 123, 124, 125, 129, 130, 141–151, 161.

Konstantinidis, Aris. *Dio Choria ap' te Mykono* (Two houses from Mykonos). Athens, 1947

————. *Ta Palia Athenaika Spitia* (Old Athenian Houses). Athens, 1950.

Michelis, Panagiotis A. *Aisthetikos.* Detroit: Wayne State University Press, 1977, pp. 18, 19, 21, 37, 42, 106, 285.

Papachadje, Nikolaou. *Pafsaniou Ellados Periegeses: Attica.* Ekdotide Athenon, Athens, 1974.

Porphyrios, Demetri. *Sources of Modern Eclecticism.* London: Academy Editions/St. Martin's Press, 1982, pp. 114, 116.

Samuels, Mike, and Samuels, Nancy. *Seeing with the Mind's Eye.* New York: Random House, 1975, pp. 239, 248.

Schildt, Göran. *Alvar Aalto as Artist.* Mairea Foundation, Villa Mairea, 1982.

————. *Alvar Aalto: The Early Years.* New York: Rizzoli, 1984.

————. *Alvar Aalto: The Decisive Years.* New York: Rizzoli, 1986.

Searing, Helen. *Speaking a New Classicism: American Architecture Now.* Northampton, MA: Smith College of Museum of Art, 1981, p. 35.

Summerson, John. *The Classical Language of Architecture.* Cambridge, MA: MIT Press, 1963.

Tatarkiewicz, Wladyslaw. *History of Aesthetics.* Warsaw: Mouton, PWN-Polish Scientific Publishers. Vol. I, 1970; Vol. II, 1970; Vol. III, 1974.

Teiji, Itoh. *Kura: Design and Tradition of the Japanese Storehouse.* Kyoto: Kodansha International, 1973.

Turner, Paul V. *The Education of Le Corbusier.* New York: Garland Publishing, 1977, p. 7.

Tzonis, Alexander, and Lefaivre, Liane. *Classical Architecture: The Poetics of Order.* Cambridge, MA: MIT Press, 1986, pp. 117, 119.

Venturi, Robert. *Complexity and Contradiction in Architecture.* New York: The Museum of Modern Art, 1966, pp. 1, 19.

Whitehead, Alfred North. *Symbolism: Its Meaning and Effect.* Barbour-Page Lectures, University of Virginia, 1927. New York: Capricorn Books, 1959, pp. 21–23.

Wittkower, Rudolf. *Architectural Principles in the Age of Humanism.* London: Alec Tiranti, Ltd., 1952.

# Chapter 9 Mimesis and Literal Interpretation

*I contend for Greek principles,
not Greek things.*

Horatio Greenough

The Corinthian capital was created, according to a myth, as the result of a sculptor's inspiration at the sight of a basket covered with a stone and surrounded by thorns on a young girl's tomb in Corinth. According to Vitruvius, the nanny of a young girl who had died had placed by her tomb a basket filled with gifts and had covered it with a square stone to protect the contents. The stems of acanthus grew around the basket and upon reaching the corners of the covering stone, turned around in spiral. This was seen one day by the sculptor Kallimachos, and he created the capital later known as the Corinthian capital.

Mimesis signifies imitation and was a term adopted very early in Greek aesthetics. According to Tatarkiewicz, it was initially applied to dance to signify "the expression of feelings and the manifestation of experiences through movement, sound, and words." This concept of mimesis exists even today; a mime is a special performer (like the famous Marcel Marceau) who imitates through facial expressions, movement, and gestures, life, situations, feelings of pleasure, sadness, melancholy. The unification of an audience under the spell of an exceptional mime is proof of the power of mimesis. In this sense, imitation as expression of feeling is a welcome condition, since architecture aims at the evocation of feelings, especially emotional and spiritual feelings.

## ATTITUDES TOWARD MIMESIS

In architecture, there is a widely accepted notion that imitation cannot produce creativity. The noted Greek aesthete Panagiotis Michelis has argued convincingly against the acceptance of the myth regarding the creation of the Corinthian capital and has further argued that Vitruvius suffered from misconceptions regarding artistic creativity.

Along with imitation, concepts such as borrowing and derivation have been controversial throughout the history of architecture, in pure studies of aesthetics as well as in critical works. There is certainly no argument regarding the negative connotations of copying or even the deplorable case of plagiarism. Imitation, however, has been generally considered a dirty word; for the majority of pure aesthetes of the modern movement, purely imitative creations are aesthetically inferior. Equally bad, in their view, were the terms "eclectic" and "derivative," which were considered attempts at pure escape.

**Fig. 9-1.** *Overview of key mimetic examples in the evolution of architecture.*

One of the major themes underlying Horatio Greenough's argument in his famous book *Form and Function* has to do with mimesis and rationality about copying the images and styles of the ancients. On several occasions he sounds like Le Corbusier, pointing to the beauty of forms that are results of, as well as expressive of, the potential and the technology of "rhetoric" in stone. He wrote: "The men who have reduced locomotion to its simplest elements, in the trotting wagon and the yacht *America,* are nearer to Athens at this moment than they who would bend the Greek Temple to every use. I contend for Greek principles, not Greek things." Perhaps his strongest endorsement of individual orginality versus the imitative disposition was exemplified through his telling of the story of Michelangelo's departure from his native Florence on his way to Rome, where he was about to finish St. Peter's. Turning back his horse and gazing upon Brunelleschi's dome at Santa Maria del Fiore, he said: "Better than thee I cannot; like thee, I will not."

Greenough admires St. Peter's dome as eventually built by Michelangelo and didactically concludes: "Implicit conformity to precedent obliterates and annihilates the individual; violation of it, not justified by theory, or by practical result, sets the individual on no enviable pedestal. A throne may become a pillory." Greenough's answer to senseless imitation was that works of art (including architecture) should be " . . . embodiments of thought . . . and feeling" or embodiments of theory, as were the tombs of the Medici, which embodied the theory of Michelangelo.

We suggest that Greenough's attitude is the most convincing summary of what could be classified as *orthodox aesthetic theory on this subject.* Such aesthetics, as well as the architects who aspire to it, want the work of architecture to be the result of imitation *from within,* not from without. The argument goes that one has to create not on the basis of visual or formal imitation and external characteristics, but on the basis of genuine understanding of the internal requirements, the structure and the geometry of shells, the inherent laws of nature that help develop a certain form logically.

Architecture, on the basis of the orthodox, or the "conservative aspect of aesthetic appreciation," is in a sense poorer than other arts, such as theater, which in fact are legitimately conceived of as imitations of life. The definition of ancient Greek tragedy, according to Aristotle, had "imitation" as the central element of its conception: "Because tragedy is the imitation of an act, important and perfect" (Aristotle, *Poetics,* 1944, 9b, 23).

Inasmuch as one may want to agree with many of the notions of orthodox aesthetics, the theory of architectural creativity should not exclude any of the possible means to creativity, no matter how bad they may sound, to start with. One could perhaps find consolation in the contentions of recent aesthetes such as Rudolf Arnheim, who in a sense provides a more liberal framework (and we believe a richer one) for the appreciation of a work of art. His attitude that we should accept a work of art as an expression of the play of life is a healthy one, in absolute agreement with our own beliefs. For Arnheim, "play" (in art) as imitation of the pleasurable aspects of life is an acceptable condition. In further elaboration, he states his concept of "borrowing" for the purpose of imitation in art as the condition when one borrows "the suspense, the thrill, and the delight of victory from fighting without accepting also the cause, the harm and the pain." In this sense he makes a distinction between the essentials as opposed to the purely visual and the final result. To borrow "the stimulation of sight and the easy peace of pattern without accepting the responsibility that goes with their significance" is not acceptable.

Arnheim points to the immorality of imitation in art through "play" as an act of imitation, in the cases where the associated concept of "borrowing" is not the right one. He is similarly adamant against the associated concept of copying, finding no merit whatsoever, even with regard to realistic representation. He argues that "there is no such thing as the faithful copying of physical reality." Copying is not a substitute to the thoughtful effort to understand and present the essence of an object or a body. If the only motive is to copy, then one "will be caught by accidental suggestions of shape and color found through piecemeal observation . . . the result will be one of those ugly wraiths of reality that do not belong to either science or art."

## INDIVIDUALITY VS. THE COLLECTIVE

In view of the controversial side of imitation and its associated concepts, it is important to pose and confront the issue from an angle that has not yet been tackled in literature. This is the topic of the cross-cultural predicament that poses the question of individuality vs. the collective. Certain cultures put extraordinary emphasis on individuality, requiring that everything, every work or form, possess its own individuality and spirit, and that these be revealed or discovered in time, offering a surprise to the spectator. In certain cultures people feel at ease when they recognize signs, symbols, and forms that are familiar and common to all members of the community.

Architects, both instructors and students, may have their own preferences with regard to this question: some may be of the individualistic persuasion, others of the collective. Yet everyone should realize that if he or she is to follow the route of imitation, the risk is satisfying one audience while displeasing another.

In the cases of work in historic environments, we may be bound (or forced by existing codes and ordinances) to resort to imitative work. In the first place, the existence of such codes should be a clear indication that we are confronted by a community where the collective sense is paramount (Santa Fe, New Mexico; Hydra/Mykonos, Greece). One will have to compose on the assumption that the creative product will have to depend on imitation of morphological elements, or even styles that were developed in that place in the past. The task in such cases becomes exceedingly difficult; it becomes a case of self-searching for the architect concerned for truth, and it becomes exponentially difficult for the architect who may subscribe to the idea of individuality and the supremacy of uniqueness.

Once we believed that to build in historic settlements, following the styles of previous generations, as determined by the codes of those settlements, was immoral. We view such situations today as challenges, and we believe that they represent perhaps the most difficult test for the thoughtful and talented architect. This designer will consider the disposition of the client; will take the appropriate sides on the issue of individuality versus the collective as perceived through study of the client and the community he or she builds in, and will eventually create a work that will transcend visible signs of the imitative aspect of the project. Even the external elements of the building, although prescribed by code (officially enforced imitation), may be related among themselves in such subtle ways that they compose a new synthesis.

The "enemy" of traditional settlements that have adopted ordinances to enforce imitation of the old is the architect who avoids the problem, or the "bad" architect who will do anything, offering clients easy-to-copy containers, without any thought of animating the interior and without any effort to create new life out of the old. The world is certainly not perfect, and one may not have it always one's way. Imitation is certainly not conducive to individuality, yet one can, and should, be able to work with it, if it is necessary. One should do one's best to elevate the commission to "architecture." As Amos Chang, the author of the inspirational book *The*

*Tao of Architecture,* has said, "Creation somehow is a matter of consciously avoiding repetition or subconsciously searching for truth." The task becomes to find truthful and honest answers in situations where imitative repetition of a style is forced upon one from above. One can produce a synthesis in which such repetition ultimately disappears, or becomes insignificant due to the overall merit of the "new" work.

## INCLUSIVITY, IMITATION, AND ASSOCIATED CONCEPTS

The theoretical as well as the pragmatic aspects of the controversial and exceedingly complicated difficulties that surround the concept of imitation (and its associated concepts) support the skeptical attitude we have adopted thus far, while they reinforce our inclination toward permissiveness and inclusivity. Thus, even if imitation from outside is not able to produce acceptable results after critical scrutiny, it will still have provided concrete statements for further support of the orthodox position. Much of the new evolves through breaking the rules of orthodoxy, protest and exploration of the unorthodox, or inclusivity with regard to already existing more liberal attitudes.

The student of architecture should therefore be encouraged to indulge in imitative, derivative, and eclectic exercises, as opposed to abstaining and conforming to a dogma, whether it may be logical today or not. We certainly endorse the attitude that copying is unacceptable and plagiarism deplorable. However, attempting to do exercises "in the manner of certain masters" in an effort to understand their secrets and to learn through comparison is not "a sin," provided one is careful to give clear references and to credit one's sources of inspiration.

## ON LITERALITY

Literal interpretation—that is, imitation by reference to specific images as generated by specific concepts—should not be excluded as a means to creativity, although one should be extremely careful regarding problems of "literality." We have notorious examples of buildings that look like boats, elephants, or hot dogs, or that carry other images, perhaps more universal and difficult to achieve, such as the house with a human face by Minoru Takeyama, the house for an archeologist that looks like a broken column by Boullée, and the series of houses of ill repute by Ledoux which are phallic symbols. In many of these instances there may have been an initial humorous disposition, which in itself might have been worth keeping, but in most cases it is a naive effort at creativity which, in the absence of anything more relevant, resorted to the gimmicks of literality and visual mimicking.

Literality degrades imagination. Architects who employ literal interpretations or resort to direct visual imitation underestimate the ability of the mind to perceive and create broader concepts out of parts or abstractions of parts of buildings that have been built. As Frank Lloyd Wright put it, "Human life itself is being cheated through senseless imitation"; he was referring to the same issues addressed by Greenough regarding the use of the classic in American architecture.

### Kinds and Forms of Literality

There are two aspects of literality: the visual and the meaningful. As Arnheim has put it: "as it looks and as it is." In literality, the "look" overlaps with the "is," that is, the visual form is an explicit statement of what it is. Such forms leave nothing for the discovery or the stimulation of the mind.

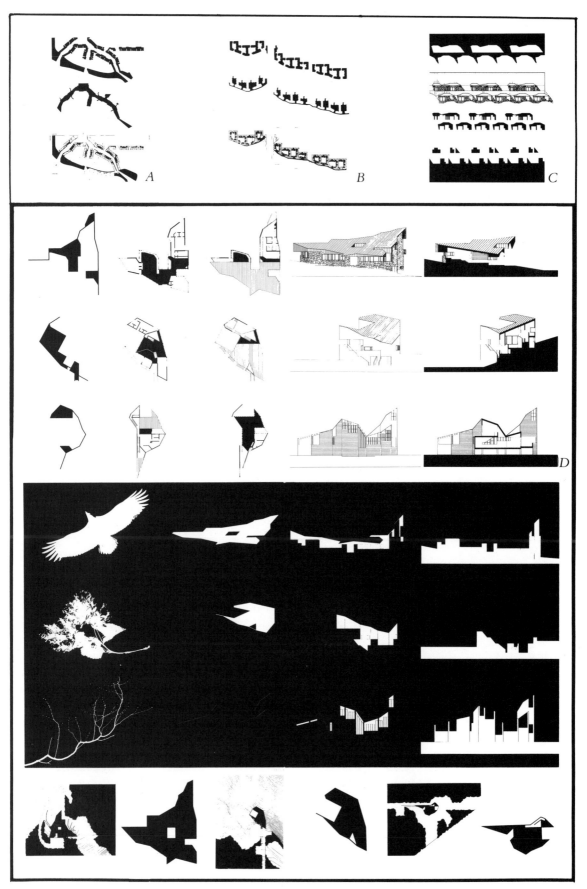

**Fig. 9-2.** *Projects by students of Martin Price inspired by nature.* **A.** *Student housing: Russell Claxton, Robert Meckfessel.* **B.** *Student housing: Ron Horton.* **C.** *Housing in Dallas: Randall Byrd, Kevin Crumpler.* **D.** *Proposals for three houses: Martin Price, architect. Martin Price exhibition, Miten Luonto Muovaa (How Nature Forms), Museum of Finnish Architecture, 1983.*

This idea should not be confused with the great difficulty most people have in "reading" or perceiving drawings or architectural models; literality becomes harmful when the buildings are finally built, which is the only time they can be "read" and understood by most people. And even in this case there will be people who are not able to "see" anything, although they will be subject to the bad effects of literality through the workings of the subconscious. Literality has the negative potential to enlarge the crowds of unstimulating, unimaginative people. For this reason, it should be avoided by architects.

Imitation and literality can take many forms depending on the origin of the stimulation. Imitation based on historical precedent may result in historicism and eclecticism. Imitation based on nature may produce "romanticism," whereas if the imitative departure is the work of admired architects, the result may suffer from the handicap of copying and even plagiarism. If the stimulation was caused by objects or forms in the environment, there is an extraordinary danger of creating works that have problems of scale. One should take all these traps into consideration and try to avoid them by constantly questioning literality and converting the inherent problems into lessons and originality.

If one were to classify the various channels one could follow in the struggle to creativity, one could separate them into *active* and *passive*. Among the passive ones, and along with others that rest on derivation and excessive reference to the past or to the works of others, literal interpretation and creativity through visual mimicking would rank very low. The reason is that all these methods exclude the possibility of the "genuinely original," since they rest on works done by others. It is possible, on the contrary, that some works of others or forms may inspire, even though this inspiration may start from purely visual and formal references.

**Fig. 9-3.** *Literal mimetic applications: naive. Motel "S. S. Galveston" in Galveston, Texas, with boat silhouette. (Photo courtesy of Dimitris Vilaetis)*

**Fig. 9-4.** *Literal mimetic applications: advanced. Lotus canopy in the Forum of Les Halles, Paris.*

**Fig. 9-5.** *Literal mimetic applications: advanced. House as a piece of sculpture: a large-scale sculpture indeed, with the scale and functions of a house. Robert Bruno, owner-sculptor. Lubbock, Texas, under construction.*

**Fig. 9-6.** *Literal mimetic applications: transcended. Column imitating tree with branches, suggesting that even literality can be elevated to high art. University of Stockholm Library, Ralph Erskine, architect.*

It is exactly for this reason that they should not be excluded as possible tools and that the intuitive teacher of design should be alert to their possibilities. Many architects have been inspired by visions from nature, by animal or tree formations, by objects, and so on. This, of course, was the case for the architect travelers of the past, who learned from landscapes and from exotic environments, as well as from the ways of others or the paintings of others.

## Architects and Literality

Alvar Aalto also was influenced by nature. He sketched and observed it and in the process transformed the visions of his various studies into generic form determinants for buildings. The same was true for Reima Pietilä and Jörn Utzon; both did not exclude the possibility of creation through mimicking hills, clouds, or natural phenomena. Utzon, in fact, created an extraordinary series of expandable furniture inspired by the silhouette of the swan. The sofas looked like swans in cross section.

Few design instructors have been influenced by these original creators. The very few whose works we have studied have achieved exceptional results. Martin Price, a design instructor at the University of Texas at Arlington, ranks at the top in this respect; his personal work as well as the projects of his students have drawn inspiration from natural elements, such as flying birds, animal formations on a prairie, a leaf on the ground, a portion of a tree branch, and so on. These projects, some of which appear in Fig. 9-2, were large gestures in which the bulk of the buildings and their plastic forms were attempts to integrate building with landscape and at the same time to abstract in an expressionistic way the naturally derived form. The results were acts of creativity in architecture never seen before.

There is no doubt that there are problems with such efforts. One has to be extremely cautious about the discrepancy that may occur between "practicality" and "vision." The implementation and buildability of the design is the ultimate test of the validity of such proposals, although it is always possible to construct almost any vision. So we should not exclude the possibility because of its translation difficulties; but these problems should be *resolved*. The resolution can occur through extra work in the structuring of the project, extra thought to standardize the details, and the extra discipline in the budget. We encourage such efforts, and condemn as counterproductive "loose-ended" visionary design efforts that do not pay proper attention to and do not devote the necessary time to the resolution of the pragmatic difficulties. Anything that has the potential to inspire should be sought after, and good schools of architecture should leave room for any channel to creativity.

A strong insistence on the realistic end of the design process is the key to freedom in challenging the imagination. A realistically inclined architect will undertake the extra discipline and the extra time necessary to resolve all the problems and turn even the most daring vision into reality. An undisciplined architect will most certainly fail. Alvar Aalto is the best example of the disciplined model, while Reima Pietilä represents the typical case of expressionistic literality to be avoided. The excess detailing complicating his Dipoli student union project, the first in a series of expressionistic projects, make it typical of what to avoid unless a whole country is willing to invest in a complicated and expensive implementation once in its history, or in an effort to impress the world by having done the impossible (as was the case with the house of the Finnish president, a Pietilä project).

It is exactly for the purpose of examining what society currently considers "untouchable" that institutions of learning and people aiming at creativity should not exclude anything and should be as permissive and daring as possible when it comes to creating. If such creative efforts come from within, if indeed a student or an architect feel the urge to look in nature or anywhere else for inspiration and creative expression, the results will be beneficial. If the case is the contrary—that is, if derivative expressionism or literal interpretation, or anything else for that matter—were to be dictated from above, through a client's brief or an instructor's handout, it is certain that the experience will be frustrating, that the product will not be the result of one's own probing and intellectual work. It will probably be the creation of the dictating authority. This is certainly why countries with very tight building permit requirements and bureaucratic due process in regard to aesthetic controls and building permits have such monotonous, nonintuitive, "boring" architecture. It is unfortunate that with computers and computerized problem solving, creative expressiveness has been discouraged and many people criticize the few who may still be visionary expressionists. One must be very critical and very tolerant at the same time.

## Mimesis and Literality in the Studio

When an instructor finds a student who may be exceptional, who may want to do buildings that look like grape leaves or birds with their wings spread, and if this instructor does not agree with these ideas, or does not have the ability to coach the student in this direction, the instructor should not try to discourage the student or attempt to prove to him or her that the attempt is futile. If there is no colleague who might perhaps feel otherwise and be more in tune with this student's inclinations, the instructor should keep the student in his studio and challenge himself along the student's lines; the chances are that the student's visions and the instructor's experience and knowhow will produce something good for both—perhaps an expressionistic project with buildable dimensions.

The creative design instructor should be more inclusive than the philosopher-aesthete; he or she should side with the "liberal" among the aesthetes, for only liberalism fertilizes art and the imagination. One should not deny the possible merits of design explorations through imitation, derivation, and even eclecticism. The goal should be to elevate the art of

**Fig. 9-7.** *"Transcendent literality": where the thrust of the boat through the waves and the shaping of its form as a reaction to the multiplicity of forces, such as wind, water pressure, and the impact of the waves, elevated the building conceived under the influence of such ideas into a work of art. Viking Museum by Cameron Potter, from the design class of Martin Price, UT Arlington, 1988. (Photo courtesy Martin Price, © copyright Craig Kuhner)*

architecture to the level of other mimetic arts such as the theater, an art of genuine imitation (and self-reflection) of the essentials of life, devoid of the handicaps of shallow literality and derivation.

## Summary

This chapter covers the origin, definitions, and opposing attitudes of scholars and aesthetes on mimesis, literal interpretation, and their associated concepts (imitation, derivation). One should be cautious when creating through this channel, and adopt the attitude of "implementability" as a way to safeguard against the dangers of misuse while achieving useful ends from both mimesis and literality. We include a commentary on the work of architects typical of the channel, with an emphasis on the pros and cons of their respective efforts. We also make the suggestion for the adoption of a climate favoring even the excesses of such approaches as a means to idea probing and creative evolution. The use of these concepts in exercises can lead to improved design education.

## References

Aalto, Alvar. *Sketches,* ed. Göran Schildt. Cambridge, MA: MIT Press, 1979, p. 19.

Antoniades, Anthony C. "Traditional vs. Contemporary Elements in Architecture." *New Mexico Architecture,* November–December 1971.

Arnheim, Rudolf. *The Dynamics of Architectural Form.* Berkeley: University of California Press, 1977, pp. 110–124, 133, 134, 148, 153.

Butcher, S. H. *Aristotle's Theory of Poetry and Fine Art.* New York: Dover Publications, 1951.

Chang, Amos Ih Tiao. *The Tao of Architecture.* Princeton, NJ: Princeton University Press, 1956, pp. 60, 62, 63.

Ferrault, Claude, trans. *Vitruve, Les dix Livres d'architecture.* Paris: Les Libraires Associées, 1965, p. 72.

Greenough, Horatio. *Form and Function.* Berkeley: University of California Press, 1947, pp. 19, 22, 26, 28, 29.

Le Corbusier. *Towards a New Architecture.* New York: Praeger, 1960, pp. 101, 121.

Martemucci, Romolo. "Mimesis and Creativity in Architectural Design." In *Fostering Creativity in Architectural Education,* ed. James P. Warfield. Champaign: University of Illinois Press, 1986, pp. 88–91.

Michelis, Panagiotis A. *Thrile gia ten archaea Ellenike Architektonike* (Myths concerning the ancient Greek Architecture). In *Aesthetica Theoremata* (Aesthetic Theorems), Vol. III. Athens, 1972.

———. *Aisthetikos.* Detroit: Wayne State University Press, 1977, pp. 189, 191, 216.

Plato. *Republic* (tenth chapter) and *Timeos* (fifth chapter).

Price, Martin. *Miten Luonto Muovaa* (How Nature Forms). Exhibit, Museum of Finnish Architecture, Helsinki, 1983, p. 6.

Simmons, Gordon B. "Analogy in Design: Studio Teaching Models." *Journal of Architectural Education,* 31,3 (month, year), pp. 18–20.

Tatarkiewicz, Wladyslaw. *History of Aesthetics.* Warsaw: Mouton, PWN-Polish Scientific Publishers. Vol. I (1970), Vol. II (1970), Vol. III (1974). Vol. I, pp. 16–17.

Wittkower, Rudolf. "Imitation, Eclecticism and Genius." In *Aspects of the Eighteenth Century,* ed. XX Wasserman. New York: Columbia University Press, 1949.

Wright, Frank Lloyd. *A Testament.* New York: Bramhall House, 1957, p. 21.

———. *In the Cause of Architecture,* ed. Frederick Gutheim. New York: Architectural Record Publishers, 1975.

# Chapter 10 Geometry and Creativity

Lines and shapes can be described in two ways: (1) through mathematics via analytical equations (algebra), or (2) through direct geometric depiction with the help of geometric instruments. In the first way, they are described, drawn, and redrawn through reference to a system of coordinates. This is obviously a difficult proposition, time-consuming and inexact; one can always measure wrong, miss the exact location of a point, come up with a wrong outline. To "draw" this line on a piece of land, on the basis of the mathematical formula, is even more difficult.

Shapes composed of complex, arbitrary lines are obviously exceedingly difficult to depict. Less complex lines and shapes can be described much more easily, and even drawn on the ground with great precision, through the help of geometric instruments and without the need for mathematical equations. The straight line, the circle, and the equilateral triangle are among the most obvious. The center of a circle and the length of its radius are all it takes to describe a specific circle; you can rest assured that you will always have the same circle and no other. Shapes that possess the element of undeniability and precision can also be described through mathematical formulas, but those who must carry out a construction project have always trusted the straightforwardness and precision of geometric instruments, rather than the abstractions of numbers and equations. Humans have thus been attracted to geometry as opposed to mathematics:

- Geometry affords us the power to realize geometrically conceived forms with ease.
- It gives us the ability to describe form with precision.
- It can make every person enjoy a sense of divinity by the mere existence of the undeniability and perfection of the geometric shapes.
- It has solved the problems inherent in the geometry of shapes, thus giving us sets of ready-made forms that can be manipulated in a variety of ways.

The whole history of architecture can be viewed in the light of the two possible realizations for lines and shapes described above. Those who follow the mathematical way look for the abstraction of numbers, the formulas that describe them, and the elegance of the relationships of the numbers. This was the attitude of architects in the Renaissance. The other attitude bases its architectural decisions on the shapes and solids (geometric shapes in three dimensions); it looks for the divinity of precision afforded by the rules of the selected geometric figure and its inherent spatial properties.

A square is that square and no other
A circle is that circle and no other
A rectangle is the particular rectangle derived through the relationships of its sides

There is no argument with the square and the circle; there may be argument regarding the proportional relationship of the sides of the rectangle and the relative appeal one may derive from that particular relationship. We can safely say that aesthetics starts with the rectangle; it becomes more elaborate with the more complex geometric shapes. There may be as many opinions as human beings; the more one distances oneself from the use of shapes that carry within themselves the element of formal undeniability, the more tedious the task of agreement of people becomes. No such problems exist with squares, circles, or other geometric shapes that carry within them the properties of generic undeniability (uniqueness).

Formal undeniability, whether inherent or man-made, has been a central theme for philosophers, architects, and aesthetes since ancient times. It is man's conquest over nature, yet a conquest of divine qualities. Plato was the first to address the inherent "undeniability" and the laws that govern geometric solids. They were named after him—the Platonic solids. Other proportions share the oblivion of vernacular humanity; nobody knows who invented the "divine proportion" or the "golden section."

From the analytical standpoint, there is no arbitrary shape; one can always describe any point of any line. Yet we tend to call "arbitrary" those lines or shapes whose points do not follow the same analytical formula. By "arbitrary" we mean lines that can be described through different mathematical equations or geometric instruments and follow no apparent reason or order in the sequence of the formulas.

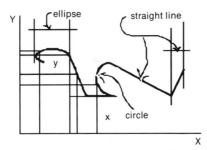

Composite line out of other lines of known algebraic description. Placement of points is predictable.

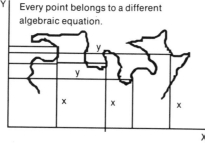

Arbitrary line: Each point needs to be described through unique coordinates of no apparent algebraic consistency.

**Fig. 10-1.** *Composite and arbitrary lines.*

The "line" to the right is an arbitrary line, a composite line of no apparent logic; it requires much explanation in order to communicate the reason for its configuration and to convince us to accept its existence. Why this particular sequence of moves and no other? Why this, why that? Of course there may be many answers; the irregular topography of traditional settlements that forced humans to adjust their buildings to their sites, to follow the topographic contours and the irregularity of the terrain, is one. Humans were smart enough to use very simple lines for individual buildings, and equally wisely gave in to topography. The *individual building* has been predominantly a geometrically conceived proposition, while the *town* has occasionally been the result of combination, a sequence of the "arbitrary" (usually dictated by nature, topography, etc.) and occasionally the divine (Hippodamean grid, squares, etc.). The Mediterranean and Italian hilltowns belong to the first category, and the towns of Miletus, Priene, Piraeus, Rhodes, Savannah (Georgia), and Philadelphia belong in the second category.

All of these ideas—mathematics vs. geometry, undeniable vs. arbitrary—have been in the forefront of our attention when dealing with the task of drawing, building, and design. Geometry, however, had an extraordinary appeal, so much so that it constitutes a distinctive channel to architectural creativity. We will address the most important issues below in an effort to reach an inclusivist appreciation of geometry.

## THE APPEAL OF GEOMETRY

Geometry has fascinated humans since ancient times. Philosophers such as Plato, Pythagoras, and Archimedes; kings such as Ptolemy, and architects such as Imhotep, Iktinos, Anthemios, and Isidoros were great mathematicians and geometers. Geometry was considered a science, property, a "secret weapon" of the priests and the pharaohs to maintain their dominance over others. They could use it to survey their lands, to measure the distance of the stars, to navigate. Initially geometric tools were like weapons, the use of which was familiar to only a few. Besides its actual usefulness, it gave psychological distinction to those privy to its secrets. It became the preoccupation of certain monastic orders (Jesuits) who questioned its suppositions, and immortalized themselves with new interpretations; they advanced new ways to solve problems and subsequently established doubts about the universality of previously held positions. Architects have always been devotees and applied users of geometry. They found in the Euclidean geometry a whole system of rules and truths on the basis of which they could make practical decisions and eventually build buildings. Geometry appealed to architects for a variety of reasons as well.

1. It afforded them a palette of shapes of rational undeniability (shapes that carried within them the proof of their formal existential reasoning).
2. It made them feel comfortable with the use of shapes that could be copied and repeated if needed, without fears of practical error.
3. It offered them extraordinary freedom even within the constraints of a preselected form (the rectangle can take infinite proportional interpretations; so can any other shape).
4. It offered them discipline with regard to the mundane, while it opened to them the metaphoric possibility to reach God and the divine when they used shapes of universal undeniability (squares, circles, spheres).
5. It offered psychological assurance, while it permitted a variety of psychological stimulations through the different feelings that could be generated with the different proportions given to the shapes.

6. It provided a unifying power of inner communication between those privy to its secrets and thus was a means of identification, of social and professional distinction.

7. It offered them more time to think and explore the manipulation and optimum use of preselected shapes, rather than wasting their time inventing new shapes each time.

## GEOMETRIC FORMS

We distinguish three categories of geometric forms from an architectural standpoint: (1) the "divine," the form whose existence is "undeniable"; (2) the "free form," whose existence is based on the personal decision of the designer (curves of no apparent origin, unfamiliar shapes); (3) the combinatorial form, geometric shapes composed of parts of the "divine" and parts that may belong to the "free." It would be pointless to repeat the arguments stated by Plato in *Timeos*, the dialogue about the universe in which he addresses the properties, the beauty, and the undeniability of shapes of the divine; the reader should refer to the original for details.

With regard to the free form, it will suffice to summarize as follows:

1. It is unpredictable.
2. It is difficult to justify.
3. It is often very difficult to draw and even more difficult to construct.
4. It does not have a unifying power among the people because it comes across as absolutely "individualistic" and in the absence of apparent logic tends to alienate and separate people.

The combinatorial category combines the "divine" and the "free" in order to accommodate the complexity of the occasional architectural problem.

Each one of the geometric categories above is better suited for certain building types than others. They have been used in the following types:

1. In monofunctional buildings conceived as large-scale geometric acts
2. In complex building types via known geometric shapes and families of geometric fields of varying modular articulation
3. In literal combinations of free and divine, in either monofunctional or multifunctional building complexes
4. In the arbitrary combinations

Each of these has ramifications for all aspects of the composition of a building, in two as well as in three dimensions. The *structural organization*, the *visual unity*, and the *scale* of the building are among the more important effects a particular use of geometry may have on the overall architectural artifact. The overall critical issue focuses on the supremacy of form over inclusivism. We address some of these ramifications below, and we call attention to some key architects and their works.

## GEOMETRY AND THE MONOFUNCTIONAL BUILDING

The monofunctional building has been with us through history. The megaron, the pyramid, the temple, the stadium, the basilica, the airplane hangar, the airplane pavilion, the greenhouse, and the suspension bridge are vivid examples of monofunctional types. Such building types often occupied the attention of scholars and aesthetes; geometer architects, and occasionally engineers, excelled in their use.

The *megaron* employed the simplest of lines, the straight line, and the most undeniable natural law, the law of gravity. Through its post and beam construction, it became the historical precedent of most of the world's

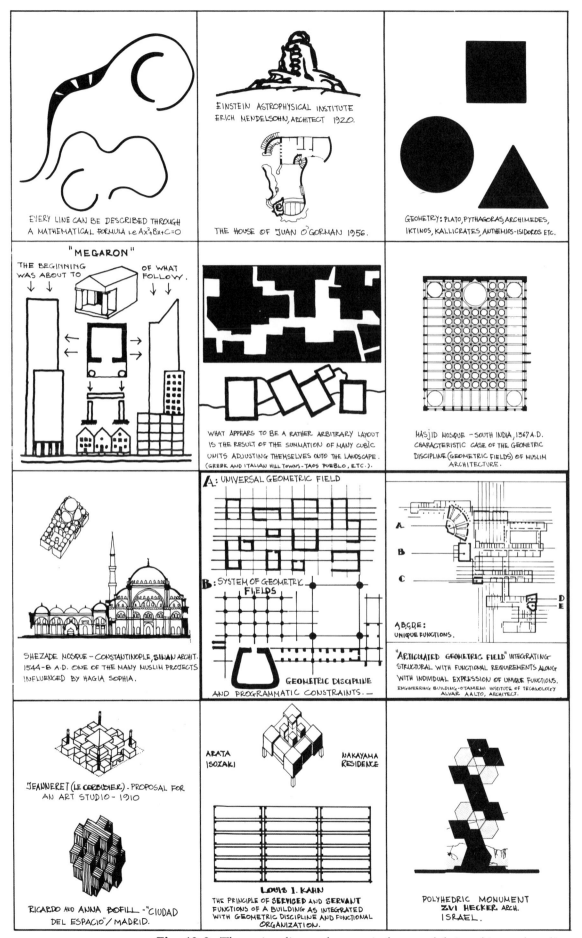

EVERY LINE CAN BE DESCRIBED THROUGH
A MATHEMATICAL FORMULA i.e $Ax^2+Bx+C=0$

EINSTEIN ASTROPHYSICAL INSTITUTE
ERICH MENDELSOHN, ARCHITECT 1920.

THE HOUSE OF JUAN O'GORMAN 1956.

GEOMETRY: PLATO, PYTHAGORAS, ARCHIMEDES,
IKTINOS, KALLICRATES, ANTHEMIOS-ISIDOROS ETC.

"MEGARON"
THE BEGINNING
WAS ABOUT TO          OF WHAT
                      FOLLOW.

WHAT APPEARS TO BE A RATHER ARBITRARY LAYOUT
IS THE RESULT OF THE SUMMATION OF MANY CUBIC
UNITS ADJUSTING THEMSELVES ONTO THE LANDSCAPE.
(GREEK AND ITALIAN HILL TOWNS - TAOS PUEBLO, ETC.).

MASJID MOSQUE - SOUTH INDIA, 1367 A.D.
CHARACTERISTIC CASE OF THE GEOMETRIC
DISCIPLINE (GEOMETRIC FIELDS) OF MUSLIM
ARCHITECTURE.

SHEZADE MOSQUE - CONSTANTINOPLE, SINAN ARCHIT.
1544-8 A.D. ONE OF THE MANY MUSLIM PROJECTS
INFLUENCED BY HAGIA SOPHIA.

A: UNIVERSAL GEOMETRIC FIELD
B: SYSTEM OF GEOMETRIC FIELDS
GEOMETRIC DISCIPLINE
AND PROGRAMMATIC CONSTRAINTS. —

A, B, C, D, E:
UNIQUE FUNCTIONS.
"ARTICULATED GEOMETRIC FIELD" INTEGRATING
STRUCTURAL WITH FUNCTIONAL REQUIREMENTS ALONG
WITH INDIVIDUAL EXPRESSION OF UNIQUE FUNCTIONS.
ENGINEERING BUILDING - OTANIEMI INSTITUTE OF TECHNOLOGY
ALVAR AALTO, ARCHITECT.

JEANNERET (LE CORBUSIER) - PROPOSAL FOR
AN ART STUDIO - 1910

RICARDO AND ANNA BOFILL - "CIUDAD
DEL ESPACIO"/ MADRID.

ARATA        NAKAYAMA
ISOZAKI      RESIDENCE

LOUIS I. KAHN
THE PRINCIPLE OF SERVICED AND SERVANT
FUNCTIONS OF A BUILDING AS INTEGRATED
WITH GEOMETRIC DISCIPLINE AND FUNCTIONAL
ORGANIZATION.

POLYHEDRIC MONUMENT
ZVI HECKER, ARCH.
ISRAEL.

**Fig. 10-2.** *The various lines and geometric shapes and their architectural application through time.*

utilitarian architecture. The highrise building is a direct descendant of the ancient megaron; both get their power through the divinity of the straight line.

The triangle is obviously encountered in the pyramid, while the circle, the square, the rectangles, the cylindrical drum, the sphere, and semisphere are encountered in Christian churches—the Byzantine, the Gothic, the Romanesque—and the Muslim architecture. In all these instances, the "big Idea" of the geometric form originated for symbolic reasons (sky, universe, cross). Structure and symbolism were afforded a complementary fit because of the particular geometric shapes selected. The discussion of the aesthetes therefore focused not on a debate as to the appropriateness of the forms employed, but rather on the subtleties of the occasional application. Attention was paid to the visible elements of such buildings, the subelements of their elevations, and the "agreement" (or not) of the parts to the whole.

If a rule was found, a module or a proportional agreement between the parts and the whole, the composition was considered to be a *symphonic composition*, one in which everything is in agreement with everything else, where the parts follow the same rules as the whole, and vice versa. The idea of the symphonic composition has been accepted as a positive quality of architecture since the time of Archimedes; he was also the first to use the term. Such buildings were viewed in musically metaphoric terms; their façades were scrutinized, their proportions were questioned, and the observed proportional relationships between the solids and the voids, between the modules, or between the sizes of the structural elements and the "scoring" of the surfaces and materials were viewed in the light of musical beats, tones, spacing, and rhythm.

The whole debate on the aesthetics of classical architecture and the architecture of the Renaissance has been a debate over the monofunctional building and the concept of the symphonic. From Palladio to Serlio during the Renaissance, Matila Ghyka and Whittkower to Alexander Tzonis and Liane Lefaivre in the twentieth century, the debate has been over the subtleties of the relationships of the parts to the whole, and the perfection of the symphonic achievement. The central theme in the whole discussion has been the theme of proportional series. Although this literature is fundamental for every architect (some books by these writers must be read by the design student), it is nonetheless a literature of partial focus on architecture and geometry, since it does not look at the building as a whole.

Modern architecture, in its preoccupation with making more economical buildings through the use of machine techniques, deprived the monofunctional building of the subtleties of the detailing of its façades; it focused instead on the overall geometric configuration. This had certain consequences: the creation of buildings devoid of human scale. The result was frequently monotony, either through excessive repetition of the same beat of the structural module, or through the existence of only one beat. Many monofunctional buildings of modern architecture became "objects," sometimes sculptural and appealing, sometimes not. Among the appealing cases were buildings whose geometric configuration had structural undeniability (shells, stadiums). But despite their sculptural appeal, such buildings had *no human scale*, and were often psychologically negative. It is quite inappropriate to enlarge a geometric form without solving the issue of scale—that is, providing elements that are familiar to the human being so that he is able to establish the right feeling with regard to the size of the building compared to his own dimensions. In the absence of such considerations, the use of geometry in the monofunctional building of modern architecture was, to say the least, simplistic. A few engineers excelled in this respect, because the divine undeniability of the geometric forms they employed stifled any arguments. Robert Maillart (1872–1940), a Swiss, and Eugène

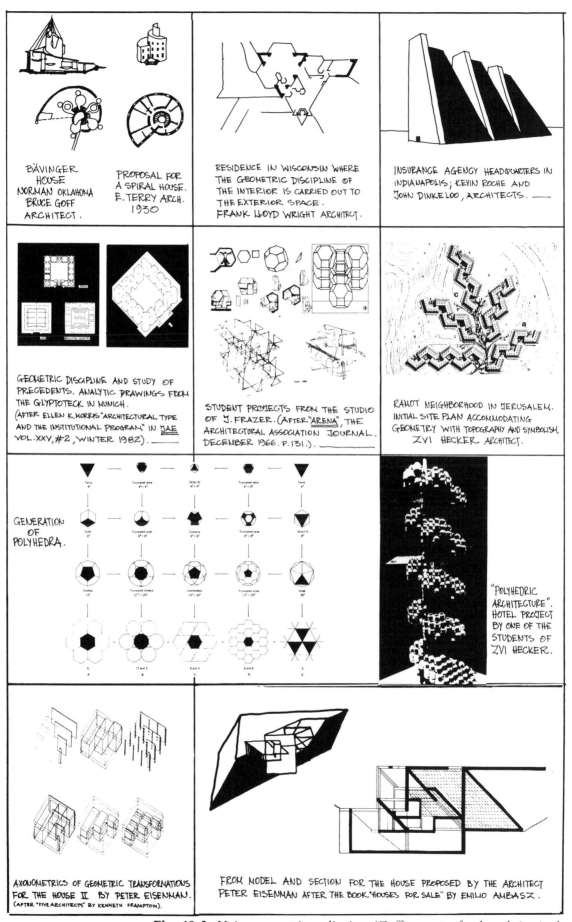

BÄVINGER HOUSE NORMAN OKLAHOMA BRUCE GOFF ARCHITECT.

PROPOSAL FOR A SPIRAL HOUSE. E. TERRY ARCH. 1930

RESIDENCE IN WISCONSIN WHERE THE GEOMETRIC DISCIPLINE OF THE INTERIOR IS CARRIED OUT TO THE EXTERIOR SPACE. FRANK LLOYD WRIGHT ARCHITECT.

INSURANCE AGENCY HEADQUARTERS IN INDIANAPOLIS; KEVIN ROCHE AND JOHN DINKELOO, ARCHITECTS. ___

GEOMETRIC DISCIPLINE AND STUDY OF PRECEDENTS. ANALYTIC DRAWINGS FROM THE GLYPTOTECK IN MUNICH. (AFTER ELLEN K. MORRIS "ARCHITECTURAL TYPE AND THE INSTITUTIONAL PROGRAM" IN JAE VOL. XXV, #2, WINTER 1982). ___

STUDENT PROJECTS FROM THE STUDIO OF J. FRAZER. (AFTER "ARENA", THE ARCHITECTURAL ASSOCIATION JOURNAL. DECEMBER 1966. P. 131.). ___

RAMOT NEIGHBORHOOD IN JERUSALEM. INITIAL SITE PLAN ACCOMMODATING GEOMETRY WITH TOPOGRAPHY AND SYMBOLISM. ZVI HECKER ARCHITECT.

GENERATION OF POLYHEDRA.

"POLYHEDRIC ARCHITECTURE". HOTEL PROJECT BY ONE OF THE STUDENTS OF ZVI HECKER.

AXONOMETRICS OF GEOMETRIC TRANSFORMATIONS FOR THE HOUSE II BY PETER EISENMAN. (AFTER "FIVE ARCHITECTS" BY KENNETH FRAMPTON).

FROM MODEL AND SECTION FOR THE HOUSE PROPOSED BY THE ARCHITECT PETER EISENMAN AFTER THE BOOK "HOUSES FOR SALE" BY EMILIO AMBASZ.

**Fig. 10-3.** *Unique geometric applications (Goff), aspects of scale and size in the geometric application (Roche), use of polygonal and polyhedric systems (Wright, Goff, Hecker): efforts to address issues of non-Euclidean geometry.*

Freyssinet (1879–1962), a Frenchman, with their bridges and their concrete shell structures, either as exhibition halls or aircraft hangars, along with Pier Luigi Nervi with his stadiums, are the key characters in this exception.

The large-scale monofunctional building, either as high-rise office building or a low-rise horizontal complex, was certainly diagrammatic, loaded with negative connotations of monotony, boredom, and boxiness. The literature on geometry is generally the literature of the monofunctional building. The experimentation with proportional systems, the exhaustive explorations of the articulation of elevations, and the constant debate over the symphonic issues have always been the focus of this literature. The summary tables on the proportional properties of rectangles from Matila Ghyka's landmark treatise *The Geometry of Art and Life*, along with the direct reference to this classic, should be constant inspirational landmarks for the important subject of the symphonic if one is to avoid making monofunctional buildings that are boring and out of scale.

## COMPLEX BUILDINGS AND GEOMETRIC FIELDS

The contemporary building is characterized by complexity of functions; the gathering of many functions in one building has become mandatory for operational as well as economic reasons (cost of land, cost of construction). A university faculty building or a downtown office/ commercial/ entertainment complex are examples. There is hardly a contemporary building type that does not call for diversity of functions, variety of structural requirements (spans of spaces), and complex circulation and mechanical requirements. There is also no contemporary building whose parts do not fit specialized functional requirements (such as acoustics). This specialization brings extra dimensions to the debate on the advantages and disadvantages of the architecture of "geometric combinations" and the architecture of "geometric fields." Such projects can be approached through a number of strategies, including the following:

1. Through accommodation of the diverse functional requirements under an overall solid (of the dimensions of a city block). Key issues to which the designer must pay special attention are functional/structural coordination and scale. The Chicago auditorium by Louis Sullivan (1887–89), and the Dentsu Building in Osaka by Kenzo Tange (1960s) are good examples. Both occupy large sites, both accommodate diverse functions in a compact manner, yet both are expressive of their diversity through appropriate structural and formal articulation.

2. Through clear separation of the various functional parts, geometric accommodation as required by the individual functional requirements of each use, and appropriate expression of each geometric element as part of the overall composition. In this case, attention must be paid to the relative degree of unity. The structural modules might not be a means toward overall unity, since they may vary because of the different structural requirements. Materials and texture might be the way to unity in this case.

Two major issues for the designer emerge in this particular case: One is whether to incorporate and externally express forms appropriate to the optimum performance of the particular use (to express the "acoustic" solid of a particular amphitheater). This is very similar to playing with building blocks, except that the architect must make certain there is an absolute fit between each "block" and functional performance. The second is not to express these aspects, but rather to incorporate the functionally optimum solid into a more generous Cartesian solid, allowing for accommodation of specialized requirements by means of interior design, such as suspended ceilings. The preference of most practitioners is to use rectilinear rooms of larger volumes and to take care of the specialized requirements later. This

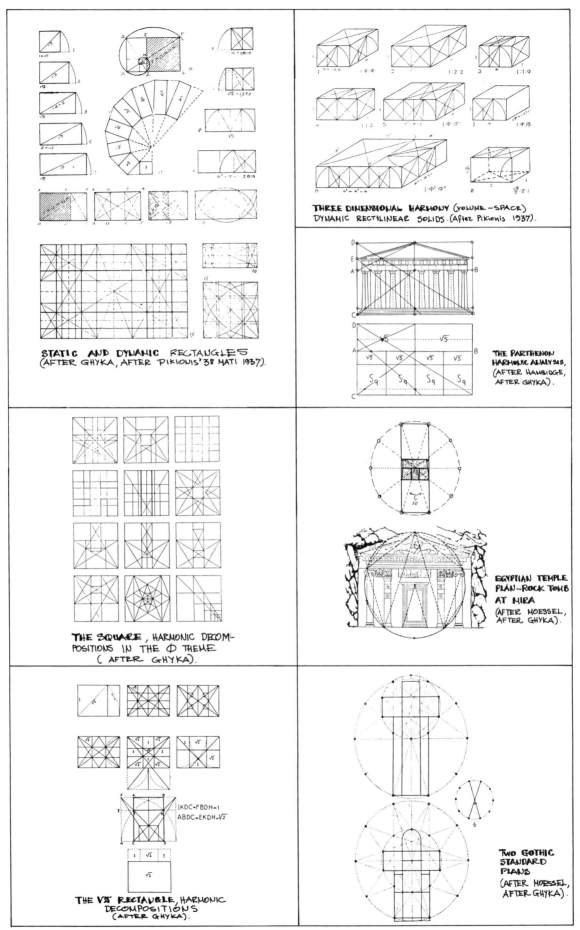

THREE DIMENSIONAL HARMONY (VOLUME-SPACE)
DYNAMIC RECTILINEAR SOLIDS. (After Pikionis 1937).

STATIC AND DYNAMIC RECTANGLES
(AFTER GHYKA, AFTER PIKIONIS'38 MATI 1937).

THE PARTHENON
HARMONIC ANALYSIS.
(AFTER HAMBIDGE,
AFTER GHYKA).

THE SQUARE, HARMONIC DECOM-
POSITIONS IN THE Φ THEME
( AFTER GHYKA).

EGYPTIAN TEMPLE
PLAN-ROCK TOMB
AT MIRA
(AFTER MOESSEL,
AFTER GHYKA).

THE √5 RECTANGLE, HARMONIC
DECOMPOSITIONS
(AFTER GHYKA).

TWO GOTHIC
STANDARD
PLANS
(AFTER MOESSEL,
AFTER GHYKA).

**Fig. 10-4.** *Summary of geometric basics after Matila Ghyka. After the original publication in French, Ghyka, 1931.*

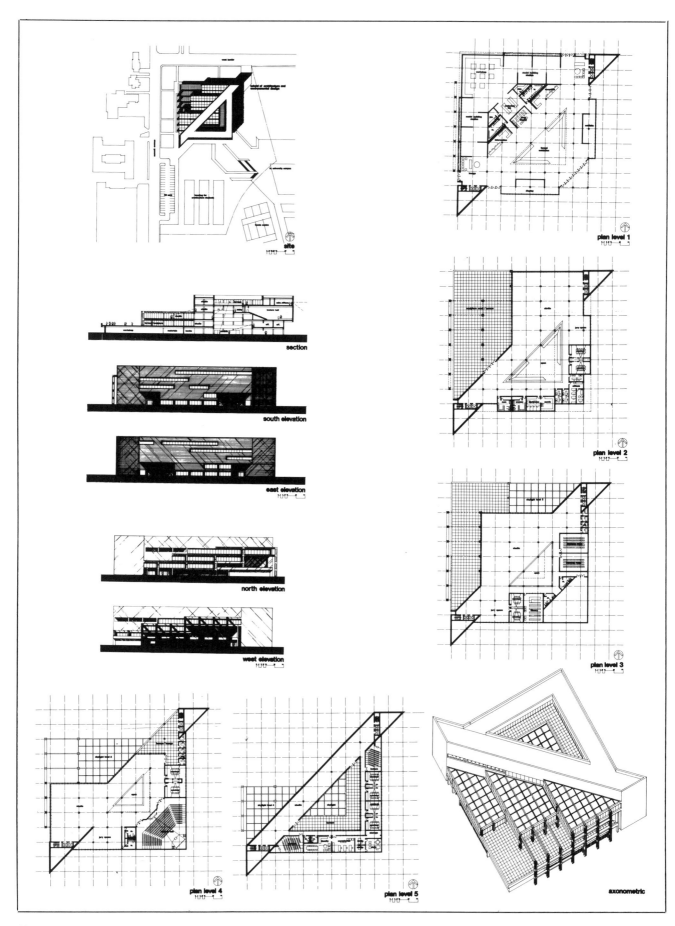

**Fig. 10-5A.** *A project for a School of Architecture building based on the geometric channel by Craig Blackmon. The author's fourth-year design studio, UT Arlington, spring 1978.*

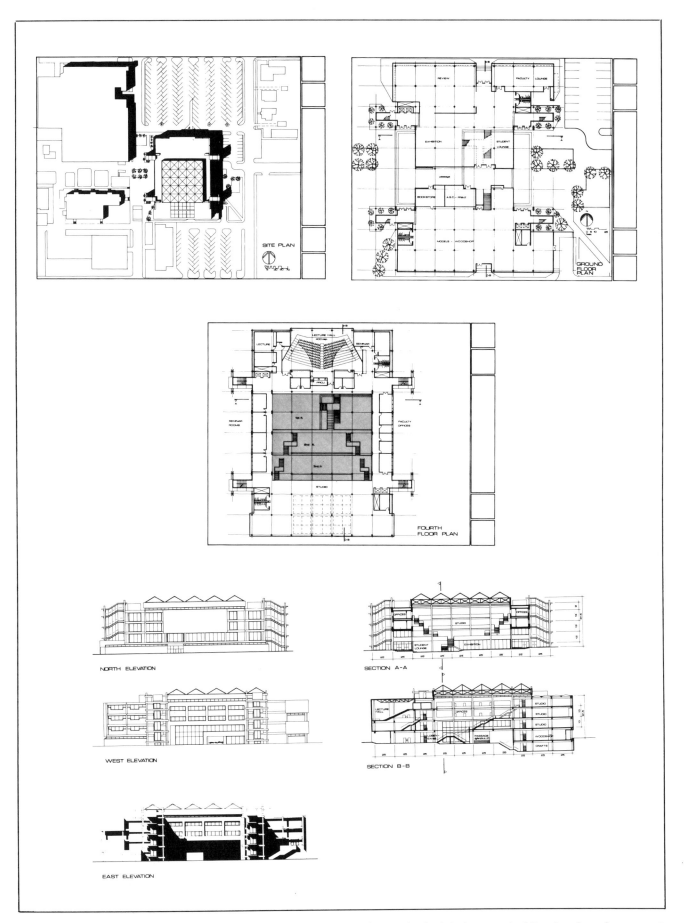

**Fig. 10-5B**. *Project for a School of Architecture building based on the geometric channel by John Frederickson. The author's fourth-year design studio, UT Arlington, spring 1978.*

has been found to be more efficient, especially in periods of unpredictability about the future life and use of buildings.

The Modern movement supported the articulation of complex buildings via individual solids expressive of function. Architects today have learned that the functional specialization is a dangerous proposition; it is far more important to focus on the aspects of unity, scale, rhythm, and the dialogue between the visible parts of the building complex for contextual and purely compositional considerations. The complex, large-scale contemporary building has become a good candidate for symphonic compositions on an urban scale, exactly the same way as the façades of monofunctional buildings in the past. The concept of the geometric field has been of great help in the achievement of such a goal.

## GEOMETRIC FIELDS

The Hippodamean grid is a geometric field of 90 degrees. The mandala patterns are polygonal geometric fields. One can also speak of combinatorial geometric fields with 90 degree angular and circular components. These fields can be monotonic (or monomodular), and rhythmic (or polymodular). The monotonic is based on a single module. Rhythmic fields are composed of a variety of modules with a modular denominator; they can accommodate a variety of sizes.

Geometric fields possess fascinating possibilities for order, achievement of unity (all inherent properties of the fields), and rhythm. They have fascinated architects since ancient times, and certain architectures have excelled in this respect. Muslim architecture has often shown the way. It incorporated monotonic geometric fields to achieve functional results, "equipotentiality" and "universality" while at the same time taking advantage of the scarcity of structural materials. The mosque is a case in point: it is a universal space for a variety of functions (a place of prayer, overnight accommodation, business) achieved by means of stones and concentric circles resting on polygonal or orthogonal tie beams. In some mosques, the monotonic characteristic of the grid became an asset rather than a liability. The impact was so strong that the blanket unity of the grid created a spatial ambience all its own. The Cordoba mosque is an example. But one must be careful since the monotonic grid can produce simply monotony and cause functional problems when dealing with the multiple functional requirements of today's buildings.

Muslim architecture has again shown us the way in this respect, through a variety of historical precedents as well as through the mosques of Sinan, the champion architect who introduced the polytonic mosque in the sixteenth century. The Suleiman Mosque in Istanbul is the most representative of an advanced geometric field. Geometric fields were rotated and violated for purposes of orientation (the Grand Mosque at Isfahan, for example), to adjust to the site (the whole layout of the precinct in Granada is a combination of the free and the irregular), or for the creation of a spatial dialogue. An extraordinary contemporary building complex with an orthogonally rhythmic geometric field is the Parliament in Riyadh, Saudi Arabia, by Jörn Utzon. Striking for its purity, it evokes the ambience of an oasis achieved via the serenity of geometry and the dynamism of contemporary technology. Some other recent architects who have used geometric fields are Louis Kahn, Moshe Safdie, Aldo Van Eyck, Mario Botta, and the two Israeli architects Alfred Neuman and Zvi Hecker. The latter has been the most persistent devotee of polygonal geometric fields and polyhedric solids. Hecker's Town Hall of Bat Yam and the Ramot neighborhood in Jerusalem are inspired by the chemical equations of Pauling and the domes of Afghanistan.

Bruce Goff has been a master in the use of combinatorial geometric fields. In spite of his occasional overindulgence in detail, he has proved a giant in the employment and successful combination of varying geometric shapes without ever compromising function to geometric preconceptions. Goff was able to adjust and to combine geometric systems appropriately in order to integrate them with functions. One is inclined to suggest that Bruce Goff was far superior to Frank Lloyd Wright in the use of geometry, in spite of the very generous assessments that have been made of Wright's excellence in the use of geometry. We believe that Wright was occasionally victimized by his frequent tendency to carry geometric fields to extremes, making every architectonic decision without ever giving in to the abstract requirements of geometry, frequently sacrificing comfort and function to abstract geometric preconceptions. One example is the Price Tower in Bartlesville, Oklahoma, where the sixty-degree field of the plan influences every element of the architecture, including the furniture and interior layout. The result is extremely uncomfortable chairs and work area layouts.

A very characteristic case of a combinatorial geometric field is the personal residence of the architect John Portman. It is a field combining squares, circles, and connecting rectangles. The large majority of the geometric fields used by Louis Kahn were untypically severe, generally orthogonal (he used triangles and combination fields only in the plan of the Government Center in Dacca). He used the difficult combination of the "two," and assigned broad functional destinations to the elements of his field (serviced and servant elements of the plan). Yet he achieved "divine" ultimate results, and I believe the Kimbell Art Museum in Fort Worth, Texas, to be a masterpiece in this respect.

A prototypical case that demonstrates the degree of possible freedom, the spatial possibilities, and the achievement of highly involved rhythmic situations from orthogonal geometric fields is the Children's Home in Amsterdam by Aldo Van Eyck. It is a precedent that could be very useful for a great variety of contemporary building programs. Kahn, Utzon, and Eyck have achieved with their buildings an excellence we like to call the "first degree of geometric inclusivism." Mario Botta for the orthogonal and Zvi Hecker for the polygonal do not rank so high overall; they frequently sacrificed the overall architectonic resolution to formal expediency.

All these architects have used geometry and the geometric fields with what we could call the "traditional Euclidean attitude." More recent efforts by Peter Eisenman have attempted to question the Euclidean framework and to achieve new perceptual experiences by a search into the unknown geometries of the present. The Eisenman fields call for further clarifications that have to do with the whole philosophical framework of geometry and the complexity of the cosmos, issues we address later.

Geometric fields provide discipline as well as freedom. Yet one always faces the danger of becoming overly obedient to the field and sacrificing comfort and functional efficiency to geometric formalism. It is only through an attitude of geometric inclusivism that the problems of form can be avoided; on the other hand, the inherent qualities of geometry can greatly enhance the final design.

## GEOMETRIC INCLUSIVISM

It is important to end this chapter with a discussion of what I consider to be the most wholesome, the freest, and the most appropriate use of geometry for the purposes of architectural design, without abstract generalities and theoretical elegance. This is the path of "geometric inclusivism," which is an attitude rather than a dogma.

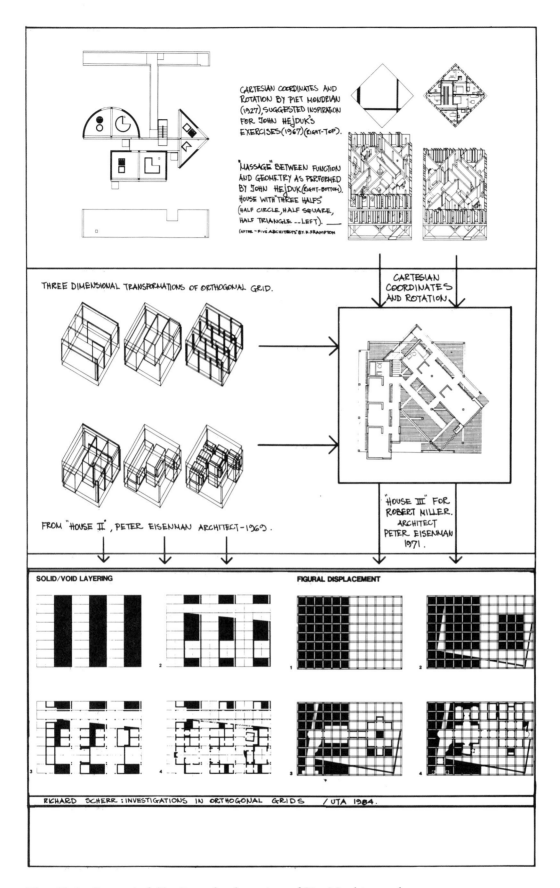

CARTESIAN COORDINATES AND ROTATION BY PIET MONDRIAN (1927), SUGGESTED INSPIRATION FOR JOHN HEJDUK'S EXERCISES (1967) (RIGHT-TOP).

"MASSAGE" BETWEEN FUNCTION AND GEOMETRY AS PERFORMED BY JOHN HEJDUK (RIGHT-BOTTOM). HOUSE WITH "THREE HALFS" (HALF CIRCLE, HALF SQUARE, HALF TRIANGLE ... LEFT). ___
(AFTER "FIVE ARCHITECTS" BY K.FRAMPTON)

THREE DIMENSIONAL TRANSFORMATIONS OF ORTHOGONAL GRID.

CARTESIAN COORDINATES AND ROTATION

FROM "HOUSE II", PETER EISENMAN ARCHITECT - 1969.

"HOUSE III" FOR ROBERT MILLER. ARCHITECT PETER EISENMAN 1971.

SOLID/VOID LAYERING

FIGURAL DISPLACEMENT

RICHARD SCHERR : INVESTIGATIONS IN ORTHOGONAL GRIDS / UTA 1984.

**Fig. 10-6.** *Geometric fields: From the abstractions of Piet Mondrian to the exercises of John Hejduk, and from the early efforts of Peter Eisenman to the Design Studio (Rich Scherr). The "Fox Trot" by Piet Mondrian was the suggested initial stimulation for the early rotational exercises by John Hejduk and his followers. For more, see Kenneth Frampton, "Frontality vs. Rotation," in* Five Architects. *New York: Oxford University Press, 1975.*

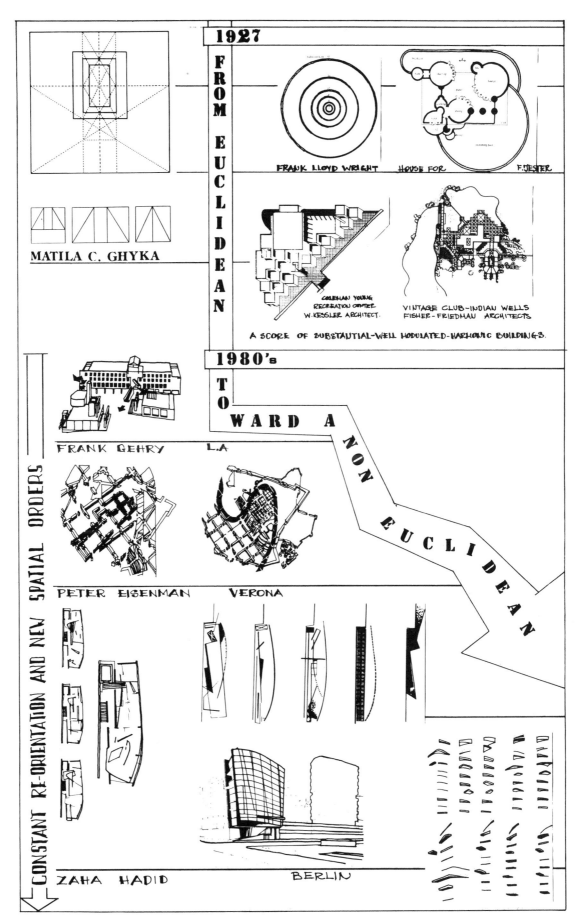

**Fig. 10–7.** *From Ghyka and the Euclidean practices of the Modern movement to the explorations of the "apparent" non-Euclidean by Postmodern pioneers of the non-Historicist stock. Eisenman, Gehry, Hadid.*

It is a combination of the "geometric free" with "geometric fields." It is best exemplified by several key Alvar Aalto buildings, such as the Otaniemi Engineering Building, the Finlandia Hall, and the Seinäjoki Library. All demonstrate the architect's license to bring together families of geometric orders, all rational and expressive of function, while at the same time functionally self-sufficient (e.g., a cross section of the library works both internally and externally).

This use of geometry requires exhaustive explorations on the part of the designer, since its goal is to achieve a harmonic fit of geometric orders in plan as well as in section, while at the same time resolving the problem of structural coordination among the diverse functions of the buildings, without losing sight of the external appeal of the building (through unity, complement or opposition), and the proper scale. Alvar Aalto has relied on the microscale, texture, and the use of detailing. An advanced Aalto building is a highly disciplined case of combinatorial geometric orders. It may appear "arbitrary" to the uninitiated, but it is highly controlled and total if looked at carefully. Such buildings obviously reject the diagrammatic modulation of fields, and so are more expensive to build and require extra care in working drawings and the construction process. They are expressive of a society that is willing to invest for the achievement of plasticity and smoothness, qualities to be found in certain natural forms and in the use of geometry by nature.

Nature is the case that knows no abstractions; it is the ultimate in the geometrically combinatorial. The idea of the "natural form" has often been abused, though; my position is that there is great difference between "the natural form" conceived through the notion of geometric discipline and the "romantic" notion embraced by those who view "nature" as the result of arbitrary phenomena. We believe this issue needs to be addressed here, because the "arbitrary" is still, we claim, part of the inquiry of geometry, except that it is so peculiar and so inappropriate for the universal practice of architecture that for all practical purposes, it should be avoided.

**Fig. 10-8.** *Otaniemi Institute of Technology, Alvar Aalto, architect. A paradigmatic case of a geometric field in the service of a polyfunctional building.*

The arbitrary certainly has negative connotations; it is the free form of the ongoing and unjustifiable (or of the difficult to justify), the geometric evolution of form whose subtleties go unnoticed and with not much effect on the whole even if they are noticed. It is the individualistic geometric whim, often the result of extraordinary esotericity—that is, it is highly uneconomic to achieve; has extraordinary joinery problems (that are multiplied with the increase in materials); generates difficulties in structural/functional coordination; and is broadly unacceptable, unless convincingly argued and adequately presented.

There is no better example of this than Reima Pietilä's Dipoli Student Union Building on the Otaniemi campus in Helsinki, Finland. Similar buildings by the same architect are the residence for the president of Finland and the Finnish embassy in New Delhi, India. Pietilä, of course, never claimed that geometry was the foundation of his architecture. His conceptual departures were metaphoric, symbolic, based on the inspirational channel of nature and the natural form. Of course one would have reservations if the whole urban environment were to be built with the nature-inspired arbitrariness of Dipoli, as one could never find one's bearings in a environment that lacks the presence of divine identity, and that does not possess an area of clearly identifiable and undeniable presence. One could have similar reservations if the whole environment were built with the opposing strategy of unending evolution by means of monotonic fields (the grid system, Wright's never-ending Broadacre City). Both represent cases of the extreme through geometric application, suggesting that the desirable point is somewhere else. I believe this "somewhere else" to be the Aalto geometric inclusivism and the spirit of the symphonic.

## RECENT EFFORTS: BEYOND EUCLIDEAN GEOMETRY

The whole body of Euclidean geometry and particularly its postulate no. 5, which suggests that two parallel lines never cross, has been challenged repeatedly, particularly during the last two hundred years. Our period has challenged the whole body of mathematical and geometric knowledge, and has probed deeper than previous eras into new geometric and mathematical horizons. Very few architects are familiar with the concepts and applications of non-Euclidean geometries—that is, the state of the art of geometry in our time. Perhaps if one were to look into geometry again, particularly into today's geometries, then one would have to align oneself with the concerns, anxieties, uncertainties, and at the same time the dynamism of architecture to explore new horizons, reach new limits.

Yet one has to know the basics; Euclidean geometry cannot be challenged if one does not know it. Unfortunately, the focus on the basics has been so obscured that classics such as *The Geometry of Art and Life* by Matila C. Ghyka, who advocated that geometry " . . . far from narrowing the creative power of the artist, opens for him an infinite variety of choices within the realm of symphonic composition," have disappeared from the design curriculum. We believe that Ghyka's book should be used once again to inspire future architects; for it is only after understanding and having a solid foundation in the basics that one can begin to grasp "imaginary geometries" and the philosophical probing into the spatially obscure and currently incomprehensible. There is indeed a whole new field out there; there must be architecture in the realm of "imaginary geometry," that non-Euclidean geometry of Bolyai and Lobachevsky.

As for my part, I feel awe at the findings and the possibilities of these still incomprehensible approaches. Yet I feel sympathy for the idea that something other than the orthodox (Euclidean) geometry may exist. This notion was reinforced with the first personal encounter I had with Frank

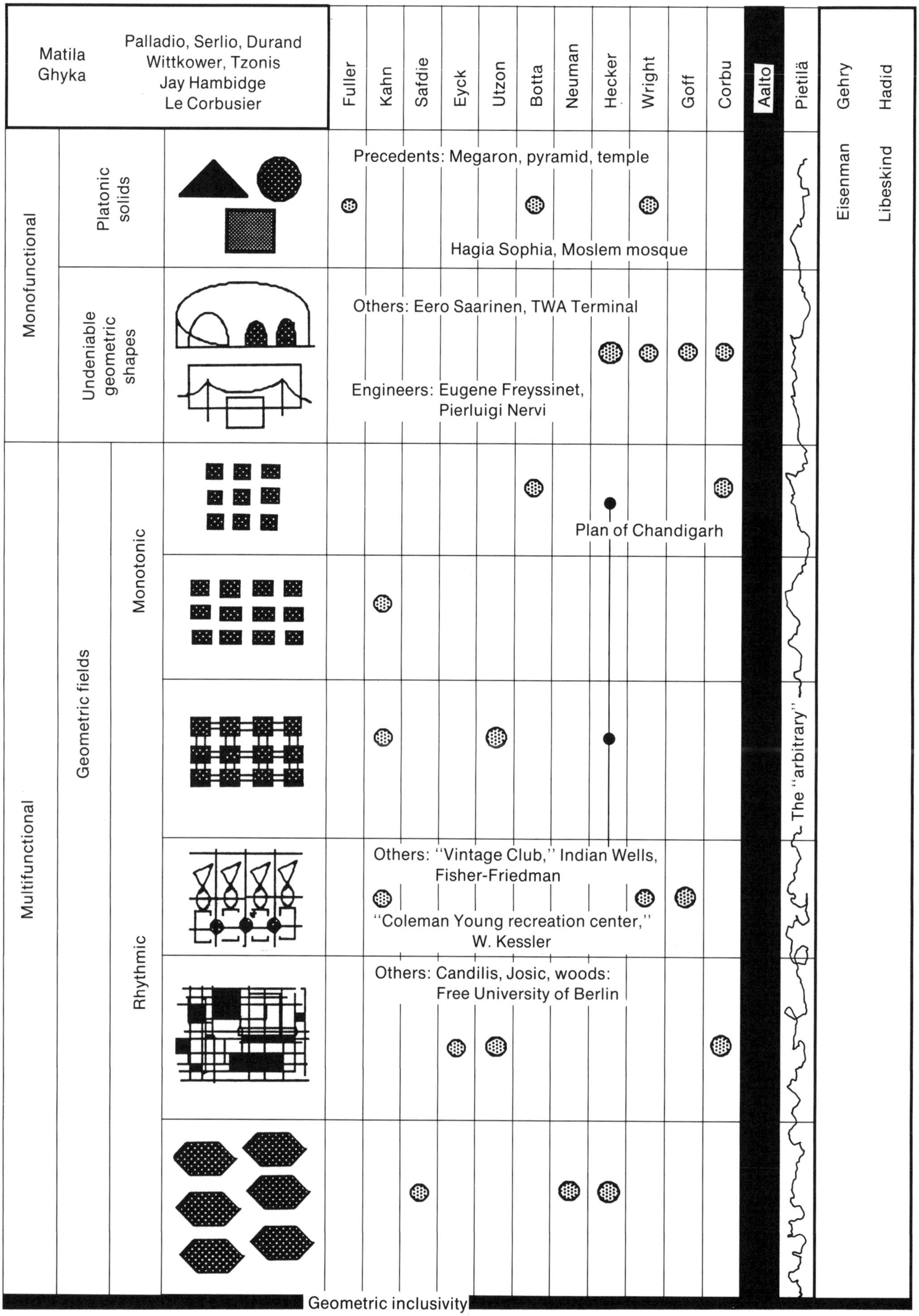

Figure 10-9 — Summary of the ways different architects have used geometry.

| Matila Ghyka | Palladio, Serlio, Durand / Wittkower, Tzonis / Jay Hambidge / Le Corbusier | Fuller | Kahn | Safdie | Eyck | Utzon | Botta | Neuman | Hecker | Wright | Goff | Corbu | Aalto | Pietilä | Gehry / Eisenman | Hadid / Libeskind |
|---|---|---|---|---|---|---|---|---|---|---|---|---|---|---|---|---|
| **Monofunctional** — Platonic solids | Precedents: Megaron, pyramid, temple … Hagia Sophia, Moslem mosque | ◉ | | | | | ◉ | | | ◉ | | | | | | |
| **Monofunctional** — Undeniable geometric shapes | Others: Eero Saarinen, TWA Terminal — Engineers: Eugene Freyssinet, Pierluigi Nervi | | | | | | | | ◉ | ◉ | ◉ | ◉ | | | | |
| **Multifunctional** — Geometric fields — Monotonic | Plan of Chandigarh | | | | | | ◉ | | ● | | | ◉ | | | | |
| **Multifunctional** — Geometric fields — Monotonic | | | ◉ | | | | | | | | | | | | | |
| **Multifunctional** — Geometric fields — Monotonic | | | ◉ | | | ◉ | | | ● | | | | | | | |
| **Multifunctional** — Rhythmic | Others: "Vintage Club," Indian Wells, Fisher-Friedman — "Coleman Young recreation center," W. Kessler | ◉ | | | | | | | | ◉ | ◉ | | | | | |
| **Multifunctional** — Rhythmic | Others: Candilis, Josic, woods: Free University of Berlin | | | ◉ | ◉ | | | | | | | ◉ | | | | |
| **Multifunctional** — Rhythmic | | | | ◉ | | | | ◉ | ◉ | | | | | | | |

Geometric inclusivity

The "arbitrary"

**Fig. 10-9.** *Summary of the ways different architects have used geometry.*

Gehry's Loyola Law School in Los Angeles. My earlier affinity for Euclidean and Cartesian orthodoxy, due to my training, conditioning, and experiences, was put to a test by the impact of this project upon sight. Repeated visits and contemplation, along with a personal struggle to theorize and "understand," were finally successful upon reading a statement included in a letter written by Carl Friedrich Gauss to his friend Olbers. Gauss, one of the noted mathematicians of the eighteenth century who influenced thought towards non-Euclidean geometry (Gauss influenced Bolyai), stated in this particular letter that he knew he was after something, but he could not prove it. "I am ever more convinced, " he wrote, "that the necessity of our geometry cannot be proved, at least not by, and not for, our HUMAN understanding. Maybe in another life we shall attain insights into the essence of space which are now beyond our reach. . . . " One could perhaps paraphrase and substitute the word "architecture" for the word "geometry": "I am ever more convinced that the necessity of our architecture cannot be proved. . . . " This leads me once more to my favorite attitude of giving the benefit of the doubt to that which may exist, which may be there (in fact, some may believe it is indeed there) and which we may find it difficult to follow due to lack of knowledge or lack of effort. At the same time, we have to be extremely cautious; architects have to graduate to the spheres of imaginary geometry.

We propose that the emphasis on geometry during the late fifties early sixties was a well-conceived one. Schools should look back and study that period more carefully as a first step prior to proceeding to more advanced and complicated states. The social awareness that prevailed among architects at that time, along with their concern for the exploration of technology and prefabrication, made them seek molecular/stereometric repetitive organization (generic geometric fields), composed of prefabricated stereometric shells. Many schools were involved in research, and projects focused on repetitive geometries and stereometries were among the most intuitive and progressive of the time. The pioneering role of the Architectural Association in London in this respect was matched by pioneer instructors such as John Frazer, Chris Dawson, and Henry Hertzberger. The idea that the geometry must satisfy anthropometrics, structure, assembly, flexibility, and so on was a major goal of the exercises. Human scale and geometry have to be complementary. Technology and geometry should serve humanity. The sixties was a time when building technology and construction were served by great engineers such as Nervi, and it was after his challenges and suggestions that architects once again got involved with rigorous geometry, as their Gothic predecessors had been. It was the influence and collaboration of another engineer, August Komendant, that made Louis Kahn look into geometry, as a discipline of structure, order, and rhythm for his major building organizations.

With the notable exception of Herman Hertzberger in the Netherlands, geometry as a means to construction, repetition, achievement of economic ends, prefabrication of modules, and repetitive entities has been neglected recently. Geometry in the studio is used only for beautification, as a tool in the achievement of plasticity. Another recent use has been purely abstractive, focusing on the two-dimensional possibilities of geometric fields and attempting compositions devoid of function or social destination. Even though abstract exercises in geometry and stereometry are certainly beneficial, they do not serve the goal of architecture, which also has functional and technological dimensions. Yet deeper involvement and concentration on the geometries of the present will probably produce exponentially significant creative results in the future. This will probably start with the study of the philosophy of geometry, which along with the reintroduction of aesthetics and morphology, would upgrade architects' involvement with

A

B

**Fig. 10-10.** *Frank Gehry: toward new geometries. Experimentation with the as yet incomprehensible.* **A.** *Aerospace Museum, Los Angeles;* **B.** *Loyola Law School, Los Angeles.*

geometry (this time the geometry of the era). Through focused study, one will find that the whole body of geometry today, both the Euclidean and the non-Euclidean geometries, collectively considered, are as inclusivist in concept as inclusivist architecture has always aspired to be. Even the most doctrinaire architect who follows the Euclidean and Cartesian systems will find that other elements, such as time, experience, movement, and even body and bodily contact have been concerns of geometric systems of the past. Ideas such as "depthless surface," "widthless line," and "dimension-less point" have been around since the eighteenth century, and may perhaps be the inspiration for the architectural concepts such as "absence of pres-ence" and "presence of absence." The last two statements, expressing ideas developed and sought after as architectural qualities by Peter Eisenman, should be viewed carefully and with respect, as they may constitute the hybrid beginnings of things we do not understand today.

To approach architecture once again, and once in one's career through the discipline of geometry, is like reintroducing the element of constructive play into the creative process. This kind of play enhances creativity through the self-assurance it provides.

Geometry as the constructive toy of architects is a powerful creativity channel because no matter what happens, a cube or a cylinder carry with their very presence and stability the self-assurance recognized by "children" of all ages. All one has to do is pick up the solid, rearrange it, and make life easier. The child is given more time to think of new arrangements, and so is the architect. More time is given to the imagination to explore new variations, to advance the properties of the preselected "ready-mades" fur-ther. Geometry offers its ready-mades to the service of creativity. It should be encouraged as a creative channel, because only through it will the archi-tect move on with maturity and experience into the realm of "imaginary geometry" and the state of inclusivist design.

## THE DESIGN CURRICULUM

The design curriculum should include exercises in all areas of geometric exploration; complexity, however, should advance incrementally, along with the growth of the designer's critical faculties. To ask young designers to indulge in rotational exercises and excessive breaking of the rules of the occasionally assigned fields, without apparent reason and lack of solid foun-dation on the need for circulation clarity and the psychological effect of the ability to "read" a building, would be counterproductive. Students would get into the bad habit of accepting spatial complexity for the sake of com-plexity and in the interest of well-crafted three-dimensional models. It is astonishing how "beautiful" some of these models are, especially under the auspices of studio instruction, where there is special emphasis on the craft-ing of models, yet how deceptive and bad they can be if students do not learn to see them as spaces where people live, walk, and find their way around. The goal should be to *view geometry as architecture,* to exploit it rather than becoming its formal victim. Because geometry can become like the spider's net in which, unlike with the spider, the first victim will be the architect who becomes known for trapping people and functions into life-less buildings.

It is not an easy task to attempt to cram complex functions into pre-conceived geometric shapes for the sake of having made a "round" or a "triangular" building. Although this should be regarded as an antiquated ambition of architects of the past, who could not be happy unless they had done their circular, or other straitjacketed building, students should try such exercises. They can learn through them that one cannot have every-thing one's way, and that abstractly superimposed forms do not work

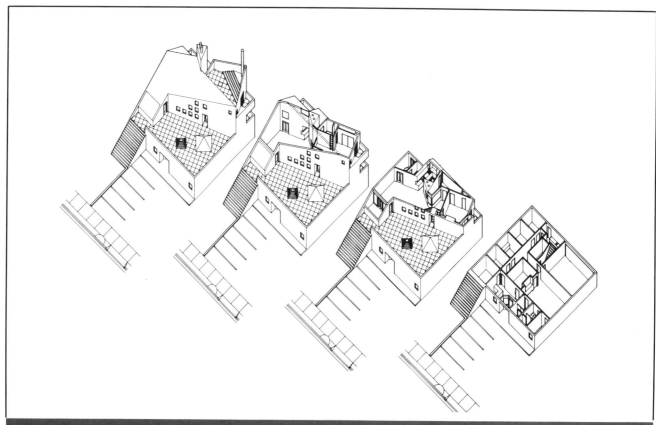

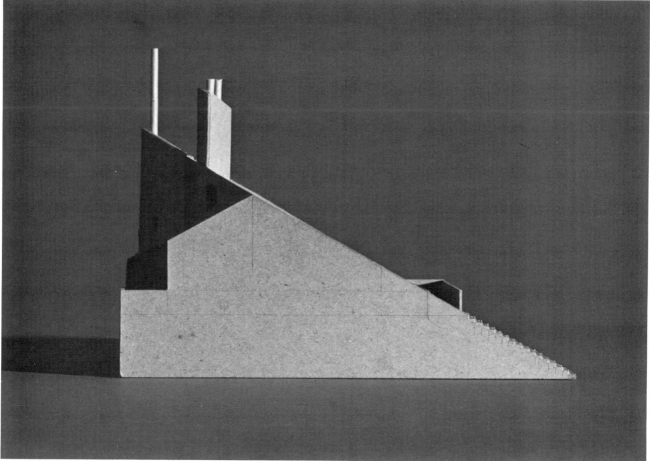

**Fig. 10–11.** *Medical clinic in Albuquerque, New Mexico, where very elementary geometry and minute geometric collisions contribute to the creation of "spatial diversity" out of the basically and economically minimal. Antoine Predock, architect. (Photo by Robert Reck)*

unless there is a reasonable fit between the inherent properties of the selected geometries and the functional requirements.

Geometric fields are the easiest to handle, more adaptable to today's complex building types, more assuring and instructive. Such exercises can be linked with occasional exercises on monofunctional buildings, and issues of "symphonic composition" (exploring the various proportional systems with Matila Ghyka as key reference). My goal is to help students to "graduate" to the attitude of geometric inclusivism, where geometry offers the opportunity to reiterate arguments on creativity also encountered in the channels of nature and the arts, eventually resulting in buildings that are acts of constructive implementability, devoid of the romantic and "arbitrary naturalness." Rather, they are architectural acts *on* nature, the divine *out of* the man-made.

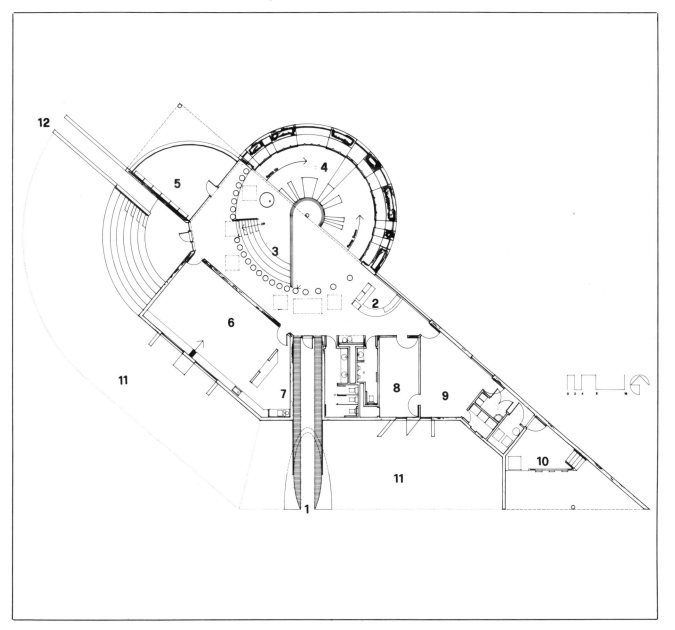

**Fig. 10-12.** *Basic geometric exercises can result in buildings of superior architectonic appeal if articulated appropriately, with concern for the topography and the overall environmental constraints. Rio Grande Natural Conservation Center, Antoine Predock, architect.*

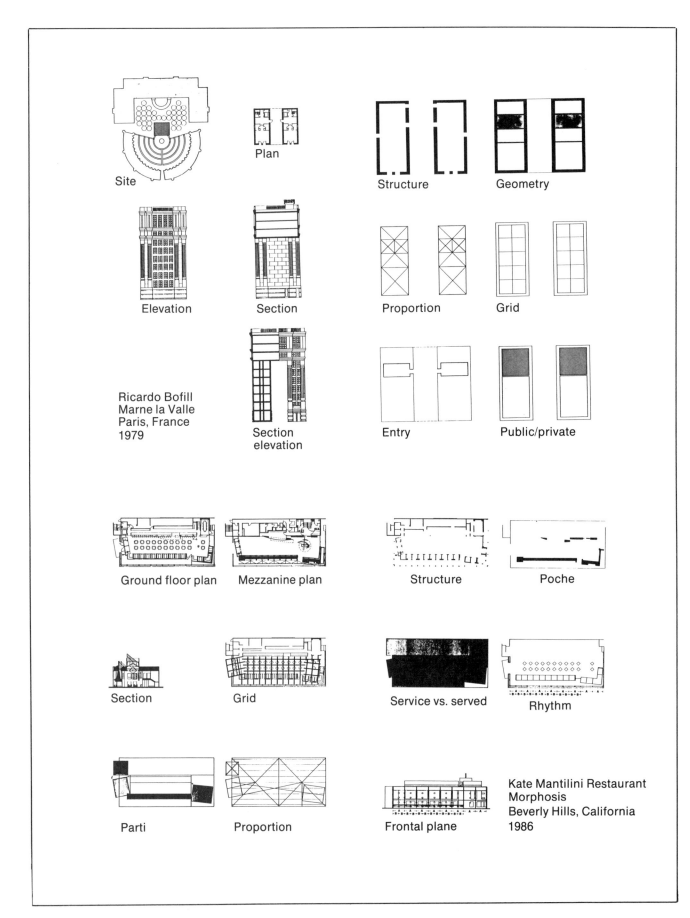

Site

Plan

Structure

Geometry

Elevation

Section

Proportion

Grid

Ricardo Bofill
Marne la Valle
Paris, France
1979

Section
elevation

Entry

Public/private

Ground floor plan

Mezzanine plan

Structure

Poche

Section

Grid

Service vs. served

Rhythm

Parti

Proportion

Frontal plane

Kate Mantilini Restaurant
Morphosis
Beverly Hills, California
1986

**Fig. 10-13.** *Analytical exercises by students on the "geometric" generics of recent buildings. From the third-year design classes of Lee Wright.*

## Summary

This chapter addresses the supremacy of geometric over analytical depiction, and the reasons for the appeal of geometry over the years. The early emphasis of aesthetes on geometry was partial, with a focus on elevations, proportional systems, and the concept of "symphonic composition." We discuss the relationship of the various building types and their corresponding fit with geometry and the concept of "geometric fields" is viewed through both historical examples and contemporary complex building types. The caution is that geometry can be misused when the emphasis is on form as opposed to the inclusivist concerns. There are emerging "new geometries," but strength in the basics of the Euclidean geometry is still the foundation of the inclusivist attitude toward geometry.

## References

Billington, David P. *The Tower and the Bridge*. New York: Basic Books, 1983.

Derrida, Jacques. *Edmund Husserl's Origin of Geometry: An Introduction*. Translated, with Preface and Afterword, by John P. Leavey, Jr. Lincoln and London: University of Nebraska Press, 1989, pp. 127, 128.

Doxiadis, Constantinos A. E. "Theories ton armonikon charaxeon es tin Architectonike" (Theories of harmonic proportioning in architecture). *3° Mati,* 7–12, 1937, p. 218.

Cook, Jeffrey. *The Architecture of Bruce Goff*. New York: Harper & Row, 1978.

Coulton, J. J. *Ancient Greek Architects at Work*. Ithaca, NY: Cornell University Press, 1977, pp. 26, 117.

Eisenman, Peter. *House X*. New York: Rizzoli, 1982.

Frampton, Kenneth. "Frontality vs. Rotation." In *Five Architects*. New York: Oxford University Press, 1975.

Ghyka, Matila C. *L'Aesthetique des Proportions dans la nature et dans les arts*. Paris: Gallimard, 1931. Also published as *The Geometry of Art and Life,* New York, Sheed and Ward, 1946, 1962, (1962 pp. 5, 124, 126, 127, 128, 129, 154, 174).

Kepes, Gyorgy. *Structure in Art and in Science*. New York: Braziller, 1965, p. 96.

Komendant, August E. *18 Years with Architect Louis I. Kahn*. Englewood, NJ: Aloray Publishers, 1975.

March, L., and Steadman, P. *The Geometry of the Environment*. London: RIBA Publications, 1971, p. 24.

Pinno, Andrzej. "Between the Ends and Means of Architecture." *Proceedings of the Seventy-sixth ACSA Annual Meeting,* Miami, March 1988.

Plato. *Timeos*.

Torretti, Roberto. *Philosophy of Geometry, from Riemann to Poincaré*. Dordrecht, Holland: D. Reidfel, 1978, pp. 55, 64.

Tzonis, Alexander, and Lefaivre, Liane. *Classical Architecture: The Poetics of Order*. Cambridge, MA: MIT Press, 1986.

Valéry, Paul. "Eupalinos ou L'Architecte." In Oeuvres II, édition établie et annotée par Jean Hytier. Paris: Gallimard, 1960, pp. 82–147.

Wittkower, Rudolf. *Architectural Principles in the Age of Humanism*. London: Alec Tiranti, 1952.

*Note:* It is extraordinary that although geometry has been at the heart of the formal structure and rhythmic essence of architecture, no recent treatise (and there have been several) other than that of March and Steadman has done justice to the subject from an architect's standpoint. The work of Matila Ghyka is still the best reference on the topic for basic design training; it is simply the classic reference on this subject. There is as yet no textbook that presents a simplified and convincing argument on the "non-Euclidean" space currently pursued intuitively by the Deconstructivist architects.

# Chapter 11 Focus on Materials

On the island of Hydra in Greece, even today materials for construction must be carried to the site by mule. The same is true for a number of other very beautiful and unspoiled historic settlements, the few that have been as yet untouched by "progress." One perhaps could find no better project managers than the artisans and local contractors in these places. They have to coordinate everything on the basis of many unknowns: the winds that may prevent arrival of the boat and the delivery of concrete, the rain that may make the steep hill unsafe for the animals, the neighbors who want to make sure they remain undisturbed by the spilling of lime and the singing of the masons. Under circumstances such as these, exotic perhaps for most people, but absolutely real for the twentieth-century Hydriot, Egyptian, or the Afghan mason, wisdom and concern for the selection of materials, and their delivery and appropriate use become issues of paramount significance for the success of the project.

The scarcity of materials, the use of mostly what is available in the area, and the handling of these materials as observation and experience has taught people to use them is a rare remnant of continuity with the past.

It is a delight today to become aware of the diligence, care, and ingenuity of the ancients in the ways they went about using materials. Two volumes by the late Anastasios Orlandos are unique for their specificity, scholastic merit, originality of visual presentation, information from other scholars, and statements of personal hypotheses regarding methods of construction, transportation, and so on. In this monumental effort, entitled *Construction Materials of the Ancient Greeks, according to Writers, Inscriptions, and Monuments* by a member of the Greek Academy and professor of the history of architecture at the Polytechnic in Athens, Orlandos, provides a taste of the ingenuity of the ancients. French-speaking readers will be equally charmed by the earlier treatise on the subject and the tables prepared by J. F. Blondel and continued by M. Patte in the fifth volume of their architectural series from the Ecole des Beaux-Arts in Paris.

Another source of information and delight is Alberti's narratives, available in English translation. Alberti was fascinated by the study of Pliny, Diodorus, Theophrastus, Hesiod, and others, who were the first to write on the subject of materials. There is no more entertaining and moving reading than Alberti's Book II of his *Ten Books on Architecture*. The trees, the best time to cut them, their fluids and their juices; the stones, those that grow, those that are unfit for bonding with cement; the marbles and the best places to find them; the same for sand and lime, stones and bricks, the whole range of the materials of the ancients—humans have developed a

**Fig. 11-1.** *Delivery of materials and methods of construction in the difficult and inaccessible sites of the Greek islands.*

whole mythology about the materials of construction. Alberti has invested them with magic and life. He has treated the inorganic in an anthropomorphic way: materials live and grow and react and are responsive to seasons, they shrink and dry, or they are durable and help us. One should cut the elm at certain times of the moon, otherwise one might become bald; one should make absolutely sure not to cut his ". . . nails or hair while the moon is oppressed or ill disposed." Tinos in Greece and Carrara in Italy became famous for their marbles, Rome for travertine, Pozzuoli near Naples for *pozzolana,* a bonding for stones, Oropos and Aulis in Greece for petrified products washed by the sea, India for the ribs of the whale, with which, according to Alberti's research, they used to build palaces (Alberti, 1965).

Materials and their use express the character, the attitude toward eternity, and the love of nature, other people, and the "good." Through the use and the choice of materials, you can tell a lot about the discipline, the patience, the wisdom, the whole range of the values of the creator. There are no easy rules in this regard. An artisan who cares will know and do well with whatever materials he or she may use; an ignorant one will make a mess no matter how good the materials are. Frank Lloyd Wright and Alvar Aalto, for example, almost always did well with everything.

## ON THE MORALITY OF CONSTRUCTION

The German architect Egon Eiermann was unique in his teaching of architectural design. He could function comfortably in many channels of creativity, both tangible and intangible. He used to consider any project of any scale appropriate for any level of design instruction. An unresolved museum project had no chance of getting approval for the awarding of a thesis degree, whereas a well-thought-out and well-coordinated small cabin of even 5 by 5 meters would certainly qualify for approval as a master's project. Eiermann's emphasis was primarily on the understanding and appropriate use of materials, the proportioning of the project in relationship to the dimensions of the materials used. A house made of concrete block, for instance, could not be tolerated unless its length and height, along with the sizes of windows and other openings, were not multiples of the dimensions of the concrete blocks.

Although there is a widespread tendency among many architectural instructors not to consider materials and details fundamental in the process of architectural conception and although even several well-known architects, noted for their overall creations, were extremely weak in handling materials and architectural details (Rudolph Schindler, Le Corbusier), it is nonetheless true that the appropriate use of materials will make the difference between a long-lasting project and a short-lived one.

Use of appropriate materials will make the difference between a real building and a "set design." Materials have not only dimensions and thickness, but strength and "sound." Knock on a stone and knock on a paper imitation of stone—they sound different. Knock on a masonry stucco wall and then knock on a stucco wall made out of $2 \times 4$ and gypsum board— again, the sound is different. It is even worse when there is no stucco, but some other application and color on the plywood. The result is something that looks like masonry but at a touch, or when something crushes it, makes a sound like a suffering drum.

This is certainly the case in many recent historicist buildings where the imitation of past forms has been achieved through the use of inappropriate materials. The Library by Michael Graves in San Juan Capistrano is a glorious example. You can walk along a colonnade that wants to be magnificent, yet the sound of the hollow plywood columns brings you to the

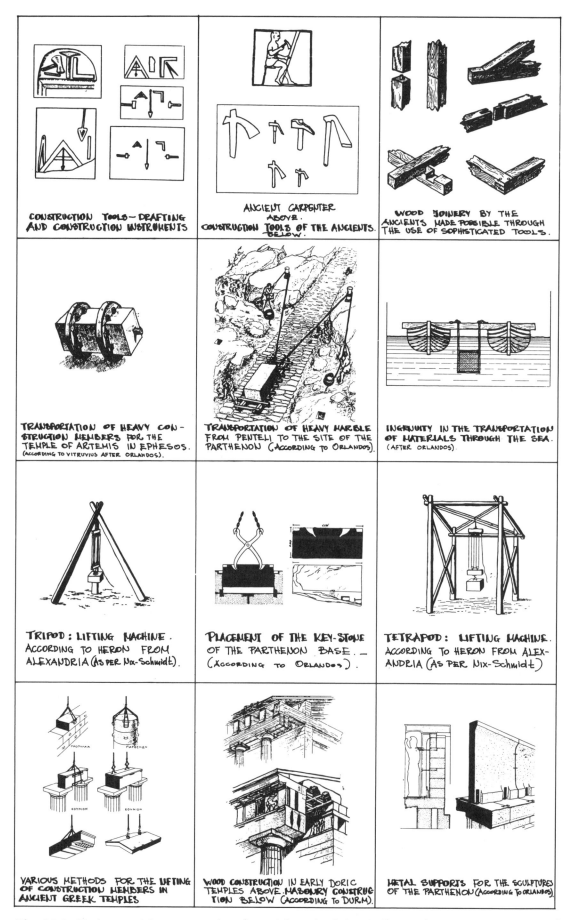

**Fig. 11-2.** *Tools, materials, transportation of materials, and techniques of material handling by the ancients, according to Anastasios Orlandos and other scholars. (After Orlandos, 1958)*

reality of a "fake present," as opposed to the real and honest past of buildings of similar design that preceded it. It is astonishing that the American Institute of Architects gave some of its best awards for 1983 to buildings of Postmodern direction such as the YWCA in Houston by Taft Architects; the building, just one year old, had already cracked. Water had run down the expansion joints, which were used as a means of separating the many materials that were applied on the elevations.

One must always take into account the country in which an architect practices, the building technology, and the standards which people there use. The higher the technology level, the higher the level of expectation with regard to detailing and trim work; the greater the number of materials, the more complicated the selection process and certainly the more expensive the initial cost. Some of these problems are magnified by the proliferation of materials and product-promoting magazines that aim at the seduction of clients. Forty-five years ago, architects in advanced countries could count on choosing from approximately 100 building materials; now these architects have to choose from over 1 million available materials. The fact that architects in technologically less advanced countries and countries of the Third World still have very few materials points out the vast differences between the two groups of architects. In this sense, one could argue that unless the type, performance, number, and method of use of materials is taken into consideration, one cannot speak of architecture in universal terms. Building technology and materials may therefore become the common denominator on the basis of which we can make comparisons, differentiate, or draw universal conclusions with regard to architecture beyond the generic qualities of space, and the broad issues of structure and rhythm.

**Fig. 11-3.** *The library of San Juan Capistrano, California. Michael Graves, architect.*

## STRUCTURAL AND AESTHETIC DIMENSIONS IN THE USE OF MATERIALS

Two broad categories of materials have consequences for the general issues of architecture: (1) those that may affect the structural system and the functional organization, and (2) those that may affect the microscale of architecture, the exterior and interior textures, the finishing and trimming details. The first category has an effect on the general character of buildings, affecting the structural organization, the proportions, the rhythmic quality (solids vs. voids) and the weight of a building; the latter has an extraordinary effect upon the overall cost of the construction, and is perhaps a unique indicator of cost-efficient architecture.

One does not necessarily have difficulties in the selection of the first category of materials; basic practice, experience working in a particular area, and basic research on particular building types can provide solutions for the optimum selection. Structural consultants are certainly indispensable in this respect. It is the microscale in the use of materials that poses greater problems with regard to selection. This scale affects the general texture of the building, its play with the sun, its visual subtleties, externally as well as internally. Furthermore, these materials, the compatibility among them as well as their compatibility with the heavier materials used for the structure, will affect the visual quality of the building in time, its weathering and its resistance to climatic conditions. They may help reduce energy costs in the long run, or they may increase them.

## ATTITUDES OF ARCHITECTS TOWARD MATERIALS

The proper use of materials has varied among architects. Several of the best-known architects of this century had difficulties with them, both in the larger scale (structure) and in the microscale. Paul Rudolph called attention to Frank Lloyd Wright's occasional failure to give priority to the correct use of materials, and sometimes there had to be a decision between spatial and aesthetic qualities versus materials. Singling out the structural planes of Taliesin West, Rudolph concluded that Wright's feeling for materials ". . . is more in his books than in his architecture."

Le Corbusier and Rudolph Schindler were notorious for their problems with materials in the microscale. Paul Rudolph once again: "It took Le Corbusier twenty-five years to learn the secrets of materials"; while Rudolph Schindler, in spite of his divine performance in the broad aspects of architecture, never managed to reach a level of acceptable standards and detailing in the microscale. Schindler's Lovell Beach house is not only one of the neglected and yet truly deserving masterpieces of the Modern movement, especially with regard to the properties of reinforced concrete, or proof of the possibilities of good client-architect cooperation, but it is on the other hand a typical example of an inappropriate combination of materials for the particular case.

Although architects may be overly anxious to see their conceptual, spatial, contextual, and poetic performance, it is the clients who have to live with the buildings, the weathering and the leaks, the costs of inappropriate workmanship and the quality of performance. It is also true, however, that many substitutions are made in order to meet the budget or at the request of clients (often on the construction site), without due thought and a specifications check at the drawing board. It is also true that the architect's desire to please clients may lead to regrettable decisions that will become apparent with the first winter and the effect of time. It requires experience, in-depth study, and extraordinary abilities to convince clients with regard to the selection of materials, especially the finishing ones.

"Artists renderings" and elevation drawings are not enough; it will be the total, the honest, and the multilayered rationalization of materials that will eventually convince the client and produce excellent buildings.

Alvar Aalto's work demonstrates the best fit between excellence in detailing and spatial and aesthetic appeal. Louis Kahn has produced buildings distinguished for the optimum use of materials and finishes that contribute much to the final formal and aesthetic resolutions of his buildings. Whether it was the use of masonry materials, such as concrete or brick, or others such as steel and wood, Kahn demonstrated care and know-how unequaled by other architects of this century.

One can hardly find any merit in Postmodern architecture with regard to its use of materials. In fact, the difference in the use of materials constitutes in my opinion the key difference between the two architectures. The identity of the Modern era was largely established through the simple expression of the materials used, the restraint in their number, and the lack of ornament. The Postmodern identity, especially Postmodern historicism, was established via the mixing of materials on the façades, the use of veneer and appliqué as well as fake materials, imitations of the originals, disproportionality in the detailing and excess joinery and decoration. In spite of our critical stance toward Wright's rhetoric, he is still a master, a leader in the use of materials expressive of their true and inherent properties and nature. We find only the opposite among the "masters" of the Postmodern group.

## ARCHITECT EXEMPLARS AND MODERN VS. POSTMODERN ARCHITECTURE

Henry Hobson Richardson, Frank Lloyd Wright, and Louis Kahn are, in my opinion, the key architects who created what we might call *correct and coordinated architecture,* including the *correct use of materials.* Richardson's load-bearing walls were the result of the very disciplined and studied expression of cut stone exposed to its natural state; the openings in the walls obeyed the integral modulation of the stones, exposed on the outside and resting solidly on the sides on supports visually and statically strong for the weight of wall, or of the building carried above. The use of few materials enhances the feeling of internal strength within the structure.

Frank Lloyd Wright broke down the Romanesque-like identity of the Richardsonian expression to the microscale of separate architectural elements: the wall, the roof, the eaves, interior and exterior planes, the pivotal masses of chimneys, cantilevered balconies or floors, fenestration or roof assemblies. His Kaufmann Fallingwater house, his first dwelling in reinforced concrete, was a major poem composed as a composition of "assemblies." A score of Wright pieces clearly demonstrate the discipline of his grammar in materials: He never mixes in a sentence stated in one language words of other languages; he never mixes materials of a particular architectural entity (such as a wall) with materials alien to the nature of this entity. Wright did not hesitate to experiment. In fact, he remains unique for his inventions. The concrete blocks and the reinforcing methods he devised for several of his houses, along with his attitude toward the use of new materials produced by industry, demonstrate an architect open to possibilities, eager to solve broader problems, for whom materials are conceived as molecular problem-solving devices. His concrete blocks were employed to solve problems of low-cost housing and construction efficiency.

Wright's experimentation with new materials was an extremely careful affair. He used as few as possible, thus limiting the joinery problems inherent in the use of a multiplicity of materials. His concrete block buildings, perhaps most characteristic of his experimental projects, were in fact Ri-

# MODERN

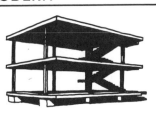

DOM-INO HOUSE, REINFORCED CONCRETE FRAME LE CORBUSIER.

DYNAMIC EXPRESSIONISM OF STRUCTURE THROUGH THE "MONOLITHICITY" OF REINFORCED CONCRETE. NEWPORT BEACH HOUSE BY RUDOLPH SCHINDLER.

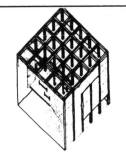

"FESTIVAL", NAHA OKINAWA TADAO ANDO ARCH.

STRUCTURE BASED ON THE EMPHASIS OF THE MATERIAL AND OBEDIENCE TO THE LAWS OF GRAVITY AND THE INHERENT STRENGTH OF MATERIALS. **USE OF ONE MAJOR MATERIAL!**

LOUIS SULLIVAN RICHARDSONIAN. WALL FROM THE AUDITORIUM BLDG. CHICAGO 1886-89.

LIVING ROOM — TALIESIN WEST F. L. WRIGHT 1958.

MORSE AND STILES COLLEGE, YALE EERO SAARINEN, ARCH.

STRAIGHTFORWARD AND **STATICALLY SOUND USE OF MATERIALS** AS PER THEIR PRIMORDIAL USE.

FAGUS FACTORY, 1911. WALTER GROPIUS WITH ADOLF MEYER.

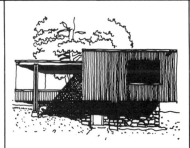

CHAMBERLAIN HOUSE SADBURY, MASSACHUSETTS — 1939 WALTER GROPIUS WITH MARCEL BREUER.

MUMMERS THEATER, OKLAHOMA CITY JOHN JOHANSEN.

USE OF "NEW" MATERIALS AND "HIGH-TECH" OF THE ERA EXPRESSIVE OF COMPATIBILITY, COOPERATION AND LEAST ENERGY.

GOVERNMENT BUILDINGS BRAZILIA. OSCAR NIEMEYER ARCH. 1956-60

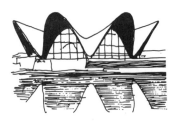

RESTAURANT, XOCHIMILCO — MEXICO CITY FELIX CANDELA AND ALVAREZ ORDONEZ 1958.

SYDNEY OPERA HOUSE 1970 JØRN UTZON ARCH.

PUSHING **STRUCTURAL TECHNOLOGY TO ITS LIMITS.** NEW BUILDING FORMS EXPRESSIVE OF THE POTENTIAL OF NEW STRUCTURAL TECHNOLOGIES (i.e SHELLS).

**Fig. 11-4.** *Broad issues of concern regarding materials and the respective attitudes of architects of the Modern and Postmodern movements. (Figure continues)*

**POSTMODERN**

"54 WINDOWS" OR "TOKYO BOOGIE-
WOOGIE".
KAZUHIRO ISHII 1975.

MEDICAL STUDENTS DORMITORIES.
LUCIEN KROLL /UNIVERSITY OF
LOUVAIN BRUSSELS. 1977.

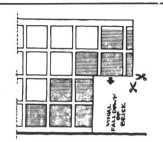

THE CLORE GALLERY/TATE GALLERY.
JAMES STIRLING, MICHAEL WILFORD
LONDON 1986.

PROGRESSIVE ATTEMPTS TO GO BEYOND STRUCTURAL EXPRESSIONISM. EVEN TO THE POINT
OF DEFYING THE LAW OF GRAVITY. USE OF MANY MATERIALS

THE BYKER WALL-NEWCASTLE UPON
TYNE. RALPH ERSKINE 1968.

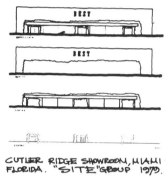

CUTLER RIDGE SHOWROOM, MIAMI
FLORIDA. "SITE" GROUP 1979.

THE FINNISH EMBASSY IN NEW DELHI.
RAILI AND REIMA PIETILÄ 1983-86.

COMPLICATED AND "TORTURED" USE OF MATERIALS ESPECIALLY AS "STRUCTURAL" AGENTS.
"DEFORMED" SECTIONS AND EXCESSIVE SIZING.

AEROSPACE MUSEUM IN L.A.
FRANK GEHRY.

TOM CRONDONA'S CLAUDIAS
BAKERY-HORTON PLAZA/SAN
DIEGO 1985.

"PETAL HOUSE"- LOS ANGELES.
ERIC OWEN MOSS ARCHITECT.

FORCED RELATIONSHIPS IN THE USE OF "HIGH-TECH". BUILT-IN TENSIONS IN THE JOINTURES OF
MATERIALS. FREQUENT INCOMPATIBILITY OF MATERIALS AND DECEITFUL EXPRESSION. ____

AT&T
NEW YORK
PHILIP
JOHNSON/
JOHN
BURGEE

PORTLAND SERVICES BUILDING
MICHAEL GRAVES, ARCH.
(AFTER MICHAEL GRAVES).

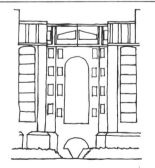

"AQUEDUCT"-HOUSING DEVELOPMENT
IN SAINT QUENTIN-EN-YVELINE
RICARDO BOFILL

POVERTY IN THE ADVANCEMENT OF "NEW" FORMS EXPRESSIVE OF THE STATE OF THE ART OF
STRUCTURAL TECHNOLOGY. LOSS OF STRUCTURE AND EMPHASIS ON "ORNAMENTAL" PRACTICES. —

**Fig. 11-4** *(Continued)*

# MODERN

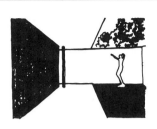

BARCELONA PAVILION, DETAIL.
MIES VAN DER ROHE 1929.

CHAPEL OF NOTRE DAME-DU-HAUT,
RONCHAMP. LE CORBUSIER 1955.

SKETCHES FOR EINSTEIN TOWER
ERICH MENDELSOHN -1919-21

PLANAR OR MASS PLASTICITY BASED ON THE CONSTRUCTIVE USE OF MASONRY
MATERIALS.

SÄYNÄTSALO TOWN HALL-ALVAR AALTO
1952.

MORRIS SHOP-SAN FRANCISCO
FRANK LLOYD WRIGHT

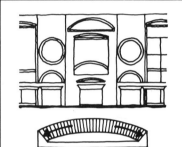

INDIAN INSTITUTE OF MANAGEMENT
AHMEDABAD. LOUIS KAHN 1963.

LOGICAL USE OF BRICK AND STRUCTURALLY SOUND ARTICULATION OF OTHER ELEMENTS OF
STRUCTURE TO PERMIT STATICALLY CORRECT ACCOMMODATION OF FORCES.
THE "ARCH" IS STILL AN "ARCH" AND THE LINTEL IS ACCOMMODATING THE FORCES(i.e. Louis Kahn).

SECTION OF PIERS FOR S.C.JOHNSON &
SON INC. ADMINISTRATION BUILDING.
RACINE WISCONSIN. F.L.WRIGHT 1936-39

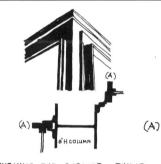

TURNING THE CORNER - PHILIP
JOHNSON GLASS HOUSE NEW CANAAN
CONNECTICUT.

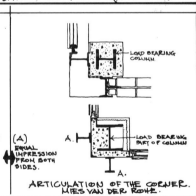

ARTICULATION OF THE CORNER.
MIES VAN DER ROHE.

INNOVATIONS IN THE EXPRESSION OF STRUCTURAL MEMBERS AND EVEN "DECORATION" THROUGH THE
APPROPRIATE PLAY BETWEEN THE ELEMENTS OF STRUCTURE, ALWAYS IN THE REINFORCEMENT OF
FEELINGS OF STABILITY AND TRUTH.

BAGSVAERD CHURCH NEAR
COPENHAGEN. JØRN UTZON ARCHITECT.

INTERIOR SPACE OF
BAGSVAERD CHURCH.

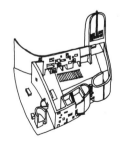

3 DIMENSIONAL CUT OF NOTRE
DAME-DU-HAUT. LE CORBUSIER 1955.

OPTIMIZATION OF THE CAPABILITIES OF AVAILABLE MATERIALS AND THE ACHIEVEMENT OF HIGHER DEGREES
OF PLASTICITY THROUGH APPROPRIATE MATERIAL CO-OPERATION. RICH INTERIOR SPACE RESULTS IN THE
GENERIC SENSE OF SPACE. LOGICAL AND SOUND DETAILING.

**Fig. 11-4** *(Continued)*

# POSTMODERN

ONE OF THE FIRST BUILDINGS BY "BITE" FOR THE "BEST PRODUCTS" CHAIN. SUPPOSEDLY COMMENTARY ON TRADITIONAL WAYS OF BUILDING YET A CORRECT MORPHOLOGY NONETHELESS.

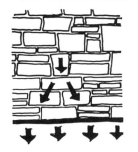

CORRECT MORPHOLOGY OF MASONRY CONSTRUCTION OBEYING TO THE LAW OF GRAVITY.

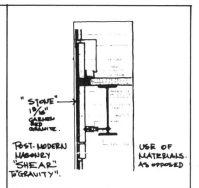

POST-MODERN MASONRY "SHEAR" TO "GRAVITY".   USE OF MATERIALS. AS OPPOSED

DEFIANCE OF THE LOGIC OF MASS. "DESTRUCTION" AS OPPOSED TO "CONSTRUCTION". USE OF STONE AS APPLIQUÉ IN INSIGNIFICANT NON-LOAD BEARING THICKNESSES. CONTRADICTION BETWEEN EXTERNAL APPEARANCE OF MASONRY ELEMENTS AND ACTUAL STRUCTURAL PERFORMANCE. ——

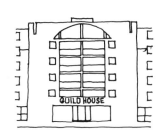

GUILD HOUSE, ROBERT VENTURI AND DENISE SCOTT-BROWN 1960-63.

BRICK ARCH THAT DOES NOT CLOSE, THUS NOT AN ARCH, EVEN BY ARCHITECT SUCH AS ROMALDO GIURGOLA.

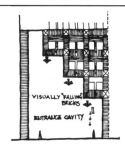

RANSILA OFFICE BUILDING. LUGANO SWITZERLAND. MARIO BOTTA, ARCHITECT 1985.

DECEITFUL USE OF "STRUCTURALLY SOUND FORMS" (i.e. ARCH). USE OF BRICK AS APPLIQUÉ (OR INSULATION DEVICE) AND INAPPROPRIATE EXPRESSION OF ITS PRIMORDIAL STRUCTURAL POTENTIAL. EXTRA — REAL STRUCTURE IS NECESSARY IN ORDER TO PERMIT THE "STRUCTURALLY SOUND-LOOKING" NON-STRUCTURAL VISUAL RESULTS. DEFIANCE OF THE "ARCH"-MORPHOLOGY OF "SHEAR" FORCES.

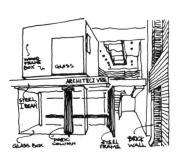

OFFICES OF THE MINNEAPOLIS SOCIETY OF ARCHITECTS. COLLABORATION OF TWO ARCHITECTURAL OFFICES — MIX OF STYLES.

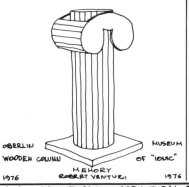

OBERLIN WOODEN COLUMN   MUSEUM OF "IONIC" MEMORY ROBERT VENTURI 1976   1976

PIAZZA D'ITALIA, NEW ORLEANS CHARLES MOORE 1977-78 (WITH FILSON, PEREZ, HEARD, ESKEW)

EXCESSIVE USE OF FREQUENT AND UNNECESSARY STRUCTURAL ELEMENTS. USE OF FAKE MATERIALS, INAPPROPRIATE FOR STRUCTURAL PURPOSES (i.e. PLASTER "ANCIENT"-LOOKING COLUMNS, "COLUMNS" OUT OF PLASTIC ETC.). THE "RIDICULE" OF HONESTY AND LOGIC.

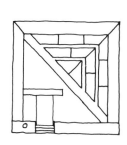

"ANTI-DWELLING" BOX-HOUSE BY MONTA MOZUNA—HOKKAIDO 1971.

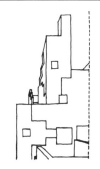

PAINTED STUCCO SURFACES. "THE BEACH", ANTONE PREDOCK 1985

HOLDING FROM A ROBERT STERN HOUSE.

MATERIALS USED AS "DRAFTING" DEVICES TO EXPRESS DESIGN INTENTIONS. FREQUENT UNNECESSARY DETAILING IN NON-FUNCTIONAL RESOLUTIONS ("FUNCTION": SO THAT THE DETAIL MAY WORK). LACK OF PLASTICITY BUT CREATION OF LARGE SCALE DECORATIVE EVENTS INSTEAD.

**Fig. 11-4** (Continued)

chardsonian in their monolithicity, creating an expression analogous to the tradition vernacular architecture of regions. In this respect his experimentation was realistically and universally restrained, in contrast to the attitude of experimentation of recent Postmodern efforts such as those by Frank Gehry, who experiments with a multiplicity of materials (plywood, asphalt shingles, chains, varnishes) that run the risk of incompatibility.

The nonexperimental palette of Frank Lloyd Wright was carefully chosen of only compatible materials. They also had to be available in the region of the construction of the building. In this sense, his architecture was a decisively selective process of material combinations, imposed by the architect and always controlled by him. The "regionalism" of Frank Lloyd Wright is not therefore one that negates technology while sticking to whatever is necessarily native to the region—as is, for instance, the architecture of Hassan Fathy—but it is a *created regionalism,* the result of a selection process that has the goal of achieving a regionally responsive composition of compatible assemblies. In this sense Wright points to an open-ended path, one that does not deny technology, yet one that eventually has to be characterized by the discipline, the rules of the "grammar of the optimum," whenever that optimum is found, or thought to have been found.

Based on all this, I believe Frank Lloyd Wright should still remain the model with regard to the use of materials, as his openness to new technologies and the new will always point toward hope for the solution to more problems, whereas the romantic regionalist attitude and unquestionable attachment to what already exists may never permit us to solve problems. Louis Kahn is also a key figure, precisely for some of the reasons stated above. He was more disciplined with regard to selection when contrasted to Wright. He was also less prone to experimentation, and therefore not necessarily the best leader in the broader area of materials; yet he was perhaps the best among the architects of this century to illustrate expressive honesty and integrity with regard to the coordination of materials with a total architectural vision.

Louis Kahn's Kimbell Art museum in Fort Worth is a masterpiece in this respect. A survey of the numerous studies of the building demonstrate a care for "fit" that can only be compared to the perfection of the classics, especially the Greek classics. Kahn put the use of tools and machines to the ultimate architectonic end; with them he produced buildings that were composites of parts working in total harmony among themselves and with the whole. There is no Kahn building that does not give evidence of his genius in the use of materials. He has achieved perfection in buildings with all sorts of budgetary constraints, from the most modest to the monumental. His Trenton bathhouse is the best example of the low-budget project, while various museums and the capital complex of Bangladesh in Dacca cover the last categories. The subtlety of the curves of his arches, the articulation of the ends of his concrete lintels, the perfect use of brick, rightfully elevate him to the levels of Doric and (for those who may prefer it) Roman divinity.

We do not believe that Le Corbusier has much to offer in the way of example in terms of materials, except his enthusiasm for the new, his infatuation with materials used in cars, airplanes, and trains, and perhaps the attitude that detailing was secondary to the conceptual aspects of architecture.

The European counterpart to the American architects discussed earlier is Alvar Aalto. With the exception of Aalto and most of the Scandinavian architects, European architects of the Modern movement or after did not reach the excellence in the use of materials of their American counterparts. They were certainly surpassed by the Postmodern Japanese, especially Kisho Kurokawa, Arata Isozaki, Kazuhiro Ishii, and Kazuo Shinohara. Yet

Alvar Aalto is, I believe, the epitome in terms of the proper use of materials. He was the architect who learned from others, while he undoubtedly influenced his distinguished colleagues. We can conceive of Aalto metaphorically as the "filtering source of knowledge" for the proper use of materials. The Wrightian, the Northern European, and the Oriental were transformed and elevated through his problem-solving capacities and ingenuity into the most inclusivist case of detailing. Aalto used materials as a means to the ultimate sensual, emotional, and poetic end. For him, the materials were also the beginning and end of architecture: "An ordinary brick . . . a primitive product . . . if it is made correctly, properly processed from the country's own raw materials, if it is used in the right way and given its proper place in the whole, then it constitutes the basic element in mankind's most valuable and visible monuments and is also the basic element in the environment that creates social well-being" (Aalto, 1979, p. 127).

Speaking of Postmodern architecture, we can safely generalize, suggesting its total failure from the point of view of materials, even though in some cases clients went to extraordinary expense to give their architects generous budgets for "wild" material combinations, costly afterthoughts, oversize details and moldings, things appropriate to various styles of the past that had to be applied to the enormous versions of today, along with an excess in the number of material combinations. Monuments of this kind of project are the Piazza d'Italia by Charles Moore, the Crescent in Dallas by Philip Johnson, and the Horton Plaza in San Diego by Jon Jerde.

## MATERIALS VS. OVERALL SYNTHESIS

Our discussion thus far has focused on materials as supreme, with everything else as secondary. Yet we must never lose sight of the responsibility of the architect, which is a total design. Only in the broader inclusivist framework will materials, or anything else for that matter, make sense. We must therefore consider the attitudes of both architects and critics on these matters before suggesting ways for the use of materials in inclusivist design education.

Important architects, as well as their critics, seem to have looked at materials differently. The architects, especially the "artist-architects" as opposed to the "architect-engineer-businessmen," have paid attention primarily to spatial and broader goals, and been quick to disregard materials and construction inefficiencies, to adopt the route of economy that will permit them to build their broader visions. As David Gebhard has argued, Rudolph Schindler "had embraced the impermanent . . . as a means of realizing his forms. If his client's budget were restricted and limited (as it usually was), he would pare the structure to the bone so that he could obtain the formal and spatial aspects he was seeking." It requires very sophisticated critics and especially strong and honest clients to eventually evaluate the project within the context of the initially accepted strategic issues, taking into consideration the extra effort on the part of the architect to meet the budget. Unfortunately, as a rule the initial efforts of the design process to meet the budget are forgotten and the verdict is negative if something goes wrong, if a particular detail or a construction method fails. Furthermore, it requires extremely strong architects, artist-architects who stick to their priorities on the need for design supremacy, for only this outlook will help advance architectural inclusivity.

Viewing materials and construction methods only from the point of view of their ultimate narrow performance, disregarding the framework of the broader architectonic goals and the "economics of architectural aesthetics" has done more harm than good. Such attitudes have created architectural sterility. On the other hand, careful consideration has proved that

eventual technological innovations began with the occasional failures of the artist-architects who took the risk of exploring the new, even though it did not always work in the first application. Rudolph Schindler discovered the four-foot modular system in the use of stucco-sheathed wood frame; Frank Lloyd Wright discovered the reinforced concrete block and the floor-heated convection system; Paul Rudolph initiated corrugated concrete and what he called "twentieth-century brick," the ultimate metaphor of the brick as a prefabricated mobile home unit that could be stacked and arranged in a site plan for the purposes of low-cost housing. Although several of these efforts, such as Paul Rudolph's, did not succeed, the concepts were valid. Industry picked them up, capital was invested, research took over, and the earlier experiments resulted in new solutions in common practice. Pioneering architects have consistently carried out Picasso's dictum: "We do it first, and then others make it pretty." For architecture, one could say: "We do it first, and then others make it work."

It requires initial poetic vision, the broad inclusivist concept, the synthesis of the whole that will justify rationalization of the generic module, if the module (and the detail) are to be correct. The opposite, engineering and "efficiency," will not guarantee success; it usually results in components that may work separately, yet will not be in harmony when put together. The materials have to serve the poetic vision if architecture is to remain art.

**Fig. 11-5.** *The monolithicity of reinforced concrete. Lovell house, Newport Beach, California. Rudolph Schindler, architect.*

## THE EDUCATIONAL ENVIRONMENT AND THE USE OF MATERIALS

I believe that the use of materials, as well as building technology, especially in advanced countries, is today the major weakness of architectural design education. Although there are scores of "good" buildings, most of them non-glamorous, but innovative in the proper use of materials, they are products of sophisticated organizations that have nothing to do with academic research or experimentation at the university. One could say that the laboratory for materials in the United States is the liability-conscious large-scale practice. Large firms and busy architects are ahead with regard to knowledge in the use of new and more efficient materials. It is also true that with very few exceptions, the use of this knowledge does not go along with great attention to overall design excellence; there seems to be a split over concern for overall design issues, theory, and the broad aspects of space on one hand, and building technology on the other. Schools of architecture seem to care for the first, while the large practice seems to care for the second. This is rather unfortunate, as it deprives the student of an organic synthesis of the two, something that should take place in the years of attitude formation, which happens at school. The resentment toward the overall integration of these issues and the attitude that synthesis is the role of schools while "working drawings" (and in extension materials) is the role of the office, weakens the education of designers.

A

Fig. 11-6. New materials, new "freedoms," new morphologies (or old ones with new technologies), new costs, new liabilities. The architect's role is becoming progressively more difficult in the effort to resolve the many considerations posed above. A. Curved steel sections for the United Airlines terminal at O'Hare Airport, Chicago. Helmut Jan, architect. B. Structural and material freedom and "gymnastics," Lloyds Building, London. Richard Rogers Partnership, architects.

B

Education that includes materials does not mean that schools of architecture should turn themselves into laboratories, although it would be a blessing if some could develop such laboratories under their auspices and strict supervision, integrated with experimental studio work. All schools should have exhibitions and assemblies of materials compatible with their regions. But it is the broader attitude of the design instructor that concerns us here. My personal belief is that a constant return to the basics, a strong effort to point out the way of the simple and logical, accompanied by reference to the work of such masters as Richardson, Wright, Kahn, and Aalto, accompanied by occasional exercises where the focus on materials is paramount, will be good for instructors and the curriculum. Reference to the basics should include rules of thumb as well as examples of vernacular and regional architectures. Exercises of an exotic and multicultural nature will stimulate questions of form and fit, especially for students in technologically advanced countries. One is deprived of the extraordinary wealth of progress if one is thrown into a pool of "riches" and does not know how to handle wealth unless one has taken part in making it. It is not "rediscovering the wheel" but "what it takes to discover the wheel" that it is at stake here.

A theorem I often hear regarding materials is "avoid using more than three basic materials in any building." The logic behind this, of course, is that the materials have different properties for contraction and expansion, and as a consequence, one material might push the other and thus create cracks or construction tensions. In climates with extreme variations of temperature between day and night, or even between seasons, the problems of mixing materials are noticeable.

**Fig. 11-7.** *Materials beyond the utilitarian. Muraatsalo: Alvar Aalto's retreat home-studio.*

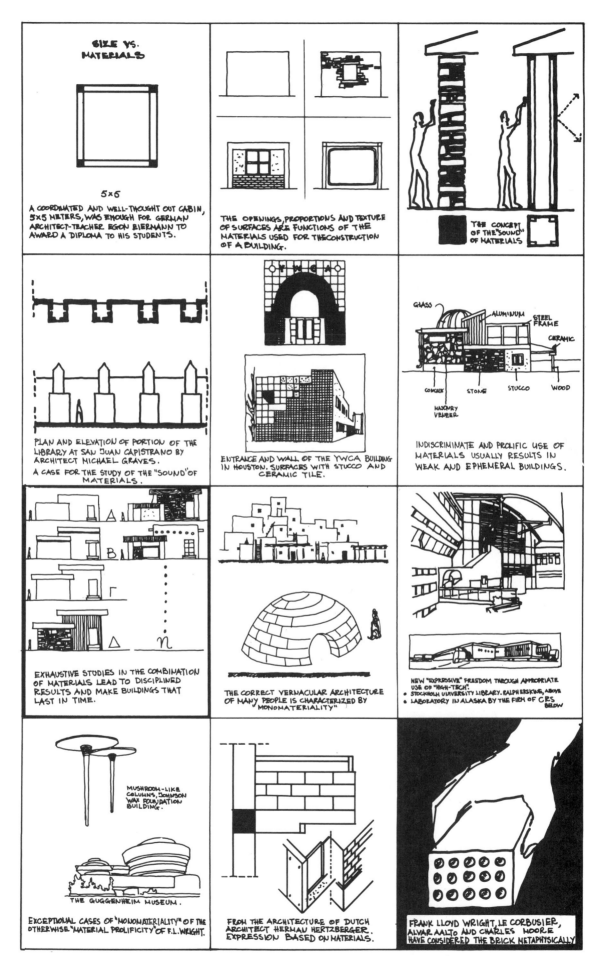

**Fig. 11-8.** *Summary of didactic commentary on the use of materials.*

**Fig. 11-9.** *Excess in the use of materials. Student housing at the University of Louvain, Belgium. Lucien Kroll, architect.*

*A*

*B*

**Fig. 11-10.** *Even the excellent among architects may have occasional problems with materials, despite regular successes: A. Resolution of stairway handrail termination where the wood changes to brass, so that the handicapped may appreciate through the difference in touch the end of the handrail and the landing approach. B. Failure: the cracked marble veneer slice of column "dressing" in an office building in Helsinki. Both projects, Alvar Aalto, architect.*

This is why the conventional wisdom and vernacular experience decrees a very limited use of materials and adopted universal applications of one and only one material, usually the one available—that is, the one that is part of the ecology and climate of the vicinity. This is why the architecture of New Mexico, a region with extremes between day and night (hot during the day, cold at night) has generated a mono-material architecture based on adobe units, and this is why the architecture of the Eskimos is based on the use of one and only one material, ice.

Extraordinary technologies of material "giving in" and "tolerance" are necessary if one is to attempt to use a variety of materials in extreme climates. Although such technologies exist, they are very costly and they are not taught in schools of architecture. In this case, the consultants to the architect should be aerospace and space engineers, the only ones qualified at present to work with extremes. If there is correct use of materials, the building will look new, look fresh, will be something we have not seen before. This is why the recent laboratory in Alaska developed by CRS is as pioneering and as pleasing as anything can be, because its form conveys the undeniability of its existence as a means to respond to the extremes of Alaskan climate, to melt the snow and to attract solar radiation.

The climate and the appearance of buildings due to material combination will eventually be a strong factor in the life span of the Postmodern collage fury, especially in the hands of inexperienced young architects. On the other hand, in the hands of willing investigators and wealthy clients, it might produce images of the "new," but only when appropriate research is invested in the fit, joinery, and connection problems. An exceptional building in this respect is the Petal House by Eric Moss in Los Angeles. Moss, in his wisdom, sought advice from experienced architects and contractors and with a generous budget, was able to produce a vibrant, multi-material, poetic collage, intermarrying the Petal House with the extraordinary citrus tree on the site. Although the project was not generated through concern for materials, but conceived through the channels of creativity that indulge in metaphors for inspiration, it could have never been achieved and it would never possess the quality it demonstrates, if it were not for the rational and constructive use of materials.

In education, instructors could assign design projects, especially in early design studios, that focus on materials. Their properties could be discussed, within the context of climate conditions. One could then go further and offer cross-sections of buildings that were successful in articulation and flashing detailing. One could ask students to attempt formal explorations and programmatic resolutions through the isolated discipline of material exploration. The focus on a series of design problems emphasizing materials will not only provide an understanding of the fundamentals of construction, but will introduce a needed aspect of reality—perhaps the closest one can get to reality in education. The design instructor who may want to use such exercises will have to have a personal and applied knowledge of what he is talking about himself. He must be willing to refresh his memory regarding his own courses in technological subjects and materials, and he will have to do his own research regarding good examples. The student should also be exposed to good examples of inclusivist architects whose work demonstrates the correct use of materials. Herman Hertzberger and Ralph Erskine should be references. The former is perhaps the most successful master today whose architecture is concerned primarily with the appropriate use and expression of materials. His concrete block, concrete structure, and glass block combinations have produced buildings of diverse functions that are not only sound from the construction point of view (Hertzberger has successfully resolved the major details), but are spatially, experientially, and aesthetically appealing. Hertzberger has gone beyond the simple discipline of the use of materials and has elevated architecture to a multilayered affair of synthethically complex considerations.

The same is true for Erskine, who is equally good in low-budget as well as in high-tech buildings. His Bycker Wall in Newcastle upon Tyne is an exemplary complex showing ingenuity in the use of materials; the total texture and "grain" of the project is achieved through the central exploration of fit, textures, compatibility, and artistry in the workmanship. There are certain brick walls in this project with an embroiderylike quality that has not been seen since Byzantine times. Erskine's library at the University of Stockholm is his masterpiece at the other end, the aesthetics of high tech.

The existence of contemporary architects such as these two who are exemplary in their adherence to the basics and the "primordial" while at the same time managing to achieve a balance between "art" and "construction" makes one skeptical about other masters who tend to ignore materials. I believe it would be ideal if the rhetoric of Le Corbusier, who once confessed, "When I held a brick in the palm of my hand, it frightened me. Its weight was petrifying," were to reach the overall synthetic resolution of a Hertzberger or an Erskine, we would have a much better model to aspire to. This was certainly the model favored by the best among the architects of the "critical regionalist" category with which Kenneth Frampton closed the second edition of his critical history of Modern architecture. Tadao Ando, as well as Dimitris and Suzanna Antonakaki, are typical examples of architects who embraced the lessons of the Modern movement (Aalto was Ando's major precedent, while Mies was the respective for Atelier '66) while, by adhering strictly to the materials and the overall circumstances of their regions, created works of evolutionary inclusivity through materials. To these architects we should add Antoine Predock, perhaps the best architect in the United States today, who exemplifies the harmonious blending of Modernism (in the control of the overall composition) and Postmodernism (in the use of metaphor and narrative) inclusive of regional parameters and integrated into a synthesis of the highest material, textural, and conceptual appeal.

Yet for the overall synthesis to happen, before the inclusivist interweaving of the metaphysical and the physical, as Predock has managed to achieve, one should gain a solid foundation in and concrete awareness of the physical; ignorance of the physical properties and the dimensions of materials, the dimensions of bricks and concrete blocks, could prove to be great handicaps in the discipline and the freedom of design. Thus, before

**Fig. 11-11.** *Herman Hertzberger's commercial mall/symphonic hall in Utrecht, Holland.*

one refers to the great masters on materials, one should learn the dimensions of a brick and of a concrete block. And incidentally, Charles Moore, that prolific, exuberant, and ironically so unsuccessful architect in the use of materials, once said to me: "The first thing I want my students to know is the dimensions of a brick." Isn't it worthwhile to try to make a simple cabin of 5 × 5 meters out of simple bricks and concrete lintels and make it right?

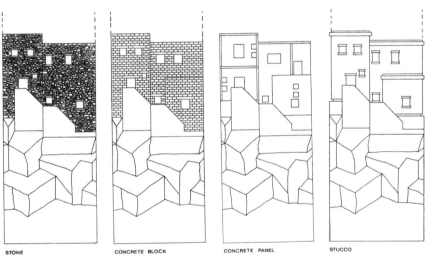

**Fig. 11-12.** *Appropriate use of materials, excellence in crafting, and correct use for the provision of identity in the various functional parts of architecture. Ralph Erskine, detail from Student Union Building, University of Stockholm.*

STONE CONCRETE BLOCK CONCRETE PANEL STUCCO

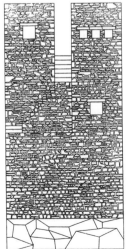
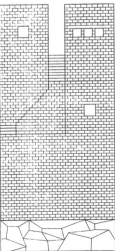
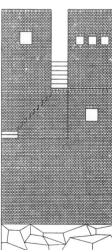

**Fig. 11-13.** *Intentional discipline for the exploration of various materials must become the preoccupation of architects from the very beginning of their studies. Material explorations from the author's second-year design studio (basic design).*

## Summary

Materials are the flesh, bones, and skin of architecture. Their proper use and selection has preoccupied architects through the ages. Their use and relativity of emphasis distinguish architects and architectures. The Modern and Postmodern movements differ with regard to the criterion of materials as "day" and "night," the Postmodern being total failure in this regard. Our discussion focuses on the use of materials by successful architects such as H. H. Richardson, Frank Lloyd Wright, Louis Kahn, and Alvar Aalto. We also discuss architects whose weakness in the use of materials was outweighed by their exceptional artistic talent. The discussion ends with suggestions for the enrichment of design education by extra emphasis on materials through their incorporation into design studio work.

**Fig. 11-14.** *Tools for masonry work, according to J. F. Blondel. (Courtesy Dr. Renaldo Petrini, from his collection of rare books).*

# References

Aalto, Alvar. "Art and Technology." In *Sketches,* ed. Göran Schildt. Cambridge, MA: MIT Press, 1979, p. 127.

Alberti, Leone Battista. "Book II." In *Ten Books on Architecture*. London: Alec Tiranti Publishers, 1977.

Billington, David P. *The Tower and the Bridge*. New York: Basic Books, 1983.

Coulton, J. J. *Ancient Greek Architects at Work*. Ithaca, NY: Cornell University Press, 1977.

Fathy, Hassan. *Architecture for the Poor*. Chicago: University of Chicago Press, 1963.

———. *Natural Energy and Vernacular Architecture*. Chicago: University of Chicago Press, 1986.

Frampton, Kenneth. *Modern Architecture: A Critical History*. London: Thames and Hudson, 1980, 1985.

Gebhard, David. *Schindler*. New York: Viking, 1971, pp. 69, 90, 99, 117.

Moore, Charles. Conversation with the author and a group of students. ACSA Conference, Asilomar, California, March 1982.

Orlandos, Anastasios K. *ta Ylika Domes ton archaeon Ellinon kata tous sygraghis, tas epigraphas ke ta mnemia*. Part A. Athens: Library of the Archaeological Society, no. 37, 1955, 1958.

Rudolph, Paul. "To Enrich Our Architecture." *Journal of Architectural Education,* 13,1 (Spring 1958), p. 12

———. *The Architecture of Paul Rudolph*. London: Thames and Hudson, 1970, p. 218.

Sarnitz, August E. "Proportion and Beauty—the Lovell Beach House by Rudolph Michael Schindler, Newport Beach, 1922–26." *Journal of the Society of Architectural Historians,* 14,4 (1986), p. 383.

Suckle, Abby, ed. *By Their Own Design*. New York: Whitney Library of Design, 1980, pp. 47–66.

Wright, Frank Lloyd. *The Nature of Materials*. New York: Duell Sloan and Pearce, 1942.

———. *The Natural House*. New York: Horizon Press, 1954.

———. *A Testament*. New York: Bramhall House, 1957, p. 231.

# Chapter 12 The Role of Nature in Architectural Creativity

*For the artist, communication with nature remains the most essential condition. The artist is human; himself nature; part of nature within natural space.*

Paul Klee

Nature is everywhere. It affects and can be found in every inquiry of creativity. Humans have imitated nature; they have learned from trees to build adobe; borrowed the visions of wildflowers to create capitals for columns. The waves of the sea gave them motifs for moldings and decorative details. Nature is central in mimesis. Nature is obviously central in the metaphor. Perhaps the greatest metaphor of them all, Nature is a source of many metaphors of varying significance. It lends its characteristics and its ingredients for contemplation of serenity, hardness, and sublimity—the calm of the sea, the sound of the waves, the shape of the land, the mood of the seasons.

Nature is present in the poetry of the poets, and it is certainly present in the poetry of any poetics. It has lent its name ("natural," "naturalistic") to everything that appears "real"; it is the source of emotions, moods, and the aura of space and time. Many of the emotions generated by nature are intangible: the changes of the hour, the passage of the time as seen through the colors of the elements, the mountains and the sky, the filtering of light through the clouds, the moon and the sunset. All of these are intangible situations that make their presence felt via observations or the influence exerted on us by the tangible elements of nature (mountains, sky, sea, valleys, animals, organisms).

Nature is in a sense unclassifiable, for it touches everything, giving the blow of life and shaping the prerequisites for the existence and the growth of things. It is the reason for every transformation, while at the same time it is the hiding place of the obscure, the forest of the unknown. It belongs to the intangible as well as to the tangible. Its "everpresence" and its "unclassifiability" make it necessary that discussions on nature cover all the topics of creativity, be they tangible or intangible. The didactic potential of nature in the visual, spatial, and constructive sense makes it possible, on the other hand, to address it separately, under the umbrella of the tangible channels.

We focus on this aspect here, although it is inevitable that any inquiry into nature will occasionally have to address both issues (tangible and intangible). It is a matter of didactics as well as of value that we have decided to address nature separately and to focus on it through the lens of the tangible. We believe there is extra need for renewed attention to the tangible ingredients of nature, because we hope that the mood, the feelings, and the auras that can be grasped by the inquiring architect will bring about an antidote to the current state of alienation to which both architects and the architect-created environment have been subjected during recent years.

## THE PRIMORDIAL INFLUENCE OF NATURE

Nowhere will one find a stronger inspiration of nature exerted on human artifacts than in ancient Greece. The Greeks revered nature. They celebrated the seasonal changes and integrated them into their lives with annual ceremonies and festivities. There were gods and semi-gods for the forests, the earth, the sky, the water, and fertility. The muses, imaginary ladies of inspiration who gave their collective name to music and to eternal creativity, lived in natural domains in creeks or in the dense forests.

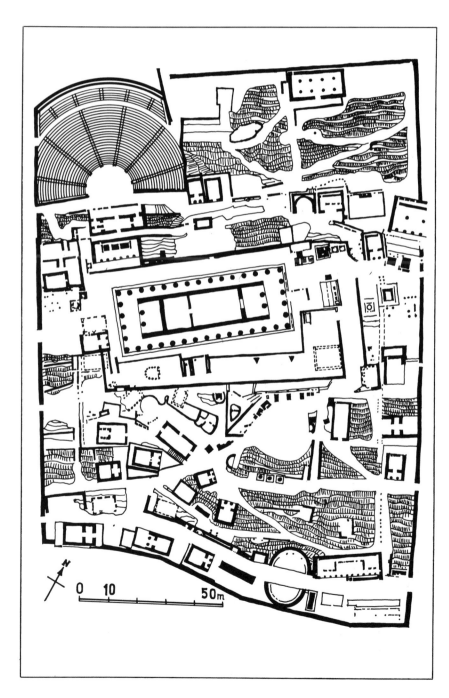

**Fig. 12-1.** *The sanctuary of Delphi: The best example of ancient Greek town planning with the strategy known as the "Attikos tropos of building"; the man-made structural and building system adjusting itself to the dictates of nature, according to the best use of topography, contours, and animal trails.*

Nature could speak to man, and vice versa. Young men and women were transformed into elements of nature. Greek mythology is full of myths of this duality.

> The mountains all were calling and the oak trees answering,
> Oh, woe, woe for Adonis. He is dead.
> And echo cried in answer. Oh, woe, woe for Adonis.
> And for the loves wept for him and all the muses too.
>
> (Edith Hamilton)

Apollo's friend, the young Hyacinthus, dies a tragic death as his god friend hits him by mistake with the discus. The boy dies, and a wildflower is born. The nymphs, the muses, the other wildflowers cry. Narcissus, Hyacinthus, Dimitra, Persephony, Beauty, or evil, the earth, the seasons, life and death, man and nature, exchange roles and are interdependent in ancient Greek mythology. Ovid in his "Metamorphoses" transformed them into a poem (epic). The sea world, the waves and dolphins, octopuses and seashells, gave their geometric forms to the decoration of the palaces of Crete and Mycenae. The wildflowers and the thorns became, according to the myth, Corinthian capitals; the helix, natural form of proportionality and growth of life, offered its image to the ionic capital.

The natural beauty of ancient shrines was exquisite; next to tree-shaded springs, above olive-carpeted valleys, in the shadow of majestic mountains (Delphi), or by rolling rivers (Olympia), looking at the setting sun by the sea (Sounion), and so on. Olympus, the metaphor for the home of the ancient Greek gods, was the country's highest mountain; Parnassus, another mountain of highly articulated beauty, more easily accessible to humans was for the poets the home of their eternal retreat.

Nature had a dual character for the ancients: the "sensual" and the "cosmic." The first aspect included everything they could see, feel, and experience. They built on the surroundings they could see and feel, they enjoyed, played, prayed to their gods and revered every "natural beauty mark" and every unique natural formation. The second was the remote universe, the cosmos; they tried to grasp it with their minds and express it with their art.

The first was a tangible appreciation, and they built by respecting the tangibles of nature; they conserved it, keeping what was best for agriculture and livelihood intact, while building houses along the topographic contours, on gentle hills and mountains, in social, economic, and energy-efficient ways. They followed the natural laws of least energy and waste. They learned from their goats and sheep, and followed their paths to cut roads. And they were very careful with their settlements to observe the holy views, east and west, and to place the important buildings of their holy precincts accordingly. The "Atticos tropos of building" (that is, the way they used to build in the province of Attica, where Athens is located) was a way of respecting the laws of natural building, yet at the same time revering views and the holiness of the Athenian cosmos. The view to the holy Mount of Hymettus to the east was carefully preserved through considerate placement of the Parthenon and the Erechtheion. Doxiades found through his measurements that the "Atticos tropos of building" was a universal design practice dependent on the important poles of access to a complex of public buildings or to a holy compound. Most history of architecture texts open with these particular topics. The most sensual and inclusivist of them all is *The Earth, the Temple and the Gods*, by Vincent Scully.

It was the concern for the intangible side of nature, however, that constituted perhaps the greatest glory of the ancient Greeks; they conceived it sometimes through visible elements, such as the stars, the moon, and the sun; at other times they felt it, perceiving it as pure spirit, often intoxicated by it. Elpenor, one of the comrades of Ulysses, lost his life while under the spell of the beauty of heaven filled with stars. He fell off the flat roof of the adobe where he had lain down to sleep and never returned to his beloved island, eternally captive to the land of Circe, sacrifice to the testimony of the celestial adoration. Such personal instances of the inexplicable gave birth to the sciences and philosophy. The whole civilization started as the human effort to communicate and understand the part of nature that was not readily comprehensible. One could say that the whole process of human development and evolution was the product of a love affair with nature; a continuous effort to communicate with its universals and laws, and through them, to communicate with the other human beings.

## NATURE'S POWER

If one accepts that the essence of aesthetic delight is the ability of a work of art to stimulate similar feelings and emotions in people and to make them communicate with the work of art, and through it with the artist and all the others, then nature is certainly the ultimate communication of aesthetic power.

Cognition of the visible world became possible through the existence of light, through human attention to nature; it subsequently gave birth to the arts. Leonardo Da Vinci believed in and revered nature. Using words similar to Dante's he wrote that "painting is the grandchild of nature." And perceiving nature's eternal endurance, he went as far as to suggest that "painting endures (as it comes directly from nature), while music dies immediately after the performance." This suggests his rather fanatical reverence for nature, something that often characterizes those who speak openly on its behalf in theoretical terms. For Leonardo, art should be consistent with nature. His concept of creativity was one of "inventiveness in maintaining fidelity" with nature.

This attitude was important for it was adopted later in history and generated one of the two major poles of the naturalistic versus abstract inquiry, the dialectic of which brought about the evolution of art. Interrelated with the cognitive power of nature, the power that gives the artist the ability to "see," are the concepts of perception, the eye, and the brain. Both together are the filters of human appreciation of the natural didactics.

There are whole theories suggesting ways to enhance a wholesome development of the two, particularly the mind, and there are suggestions that we perceive differently with the two distinctive sides of the brain. The debate over the eye versus the brain in terms of perceptual supremacy has always preoccupied artists, and frequently affected their work habits, the way they went about studying and sketching nature, the eventual process of their creativity. For Leonardo as well as for Michelangelo, the eye and the brain were more important than the hand, the tool for the ultimate execution of art. Michelangelo wrote: "One paints with the brain, not with the hands," and he held that "the criterion of art consists not in universal principles, but in individual ones, the concrete judgement of the eye." He concluded that only after many years of searching and effort is the artist able to embody his thought in stone.

Scores of artists subscribe to the power of the brain; in fact, much of the art done in the studio, away from the immediacy of the object that might have stimulated a work, is due to the training of the eye to see, and the ability of the brain to store and carry the visions for some time, waiting for the moment of eventual expression. Wassily Kandinsky said in this regard when speaking about his childhood that he could see with his brain. He passed his exams in statistics only when he managed to see and register the whole page in his brain. He applied this technique to his study of nature;

he loved it, wandered around it, saw and stored it in his brain: "Years later I managed to paint a landscape much better through my memory in the studio rather than staring at it in the countryside."

We wholly endorse these attitudes and suggest that one should ask oneself to just "see," and always try to "explain" what one sees. It will be our personal perception and our personal explanation of things that will eventually prepare us to enter into the broader debate at the highest levels of aesthetics. And we must learn to see what interests us as architects the most: the shapes, the formations of the various natural entities, the light and its filtering through the elements, the materials. Both architects and artists of the caliber of the ones cited here have looked into nature as part of their immediate interests. We can safely suggest that the cinematographer is at this time the more inclusivist, since the filtering of light through the atmosphere is perhaps more important than the marble was in the time of Michelangelo.

Michelangelo believed that the form the artist imparts to his material preexists not only in the mind of the artist, but also in the material. The artist is therefore in an ongoing metaphysical struggle with the form and the secrets of nature, a process of disciplined discovery through which he or she tries to find the commonality of the form that was in his or her brain as well as hidden in the material. Perhaps this was all Frank Lloyd Wright was trying to say when he addressed the subject. Only Wright, though an extraordinary lover of nature, never found the extraordinary nature of materials the way Michelangelo did. He occasionally failed, contrary to his claim to understand. Perhaps architects are doomed to failure because of the peculiar nature of the discipline. It has to deal with many materials, as opposed to the one (or the very few) of the sculptor. Yet Wright, as well as the many other architects who sought to learn through nature, learned many of its secrets, the many aspects of the blending of nature with the site, the placement of a building on it, its orientation, the thermal and climatic repercussions, sometimes even the formal aspects of architectonic genesis.

## THE CONCEPT OF THE ROMANTIC

Humans, especially primitive humans, lived wisely with nature. Some great works of art, poetry, literature, and architecture have been the results of our absolute love and longing for a symbiotic relationship with nature. There were times when this love took the form of art movements, as was the case with what is known as the Romantic movements in art and architectural history. These issues must be addressed carefully because the didactics and usefulness of nature as a design channel are dependent on the well-conceived as opposed to what we consider to be the ill-conceived appreciation of the Romantic lens.

The second, the fifteenth, and the nineteenth centuries experienced Romantic attitudes in the arts—literature, poetry, and music, as well as architecture, became fascinated with an artistic sensibility toward the remote, the distant—both in time and place—to the strange and unfamiliar, rather than the current, the relevant, and the familiar. Artists revered the past, the strange, the exotic. And the summary of all the Romantic movements, both in Europe and later in America, was ancient Greece, and the attitude of its people toward nature.

It can be easy to oppose romanticism, especially on the grounds of expediency and currency; it is more difficult, however, to understand that it is probably the dissatisfaction with the compromises and solutions of the contemporary practices that brings people to dissociation from the status quo and its operations and makes them seek answers elsewhere, in earlier times, when things were always "better." One could build out of compassion a very strong argument in favor of all the romantic people of the past and the present if one were to admit the unpleasantness of today and make just a simple suggestion about the beauty of ancient Athens and its contemporary counterpart. Yet one could make an equally strong argument against such attitudes based on unrealistic romantic propositions, the antiquarianism at their base and the danger of submitting the present to cults of the extinct. We realize all this, and yet we prefer to take the attitude that romanticism has been a soothing antidote to the vulgarities of the trivial and the occasional shelter of those who always believed in a better, poetic, and idealized world.

We regard the various Romantic movements as the constant opposition to the trivial, the compromised professional, the strictly constructural and the one-sided. Anyone who believes as I do, as Cassirer and Vico did, that human creativity is largely dependent on the mythical and the primordial, will have to be a Romantic of sorts. Anybody who believes that architecture should satisfy the emotions above all else is a Romantic of sorts. In this sense, all the Romantics and Romantic movements, especially in architecture, performed an extraordinary role in bringing architecture back to poetry, helping to push architecture a step forward and away from the trivial. Nothing is lost in this sense, as the critical resolution of the arguments from either side will eventually bring about new understanding and critical evolution.

Arcadia, one of the real provinces of the Peloponnesus took on mythical dimensions in the minds of Romantics of all centuries, symbolizing the idealized element in nature. Arcadia and Paradise became synonymous, and poets such as Milton attempted to capture it in words. Arcadia, or what became in the longings of mortals "the Arcadian dream," symbolized the ideal natural environment of a happy existence in nature, as opposed to "Pandemonium," the "disorderly and incomprehensible landscape," an environment of claustrophobic building, "inadequate to contain the angels," with inappropriate lighting and a chemical atmosphere.

The most significant theoreticians and aesthetes of the past, especially John Ruskin and Geofrey Scott, aligned themselves with nature and took an active part in the Romantic issue, either as advocates (Ruskin) or opposers (Geofrey Scott). Ruskin is more significant for architects because he saw ways to look at nature from every possible angle—by searching through landscapes, clouds, the mountains, or looking at details such as the petals of flowers, birds, or natural "obscurities" such as the eagle's nest. The sketches Ruskin did are paradigmatic of the discipline every designer should have. Scott became Ruskin's opposition, charging him with diverting attention from the present through a focus on the antiquarian and the remote, what he described as the "fallacy of romanticism." Scott's criticism was only one incident in the ongoing dialectic of the evolution of ideas about the influence and effect of nature on architecture and the arts. The two key poles of this debate have been *nature* on the one hand and the *man-made* on the other.

Although romanticism has come to have rather negative connotations today, especially to those who are committed to reality, it has been an ingredient in the making of almost all the important architects of this century. All of them have been Romantics of sorts in the natural, Arcadian, and didactic sense. The best among them have had a very clear and concrete understanding of the era they lived in. None of the pioneering architects of the twentieth century were Romantics in the antiquarian sense, although all of them were Romantic with regard to the idea of the Arcadian, the Paradisiac.

Ruskin's concept of the formation of the mountain as a series of books next to each other.

 Edges of "books" as if torn by time and dampness.

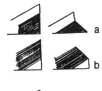

a

b

c

Hypothetical reality of the mountain as a series of layers of formations: (a) soft layers below and solid layers above; (c) soft above and solid below. Resulting configuration in time shown in b and d. More complicated condition in e and f.

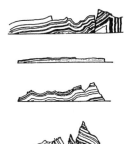

Ruskin's sketches for the geological formation of the mountain.

Rocks. Particles of torn-apart edges of the "book pages," resting gently on intact back of next "book." Often the "book" to be found in distance away. Ruskin made reference in this respect to the valley of Cluse on the way from Geneva to Chamonix.

Influence of the perception of mountains at a distance according to Ruskin.

Point top    Crest    Cliff

Typology of mountains according to Ruskin.

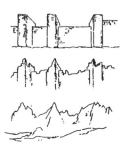

Observations on the perception of the mountain. The false impressions caused to the viewer (because of perspective) and thus the "mystery" of the mountain. Ruskin equates the mountain with the fortified wall in ruinous condition.

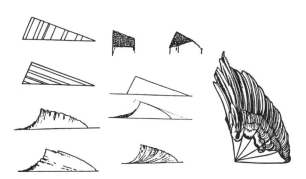

Typologies and graphic explanations regarding the evolution of a "crest." The dynamic quality of the crest, equated to that of the birds' wings.

**Fig. 12-2.** *From John Ruskin's studies on nature. (After T. K. Papatjones, 3° Mati [1–3], Athens, 1937)*

A

B

**Fig. 12–3.** *The poetics of nature and the poetics of man go hand in hand in Mesa Verde, Colorado.* **A.** *Natural landscapes.* **B.** *The Cliff Palace, the cave city of the Anasazi Indians.*

## WELL-CONCEIVED ATTITUDES TOWARD NATURE: FROM THE POETIC SULLIVANESQUE TO AALTO INCLUSIVISM

The examples of Louis Sullivan, Frank Lloyd Wright, Le Corbusier, Eliel Saarinen, Gunnar Asplund, and Alvar Aalto assure us today that to be a Romantic in the non-antiquarian sense does not represent a fallacy or a weakness. On the contrary, it strengthens architecture, enriching it with feeling and sensibility. We will call such appreciation of nature a case of "the well-conceived Romantic." The attitude accompanied by antiquarian formal expressionism we would classify as "ill-conceived." The first sign of a person's "well-conceived" Romantic impulses is to make it a goal to seek exceptional natural surroundings for his or her own habitat. Given the opportunity, all creative people seek living in nature as a means to fruitful inspiration. Architects and poets are primary examples. Those who, for one reason or another, could not achieve a personal habitat in exceptional natural surroundings took to the road to discover the secrets of nature and the uniqueness of the land. Walt Whitman and John Steinbeck are examples.

It is not accidental that most creative artists seek exceptional natural surroundings for their own habitat. Picasso, in a sense, equated nature to his art and to his goal of life. When he bought his estate in southern France, he called his dealer in Paris to inform him that he had purchased a Cezanne. The dealer asked, "Which one?" Picasso replied, "The original." He had just bought a property in a landscape that had been drawn repeatedly by Cézanne.

George Braque, Wassily Kandinsky, Paul Klee, and a great many other painters, as well as architects such as Luis Barragán, Lawrence Halprin, Dimitrios Pikionis, and Miguel Angel Roca, have learned from nature and demonstrated its lessons through their work and writings. Sketching nature and natural formations has been their favorite way of studying; living in close proximity with nature for prolonged periods of time has been equally significant. Sometimes, a special association with nature became a turning point in an artist's life. This was the case with Kandinsky. He had always felt that his personal ability was weaker than anything done by nature. He finally got reassurance and strength from trips to the Russian countryside and prolonged study and observation of its lines and planes, and their intensity and definition.

Yet I believe that nobody sees nature in more dynamic ways than architects, because they are looking at it from so many more points of view. They care about the ways and laws of the construction of the various natural elements, and they care equally about the "whys" of the changes and the dynamism of natural phenomena. The reciprocal relationship of architects with nature has occurred at the intangible as well as the tangible levels. They have reacted to it intangibly

- Through metaphoric inspiration
- Through mental association
- Through ascetic reliance, personal adoration, and even personal "sacrifice"

They have reacted to it tangibly

- Through buildings integrated with the lines of the terrain, in plan as well as in section
- Through "enhancement" of the lines of the terrain by opposing lines to those of the predominant configuration of the site, or by creating tension to neutral and uninspiring natural conditions.
- Through direct man-made opposition to the terrain, in plan or in plan and section

- Through total subordination to nature, leaving the terrain profile intact, while "berming" or "submerging" the building.
- Through unification of the interior with the exterior, either through view and fenestration strategies, or through incorporation of elements of the exterior in the interior
- Through reliance on materials
- Through imitative reaction, as follows: literal interpretation of nature, or substantial/existential interpretation of qualities and laws of nature
- Through an "inclusivist" reaction, where all of the above merge into one interrelated system of reciprocal relationships, incorporating both intangible as well as tangible considerations.

It has been customary to study all of these possibilities through reference to examples from vernacular and regional architecture. We suggest here attention to cases of specific architects of this century, rather than to the vernacular model, because we believe it is more important to study nature through examples of people who work within the highly pragmatic, the urban, and the technological, the framework for the professional involvement of most architects anyhow.

Louis Sullivan will always be among the greatest architects, a great pragmatist and innovator, yet one who saw nature in its most dynamic spiritual and metaphoric way. He "saw" the storm, the various seasons. He let the moods of the epochs affect his spirit. This gave "mood" and "dynamic quality" to his own work. He speaks of the silence, the bare and dusky trees, the melancholy of the day. He makes observations that only ascetics make. He meditates:

> What ineffable, what unspeakable sadness here! What miserere is Nature chanting, here, with numberless voices unbearable to our ears?"

And he equates the depression of winter to the sorrow of art throughout the land. After the sadness of winter, "Spring, Spring's the epoch of Creation!" But Sullivan also needs winter—the oppressive, unpleasant situation of the sad; he will try his soul, he will test his strength and fortify his courage.

In the process of testing, understanding, trying to understand the spirit of nature, Sullivan will become a poet. His own master showed him unhappiness in order to help him become an interpreter, a poet. In return, he will pass his passion onto others: Frank Lloyd Wright, his most important disciple, will continue this tradition, but he will get a lot more involved with the tangible; he will tell his own apprentices "Stop reading books and do nothing but study nature and sketch." He will further suggest them to continually and eternally sketch the forms of the tree. "A man who can sketch from memory the different trees with their characteristics faithfully portrayed will be a good architect!"

It has been well documented that Frank Lloyd Wright revered nature and regarded it as the source of inspiration for his organic architecture. The word "nature" was frequent in his speeches, and two of his major written works, *The Natural House* and *In the Nature of Materials,* revolved around the concepts of natural construction, symbiosis and natural harmony. He complemented nature and referred to it occasionally in order to codify his architecture. This was the case with his prairie style, inspired by the prairie to whose planes he tried to respond through an emphasis on the horizontal.

Unlike Louis Sullivan, whose love for nature resulted in naturalistic decorative motifs on otherwise robust buildings, Frank Lloyd Wright remains to this day the architect par excellence whose buildings have an absolutely symbiotic integration with nature. We can hardly find a stronger

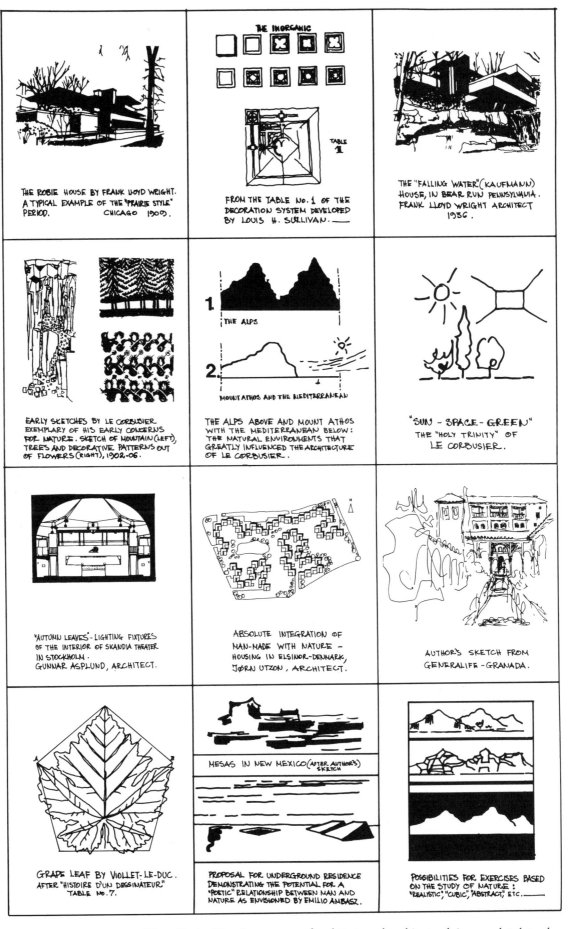

THE ROBIE HOUSE BY FRANK LLOYD WRIGHT. A TYPICAL EXAMPLE OF THE "PRAIRIE STYLE" PERIOD. CHICAGO 1909.

FROM THE TABLE No. 1 OF THE DECORATION SYSTEM DEVELOPED BY LOUIS H. SULLIVAN.

THE "FALLING WATER" (KAUFMANN) HOUSE, IN BEAR RUN PENNSYLVANIA. FRANK LLOYD WRIGHT ARCHITECT 1936.

EARLY SKETCHES BY LE CORBUSIER EXEMPLARY OF HIS EARLY CONCERNS FOR NATURE. SKETCH OF MOUNTAIN (LEFT), TREES AND DECORATIVE PATTERNS OUT OF FLOWERS (RIGHT), 1902-06.

THE ALPS ABOVE AND MOUNT ATHOS WITH THE MEDITERRANEAN BELOW: THE NATURAL ENVIRONMENTS THAT GREATLY INFLUENCED THE ARCHITECTURE OF LE CORBUSIER.

"SUN - SPACE - GREEN" THE "HOLY TRINITY" OF LE CORBUSIER.

"AUTUMN LEAVES" - LIGHTING FIXTURES OF THE INTERIOR OF SKANDIA THEATER IN STOCKHOLM. GUNNAR ASPLUND, ARCHITECT.

ABSOLUTE INTEGRATION OF MAN-MADE WITH NATURE - HOUSING IN ELSINOR-DENMARK, JØRN UTZON, ARCHITECT.

AUTHOR'S SKETCH FROM GENERALIFE - GRANADA.

GRAPE LEAF BY VIOLLET-LE-DUC. AFTER "HISTOIRE D'UN DESSINATEUR" TABLE No. 7.

PROPOSAL FOR UNDERGROUND RESIDENCE DEMONSTRATING THE POTENTIAL FOR A "POETIC" RELATIONSHIP BETWEEN MAN AND NATURE AS ENVISIONED BY EMILIO AMBASZ.

POSSIBILITIES FOR EXERCISES BASED ON THE STUDY OF NATURE: "REALISTIC", "CUBIC", "ABSTRACT", ETC.

**Fig. 12-4.** *Visual summary of architects and architectural issues related to the architecture-nature inquiry.*

case of integration of the man-made with the natural than Wright's house for the Kaufmann family in Bear Run, Pennsylvania. This house, also known as Fallingwater, is interwoven with rocks, vegetation, and the water, and set in a terrain of uncommon natural irregularity and dynamism.

In this instance Wright achieved integration with nature via the strategy of opposition, dynamic cantilevers, straight lines, and abundant use of glass in direct conjunction with natural materials such as stone. He achieved complementarity with nature in several other projects and in several other ways: in Taliesin East, via decisive Cartesian composition, in close juxtaposition with free-standing trees, bushes, and free-flowing elements of the terrain of the estate, outside the boundaries of the "house" proper. In Taliesin West in Arizona, the harmony came through the strategy of consonance; the lines of the buildings follow the lines of the desert, acting as a horizontal summarizing reference for the irregular skyline of the desert hills in the background. The materials—desert stone, wood, and canvas—act as regional catalysts, uniting the building with the place and the "light" of the region. In his Marin County Civic Center, he worked with nature by "subordinating" it: The linear buildings of the complex literally "crawl" over the serene hills of the terrain, elevating the whole into a harmonious combination of the man-made with the natural. He showed the possibility of total integration with nature through absolute submergence via buildings that are berming into the landscape (house for Mr. and Mrs. Herbert Jacobs in Middleton, Wisconsin) or others that were totally underground.

Wright attempted to universalize his love for nature and to transfer his own compassion to the American people. He wanted them to reach a life of natural and technological compatibility. His planning theory (Broadacre City) had nature at its foundation, a fact that made critics charge him with anti-urbanism and agrarian irrelevance. Wright's affinity for nature comes across as an affair of total inclusivity, the "graduate" state of the human-nature interaction, where many possible strategies can coexist in every instance with the possibility for harmonious coexistence in each and every one of them, provided the dominating synthetic spirit derives its power from nature.

Contemporary cultures that exhibit a rather "religious" attitude toward nature are the Japanese and the Scandinavian. The former has affected Frank Lloyd Wright, while the latter is best epitomized by the work of Alvar Aalto. The Mediterranean Basin has stimulated a rather diverse reaction of people toward their environment, and the human-nature equation often appears as a resolution of antithetical and often severe relationships, sometimes with "love-hate" dimensions. We can have a sense of the broad regional relationships between human and nature if we look at the ways through which some of the most important architects of our century regarded nature, and how the mobility afforded by our era and the architects' exposure to various natural surroundings and natural didactics has affected design strategies.

## COMPLEMENTARITY THROUGH ANTITHESIS

A rather peculiar case of architect-nature interaction appeared in the preceding list of tangibles. Antithesis has frequently been considered polemical, and architects who attempted buildings that oppose the silhouette of the terrain have been often considered enemies of nature. Using this generalization, most classical architecture, including the siting of the Parthenon and of other ancient temples, would be anti-natural. We are about to argue that the picturesque or the "appearing natural" are not necessarily natural and that it is indeed possible for a highly tectonic-looking form, a man-made form if you wish, to be more in tune with nature if it follows its laws, if it has internal and structural logic, and if it is the result of a "cosmotheoretical" approach to architecture.

Cubism and the whole Mediterranean attitude has been an affair with the nature of complementation through antithesis. It is the case of the geometric solid placed decisively on the natural terrain. Next to Braque and Picasso, it is Le Corbusier who is more significant for the architect in this respect. Born in natural surroundings of exceptional beauty, he was trained to love nature, to live with his classmates in the mountains of the Ura region, to sketch the trees and flowers and even to make resolutions about building monuments dedicated to nature. Both his father and his teacher at the school of art in La Chaux-de-Fonds were instrumental in guiding his attention and opening his eyes toward nature. The early sketches of leaves and flora inspired some of the decorative motifs of the Villa Fallet, one of the earliest projects of the young Le Corbusier. But we believe that the significance of his early expeditions to the mountains and the nature of Switzerland became apparent much later, when he had seen other lands and become spellbound by the intoxicating effect of the exotic Mediterranean.

We believe that it was the confining feeling of living in the subliminal spell of the Swiss landscape—humans moving in the sharply defined space between mountains—that made the youth seek other, perhaps more "liberating," spatial experiences in other lands. Le Corbusier had known the finite (spatially finite) through Switzerland, and he found the infinite (spatially infinite) in the Mediterranean, in the Greek islands. These exceptional physical environments complemented his palette on nature. Years later, the majestic mass of Mount Athos and Missolongi, subliminally "floating" on the calm of the infinite Mediterranean horizon, were transformed into the mass of the Marseilles block, the project for Algiers, or the government center of Chandigarh. The vast open spaces between the "mountain"-like buildings were playing the role of the calm sea and infinity.

Although others have argued in favor of natural insensitivity, the creation of machine objects and the anti-natural through the evident sharpness of the opposition, I am inclined to suggest that Le Corbusier, on the contrary, attempted the creation of a new state of natural equilibrium, an intermarriage of sorts: The marriage of the two landscapes of the extreme, directly out of the storage of his subconscious, the "finite" of the Swiss Alps and the "infinite" of the Mediterranean. I believe that if I were to speak of Le Corbusier's god, I would have to conclude it was nature. It was that richness he sought, those green and open spaces.

"Sun, Space, Green" became Le Corbusier's pursuit. Homes and cities had to include all three. Poetry was the means through which he sought nature. Le Corbusier's architecture was the product of a searching youth, one who looked for more than what surrounded him upon birth. His reaction to nature was universal, not regional, and so he dealt with it abstractly, often failing, or at least failing in the eyes of those who understand the human-nature interaction only as a symbiotic relationship similar to those achieved by Wright and subsequently Alvar Aalto and the other good regional architects of the world.

## NATURAL INCLUSIVITY AND THE REGIONAL INGREDIENT

There is no doubt that the nature of Scandinavia, its climate and seasonal adversities, played a significant role in the unique affinity of its architects with nature. All three major pioneers, Eliel Saarinen, Gunnar Asplund, and Alvar Aalto, had personal relationships and personal attitudes toward nature covering all aspects of synthetic and creative considerations, so as to be typical of the model of inclusivism.

For Eliel Saarinen, who had no canonical design background, nature provided a major source of learning. Along with his associates, Herman Gesellius and Armas Lindrgren, he learned everything he came to know about materials from nature. Such direct naturalistic learning inspired projects distinguished for their rusticated textures, something that appears to those who do not know as Romantic. Yet such a characterization would be unfair, as these architects created honestly, for the region, whatever they had seen and observed in the region. Theirs was not an academic abstraction, but a direct imitation of nature—Nature as they saw it and Nature as they found it expressed in the Kalevala, the epic poem of Finland. Hvitträsk, Eliel Saarinen's studio/communal residence, is the best example of the possibility for direct learning from nature and natural symbiosis (with terrain, materials and climate). Although Hvitträsk may deceive many as Romantic, no one would think the works of Gunnar Asplund and Alvar Aalto Romantic. Both architects were influenced by nature through immediate observations and a spiritual appreciation. This was coupled with a disposition to accept the technological, an attitude that leaves no doubt as to where they stood with regard to formal imitation and romanticism.

Alvar Aalto considered Gunnar Asplund "the foremost among architects." In a eulogic commentary following Asplund's death and published in the magazine *Arkkitehti* in 1940, he called Asplund's affinity for nature a source of inspiration and a path to creativity. Recollecting a personal experience with Asplund while visiting the latter's Scandia Theater a few days before it was completed, he pointed out Asplund's comment regarding his inspiration for the indigo-colored interior with the yellow light fixtures: "While I was building this I thought of autumn evenings and yellow leaves," said Asplund. It is through reference to Asplund's love and reliance on nature that Aalto eventually states his own conception of the art of architecture as an architecture for "the unknown human." Nature and architecture are inseparable: "the art of architecture continues to have inexhaustible resources and means which flow directly from nature and the inexplicable reactions of human emotions" (Aalto, 1979).

**Fig. 12-5.** *Muraatsalo, Alvar Aalto's masterpiece displaying his attitude toward the man-made and its integration with nature. Both coexist in harmony, keeping their inherent integrities. House-studio: rock on the rock; the sauna is a walk away from the house, immersed in the forest, in an ambience of absolute serenity.*

There is no doubt that Aalto himself had exactly what he had perceived as the great qualities of Gunnar Asplund. And there is no doubt that these two Scandinavian architects represent two key personalities whose work proves inexhaustible possibilities for creativity through the path of nature. Alvar Aalto lived much longer and did many more projects than Asplund to make his own case and to distinguish himself as the major architect from Europe whose creativity largely depended on his love and study of the visual characteristics and secrets of nature. He followed many strategies when dealing with nature, including topographical integration through consonance, integration through the use of materials, strategic incorporation of materials to enhance interior-exterior harmony (Villa Mairea), and even the strategy of natural enhancement, for he believed the building should sometimes become its own landscape (as in the cases of the roof of the Lapia house in Rovaniemi, and the pyramidal roof of the lecture hall/engineering building at the Otaniemi Institute of Technology). Aalto sketched and painted nature constantly, and he had very strong exposure to its temperament through living, fishing, and hunting in the countryside of his native Jyväskylä since early childhood.

He had learned to revere and treat nature as an equal. One cannot survive in the harsh Scandinavian landscape if one does not respect nature. Because of this deep knowledge, Aalto addressed issues of substance (the protection of the joints from natural adversities, the use of the right materials, the use of local materials that fit the regional climate, and so on). He went as far as the use of metaphors from nature (particularly evident in several of his buildings), never resorting to a literal interpretation of the natural, a weakness observed in the efforts of several of his disciples.

## DISCIPLINING THE INTANGIBLE INTO THE NATURALLY TANGIBLE

Reima Pietilä is one of Alvar Aalto's most celebrated disciples. He designed buildings inspired directly by metaphors from nature, and frequently resorted to literal interpretations of natural forms. His earliest such building, the Dipoli student union at the university of Otaniemi-Helsinki, was inspired by the natural metaphor of "the primitive cave," a shelter where the student, a contemporary primitive, searches for knowledge and truth. Pietilä, a "primitive hunter" himself, views creativity as a case of survival; the architect is in search of game in the jungle of ideas. Several of his buildings look like caves, undulating lakes, waving sand dunes, spiraling winds. It is admirable that the brilliant sketches of one of the most complex imaginations of the era have been translated into buildings; but the transformation of natural looking buildings into reality is a costly and unlikely "natural" proposition. For the mere fact that nature uses the law of least energy, whereas one must spend extraordinary amounts of energy to construct the natural-looking, irregular forms of the imagination. Any architectural form, no matter how much it may resemble a form that can be found in nature, or no matter how charming it may be as a statement of architectonic expressionism (as is the case with the plans of the Pietilä buildings that come across as the brushstrokes of an Expressionist painter) is inappropriate and "unnatural" if the laws of nature must be violated for its creation.

The basic laws of nature that are absolutely relevant to architecture are the following:

The law of gravity
The law of least energy
The law of attraction of opposites
The law of habitat (symbiosis, complementability of regional items)

The law of time of life cycle (infancy-growth-reproduction-maturity-
decay, death)

Of course, the human goal has been to defy death; yet "immortality" in
architecture is achieved, we believe, much more easily through the tested
natural strategy of adherence to the laws of nature, rather than by resorting
to a literal interpretation of its forms. The metaphor can take us away from
the pitfall of the literal, as it can claim its ideal through words, without
negating the architectural goal of implementability and the need to build.
So it is appropriate here to stress the superiority of the metaphor as a
creative channel, as opposed to the literal. Architects who looked at nature
through the broadest metaphorical lens, and who made buildings through
straightforward architectural and construction techniques, are on the best
track of the creative channel. Jörn Utzon is a case in point. He has been
very sensitive in his response to the pragmatic circumstantial requirements
of nature in the microscale (making his forms and spatial decisions respond
accordingly), while he has achieved buildings of communal and monumental significance inspired by natural metaphors, but transformed into most
imposing complexes of up-to-the-minute building technology and perfection. Utzon "graduated" from the expressionistic Sydney Opera House to
the highly tectonic Bagsvaerd Church near Copenhagen, where the sky-
inspired metaphor of the interior space has been achieved through the
straightforward means of post and beam construction and industrial
technology.

## TEACHING STRATEGIES

Teaching strategies in the design studio should include the following:

1. The study of and exposure to architects who, like Utzon, Le Corbusier, and Asplund, produce buildings that do not have natural-looking
form, but that logically and through materials are derived from and related
to nature. These precedents are appropriate for what we consider to be the
well-conceived model of imitation of nature. Imitation of nature should
mean understanding and imitating the laws of nature, not its forms.

2. Exhaustive discussion on the prevailing laws that were at work in
the generation of a particular form of nature should play a dominant role
in the creative process when dealing with natural phenomena.

3. The studio should include paradigms of works by Frank Lloyd
Wright and Alvar Aalto that have been totally integrated or that complement nature in subdued, nonopposing ways, even though, in certain instances, their forms may act to extend or complete the image and silhouette
of landscape configuration.

4. Discussions of regionalism, and reference to typical regional architectures, vernacular or contemporary, should be part of the same inquiry.
The core of this discussion should focus on materials and their performance
due to climatic constraints, lighting intensity, and the textural peculiarities
of a region.

5. The fifth category that should be discussed has to do with paradigms
of buildings that are totally "absorbed" by nature, "bermed," or even
buried in their terrain. Works by many energy-concerned architects should
be used, along with the habitats of subterranean animals. The architect
should constantly ask her or himself questions of a psychological nature,
such as: How would I feel if I were to spend my life underground?

## HABITS, TECHNIQUES, AND TOOLS OF TEACHING

The major thrust of the teaching strategy will be devoted to the direct
storage process, and to the direct sketching from nature. Sketches must be

done with time, effort, and discipline. Activities such as backpacking, group expeditions, mountaineering, hiking and sailing, always with sketchbook at hand, are most important. The extraordinary camaraderie that develops among the members of a studio that "adopts" a particular landscape, a mountain, or the coast of an island for the study of nature becomes a lifelong experience; personal observations, accompanied by memories, discussions, and incidents from the experiences of the group give an extraordinary human dimension to the sketches, each one of which acts as a catalyst between the divinity of nature upon sight and the human condition on the earth.

Such dynamics have been known and practiced by some of the best and most sensitive design instructors of all time and, astonishingly enough, of very different design inclinations. Highly sensitive and poetic instructors such as Dimitrios Pikionis, Robert Walters, and the diametrically opposite Mies van der Rohe sought such instructive situations for their design students through the islands of Greece, the mesas of New Mexico, and the valleys of Switzerland. Pikionis tried to make his students unravel the secrets of the microscale, the architectonic detail, the simple but so substantial element of nature, the flowers and the olive trees. Walters asked them to make buildings and cities through observation, sketching, meditation, and transformations of the rock formations of the desert and the mesas of New Mexico and Arizona. Mies would invite them to his Swiss country home and give them specific sites for on-the-spot exercises on the human-nature interaction.

These examples suggest the universality of the spell of nature for diverse people. It is the overall common denominator for all designers who must feel down deep that encountering the secrets of nature brings one into direct contact with the highest creator of them all.

Sketching and drawing are indispensable to any process of teaching through nature. Very important theoreticians and architects of the past, such as Viollet-le-Duc, John Ruskin, and Le Corbusier, occupied themselves with direct drawing from nature and natural formations. John Ruskin is very significant for the student, because his study of natural form covered a wide range, including written analysis of his personal explanations for the reasons and the phenomena that caused certain forms to happen. The formation of the rocks and their typological varieties, the curves of waves and leaves, the wings of birds, and the formation of the clouds kept him exploring. Ruskin has shown a way that can be followed by everyone: to make constant theory about the object under observation,

**Fig. 12-6.** *Kaiha and Heikki Siren: Chapel, Otaniemi University, Finland.*

**Fig. 12-7.** *We have "architecture with nature" only when the decisively man-made is in harmonious coexistence and interaction with the contours of the terrain, the orientation, the winds, the flow of water, and all other natural constraints. "La Luz del Sol" condominium complex, New Mexico. Hildreth Barker, architect.*

always with the goal of transferring the lessons to the man-made artifact or the work of art.

The study of leaves by Ruskin is perhaps more relevant for the architect. He has shown us how this simple detail of nature can be the key to the making of a building or a city. The drawing of a leaf becomes much easier if one observes the stems, the nodes, and the branching arteries than if one were to draw the outline of the leaf's shape. Drawing a leaf can help one conceive a building not as the arbitrary outline of exterior silhouette, but rather as something determined by its organizational structure, the circulation and the movements inside it. The study of a mountain can be equally relevant. Through a variety of depictions, including the naturalistic sketch, the cubic representation (where the various masses are individualized and express the role of individual parts to the whole), or the drafting of negative space, (the sky above the mountain peak and the shadows on its sides), it can reveal the interrelationship of positive and negative and the dependency of a building on its surroundings. One could finally extract details out of the whole, assign them size and function, thus training the eye and stimulating the spirit to the fit between form-function-scale as related to possible structural implications.

Le Corbusier held that nature will not reveal its secrets unless you are willing to take the time to see and study it. Le Corbusier saw in the direct drawing a means of creating. He loathed the camera, "a tool for the idlers who use a machine to do their seeing for them," while he held that "to draw oneself, to trace the lines, handle the volumes, organize the surface . . . all this means first to look and then to observe and finally perhaps to

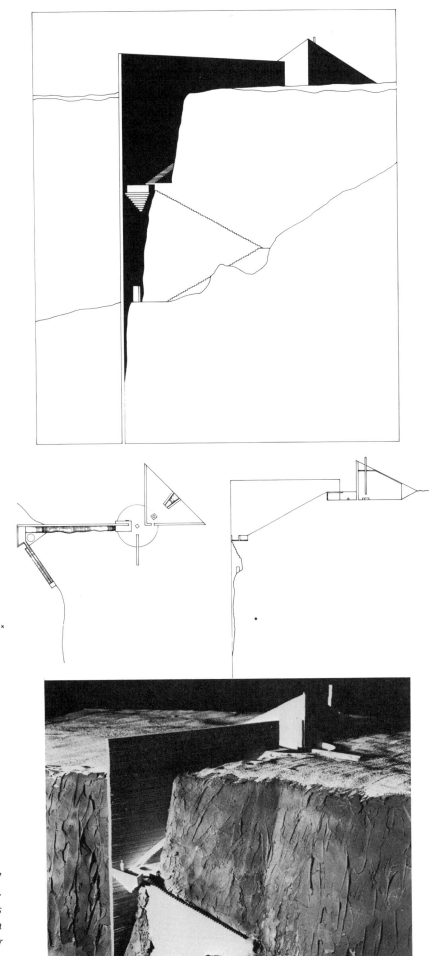

**Fig. 12-8.** *Project "X Marks the Spot" by Kramer Woodard. From the independent study projects of instructor Nicholas Markovich based on the study of nature in New Mexico. (Photo courtesy Kramer Woodard)*

discover . . . and it is then that inspiration may come." For Le Corbusier, to draw on one's own was the real and truthful education, the way out of the fallacies and the perpetuation of myths in textbooks.

The candid and honest student, after much exposure and disciplined effort to draw and "see" nature from as many angles as possible, will probably conclude that not everything thus derived can be constructed, that it might be extremely difficult and uneconomic to attempt to structure such forms, and that one ought to adhere to the laws of nature rather than defy them. It is the structural and construction impossibility which handicaps most of the literal derivations from nature that finally brings discipline into the process and prudence into the final decision.

The route to creativity through direct observation of nature, even imitative abstraction and exaggeration of scale, can be exceedingly rewarding. The instructor should attempt at least one comprehensive design exercise (including going and living for some time with the studio group on the natural site) to explore its possibilities.

## Summary

Nature influences many channels of architectural creativity. It is ever-present and unclassifiable, powerful inspirationally and as a tool. Its presence is obvious in metaphor, in mimesis, in transformation, in materials. People and architects have revered and studied it since ancient times, sometimes in well-conceived ways, other times not. This chapter addresses nature in light of the concepts of "Romantic," "pragmatic," "tangible," "intangible," and through broad reference to the strategies of "dealing with nature" used by architects such as Louis Sullivan, Frank Lloyd Wright, Le Corbusier, Eliel Saarinen, Gunnar Asplund, Alvar Aalto, Reima Pietilä, and Jörn Utzon. The focus is on the tangible and imitative didactics of nature. The stress is on the need to sketch from nature, to acquire the habit of experiencing varying natural surroundings and attempting design exercises with nature as the focus.

## References

Aalto, Alvar. "E. G. Asplund in Memoriam." In *Sketches,* ed. Göran Schildt. Cambridge, MA: MIT Press, 1979, pp. 66, 67.

Christ-Janer, Albert. *Eliel Saarinen.* Chicago: University of Chicago Press, 1948, p. 9.

Crawford, John Martin. *The Kalevala: The Epic of Finland.* New York: Columbian Publishing Company, 1881.

Duncan, David Douglas. *Goodbye Picasso.* New York: Grosset and Dunlap, 1974.

Halprin, Lawrence. *Notebooks, 1959–1971.* Cambridge, MA: MIT Press, 1972.

Hamilton, Edith. *Mythology: Timeless Tales of Gods and Heroes.* New York: Mentor, 1910, p. 91.

Kandinsky, Wassily. *Anadrome 1891–1913, Syntome Autobiographia* (Flashback 1891–1913, sort autobiography). Athens, 1988.

Klee, Paul. *Pedagogical Sketchbook.* New York: Praeger, 1969, p. 1.

Le Corbusier. *Towards a New Architecture.* New York: Praeger, 1960, pp. 32, 36, 37.

McClung, William Alexander. "The Architectonics of Paradise Lost." *VIA 8, Journal of the Graduate School of Fine Arts, University of Pennsylvania.* Rizzoli, 1988, pp. 34, 39.

Malraux, André. *The Voices of Silence.* St. Albans, Eng.: Paladin, 1974, pp. 85, 636.

Morris-Smith, Nancy K. "Letters, 1903–1906, by Charles E. Whiter, Jr., from the Studio of Frank Lloyd Wright." *Journal of Architectural Education,* 25,4 (Fall 1971), p. 104.

Pikionis, Dimitrios. *Afieroma tou syllogou architektonon ste mneme tou architek-tonos-Kathegetou Demetriou Pikioni, Akademaikou* (In memorium of the architect Professor Dimitrios Pikionis-Academecian, by the Greek Society of Architects). Athens, 1968.

Rugg, Harold. *Imagination.* New York: Harper & Row, 1963, p. 11.

Ruskin, John. *Modern Painters,* Vol. I to Vol. VI. Editions of various volumes by various publishers from 1907 to 1935. See also the Pocket Ruskin series. London: Allen & Unwin, 1925.

Scott, Geoffrey. *The Architecture of Humanism.* New York: Norton, 1974, pp. 43, 60–78.

Scully, Vincent. *Louis I. Kahn.* New York: Braziller, 1962.

———. *The Earth, the Temple and the Gods.* New Haven, CT: Yale University Press, 1979.

Sullivan, Louis H. *Kindergarten Chats and Other Writings.* New York: Wittenborn, 1947, pp. 155, 158, 174.

Tatarkiewicz, Wladyslaw. *History of Aesthetics.* Warsaw: Mouton, PWN-Polish Scientific Publishers. Vol. I, 1970; Vol. II, 1970; Vol. III, 1974.

Travlos, Ioannis. "Poledomike exelixis ton Athenon (City Planning Evolution of Athens)." Ph.D. dissertation, Athens, 1955.

Von Moos, Stanislaus. "Le Corbusier as Painter." In *Oppositions 19/20,* Winter–Spring 1980, pp. 4, 5, 6, 7, 24, 308. Cambridge, MA: MIT Press.

Wingler, Hans Maria. *The Bauhaus.* Cambridge, MA: MIT Press, 1969, p. 174.

# Chapter 13 Creativity through Association with Other Arts and Artists

It is a most difficult task to rid oneself of the usual mental blocks and preconceptions regarding generally accepted ideas. The word "skyscraper" may evoke the image of the Empire State Building in New York, while "office building" and "ancient temple" may evoke images of glass boxes (New York's Seagram Building) and the Parthenon of Athens. If one already has strong preconceptions regarding a certain ideal structure or approach, the problem is compounded. Emilio Ambasz, an original, poetic, and very disciplined creator himself, has suggested: "Every architect has an ideal house in mind when a client walks into his office." Ambasz does not question the validity or the possible problems with this attitude; on the contrary, he endorses it by suggesting: "The client is going to get the coat whether it fits him or not. If it doesn't fit him very well, then a couple of pins or a couple of stitches here and there will correct it."

But such an attitude, highly individualistic and frequently idosyncratic, may be dangerous in the hands of a novice who may not yet have a strong grasp of what it means to produce really personal and original work. Holding tight to preconceptions and early convictions may eventually produce tailors (and there is nothing wrong with good tailors) rather than architects (but it is bad to find a "tailor" when you are looking for an architect).

Architectural projects, student or professional, face the great risk of becoming encumbered by preconceptions in the mind of the creator from past experience, history, and imitation of admired models. Many original creators seeking to liberate themselves from the handicaps of creative mental blocks even go to the point of an intentional break with what is conventionally accepted, at the risk of becoming totally incomprehensible. One typical case in the 1980s was Peter Eisenman.

Original creativity can be greatly enhanced through efforts to work in other creative arts, such as painting, sculpture, photography, set design, dance, theater, movie making, and most important of all, music. All artists need this, be they architects or not; and many significant innovators in art during this century did this cross-fertilization on their own. The musician Edgar Varèse, the poet Jean Cocteau, the architects Frederick Kiesler and certainly Le Corbusier are among the more notable examples. In the 1920s, the Bauhaus institutionalized this process for its students. The entire curriculum was based on the simultaneous involvement of its students in most, or in as many as possible, of the other creative arts. The roles of the painters Klee and Kandinsky, Johannes Itten, László Moholy Nagy, Oskar Schelmer, and Joseph Albers were perhaps more important that those of Mies and Gropius, as far as the creative process was concerned. The music and the theatrical events at the Taliesin were as important for the development of students' creativity as watching Frank Lloyd Wright at work.

## PERSONAL INVOLVEMENT WITH OTHER ARTS

Simultaneous involvement with arts that use other media helps create a distance between the constraints of the real world and the frame of mind in which one should operate if one is to become creative and produce unique, meaningful work. This involvement with other arts should be in an "amateur" way, a way in which the architect does not feel obliged to produce professional-quality results. This kind of involvement helps the mind rest, while it subconsciously sharpens it and brings about the relaxed concentration that is a prerequisite for an "idea" to be born. So it is not surprising that great architects such as Le Corbusier and Alvar Aalto also distinguished themselves as painters, although painting was not the focus of their professional endeavors. The same is true for many other creative architects. Feeling unobligated to the other art, but equipped with the technical skills and an eye for painting, they offered a good deal to painting, which paid them back with relaxation that subsequently resulted in successful creative activity in their own discipline. So to use leisure time—that is, unobligated time—to peripheral artistic activities is of extraordinary value to the architect.

## SOME ACTUAL CASES OF CROSS-FERTILIZATION

There is no doubt that a general involvement with other fine arts can be stimulating. But it is possible to utilize the arts and the artists in a more immediate way, on a project-by-project basis, for the sole purpose of faster and better results in liberating an architect from predictability and preconception.

One strategy to creativity from the very beginning pairs architects with artists, be they painters, sculptors, or poets. It has proved most successful. Taller de Arquitetura initiated this strategy by including among its members people of diverse interests and artistic backgrounds, notably architects and poets. Juan Goytisolo, considered by some as the most important contemporary poet of Spain, has been an indispensable member of the team, playing devil's advocate and asking questions that trained architects may never ask. The Granbrook Academy of Design, a unique school with a one-person faculty architecture program, founded by Eliel Saarinen, has a curriculum that seeks to develop creativity through simultaneous and rigorous involvement with other arts and with philosophical and aesthetic thinking. The occasional directors of the program were people whose creative personality had developed as a result of multiple involvement in such arts and thinking (Daniel Libeskind, mathematics, architecture, painting, music; Dan Hoffmann, architecture, poetry, philosophy). Many prominent architects of our day have sought to see their problems from other perspectives in the literature of art. Giorgio De Chirico's belief, "What shall I love unless it be the enigma?" (Pikionis, 1968) has prompted many architects to look at creative results as if they were the solutions to incomprehensible enigmas.

Practicing architects are generally more advanced in this respect than students, and the best among them seek the company, the intellectual and professional collaboration of other artists. Schools cannot catch up in this respect with the profession; the teaching of architecture has spread geographically away from artistic centers like Paris and New York. Further, most schools in the United States are preoccupied with following fashions or trends rather than creating them. It would be of great creative significance to run an architectural studio in which the participating students would be architects and poets, architects and painters, or architects and musicians, and where both would be part of the brainstorming team during the conceptual stages of a design.

This involvement should not be confused with the inclusion of art in the built environment, which is another and very fundamental issue and which, at least in the United States, has been substantially confronted. The role of the artist in the case under discussion should be one of the challenger, of the layperson (as far as the discipline goes), but one who speaks a similar language and who has similar creative goals.

In cases where architects have collaborated with artists as their clients, the results have been extraordinary. Music composer Harry Nilsson's house done by architect Eugene Kupper in California is an excellent example. Nilsson, who knew instinctively what he wanted, suggested to his architect that he produce a house like the hut Nilsson's child had drawn on a piece of paper and which he had been using as the trademark for his record company. Kupper managed to create an extraordinary interpretation of this primordial archetype. Another example is the Spear house in Miami, a collaboration between architects and a writer (the mother of Laurinda Spear). It is a unique statement of what one might call a "writer's paradise."

Projects that go beyond predictable triviality—that is, that go beyond what most people understand as "real," have their origins in the surreal. They bring to the surface what has never surfaced before. Other arts are not "real" as far as one's own discipline and livelihood are concerned. And this is why close involvement with them will almost certainly prove beneficial. The Greek architect Dimitrios Pikionis, for example, used to take country walks and paint the landscape and the olive trees of his favorite sites in Attica. One day, as he was searching for a spot to place his easel, he saw in the middle of the countryside a musician playing violincello. He did not move but remained on the spot, fascinated by the vision. He did not paint that day, but returned home ready to continue work on his own architectural projects, refreshed and restored by the experience. Incentive toward creativity through observation of other artists at work is another great benefit of association with creative people.

## THE SOCIABILITY TEST

One way to test an architect's creativity would be to prepare a list of the people he or she associates with most frequently, to see who the best friends are, and who are occasionally included on the invitation list for parties. Sociability is considered a personality trait of creative people. Yet it is the type and composition of the sociability network that is important for creative purposes.

Creative architects have not ranked high in sociability, something that has also been found to be true for many other creative professionals. One often hears about artists' colonies, "closed circles," and so on. Many architects tend to cluster in such "ghettoes" with other architects or their close associates. Their parties and public activities, often reported in popular magazines, are not necessarily the social framework that will enhance honest cross-fertilization among the arts. "Intellectual," "artistic," or "elite" ghettoes are usually greenhouses for the growth of a shallow intellectual infrastructure, the exclusion of critical challenge, the alienation of the members of the circle from the rest of the population, and in the worst cases, the development of "cults."

One must associate with every creative person, from all levels of society. Pikionis gave us an example in this respect as well; he used to take his students to the local carpenter's workshop, to the local shipyard, to the local marble carver. They had drinks and discussions with them in the artisan's familiar surroundings first. Then Pikionis would invite them to the university to talk about their art and skills, thus breaking the walls of the ivory tower, that other mental handicap of intellectual and artistic cross-fertilization, often perpetuated by the closed doors of academia. Individual creative architects must seek such associations constantly, on their own. Le Corbusier almost missed his chance to address the group at the CIAM meeting in Athens in 1933 because he had talks with a local shipbuilder in Piraeus about the way he applied colors on the boats, and with a baker in Plaka who was asked to explain his particular method of making bread. It was the local cook at a countryside restaurant in Palaeochora-Aegina, who proved to be my best challenger and art critic when, with a group of classmates, I was struggling to make copies of the frescoes that adorned the walls of the small Byzantine churches of the island, to complete the requirements for an art history course.

Creativity knows no titles or social distinctions. It resides in the heart of every creative person—all, that is, who are in love with what they are doing, who are wholly devoted to it, who see it as a vocation, be it a good meal, weaving blankets, or making music. The really creative architect, the one who wants to reach beyond the narrow confines of being a "professional" (which often has the negative connotations of mediocrity and compromise), should work hard to escape the chains of snobbery and elitism. He or she should try to develop an honest network of associations with creative people of all kinds, people who are "artists of life and of their art," no matter what this art or vocation may be; only through them will the architect manage eventually to become truly a member of society, a better person and a more creative architect.

The design teacher should know this and keep the lines open to the most creative and the best among fine arts colleagues as well as among the creative people of the community. He or she should invite them to the studio as frequently as possible and let them talk to students. The design studio can become the laboratory for well-conceived architect-artist-artisan socialization, with at least one semester devoted to teaming the teacher-architect with invited colleagues and social friends as critics for the student group. It is obvious that this is extremely difficult to coordinate, but it can be an extraordinary experience for the students who may be lucky enough to participate.

Organized efforts have already been made by Gyorgy Kepes at MIT. Over the years he has brought together a good many artists from the liberal arts who created collaboratively and who produced experimental projects. The series of books published by Kepes are basic references for the instructor who seeks precedents for a discussion of aspects of creativity, perception, and imagination through the perspective of a variety of creative artists.

## CROSS-FERTILIZATION INCLUSIVITY THROUGH TIME

In the Renaissance, the architect was in most instances a painter, a sculptor, an engineer, and an inventor. Michelangelo and Leonardo Da Vinci were the most prominent examples. The advent of modern times brought about specialization and the separation of disciplines. Yet architecture, as if because of the nature of its art, could not exist in isolation. The best architects of the twentieth century felt the need for association with other arts and artists, sometimes in the most direct and collaborative ways. In terms of actual innovative architectural practice, we could find a score of significant examples, some of them legendary. Le Corbusier might never have formulated his ideas were it not for Braque and Picasso, who exerted enormous influence on the architect, both formally as well as in life style. Nor would he have gained an understanding of cubism were it not for his association and friendship with the painter Amadeus Ozenfant. One could argue that we would never have had the Barcelona Pavilion and the whole compositional vocabulary of Mies van der Rohe if we had not had the paintings of Piet Mondrian (Broadway series, Boogie Woogie series) and his association with the Bauhaus. Eliel Saarinen owed similar debts to his association with the painters and musicians of Finland with whom he shared experiences in art in a communal spirit, both in Finland and later in America. One could perhaps say the same for the effect the poet Carl Sandburg had on his cousin, Frank Lloyd Wright, and the indisputable effect exerted by the Mexican painter Jesus Reyes, who inspired Luis Barragán to search for his roots, the masses, the wall, the color, and the earth of Mexican architecture.

In the late sixties Robert Slutzky, a painter and theoretician on perception, exerted a collaborative influence on Colin Rowe, whose theories influenced a great number of students and architects in the United States and abroad. In more recent times it was Claes Oldenburg whose art and ideas on the environment, along with his personal association with Robert Venturi, produced the initial stimulation for the break from the Modern movement and the development of Venturi as the pioneer, theoretician, and creator of original American architecture (Pop, Las Vegas, etc.). It was the same artist, Oldenburg, who in the mid-eighties exerted a similarly extraordinary influence on Frank Gehry and became his collaborator in an effort to attempt a further step in the refinement of Postmodernism through the Dr. Coltello project in Venice.

Gehry, following his association with Oldenburg, spoke of "the street" again, just as Venturi had done in the mid-sixties; Claes Oldenburg was the "common denominator" for both architects as he was the first one to see the "poetry" of the street and to have produced works on the theme of streets and the urban environment. Frank Gehry has said that with his recent work, he has been trying to make us "think about what we think." Perhaps that could not have happened were it not for the painter having exerted an influence on the shaping and the thinking of the architect.

The cross-fertilization effect of the arts has been a fact throughout history. Yet despite the very tangible and easy to comprehend affinity between the visual arts, such as painting, sculpture, and architecture, there is an even stronger affinity between the arts of "time," dance and music, and architecture. Despite the fact that hardly any architects are dancers and that there are extremely few architects who are musicians, there is a need for a deeper focus on the concepts of these arts because the issue of discipline in architecture is paramount and because the aspect of harmony is equally significant. This focus at this time in history will perhaps help eliminate some recent confusions and help clarify anxieties and misconceptions regarding the discipline of architecture, its relationship to the past, and its proper place in today's world.

Of the two, music is considered to be more fundamental for the purposes of architectural creativity (and instruction), yet we should look briefly through the "gate" of dance. It will help clarify concepts such as the classical and the contemporary, while it will also prepare us for entry into the realm of music.

**Fig. 13-1.** *Multidirectional fire exit of the Loyola Law School in Los Angeles by Frank Gehry, whose architectural work in the 1980s challenged preconceived notions of composition, use of materials, and geometry, and who has been greatly influenced by his associative collaboration with the artist Claes Oldenburg.*

## ON DANCE AND ARCHITECTURE

The attention of architects to dance has not been as direct as that of painters and musicians; studies on dance from a spatial and architectural standpoint have been extremely rare. Yet there have been studies on the dance formations of the primitive peoples and on square dance, medieval dances, and Renaissance patterns.

Curt Sachs, one of the world's noted authorities on ethnomusicology and the history of the dance, in an article written for an ethnography exhibit at the Trocadero in Paris in the 1930s, provided a diagram depicting in abstract form the various dance formations that bear close resemblance to architectural plans and architectural patterns and forms. According to Sachs, it was dance that gave birth to the arts, because dance exists both in time and in space; although his comments may sound outdated today, as we are beyond the concepts of separation of the arts on the time-space issue (we believe today that all the arts have a time-space dimension; some emphasize the one and others the other), we are still attracted by his argument on the communication dynamics of the various time-experience situations depicted in his diagrams. The movements of a dance suggest characteristics and the temperament of the people, while the ultimate conclusion of the writer, based on purely ethnographic evidence, proves the overlapping of the two basic shapes of choreography: the cyclical and the linear. Sachs argues that "the whole dialectic between circle and straight line is to be found again in the two basic shapes of human habitation—the round hut and the hut of right angles—the megaron. Anthropological evidence suggests that the whole of humankind could be classified by the choreographic diagram of their primordial dances: "There are no dances of linear choreography in countries that do not know the hut with the right angles." Sachs' essay on ritualistic dance is a treasure for anyone who might want a taste of the relationship between attitudes for expression through movement and his spatial conceptions.

Perhaps the best thoughts thus far on the relationship between architecture and dance have been expressed by the late Frederick Kiesler, the architect perhaps most appreciated by musicians and dancers as well as by artists of the avant-garde from the 1930s until his death. In the section called "Dance Script" of his inspiring book *Inside the Endless House*, a work published after his unexpected death in the 1960s, Kiesler worked through the relationships among the time-experiential arts and addressed the differences between the various types of spaces, the "pictorial space" addressed by painting and "time space" addressed by dance. In his words, this difference lies in the fact that "in painting, space is entirely illusionary, and in the dance it's real." He suggests it is only through dance that we manage to experience the fluidity and the endlessness of space, the space that has become "coagulated into solid form," what was initially associated with the meaning of the outer cosmos. The space created by dance " . . . expands from the nucleus of an idea to such vast dimensions that you can 'live with it.' " Kiesler finds in dance a unique art form that involves the elements of movement, time, pictorial and thematic representation, and the fundamental element of life, a metaphoric "dance" from point A to point B.

We can push the arguments of Sachs and Kiesler further; we can try to explain architectural concepts and attitudes as applied to the twentieth century, which has added to the straight line and the circle of earlier peoples and civilizations the possibility of another "infinite" group of choreographic formations. This new third element may be any combination of the first two, while the final result of the choreography (or the work of art) will depend on the relationship of these three types and the discipline of the artist. With regard to the attitudes suggested by Kiesler, we will use the concepts of individuality, freedom, democracy, and collective good, and see how various forms of dance can provide lessons for the architect for his own encounters with spatial and life issues such as these.

**Fig. 13-2.** *The basic forms of team dancing (square dancing) are also symbolic: (1) circle: mystical society; (2) criss-crossing; (3) frontal; (4) chain; (5) fence, symbol of the moon; (6) bridge, symbol of rebirth; (7) leading to form; (8) double circle, symbol of the moon. (After Curt Sachs in 3° Mati, Athens, 1937)*

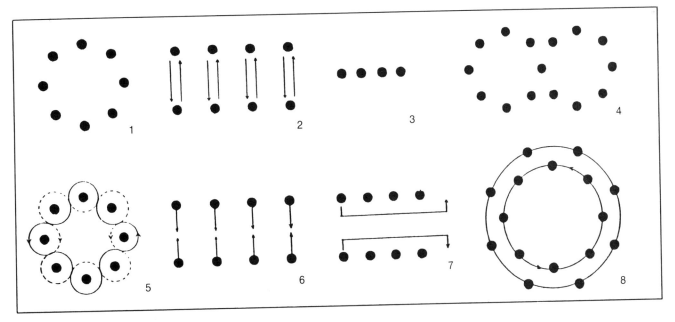

## Classical and Contemporary

In order to understand where we are today, we should try to conceive of our civilization through the lens of classical versus modern choreography, or ballet and modern dance. Let us assume that we look at a dance performance from above and that we freeze with a camera the sequence of the movement formations. In the case of classical ballet, we come out with a series of photographs depicting straight lines, alone or in groups, circles, grids, perhaps other curves, geometrical rotations. We'll have a series of pictures that show geometric patterns similar to snowflakes or other well-known molecular organisms. Only the soloists will perform the "spirals" and move in more complicated orbits. If we go back to take another set of pictures of the same classical choreography (say Swan Lake), we will end up with an almost identical set of patterns. The dancers, the corps de ballet and the soloists, will move along the same paths, forming the same circles and lines the choreographer designed. There is consistency and predictability in classical ballet. The differences, if any, will be subtle—differences of microscale, not concept. They can be observed through detailed photography that focuses on the particular interpretation of the dancers, their muscles and facial expressions. Such differences will depend on the personality, the training, and the talent of individual dancers.

Yet classical ballet is above all a time-space expression of a predictable whole and a subordination of the individual to a predetermined whole; the score of the particular choreography. It requires extraordinary discipline—total subordination of the individual to the will of the choreographer. The same is found in folk dance—in this case the discipline of the individual performers is an indication of abiding by communal covenants: to dance the same way as generations of members of the particular community had done. Further evidence of discipline is the custom of folk dancers to unpack from family trunks the costumes of their ancestors. Folk dancing is a time-space expressive ritual of a group totally tied to the past.

Modern dance is the time-space expressive experience of the free individual living in a group. It is an expression of freedom, individuality, and improvisation according to each individual's understanding of the broad context of the rules (the play), the loosely yet clearly established score, and the choreographic framework as conceived by the modern choreographer. The score may suggest broad constraints, such as that the dancers should move for a particular period of time to a particular part of the stage, while a forklift truck crosses another part of the stage; what they will do, how they will move their hands and bodies, will depend on them, on their feelings and reactions upon viewing a colleague's body lifted by a forklift truck and slowly removed from the stage into the reality of the street through the backstage service door. The score might suggest other broad movements and assign tasks to the dancers, always telling them broadly what is expected from them, yet leaving it up to them to interpret the details. Modern choreography is usually a participatory affair, the score being frequently discussed with the dancers or other people related to the performance. The choreography is a generally accepted covenant for the participation and the expression of the many; all those who have contributed to the formation and who have accepted the particular covenants, the "rules of the game," or the communal ritual. Gone is the role of the choreographer as dictator, while the dancers are free to perform movements more fitting to the physical structure of the body, as opposed to the absolutely prescribed and unnatural movements that are expected of the dancer of classical ballet.

## Postmodern Inclusivity and Modern Choreography

This discussion is intended to stress the element of broad covenants, and individual freedom, along with the element of training along the lines of nature that represent the acceptable attitude in modern dance; these two conditions are equally applicable to attitudes regarding architecture and urban design. An analysis of either of the two, classical or modern choreography, and attendance at representative performances and application of the lessons in design exercises may leave a lasting effect. Lawrence Halprin, influenced by his wife, Anna Halprin, a modern dancer, helped by his own natural affinity to nature, had developed thus far the best case of "scoring" and the applicability of modern dance choreography to architecture. His Ghirardelli Square complex in San Francisco was the first and perhaps among the most successful (to date) evidences of the possibility. The example of the mid-eighties was Horton Plaza in San Diego. In my judgment, this equally successful example of architecture as modern choreography made it possible to synthesize conceptions of individual expression from the most historicist twentieth-century derivative to pop, punk, and the "sensually stimulating" (Claudia's bakery, Tom Grondona). In Horton Plaza, there is the larger connector of a straight line gently opposed by two gentle curves, the strategically distributed parking garages, respectfully retained existing buildings of merit and a financially imaginative strategy for a mixture of compatible and complementary uses, all geared to pleasing the senses, to the sensual satisfaction of users. Jon Jerde, the architect of the total work, can be thought of as the "choreographer" of this piece of "modern architectural dance." Architects such as Tom Grondona, who were called to do individual parts of the whole, can be perceived as the "modern architectural dancers."

**Fig. 13-3.** *Detail from Horton Plaza in San Diego, John Jerde, architect/graphic designer with entrance to Claudia's Bakery. Tom Grondona, architect-sculptor.*

This project is further evidence of the power of cross-fertilization of the arts when they are used appropriately for creative architecture. Both Jerde and Grondona had training and experience in more than the discipline of architecture. Jerde was a graphic designer and artist of "urban rituals" and ceremonial events, his best-known project being the organization of the Los Angeles Olympics in 1984, while Tom Grondona was a sculptor by training, turned into an architect through the influence of and association with his contractor father.

## The Ingredient of Discipline

Constant training and devoted application are necessary for both architects and dancers. One cannot find better paradigms among the various artists than dancers, both classical and modern. As Frederick Kiesler has observed, ". . . the artists most devoted to their profession are not the architects, not the writers, but the dancers." We certainly share the admiration of Kiesler; only when one is "lost" in his art, spiritually as well as physically, through hard work and constant application, can one eventually find the secrets of the art and gain the title of artist, dancer, or architect. The biographies of devoted choreographers and dancers (George Petipa, Martha Graham, Alwin Nikolais, George Ballanchine, Pavlova, Ulanova, Nijinsky, Margot Fontanne, Rudolf Nureyev, and others) will be equally stimulating for anyone who wants to earn a place in architecture as will the study of biographies of certain architects, a topic we examine in detail later.

## MUSIC AND ARCHITECTURE

Goethe once said: "A distinguished philosopher spoke of architecture as frozen music, and his assertion caused many to shake their heads. We believe this really beautiful idea could not be better reintroduced than by calling architecture silent music." The relationship between architecture and music has been referred to repeatedly, and various students of both arts have occasionally dwelled on the point in depth, addressing common grounds, similarities, characteristics, even their occasional identities. Such instances begin during classical Greek times; Pythagoras and Plato, among the first to have formulated theories on beauty, who concerned themselves with concepts regarding the creation of the universe, were also the first to lay the foundations as well as to develop systems of proof interweaving mathematics, geometry, music, and eventually architecture.

Music was a handy reference for Renaissance theoreticians of architecture; they used to refer to it in order to make clear their architectural concepts. Alberti used the example of music to make his point regarding the achievement of beauty through variety. The architect should join and bring together "in a regular manner, things different, but proportional to each other; . . . similarly as happens with music, . . . when the bass answers the treble, and the tenor agrees with both, then arises from that variety of sounds an harmonious and wonderful union of proportions which delights and enchants our senses."

Yet the eternal affinities of music and architecture have been deemphasized recently, to the point where many people (architects included), absorbed by the recent environment of sound, visual, and value pollution, have come to possess only certain vague notions of the relationship, let alone have any creative use for the relationship between music and architecture and the use of the former for the benefit of the latter.

## Cross-Fertilization through Music

Until very recently one could point to comments in popular treatises on aesthetics, or to introductory books on music or architecture, for assurances that both arts share similarities, such as tone, beat, proportion, and rhythm. There have been several well-known works in the popular literature of architecture (Steen Eiler Rasmussen and his *Experiencing Architecture*) that addressed architecture in terms of music and pointed out the similarity of their compositional concepts. More sophisticated studies on the subject were scarce, and most of the architectural public remained unaware of the connection. The attitude that prevailed was one of a mystique; some held that if you knew music, or performed on an instrument, you would become a better architect. This public perception was reinforced by the example of several prominent architects, such as Frank Lloyd Wright and Eliel Saarinen; both played the piano and both had integrated musical activities into the educational processes they promoted. Eliel Saarinen, luckier than Wright in this respect, enjoyed the benefit of a friendship and personal relationship with Sibelius and Gustav Mahler, who even played his piano at Hvitträsk.

Musical education has been generally regarded as a cultural differential, a sign of the "gentleman" architect. Yet it is astonishing how very few architects are seriously involved with music today.

**Fig. 13-4.** *The Media House for the Yhtyneet Kuvalehdet Publishing Company in Helsinki by Ilmo Valjakka, architect. A building that inspired Harri Wessman to write a music score.*

Within the overall negative picture of architecture with regard to music and within the broader context of the architectural predicament of the 1980s, several extremely serious efforts of scholarly researchers on the music-architecture reciprocity undertaken earlier in the century remained generally unknown. There is the barely known case of Georgiades, a Greek architect of the 1930s who took up the task of correlating cannons of musical harmony with the placement of the columns of ancient Greek temples. His studies and measurements added up to a revealing conclusion which he summarized into a visual chart known as "The Architectural Canon of Georgiades"; a proof that the delight of harmony experienced by the eye when looking at Greek temples was caused not by arbitrary acts of column placement, but because the placement of these columns had a relationship of column-void succession corresponding to specific musical harmonies. Georgiades proved, at least through his specialized focus, that harmony, visually or acoustically perceived, is a guarantee of aesthetic delight. Of course, the debate as to whether these ancient Greek "frozen harmonies" were products of conscious or arbitrary and coincidental acts, as Georgiades claimed, was ended long ago, when scholars such as Ghyka gave their answers with regard to similar findings by Hambidge, Caskey, and Moessel, archeologists who looked at the harmonic rules of ancient and Gothic buildings from a geometric and proportional perspective.

## Composers of Particular Significance

Equally destructive perhaps would be an attitude that would object to explorations and scholarly studies of music done on the basis of architectural, geometric, and proportional canons of harmony. Musicians, like other creative artists, may have preferred not to talk about their work, yet scholars and students must study and try to analyze it. Both Sibelius and Béla Bartók were legendary for their silence; yet Béla Bartók, a compassionate, tolerant and caring teacher, was totally aligned with "silence" when it came to explanations regarding his own work.

It is Bartók we would like to focus on, because he among all the others has been found by scholars to have created compositions that reveal the extraordinary affinity of music and architecture. His work comes across today as the masterful blend of eternal as well as contemporary principles of composition and inclusivity. Erno Lendvai, one of the top scholars on the composer, has found that Bartók's compositions integrate principles of ancient Greek architecture, such as the golden section and the Pythagorean pentanomy, along with principles of acoustic harmony derived from Western European thinking (use of the straight line and the circle). Bartók's use of the golden section was found in the structure of whole movements, as well as in the structure of their details. Yet the melody steps of these musical golden sections (time-space intervals of varying scales) followed the rules of the Pythagorean pentanomy, ". . . the most ancient human sound system, which may be regarded as the purest musical conception of the principle of golden sections."

Yet if one were to conceive the movements of Bartók's works as individual buildings, obeying the discipline mentioned above, the totality of his compositions can be conceived of as urban design, with its own overall concept, its own intervals and intersections (the plazas, streets, and open spaces). In this respect, in the articulation of the whole and the important junctures of the parts, the beginning(s), or the end(s), the composer accepted the attitudes of his contemporaries, what Lendvai called "the wide European horizon."

Knowledge of music is necessary for the specific explanations provided by Lendvai with regard to the acoustic system and the Western harmonic

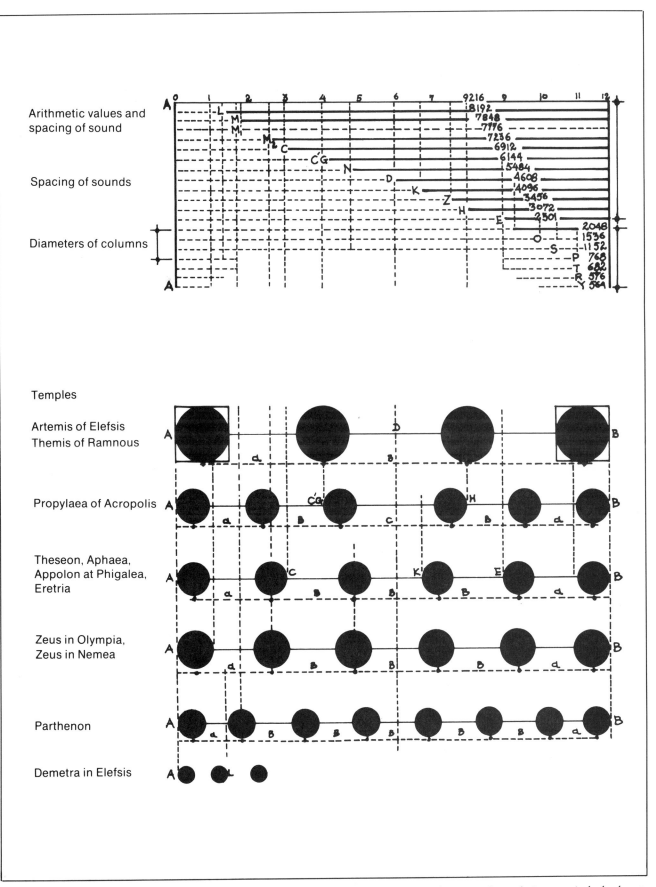

Arithmetic values and spacing of sound

Spacing of sounds

Diameters of columns

Temples

Artemis of Elefsis
Themis of Ramnous

Propylaea of Acropolis

Theseon, Aphaea,
Appolon at Phigalea,
Eretria

Zeus in Olympia,
Zeus in Nemea

Parthenon

Demetra in Elefsis

**Fig. 13-5.** *The architectural canon of Georgiades, relating musical rhythm to architecture. The base of the temple (below) is considered to be the equivalent to the musical canon (above), controlling the placement, the diameters, and the spacing between columns in such a way that the interrelationships among themselves and to the building as a whole are analogous to musical harmony. (After 3° Mati, 1937)*

thinking followed by Bartók. Yet it does not require musical knowledge to stress that Bartók has been found to have achieved a dualism in his compositions based on polarization. In this sense he has achieved an element of complexity and contradiction, yet within the overall structure of simply perceived (and organized) wholes, with parts that adhere to well-established and tested paths of harmony and aesthetic appeal. Bartók's symphonies are therefore addressed to varying points of view, to varying conditions of scale, like those sought through the architectural advocacy of Robert Venturi. Although one could call Lendvai's analysis of Bartók scientific, the student of the composer will find a lot more in the essence, content, emotionality, and feeling of an otherwise work of consciously meticulous composition, because most of his compositions were motivated by his personal perception of the world, his love for freedom, for his country, for humanity, and for those whose music he studied and tried to understand.

No Bartók project is more exemplary than his Dance Suite, the work that came to be known as the Eastern European Symphony. This was a work composed to celebrate the fiftieth anniversary of the inauguration of the towns of Buda and Pest; the birth of a great world city requires its coexistence with the rest of the world. The national and ethnic music themes integrated and transformed into this coherent whole express the composer's ideological desire for openness, understanding, toleration, and cooexistence. He filters them through his own rigorous compositional discipline. Yet it is the feeling and the concept of the whole work, not only the mechanics, the rules and composition of its form, that represent the totality, the glory of the composer. One need not be a musician or an architect to get the feeling of the multilayered comprehensivity of Béla Bartók. Yet one needs to be willing to concentrate, to be attentive and to think. Only then will the union of aesthetic delights occur.

## The Music-Architecture Analogue

The prose of Lionel Salter, quoted below, although it utilizes musical language, will best express Bartók's feelings, strategy, and inclusivist discipline. The reading of this quotation should occur before, during and after contemplative listening sessions of the composer's Dance Suite. Salter summed up:

> . . . the first section, which is full of tempo variations, is largely concerned with derivatives from the introverted, Oriental-sounding theme first stated by the bassoon (first cousin to the fugue subject at the climax of the miraculous mandarin) and is followed by the ritornello, dreamily pastoral on muted violins and then on clarinet. A change of key and a quickening of pace announce the excitable, heavily-accented second section: it is rhythmically very irregular, but melodically it is obsessed by the interval of the minor third (whose appearance on sliding trombones immediately recalls the ballet). A sharp glissando brings back the ritornello (starting on the clarinet this time) after which the bassoon introduces a high-spirited allegro vivace rondo with two subsidiary themes: this section is brilliantly scored, with a great diversity of instrumental color and suggestions of bagpipe drones. There is a sudden pause, and (without the intervention of the ritornello) the mood changes for a mysterious night-picture of strongly Arabic character, its sinuous unison melodic lines on woodwind, alternating with wavering chords on muted strings, swelling and thinning out again. A brief violin reference to the ritornello precedes the short fifth section, which is little more than a persistent rhythmic figure built up in fourths; this leads straight into the finale, in the course of whose enormously energetic progress themes from all the previous sections, except the fourth, are tossed hither and thither, the ritornello returns, and the work ends in high glee.

To read passages such as this, to listen to musical works like those described, to extract the structural, conceptual, tactile, and textural essentials and to attempt to design buildings or urban design sequences on these principles, would be a very rewarding and most creative exercise.

John Williams wrote: "In every era, composers have demanded the very latest instruments and techniques. Think of Mozart who championed the clarinet and the glass harmonica." Robert Moog, introducing one of his digital recordings in 1982 (an assembly of works appropriately called "Angels in Architecture"), wrote about his work: " . . . when we hear this new music, we have to stop and think." Considering the concerns of the composers of the late 1980s, we have to appreciate the significance of Béla Bartók and to recognize his key role in the realm of creativity through music as applied to the state of civilization, to the notions, the materials, the techniques, and the potential of the late twentieth century. If one conceives of him as the "gate" to this twentieth century through music, then the composers using the electronic musical technology of the time are the beautifully proportioned "windows" of our musical edifice, oriented to different directions, bringing different breezes and aesthetic delights.

These are extremely sensitive and yet highly disciplined people. They have been the first among the creators of the late twentieth century to have achieved "poetry" and "emotional humanity" without denying the potential and the usefulness of computers and electronics. These people speak of "landscape," "space," and "materials" almost in purely architectonic terms. Brian Eno tried the synthesizer, learned it well, used it, and yet went beyond it because of "its limited usefulness . . . its sound tended towards a diagrammatic rather than an organic quality." Eno, along with others, sought liberation from the confines of the machine; they searched for human expression as opposed to diagrammatic possibilities. Eno, unlike Bartók and Sibelius, was very articulate; he opened up about his creative process and revealed that it shifted from "the diagrammatic" constraints of the synthesizer "towards non-instruments like pieces of chain and sticks and stones."

The quality of sound "as a completely plastic and malleable material" sought by Brian Eno can be best experienced in the closing Eternal Spring (of the Silk Road II) of the Japanese composer Kitaro. The crystalline sound of water running pure and clear above creek pebbles, pierced by the shining rays of a forest-filtered sun, could very well have been in the mind of Frank Lloyd Wright when he designed the Kaufmann house. "A forest seen from the air is complex and interesting. A single tree is equally complex. One leaf, even one molecule is endlessly fascinating. That's how music should be." This statement by Eno sounds incredibly similar to the architectonic concept of Le Corbusier, who believed that the design of the doorknob is as difficult (and important) as the design of a whole town.

## Music's Direct Input to Architecture

Among the first ones to open the horizons and guide musicians to discover their "leafs" in the unexplored forests of the late twentieth century were people relatively unknown to the great masses but ascetics and pioneers in their own way. Foremost among them was the organist composer Olivier Messiaen, a musician appreciated and admired by Le Corbusier. He became the teacher of Iannis Xenakis, who while working at the office of Le Corbusier and being wholly responsible for several Le Corbusier projects, offered his knowledge of music and his personal system of notation (formalized music) in the service of the development of twentieth-century architecture. During his years with Le Corbusier, he gave evidence of his ability with numbers, geometry, and proportions and helped introduce high degrees of rhythmic order to several Le Corbusier projects. Iannis Xenakis was largely responsible (along with another Greek architect, Stamos Papadakis) for working out the mathematics of Le Corbusier's Modulor, a modular series of proportions. As Le Corbusier "had no idea of mathematics," contrary to what he professed, and as George Candilis has testified to the author, Xenakis and Papadakis (then working in his office and trained in math and geometry through their studies at the School of Architecture in Athens) got the assignment to "come up with something along these lines." And they did.

In an essay on architecture that perhaps casts the most revealing light regarding the creative, collaborative, open-minded and innovative genius of Le Corbusier, Xenakis has told the story of the design of the Monastery of La Tourette, a design for which he was largely responsible. In his biography he has told the story of the tensions with Corbu regarding the authorship of the Philips Pavilion, which was totally designed by the musician on the basis of the geometry and the score of one of the musical compositions he had prepared for this particular building. Even if Xenakis had not told us, any serious scholar of the evolution of contemporary music would perhaps have traced the origin of the rhythmic articulation of the various parts of La Tourette, especially its three façades with the four elements a, b, c, d, of the golden section and their twenty-four permutations in the "Metastasis," one of the Xenakis's early musical compositions. Le Corbusier, by accepting the young musician's suggestions (in fact, he honored him by publishing the first score of the "Metastasis" in the 1955 edition of Modulor 2), was the first to give legitimacy to the actual collaboration of kindred spirits from different arts, in this case music and architecture. Xenakis subsequently abandoned architecture to devote himself completely to music, to become the proponent of electronic music and to have France honor him with a National Pavilion at the Montreal Expo, which had an architectonic form that was perfect for the composer's electronic music.

**Fig. 13-6.** *The southern façade of La Tourette, based on a music score and designed by Iannis Xenakis; architect, Le Corbusier.*

Several other musicians reached music through architecture. Paul Simon (of Simon and Garfunkel) is the best known case in the United States. The opposite trend, for musicians to become architects, or just simply be interested in architecture, is not as marked. With the exception of Daniel Libeskind, who came to architecture via music and subsequent studies in mathematics and painting, the decades of the 1960s and 1970s were stagnant in terms of reciprocal cross-fertilization. Furthermore, the literature of architecture, not yet prepared for pioneering experimental efforts in architectural poetics, was a difficult outlet for the communication of personal or idiosyncratic concerns on the subject.

## Recent Design Lessons Based on Departures from Music

It took approximately twenty years of silence (the last important writings were summarized through the editorial efforts of Gyorgy Kepes in 1966) until Radoslav Zuk's article in the *Journal of Architectural Education*. It was basic and introductory on a subject that had to be treated as a forgotten one, yet it was inspiring and well received. Using lay terms, Zuk pointed out a whole series of music-architecture commonalities. If nothing else, he attracted the attention and stimulated the chords of creativity of students and instructors who had been brought up with the music of the Beatles, Bob Dylan, jazz, and rock 'n roll. He did not provide evidence of samples of his student projects to demonstrate the applicability and the potential of his advocacy as a channel to design.

This was left to the efforts of few experimentally inclined design instructors who were conversant with and cognizant of music. Susan Ubbelohde from the University of Minnesota and Bennett Neiman from the University of Colorado at Denver were the pioneers of the 1980s in using music as the external reference for architectural design purposes.

Ubbelohde used the relationship between music and architecture in two ways in teaching. She described the first as relatively straightforward, in that it addressed the relationship between the acoustics of a room and the visual experience of that room through a one-hour slide lecture synchronized with musical recordings. This effort, which addresses the experiential nature of room acoustics in a profound way, is perhaps the stimulating channel through which students learn not only the difficult tasks of acoustics, but are motivated for what should follow in the design studio.

Ubbelohde expands her efforts with a studio project entitled "The Sound Machine." The students are introduced to the project through a slide lecture synchronized to recordings (a carefully selected list, including music from ancient Greece, covering the evolution of music down to Varèse's Poemme Electronique (performed in the Le Corbusier–Xenakis Philips Pavilion at the Brussels World's Fair 1958) before they select a historic period. Upon selecting a period of their choice, they are asked to survey the literature of the time, both on music and on architecture. The goal is to identify the rules and canons of the time. The findings of these canons are summarized graphically, while the programming stage takes a scoring direction, based on examples from Anna and Lawrence Halprin's concepts of choreography. The project concludes with a "design by doing it" event, where the students construct their projects. "The entire school watches the process and approximately 500 are on hand for the final jury to listen to the machines" (From Ubbelohde's letter to the author and course syllabuses).

Ubbelohde realizes that the students gain and learn more about teamwork and construction than about the nature of the arts. Yet one may speculate about the valuable effects such exercises and experiences may have on the very few who might see the immensely greater potential music can exert on their design efforts. It is during the very early introductory exercises and introductory lectures that the student hears for the first time about the ideas and attributes of architecture that bear a similarity to music.

Bennett Neiman goes beyond these goals; he intermarries the references in music to architecture with the discipline and capabilities of the computer. Neiman begins with jazz scores by his favorite musicians. He encourages his students to go through the listening sessions with the goal of analyzing and depicting graphically the structure and the rhythmic sequences of the piece performed. In subsequent steps, students are asked to perform "spatial improvisations" and "spontaneous spatial moves" analogous to the structure and rhythm of the analyzed jazz piece. These improvisations are then drawn with the computer, while the computer program permits the development of many variations. The designer's mind and poetic license are used to make the final selection, which is then transformed into the desired building. Through the reference to jazz, the students are introduced to concepts and habits of discipline (for the overall structure of jazz is highly structured and disciplined), and at the same time the attitude of permissiveness and improvisation (also characteristic ingredients of jazz) leaves the field open and free for the achievement of the unique. Jazz as a departure for architecture can be very well argued as the desirable music prototype for an eventual "democratic" architecture—where everyone is playing his own instrument and compositions—within a mutually accepted structured whole.

## Toward a Model for Music-Architecture Inclusivity

Don Fedorko, one of my architectural students, has developed the most direct music-architecture working theory, and has consistently been using music as a source of inspiration and synthetic guide in his own designs. He was inspired by a comment by one of his instructors during the early years of his studies; the instructor suggested that architecture has "rhythm," like music. Fedorko, a young musician, songwriter, and vocalist, and a highly independent student of architecture, devoted his free time to developing a theory of the music-architecture relationship, the best developed and most promising thus far for actual design application. His student designs are evidence of the promise as well as the liabilities of "architecture as music" if it is not resolved in an inclusivist manner. Fedorko believes that "you can get ideas from many sources," and he encourages his colleagues to keep their eyes and ears open: "You get ideas from small instances, not when you force it . . . take an everyday symbol and exploit it."

The young composer-architect derives joy from explaining his efforts to his colleagues. It was the first time some of them really understood the music they were enjoying. Music has an extraordinary power as a tool of instruction, because if one selects musical compositions that have already had general emotional appeal to a certain audience, then the audience is sympathetic, attentive, and assimilates the analytical comments on the secrets of a composition. It is much easier to find a piece of music that has been experienced and has universal appeal to a student audience than it is to find a building that arouses such a sympathetic response.

Perhaps the most remarkable lesson I derived from students was the ambition of one to reach a point where he might be able to get a commission from a client in which he would

> write song for the client
> then design the house
> deriving form and spatial
> quality from the music of
> the song.

| A | | A | | B | A | |
|---|---|---|---|---|---|---|
| 3 | 5 | 3 | 5 | 8 | 3 | 5 |
| ensemble | tenor sax | ensemble | piano | piano | ensemble | tenor sax |

**"LESTER LEAPS IN"**
**COUNT BASIE'S KANSAS CITY SEVEN**

Count Basie (piano), Buck Clayton (trumpet),Dickie Wells (trombone), Lester Young (tenor saxophone),
Freddy Green (guitar), Walter Page (bass), Jo Jones (drums)

Formal Structure: AABA (each section is 8 measures or bars long)
Length of Selection: 4 + 192 measures

jazz arrangement, fifth chorus

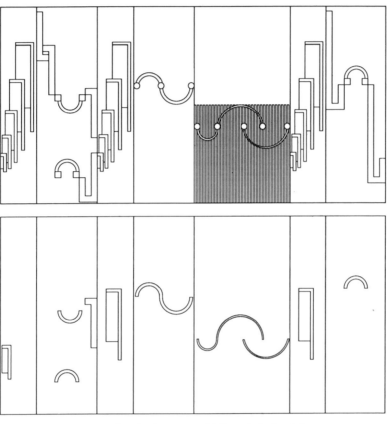

two-dimensional, computer-assisted improvisation line studies

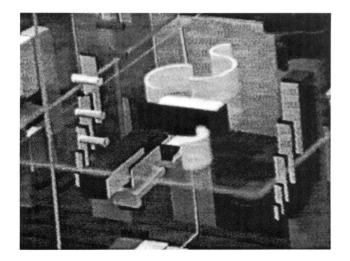 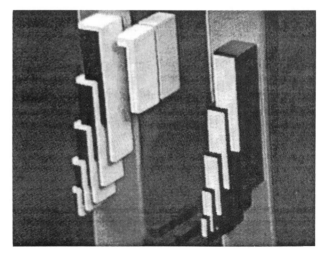

**Fig. 13-7.** *Architecture generated by music (jazz) and computers. Project by Terry Kemp from the design studio of Bennett Neiman, University of Colorado at Denver. (Courtesy Bennett Neiman)*

One could perhaps find no more inclusivist definition of architectural creativity and design as an inclusivist act than the one stated above; when the lyrics will be given life through music to be eventually frozen for eternity as edifice.

"The spirit doesn't descend upon you without some help from music." Perhaps this statement by Dr. Billy King, in his effort to explain the significance and the communal power of Gospel music, is equally applicable to architecture: Music could help the spirit come down again.

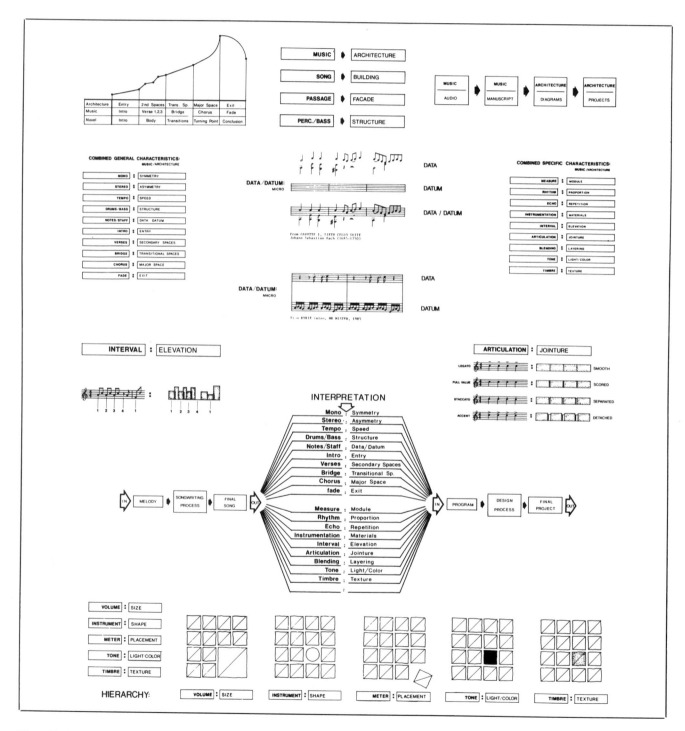

**Fig. 13–8.** *Conceptual relationships between architecture and music, according to Don Fedorko. (Diagram courtesy Don Fedorko)*

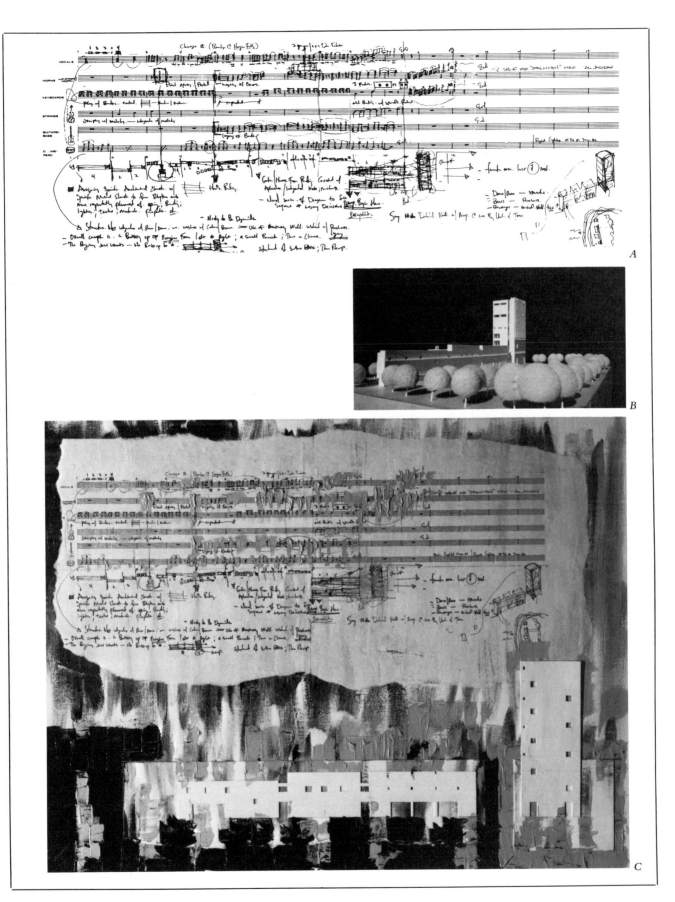

**Fig. 13-9.** *Integration of music score and architecture, with the help of painting as a means for conceptual expression during the creative process.* **A.** *Music score.* **B.** *Final architectural model.* **C.** *Conceptual painting. Project designed by Don Fedorko and inspired by the song "Niagara Falls," from the album* Chicago 18, *the band Chicago. (Drawings and photos courtesy Don Fedorko)*

## THE CONCEPT OF THE SYMPHONIC AND THE SCALES OF ARCHITECTURE

The "spirit," however, has a more complicated role to perform, as the architects of the 1990s deal with more complicated issues than before. Architecture is much larger, more complicated, exponentially more complex in scale, both physically and—more important—socially. Thoughts regarding the state of individuality, freedom, and the plurality of society pose additional dimensions for the music-architecture relationship. Today we face a dilemma in the applicability of the analogue between music and architecture. The argument can go like this: You cannot hear two pieces of music simultaneously. The result will be a blare. You can, however, look at two buildings simultaneously. It is possible that they may be different and yet they may complement each other. It is also possible that they may not help each other, that one may perhaps be "fighting" the other; finally it is possible that they may be unobjectionable, making no commentary on each other, while they may appear to be concerned about something else, a broader whole, idiom, or a tradition (perhaps the esoteric whim and desires of client or architect).

All these possibilities may be perceived through one visual glance. None of this can happen with the auditory analogue; the works of two composers must be experienced (and considered) separately, while the works of two (or more) architects can be experienced simultaneously. In this sense we can suggest a fundamental difference between music and architecture. Architecture can permit the simultaneous perception (or visual experience) of more than one work, so it could perhaps be considered more dynamic. One could not speak of musical pieces performed simultaneously and yet making sense. Is this a plus for architecture, or is it perhaps one of its great dilemmas? Should architects, especially in a plural society, where they may not know each other, approach individual projects as separate pieces of music, or should they be sensitive to the total harmony of the whole? Or should they perceive their projects like separate instruments playing their individual scores in a "symphony" to which they are supposed to contribute?

This question brings us to the realization that every effort to equate architecture with music and find an analogue between the two is a function of scale. In urban design, one could conceive each building as equivalent to the music played by a particular instrument, but it is also possible to consider a building all by itself and equate it to a pleasing piece of music, separately performed, experienced, and judged. Music has an inexplicable appeal, one that grows in time and is a function of several factors, some explicable, others not easy to understand. Of great importance is the effort on the part of the listener to learn to appreciate music beyond the pleasure derived through the ear, the airing of harmonies, the succession of rhythms and the quality of the sound.

Although it is more complicated at first, it is easy to approach the music-architecture analogue from the broader scale and speak about the possibility of the dilemma: You cannot listen to two pieces of music simultaneously, but you can perceive two (or more) works of architecture at the same time. Starting from the case of a musical symphony, which we will equate here to urban design, we can see that there are lessons to be learned for architecture if the architect perceives urban design acts as symphonies of building in which each project corresponds to the role played by each particular instrument. Because if a building is perceived as part of a symphonic performance it will have to be in agreement with the covenants of the whole. A *symphony* is an agreement—an agreement of harmony that has the goal of delighting. A musical symphony is therefore the togetherness of the voices of the performing instruments with the goal of agreeing in complementing others.

It is my strong belief that only with the concept of the symphony can one derive results from the music-architecture analogue. The Pythagorean, the Platonic, the Aristotelian, and the Renaissance understandings of the concept of symphonic should be studied, contemplated, perhaps tried occasionally, but always put on the side in favor of today's values, of today's complex world. The architectonic "symphony" of the late twentieth century has to include myriad "instruments." Its rhythm has to include plurality. Its rhythm should be judged on a broader scale, its score should leave room for individual expression and improvisation. It is all an issue of scale and magnitude. This is why, with the music-architecture channel to creativity, one should pay equal attention to the basics, as to the history and the evolution of the subject, as opposed to jumping unprepared (and unequipped) into the fashions and unrelated trends of the present.

The reciprocal effect of the arts has been a fact throughout history. It is surprising to many people today when they hear that the person responsible for all the work on the Acropolis of Athens, including architecture, construction process, and artistic execution, was Phedias, a sculptor by profession, who had daily discussions on art and architecture when in the house of Pericles with their mutual friend, the philosopher Anaxagoras. It might perhaps be equally surprising in the future if we were to suggest that almost all the forward steps in the architecture of the twentieth century were due largely to the influence exerted by some artists (Mondrian, Picasso, Oldenburg, De Chirico) on the architects. This should not offend the architects. They need the artists and they need the other arts in order to become better architects.

## Summary

Association, applied involvement, and a working relationship with other artists and creative people should become part of the architect's creativity enhancement strategy. Important architects have done so, with wonderful results. This chapter presents suggestions for a well-planned socialization process as a means to furthering chances for cross-fertilization. In particular, the arts of dance and music have a special affinity with architecture. Dance enhances the architect's appreciation of cross-cultural differences while it clarifies understanding of the concepts of the classical and the contemporary. We close our inquiry with an original contribution to the music-architecture cross-fertilization relationship. We present theoreticians, architects, and musicians who have been instrumental in this respect, and conclude with a suggestion for a music-architecture inclusivist approach to design.

## References

Alberti, Leone Battista. *Ten Books on Architecture*. London: Alex Tiranti Publishers, 1965. Book L, Chapter IX, p. 14.

Christ-Janer, Albert. *Eliel Saarinen*. Chicago: University of Chicago Press, 1948.

Eno, Brian. Statements in "Angels in the Architecture." Compact disc, E.G. Records, Ltd., 1987.

Georgiades, Athanasios Georgeas. "E Armonia en te Architektonike: mousike-poesis-Architektonike armonia" (Harmony in architecture: Music-poetry-architecture). *3° Mati*, 7–12, Athens, 1937, p. 197.

Ghyka, Matila. *Le Nombre D'or* (Vol. I); *Les Rhymes* (Vol. II). Paris: Gallimard, 1931.

Graves, Michael. *Le Corbusier: Selected Drawings*. New York: 1981.

Halprin, Anna. "Rituals of Space." *Journal of Architectural Education*, 39, 1 (September 1975).

Hanslik, Eduard. "The Beautiful in Music." In Kennick, 1964.

Kennick, W. E. *Art and Philosophy: Readings in Aesthetics*. New York: St. Martin's Press, 1964.

Kepes, Gyorgy. *Structure in Art and Science*. New York: Braziller, 1965.

Kepes, Gyorgy. *Language of Vision*. Chicago: Paul Theobald, 1969.

Kiesler, Frederick. *Inside the Endless House: Art People and Architecture: A Journal*. New York: Simon and Schuster, 1964.

Le Corbusier. *New World of Space*. Boston: Institute of Contemporary Art; and New York: Reynal and Hitchcock, 1948, p. 14.

Lendvai, Erno. "Duality and Synthesis in the Music of Bela Bartok." In Gyorgy Kepes, *Module, Proportion, Symmetry, Rhythm*. New York: Braziller, 1966, p. 181.

Libeskind, Daniel. "Deus ex Machina/Machina ex Deo: Aldo Rossi's Theater of the World." In *Oppositions #21*. Cambridge, MA: MIT Press, Summer 1981.

"Maker of Myths and Machines: An interview with Emilio Ambasz." *Crit*, Spring 1982, pp. 22–24.

Matossian, Nouritsa. *Xenakis*. London: Kahn and Averill; New York: Taplinger, 1986.

Neiman, Bennett. "Architectural Parallels: The Jazz Studio." ACSA Regional Conference, UT/Arlington, Texas, October 15, 1988.

Pikionis, Dimitrios. "Laika Pechnidia" (Folk toys). *3° Mati* 1, Athens, October 1935.

———. "Ideogrammata tis oraseos" (Ideograms of vision). *3° Mati* 2, 1935.

Rasmussen-Steen, Eiler. *Experiencing Architecture*. Cambridge, MA: MIT Press, 1974.

Rowe, Colin, and Slutzky, Robert. "Transparency: Literal and Phenomenal." In Rowe Colin, *The Mathematics of the Ideal Villa and Other Essays*. Cambridge, MA: MIT Press, 1976.

Sachs, Curt. "O ieros choros" (The holy dance). *3° Mati*, 7–12, Athens, 1937, pp. 259–263.

Salter, Lionel. Text accompanying digital recording of Béla Bartók's *Dance Suite*, Sir Georg Solti, conductor.

Schildt, Göran. *Alvar Aalto as Artist*. Mairea Foundation, Villa Mairea, 1982.

———. *Alvar Aalto: The Decisive Years*. New York: Rizzoli, 1986.

Tigerman, Stanley. "California: A Pregnant Architecture." Exhibit catalog essay, La Jolla Museum of Art, 1983, p. 27.

Turner, Paul V. *The Education of Le Corbusier*. New York: Garland, 1977, p. 137.

Tzonis, Alexander, and Lefaivre, Liane. *Classical Architecture: The Poetics of Order*. Cambridge, MA: MIT Press, 1986, pp. 118, 119, 120.

Van Bruggen, Coosje. "Waiting for Dr. Coltello." *ARTFORUM International*, September 1984, p. 88.

Varèse, Louise. Varèse: A Looking-glass Diary. Vol. 1, 1883–1928. New York: Norton, 1972, pp. 53, 55, 98, 110, 228.

Vasari, Giorgio. *Vasari's Lives of the Painters, Sculptors, and Architects*, ed. Edmund Fuller. New York: Dell, 1963.

Wingler, Hans Maria. *The Bauhaus*. Cambridge, MA: MIT Press, 1969.

Wittkower, Rudolf. *Architectural Principles in the Age of Humanism*. London: Alec Tiranti, 1952, pp. 115, 135.

Wright, Frank Lloyd. *An Autobiography*. New York: Duell, Sloan and Pearce, May 1958.

Xenakis, Iannis. "The Monastery of La Tourette." In *Le Corbusier: La Tourette and Other Projects, 1955–1957*. Alexander Tzonis, general editor. New York: Garland; Paris: Fondation Le Corbusier, 1984. Pp. ix–xxviii, xii.

Zuk, Radoslav. "A Music Lesson." *Journal of Architectural Education*, 36, 3 (Spring 1983), pp. 2–6.

# Chapter 14  Architectural Biographies as a Means to All-Inclusive Creativity

The first project done by the successful California architect Welton Becket was a house for a dog, an "over-privileged Great Dane" belonging to a client in Seattle. This client was apparently so pleased that he subsequently commissioned Becket to design a new house for him in the same style as his dog's, "early Swedish modern with exposed beam ceilings." The same architect had also remodeled a modest Los Angeles cafeteria during the Depression; he received his fee in the form of free meals for a certain period of time. The early difficulties were subsequently overcome, and Becket became one of the most successful and wealthiest architects in America.

The study of biographies of important architects can be a positive departure path for architectural creativity. A biography is not necessarily a boring scholastic text. Although it must tell the truth (and therefore be scholastic), it is more than anything else "human" and "personal," describing people in personal rather than impersonal ways. A biography of an architect, unlike that of any other person, acts like a model of "the human as architect" of a time gone by. If the student represents the present as an embarkation point for the future, the biography represents the past. It offers a strong awareness regarding the placement of one's personality within the historic framework of which one is a part. Architects are among the few professionals who can trace their origins to antiquity and whose contribution to civilization has been substantial and long-standing. The study of architectural biographies can provide examples for imitation. It can raise questions regarding the profession; it can suggest methods for future professional strategies and success in life. On the other hand, it may suggest the obstacles one may have to overcome.

It is creative to stay alive, and one is successful if one manages to stay creative for as long as one can feel healthy. The study of biographies will point out recurrent similarities regarding the intensive discipline, dedication, and hard work of architects of the past. It seems inconceivable that it will not have a positive effect on the creative thirst of the novice. A biography will also provide suggestions regarding the most important aspect of getting a commission, a topic absolutely bypassed in schools, yet a topic that is vital for any professional creativity. A professional has no chance to create if he has no projects in his office.

The all-inclusive architectural biography is relatively new in the architecture literature. We are in a period in which biographical research has produced a good body of work to which we can refer. The background, the social and cultural milieus of the architects, the cultural, governmental, and political dynamics under which they operated and which are prerequisites to creativity, are as fundamental for the biography as the presentation of the work of the creators themselves. Using such biographies can be much more stimulating than the works the architects produced, because the works are the product of their knowledge, education, and personality. Personality is the God-given substance through which creation is filtered and achieved. Contrary to the purist belief that the artist and his personality should not be confused with the artist and his work, it remains true that the artist is the psychic-intellectual medium through which the creative process must travel. As such, the artist is subject to a definite relationship with his or her work, and ignoring the artist's personality is like ignoring the source of the creative process. One could not conceive of nature if one were not able to concern oneself with God and his attributes.

The study of architectural biographies may not have a direct, specific effect on particular design projects in process, but it will have a long-lasting effect on the shaping of the creative personality, and on creative habits and discipline of the person. A whole range of attitudes is available today through a rather extensive bookshelf of architectural biographies. In my opinion, some of the best biographies around are on architects such as Gunnar Asplund, Hans Scharoun, Constantine Melnikov, Welton Becket, Enri Sauvage, Le Corbusier, Frank Lloyd Wright, Mies van der Rohe, and Alvar Aalto. There are also several autobiographies or personal accounts of architects on specific projects and portions of their creative lives. Among these we would have to include Louis Sullivan, Le Corbusier, Frank Lloyd Wright, and George Candilis, along with Hassan Fathy and Ricardo Bofill. The content of many of these books is highly inspirational. They can hardly be dismissed as stimulants, but one must be cautious about the usefulness of autobiographies or biographies by third persons in praise of their subjects. As we will see below, the inspirational ingredient of a biography may even be counterproductive for instruction purposes if the biography lacks other fundamental ingredients, such as an infrastructure of truth on which it builds the subject's image and develops the biographer's arguments.

## SCHILDT'S EXEMPLARY BIOGRAPHY OF AALTO

No definitive history and criticism of architecture will ever be written unless the critic has all the facts at hand, including recent reports by the analyst of the architect under scrutiny. No critic or historian has been as fortunate thus far to have been privy to such information as was Göran Schildt, the biographer of Alvar Aalto. Schildt had access to the whole archive of the architect, his correspondence, writings, sketches, and drawings, along with some correspondence by an Aalto-related psychoanalyst. This material permitted him to cut through sensitive areas in formulating opinions, developing hypotheses, and making suggestions regarding the factors and dynamics that were at work in shaping Aalto's personality and making Alvar Aalto.

In this three-volume biography, Schildt does not mince words; nor does he become the victim of the idol trap. He is honest and unhesitant in pointing to his subject's weaknesses whenever appropriate and in correcting false impressions held by others—victims, perhaps, of Aalto's occasional tactic to mislead those he felt he should take lightly. Through Schildt's pen and his evidence, Aalto was never a great student, he was never a prize-winning student, or a good draftsman in the conventional sense of the period. He had a rather anxious "country boy" mentality in the early years, and throughout his life he was inconsistent in relaying facts, even about his own life. All these are surprises for the student or anyone who may have experienced the prevailing attitude of parents and many teachers that only high marks and overnight achievement of "excellence" are needed for eventual success in life. On the contrary, these are gained in time, through a life-long process of discipline and creative advancement.

As we can learn from biographies, not all great architects were great talents and overnight successes. Schildt was consistent in his critical approach throughout the treatment of his subject's life. He proved through ample evidence a whole array of notions held by many regarding the importance of early childhood influences as well as subsequent activities and preoccupations. We are now certain that everything was right in the shaping and making of Alvar Aalto and that in extension, the caring, ambitious, and supportive parents (in the case of Aalto it was his supportive father), along with the circumstances of a family life of constant social mobility, can be decisive for the future evolution of a creative youth. Early lifestyle and schooling can also be helpful along with the uniqueness of the natural environment. The international, national, and regional circumstances, handled appropriately, may also have a decisive influence on the person's subsequent evolution. Aalto took an active stand in issues that affected his country and participated in the civil war, only to enjoy in subsequent years the benefits of these experiences through his personal associations. An early love for sports, hunting and fishing, the theater and the arts are good signs that love for architecture may follow in later years. Such conditions can be encouraged by the family, a sport- or nature-loving father, an art-loving mother; they are among the sure requisites for a life through creative endeavor in the future.

In the second volume of Aalto's biography, Schildt establishes the processes at work in the shaping of Aalto's creative personality during the years of his professional establishment and his involvement with architecture on a global basis. The architect's efforts were endless and multidirectional. To *build,* to *write,* to *exhibit,* to *travel abroad,* to *participate in conferences* were decisive for Aalto and can certainly be for others. The biography also pointed out the architect's knack at selecting competent associates or his ability to initiate cultural institutions (i.e. founding the Projektio film club) and encouraging public education that could produce clients in the future. In this respect, Aalto also exhibited and constantly sought kindred people from whom he drew and gained (Asplund, Markelius, Gropius, László Moholy-Nagy).

Schildt's objective dissection was based on interviews with many surviving Aalto associates, friends, and personalities that were actors of one kind or another in the architect's life. An extraordinary evidence of humanity springs from this documentation. Aalto, admired by his assistants as the "chief," displayed one of the most fundamental prerequisites to human architecture—humanity, compassion, and good manners toward others. To create, you need to make others about you creative, to get the best out of people, to make them enthusiastic about what they are about to do, to feel it is theirs, so that they can give themselves to it wholeheartedly. Aalto was a human being indeed, in flesh and blood and spirit. Viola Markelius and Mairea Gullichsen provide some of the most spirited testimonies in this respect. The latter will offer information that will cast light on Aalto's attitude toward women, his love for and constructive dependence on them, uncomplicated and primordial. She will say: ". . . It was from them—Mama's underwear—that Alvar got the inspiration for his vases and lamps . . ."

The professional part of the biography is the second volume. It must be read by anyone who thinks seriously about professionally creative fulfillment through architecture. Schildt gets rid of false impressions regarding Aalto, talks about his defeats in competitions, and points to his subject's "pushiness" in professional as well as "self-promoting matters," his lifelong habit of never giving credit to those who influenced him or whose ideas he embraced and elaborated on, his "hypersensitive and unstable temperament," the "anarchistic imagination" and "the radical attitudes of Aalto" and his politically noncommittal attitude. Although Schildt does not seem to be bothered by the last ingredient, offering on the contrary enough evidence to justify Aalto's apoliticality in the name of doing one's best for humanity from within one's own metier, even by accepting and sending an exhibition to the "artek" in Milan in the heyday of Mussolini's fascism—he leaves it up to us to interpret or to take issue with Aalto's personality with regard to his personal behavior under various cultural, ethnic, or business circumstances. Aalto did do certain things: he would speak with the accent of a Dane when crossing the border to Denmark, or assume the mannerisms of a snob when in England, or wear a cowboy hat when in Arizona and offer hanging gondolas because "the Americans use sensational effects." These are but few examples of his ever-changing personal behavior. Lisbeth Sachs, one of his collaborators, attributed the secret of his genius to his "ability to alternate between extremes."

Could it not be that a constant process of diplomatic oscillation accompanied by great adjustability, suggests a model for professional success and advancement in architecture? This may perhaps be one of the many lessons of this volume. Aalto also worked hard on his "socialization plan." He sought his equals, he became part of the "inner circle," he took as much as he could from colleagues, artists, intellectuals, and eventually from some of his clients, whom he involved in his professional endeavors. He was constantly open and he became attached to no style while he attempted to please his clients. He worked hard, very hard.

The author of the biography, who is a literary critic and a philosopher, not an architect, is eventually elevated by the study of his subject to become one of the best architectural critics of the time. After candid critical references to many known and many relatively unknown projects and studies from the Aalto archives, he closes with a tour-de-force of very personal, deeply felt prose. He concluded that Aalto managed to bring "the deepest conflicts of our age into exemplary harmony"; and to confirm his contention that Aalto's goal was the same as of the classical Greek artists, he closes with this remark: "I stand before Säynätsalo Town Hall, Rovaniemi Library and many other Aalto works with the same inexpressible feeling of joy as before the Parthenon in Athens." This monumental biography may very well become the textbook for future biographical research and perhaps the best case study on "the poetics of architecture."

## THE USEFULNESS OF BIOGRAPHIES

The reference to the biography by Schildt reinforces our personal contention that the usefulness of architectural biographies depends completely on the credibility and the truth about the facts the biographer may have been able to establish. The writer's analytical ability, the ability to edit irrelevant information and to be able to convey the absolute truth about the circumstances under which the subject evolved as a creative being, an artist, and a professional are prerequisites to the good architectural biography. We ask for truth as opposed to interpretive poetic license because we want the biography to be *instructive*. The reader must get a crystal-clear picture of the cause and effect relationships between form-generating dynamics and form itself. If the information about the circumstances that caused a commission or made a compromise or a formal decison to happen is wrong, or even worse, if it is fictitious, then the biography is deceptive. It is a wishful projection of what architectural dynamics should be, not what they were.

People lie, and they often "cover up" collectively. They have deceived us occasionally when asked about their vernacular architecture. Nobody ever revealed the ongoing cheating and the stealing that went on (and still goes on) in the making of the vernacular settlements, and the cause of their "picturesque" images. Take a little land from here, push a little bit there, claim the absent neighbor's lot for entrance access to your own site. Plant a tree, water it, hoping that he may stay abroad for over twenty years, so that you can legally claim the land (the number of years varies). Occasionally people kill for a square meter of land. This, of course, has been the real cause of the "picturesque" and "irregular" of the Mediterranean vernacular of the Greek islands, southern Italy, Sicily, and elsewhere.

How could you stimulate similar conditions and justify the laissez-faire imagery if you have completely different generating circumstances? Whatever you may do in this respect will always be a lie, the perpetuation of the lie of ill-informed though perhaps innocent romantic critics, sketching travelers, or historians.

Architects often cheat individually; they have been notorious liars about their own lives and work, often not giving credit for the origins of their ideas, or to those whose ideas they borrowed (or simply stole). This has often made many people around them feel unhappy, oppressed, uncomfortable. Some of the best-known architects have no respect for copyright issues and act as if they invent the world daily. Plagiarism and the absence of credibility would eliminate half the names from the books of architectural acceptance if the basic laws of academic propriety were to be applied in the community of architectural creators. Paul Turner in his little known but highly deserving study *The Education of Le Corbusier* makes a clear case for such weaknesses. Le Corbusier's pretensions that "reading had never been significant to him" have been proved not to be true. Nouritza Matossian, in her biography of Xenakis, reveals information by the composer that reinforces the "cadaver stepping" personality and practices of the architect. It is only after revelations of information such as this that one can understand why Le Corbusier—the architect so many of us have come to admire in so many ways—never taught at a university or prospered in the temple of truth.

Or is it that the architecture we have come to admire through our reading of history texts is a lie? It may very well have been so—to a great extent perhaps. The Parthenon is a case in point. It was the product of many dynamics: the debate of the philosophers who at the time were debating the Athenian state, the genius of Phedias, the talent of Iktinos and Kallicrates, but also—and foremost—the personality of Pericles, who did not hesitate for one moment to deprive the treasury of cash that was kept in Delos for the defense of all the Greeks against the threat of the Persians. Do we want to become architects who believe that "the goal justifies the means"? This, of course, is an answer each one of us would have to give separately. As for me, I have selected to remain more an author than an architect, if that answers some questions.

We believe that the well-researched and substantiated biography, the one whose writer does not write to immortalize a father or simply praise a subject, but the one who has seeking truth as a central goal, will help bring about a turnaround in the appreciation of architecture. Such a biography will help people eliminate many unjustifiably praised architects and monuments of the past. Such biographies may also bring architecture back to a human scale again.

All of this of course sounds "antiprofessional" and utopian for an era conditioned by the expediencies and the practices of middle men, profit-oriented interests, and exaggerated overhead (for the running of the elaborate office, the inch-deep carpets, the intercoms and the secretaries). But in my little house in Hydra, one I designed for myself, with its square window facing the little island of St. Nicholas, and with the Macintosh SE in front of my desk, I can afford to rejoice at the thought that "truth-grounded" architectural biography of the future may help more people—architectural students at least—come to enjoy the rewards of creative productivity, even through the tiniest architectural commission, that our era deprived many of my generation of knowing.

## IN THE MANNER OF THE MASTERS: DESIGN EXERCISES

The study of biographies can be combined with an exceedingly disciplined process of design exercises based on a project that will have to be done "after" the master under study. In this case, a student will have to immerse her or himself into the persona and the design vocabulary of the master and will have to produce a building as if he or she *were* the master.

To do this, we need to study certain characteristic buildings by the selected architect, with special emphasis on his personal home. The architect's house is usually his "weapon," his way of impressing society with his architectonic ideas, besides being in the best instances a clear autobiographical statement. The architect's own house is a paradigm of the "biographic-spatial" equation.

Someone might suggest that attempting to create "in the manner of" somebody else may not be creative at all, that it may be superficial and even hypocritical, a waste of time. Many students, especially the prolific ones and those with strong personalities of their own, may resent the task. Others may try it and struggle; still others may conform and produce projects that look as if they were done by the masters themselves. Charles Moore once suggested to me that he was never able to do a building "à la" Kahn when he was studying under Louis Kahn, while in Moore's words, "Don Lyndon managed to stick with the effort and to produce a Kahn-looking building." There is no doubt that there are enormous dangers in such endeavors; yet the creative person, and Don Lyndon is an exceptionally creative architect, only learns from the opportunity and does not become a prisoner of the master's creative vocabulary.

The creative process requires that an architect evolve in life and that one graduate from one "idol" to another. Mies van der Rohe may appeal to young and professionally inclined students, while Alvar Aalto and Gunnar Asplund may appeal to those who are more mature. And as some of the great architects, such as Asplund, Aalto, Le Corbusier, Frank Lloyd Wright, and Louis Kahn, advanced in life, they changed their beliefs and styles. The same can be done by the student, who can adopt one idol after another, testing their principles, doing some projects "after" their styles, and leaving them never to return. This student will eventually find her or his own voice in time and with the accumulation of experience.

In the past, people had to cross continents in search of a sage. It is possible today to be exposed to many more sages through the ever-expanding list of good architectural biographies. In addition, a design instructor who can rely on personal experiences and who will be able to make personal references to important architects of the past will probably make a stronger impression on students' minds than others who may not be able to make such references. People more easily remember stories and incidents about the lives of others than treatises on their theories and philosophies. One can more easily comprehend Sartre by attending a performance of one of his plays than by reading his existential theories. Personal stories and jokes about architects are as important to stimulate the imagination and creative thirst of the novice as scholastic dissertations on these architects. Personal experience and research on such obscure topics as "Jokes and Anecdotes about Celebrated Architects" have enriched my ability to convince students to do further biographical study and has introduced an additional dimension into my efforts to introduce creative incentives in my studios.

## READING BEFORE DOING

The architectural biography can be further enhanced with readings that will generate an all-inclusive historical sense of the professional evolution of the art and the historical ties among the family of architects. Readings on the professional aspects of architecture from a historical perspective, more general than specific biographies, have additional power in shaping one's stand on architecture and stimulating creative impulses. General works such as Kostof's study *The Architect* and Andrew Saint's *The Image of the Architect* are essential for the beginning as well as the graduate student. Such references complete the task of giving the student a sense of history and providing a means for students to know themselves better in order to plan for the future. Kostoff's book will help create that sense of history, and Saint's book will do the same for recent times and the future. In *The Image of the Architect* one will be given the chance to see the complete model of one's future self, to see both the art and the business aspects of architecture, both of which are requisites for success in any future creative life. Andrew Saint is aware of the problems confronted by creative architects, the difficulties posed by the constant constraints of profit and loss within which they have to operate. He even suggests that "without an improved social system there can be no permanently better architecture or permanently better architects."

A totally creative life for the architect would mean a life full of commissions in which there is enough time for creative involvement, as opposed to inertia and the search for creative outlets through peripheral disciplines and other forms of expression. There is absolute truth in Saint's statement, "This is why frustrated architects so often have recourse to fantasy and to art." The far too many publication-oriented drawings of far too many architects, especially young academic architects in the United States, are a testimonial to the lack of commissions, the lack of rounded creative involvement, and thus the withdrawal into a world of creative dreamwork, fantasy, and publications.

The creativity of the architect will be wholesome only when the product of imagination and the creative search becomes created in the real world and is built, or when the architect, after he or she has built (but not before) decides to withdraw into peripheral activities, or into the "silence," and become a true artist of the twentieth century. We may not be able to change the world and get equity overnight in terms of distribution of commissions and giving every creative person the right to express these creative impulses while they are alive. Yet we may be able to define a course of life, based on the study of biographies and the cases of others, through which we may be able in due course to establish ourselves in the community, enjoy our commissions, and live a happy, imaginative, and creative life.

## BIOGRAPHY AND THE NATURE OF ARCHITECTURE

Vasari's *Lives of the Painters, Sculptors and Architects,* a task that has not been repeated since his day, is perhaps the greatest account of the High Italian

Renaissance than other treatises on specific narrow topics. The biographies reveal to the reader the framework of an era, and give an understanding of the aura, the mood, the broader artistic climate, and the social and economic dynamics that permit and nourish art.

The reading of biographies is instructive as well as entertaining. In this sense biographies help establish the context within which an architect operates as an "artist," a quality that has to remain central for architecture in the pursuit of creativity. The lives of creative people can help others become creative.

## Art vs. Science

The notion of architecture as a "science" and as an "art" has been repeatedly debated in the past; most people have been in agreement that architecture is both, yet "how much art" and "how much science" or the priority of the one ingredient over the other has differed over time, depending on the circumstances. This debate has been an ongoing one, often accompanied by severe polarization and animosities between architects. The "form" or "visual appeal" oriented architects often claim architecture for themselves, while "programming," "problem solving," "social issue oriented" or "energy conscious" architects are often put on the defensive by the former group, and vice versa. Art is more fragile than science for the comprehension of the masses, who generally can appreciate the immediate tangible effects of science on their lives, while they have no room or time to think about the effects of art, which are long range and intangible. Furthermore, society is generally split over what art is, while it is generally in agreement in accepting science.

## Beauty and the Attitude of the Artist

One of the major characteristics of art in the twentieth century is that it has challenged the concept of beauty, of the visual and formal appeal of a work of art on sight, while it has accepted new license for the performance, conduct, and role of artists in society. Through a process of cause and effect, twentieth-century civilization has created its own concepts of art from within; artists are now accepted as creators and social critics, and their relationship to their general audience is totally different from that of earlier times. The artist as an ascetic within society, in constant confrontation with the lethargic performance of others, an individual of "radical will" who denies the easy paths and who may occasionally live beyond the practice of art when he or she has achieved an understanding of artistic fulfillment, is totally different from his or her counterpart of the past. The latter's goal was the proof of achievement of excellence through the evidence of the artistic and qualitative excellence of his metier, narrowly conceived. The characteristic aim of modern art, according to the very convincing analysis of Susan Sontag, is to be "unacceptable to its audience." The artist does not accept even the presence of an audience—an audience of "voyeuristic spectators."

## Form vs. Utility

From such widely held notions, it becomes obvious that the architect as a twentieth-century artist, if he or she is to be one, faces a significant dilemma because of the nature of architecture as a utilitarian art. Should the architect care for society and its needs, since architecture must always take care of the utilitarian needs of the client, or should the architect follow the artistically accepted contemporary role and become "client careless"?

There have been indeed architects who have acted only as artists of the "twentieth century," denying the value of acceptability by their audience, caring less for utilitarian needs, and there have been many whose sole concern has been the achievement of "beauty" in its abstract formal dimensions, in the "stylistic" and "historicist" sense. The period of the 1970s to the 1980s was dominated by such attitudes.

## Architect vs. Client

We categorically suggest that a clear road to "all-inclusive creativity" depends greatly on the wholesome performance of architecture as a simultaneously integrated affair of "art and science." After practice, experience, and exposure to as many channels of architectural creativity as possible, the architect will be able to integrate multiple combinations, inluding many tangible as well as intangible parameters of architecture, using every conceivable criteria, and eventually expressed all this through sketches, concepts, and designs.

The study of the lives of architects will reveal, among other things, not only the struggle of several of the best "inclusivist" architects to reach this point, but the lifelong discipline, the failures and successes they had to endure. Inclusivity is not a textbook or an overnight affair. One of the most revealing things the school will not teach is that all the good "inclusivist" architects learned from their clients, and that the personal relationship between architect and client has been a key factor in producing good architecture. A client-receptive and caring architect will become receptive to the client's need, while a good, receptive and friendly client will eventually accept the architect's suggestions, including those of pure "art." For intuitive architecture, one needs intuitive clients. And the biography will always teach the newcomer that even great architects learned on occasion from clients who proved to be inventive and innovative. Even Frank Lloyd Wright, an architect of legendary domineering attitudes toward clients, came to learn to work with them, frequently benefiting from their inventive suggestions, their intuitive and progressive desires. He listened carefully to his occasional engineer clients, and along with them he solved their problems while at the same time achieving his highly artistic goals.

It has been unfortunate that today's form-oriented artist-architects look down on the client-concerned architects of the 1960s and 1970s. Beyond the ability of biographies to provide answers to some of the issues in the ongoing debate, they can cast light on the very important issue of the life style of the architect as a creative being. It is well known that society nourishes poetry and art and that certain life styles enhance creativity more than others. Life style, personal habitat, and the value system building process are fundamental in the development of the creative personality. The architect must become rock solid and adamant if he or she is to act as a successful harmonizer of all the complex, frequently highly antithetical and often contradictory forces that affect architecture today. The biographies of Walter Gropius, Mies van der Rohe, Alvar Aalto, and Carlo Scarpa are strong testimonies to the strength required by today's "artist-scientist-architects" to resist and to operate creatively under conditions of exile, persecution, censorship, litigation, and even professional opposition of a bureaucratic nature.

Architects, unlike other artists, have to manage to live on the edge of scientific and artistic frontiers, while at the same time they have to be able to operate and understand the mainstream and the prevailing values of society. They are to be agents of progress through constant encounter with the status quo and the implied resistance toward anything that sounds different and sinister.

## The Tragic Role of the Architect as Artist

The role of today's architects is tragic in a sense; it is the constant lament over what the artist knows (and imagines) to be "good" and which as a rule is initially resented by a society that does not seem to be ready to accept anything different. No other artist today suffers so many acts of destruction and substitution of his conceptions. And there is no artist whose art is so dependent on circumstances of budget, legalities, and construction constraints, than the architect. The textbook may suggest ways of dealing with these issues; the architectural biography will offer the compassionate precedent of the past and will prepare new architects mentally for dealing with such circumstances creatively as expectations rather than adversities.

The biography will tell, among other things, about how to deal with associates and collaborators, while it will provide precedents for behavior with one's peers. It is not accidental that architects such as Frank Lloyd Wright and Dimitrios Pikionis took the time to write their personal artistic "testaments" for the inspiration and guidance of their peers; eternity for these modern pioneers was not only the tangible buildings they achieved while alive, but the gain their own experiences could bestow on future generations on professional behavior and lifestyles.

All of this suggests that biographies can be extremely useful, provided they cover as many of these issues as possible. But the prerequisite of their usefulness, as we have already argued, is to tell it exactly as it happened, to be "true" accounts of the circumstances, to tell the truth, not praise or simply "mythify" their subjects.

## THE TEACHER'S LIFE AS AN OPEN BOOK

A teacher's own life is, of course, the best-known case that can and should be conveyed to students. The creative teacher should be an open book. Students should hear not only the story of experiences with individual buildings, but all the circumstances that led to the commissions, as well as explanations of everything regarding compromises of which only the architect is aware. It is not farfetched to introduce a system whereby the computer could be the agent for equitable distribution of public commissions among architects. Commissions for public projects depend on public money and they should get the best design; they should be results of the most imaginative and creative minds in the community. The imaginative and creative can be from any group, but the young are more energetic and have more time to refine and work harder on the conceptions of their artistic imagination. Unfortunately, the great majority of young architects seldom get any public commissions, often becoming "unknown soldiers" in the drafting rooms of large architectural corporations. This is especially true in Western countries; but socialist countries, which stand for equal distribution, have not done anything in this respect either. Their architecture lacks imagination and creativity; the only interpretation of the model of equity is one of monotony and boredom.

Japan, a country of the free world, has at this moment the best model for the equitable exploitation of the creative dynamic of its country. All the young architects who may want (and most want) to participate in public commissions have to express an interest. Upon application, their name is entered into a computer whose task is to see that there is equitable distribution of public commissions among the architects on a rotating basis. Young architects are distributed among the various regions of the country. Each region has a certain number of architects assigned, a number correlated to the size and population of the region. Architects do not have to live in the region, but they certainly have to travel there when the commission

**Fig. 14-1.** *Cover of* A + U Architecture and Urbanism *featuring a constellation of architects (July 1979). (Courtesy of the author)*

comes. Architects graduate to larger regions and perhaps more demanding and complicated projects depending on time served in the assigned region and other experience criteria. Nothing stops the young Japanese architect from accepting private commissions, while everything is geared toward decentralization of design excellence and creation of a physical environment that is the result of the imagination and creativity of the most imaginative and creative among the architects. In Japan, the Scandinavian countries, and a few countries where the general population values art and architecture for their social and cultural merit (i.e., Mexico), the possibilities for all inclusive creativity still survive. Such possibilities are grim for the rest of the world. In all these cases, the task of all-inclusive creative success will rest with the creator. This is why it is fundamental that every bit of the experiences of others be considered and this is why the path to professional, all-inclusive creativity through the study of biography can be so rewarding.

## Summary

The architectural biography can be viewed as part of the inquiry into "precedents," in this case of the human architect, not the product of his efforts—architecture. Yet the human being is certainly the main source of all creative power. Biographies can provide information on many levels about the dynamics that help develop the creative personality of architects. They can be inspirational and helpful in artistic as well as professional areas and they can be suggestive of the possibilities a future architect could take advantage of to reach creative and professional fulfillment. The biography of Alvar Aalto by Göran Schildt is exemplary as a model of the "useful" biography, one based on well-grounded research and the element of truth, not the praise of the subject. Further in the chapter, biography is presented as a means for the study of the ongoing debate on critical issues in architecture, such as the "art vs. science" concern, "form" vs. "client" and so on. We conclude the discussion with a suggestion that the life and overall professional and intellectual experience of the design instructor be an open book for students, and their first encounter with the biographical inquiry.

## References

Antoniades, Anthony C. "Architecture from Inside Lens." *A + U Architecture and Urbanism*, 3 (July 1979).

Blundell Jones, Peter. *Hans Scharoun*. London: Gordon Fraser, 1978.

Bofill, Ricardo. *L'Architecture d'un homme, Interviews with François Hebert-Stevens*. Paris: Arthaud, 1978.

Candilis, George. *Batir la vie*. Paris: Stock, 1977.

Crippa, Maria Antonietta. *Carlo Scarpa*. Cambridge, MA: MIT Press, 1986.

Fathy, Hassan. *Architecture for the Poor*. Chicago: The University of Chicago Press, 1973.

Gebhard, David. *Schindler*. New York: Viking, 1971.

Hunt, William Dudley, Jr., FAIA. *Total Design, Architecture of Welton Becket and Associates*. New York: McGraw-Hill, 1972, p. 10.

Jacobs, Herbert, with Katherine Jacobs. *Building with Frank Lloyd Wright*. San Francisco: Chronicle Books, 1978.

Kostof, Spiro. *The Architect: Chapters in the History of the Profession*. New York: Oxford University Press, 1977.

Moore, Charles. *Conversation with the Author, ACSA Conference*, Asilomar, California, March 1982.

Pikionis, Dimitrios. *Afieroma tou syllogou architektonon ste mneme tou architektonos- Kathegetou Demetriou Pikioni, Akademaikou* (In memorium of the architect Professor Dimitrios Pikionis-Academecian, by the Greek Society of Architects). Athens, 1968.

Saint, Andrew. *The Images of the Architect*. New Haven and London: Yale University Press, 1983.

Schildt, Göran. *Alvar Aalto: The Early Years*. New York: Rizzoli, 1984, p. 136.

———. *Alvar Aalto: The Decisive Years*. New York: Rizzoli, 1986.

Schulze, Franz. *Mies van der Rohe: A Critical Biography*. Chicago: University of Chicago Press, 1985.

Sontag, Susan. *Styles of Radical Will*. New York: Dell, 1966, p. 9.

Starr, Frederick. *Melnikov: Solo Architect in a Mass Society*. Princeton, NJ: Princeton University Press, 1978.

Sullivan, Louis H. *The Autobiography of an Idea*. New York: Norton, 1934.

Turner, Paul V. *The Education of Le Corbusier*. New York: Garland, 1977, p. 3.

Vasari, Giorgio. *Vasari's Lives of the Painters, Sculptors and Architects*, ed. Edmund Fuller. New York: Dell, 1963, pp. 43, 44, 61, 262.

Von Moos, Stanislaus. *Le Corbusier: Elements of a Synthesis*. Cambridge, MA: MIT Press, 1979.

Wrede, Stuart. *The Architecture of Erik Gunnar Asplund*. Cambridge, MA: MIT Press, 1978.

Wright, Frank Lloyd. *A Testament*. New York: Bramhall House, 1957.

Wright, Frank Lloyd. *An Autobiography*. New York: Duell, Sloan and Pearce, May 1958.

# Epilogue

It would be natural for some people to ask themselves if it is indeed possible to become an inclusivist architect by prescription or through adherence to the channels of creativity discussed in the book. The answer is very simple: One does not become an "inclusivist" architect overnight; one graduates to inclusivity. Time, age, and experience eventually do the job. This book outlines only the various levels of creative consideration that will eventually come into play in the progress to inclusivity. And since our age is saturated with fragmented approaches to architectural design, most of them presented by their advocates as isolated panaceas, I thought it was worth the effort to present a picture of my own personal gain through architectural design studios over the last twenty years, and to link the alternative of inclusivity with the possibility of becoming "excellent."

Inclusivity in this sense is the picture of the overall domain of ideas and creative channels through which the designer's mind will eventually "swim" to find the way to its own expression. Thus inclusivity is in a sense the odyssey of the architect who will eventually come to know what it takes, why and when one is there.

We have presented many intangible and tangible channels to architectural creativity. Each was seen within its own context, from its own vantage point. Many would argue that some of the channels are more important than others. Equally many would push for the channel of their personal inclination or affiliation. They may propagate and even fight for it, and indeed do very well themselves within the creative potential of their selected channel. But we have been very determined to prescribe none of the channels as the panacea. We do not believe, for instance, that the metaphor, or geometry, taken in isolation, will provide the solution to all problems; on the contrary, we subscribe to the belief that any problem has solutions that are affected by combinations of things, architecture being only one of the elements of life. The argument goes like this:

Architecture has been a container of life, yet it has seldom been a true reflection of life. It has the peculiar characteristic of being to a great extent a "petrified form" in space, in a particular time. Unlike other forms of life in biology, botany, or the animal kingdom, architecture is fixed in form, location, and shape; its basic organization and structure are bound to remain the same, despite minor changes, expansions, attachments, or adaptations that may occur in time. Unlike other biological organisms, and despite the metaphors we may occasionally employ, in order to excite our architectural imagination or to study the particular form or make ourselves think, the major container and structure of architecture, after a building is built, will remain the same for many years to come. Thus we realize that although the building will have a decisive effect on the users' lives, it will not change substantially throughout its life span. Occupants will come and go, functions may change and be adapted, but the building will remain virtually the same, its changes relatively insignificant. *It is in the preconstruction period, the stage of design, during which the building receives its great transformation.* From an idea or a concept, it is eventually given life through drawing and means of communication; it changes and alters, modified by all sorts of factors and reasons, until it is finally crystallized into a "petrified reality."

The dynamics of architectural poetics is, for the architect at least, to a great extent the period and the process of design. In view of the flexibility and ever-growing transformation of life in time, versus the static state of the architectural container, architects should think seriously about the repercussions of all their decisions, and make "inclusivity" the moral goal of their lives as well as the guiding attitude of their design methodology.

No creative possibility should be sufficient in isolation. All, or as many as possible should be considered, keeping from each one whatever is essential for each situation, breaking or adjusting the rules as demanded by the circumstances and the project.

Fundamental to the contemplative process of design creation should be the reevaluation of long-standing concepts about issues such as functionalism and form. Much energy should be invested in the establishment of priorities according to the unexpected destination of the building:

What should be the answer for an ever-evolving, ever-changing functionality?

How can one generate a project of "elastic" functionalism?

How can one be sure that the project will be spiritually uplifting and appealing to its immediate users and the community at large?

Perhaps the universal goals cannot be accommodated in each and every project. After all, life takes care of the evolving needs of people through its own dynamics; people move, they change habitat and location of work; they seek better environments for themselves. They seek places for their God, places for leisure and art, the community and the shopping centers. The various building types take care of the varied and the ever-growing, ever-changing needs of people.

No individual building in particular can be the answer to all problems, but all the buildings together, the city, the urban and rural environment, will serve and contain the flexible, the changing, the temperamental and growing needs of humanity as a whole.

Inclusivity will eventually permit the well-trained well-educated and imaginative architect to consider a process of design that will compose a building through the widest variety of combinatorial concerns and will produce it as a result of these factors. Architecture is not created by air or by fire, as many ancient people used to think, but by today's architects, who have to use their brains and talents to become eventually agents of the many factors that shape and enrich architecture.

We believe that architecture of recent years, as well as the criticism and theory of the 1970s, were results of minds that saw only one side of the coin. The major architects and theoreticians of the era attempted to present a case that all architecture before Postmodernism (especially the architecture of the Modern movement) was what Descartes had considered the *poisoned well,* and thus should be abandoned; Postmodernism and its advocates believed they had found the one essential item of knowledge, the Cartesian *cogito.* For the majority of them, the answer was history and historicism.

My own attitude toward this whole problem has been that of a skeptic; I have been convinced, through life, study, practice, teaching, and experience, as well through the arguments of the skeptics with regard to the

Cartesian doctrine, that there are no perfect and foolproof sources and that we should not ask from our own personal sources for more than they can ever deliver. I have thus attempted to present arguments that will show some ways to help the genuinely searching architect to find his or her own truth.

I believe it would have been ill-advised to rule out the prospect of obtaining knowledge even from sources that I consider imperfect, sources that might be imperfect indeed. People can always tolerate some indigestion; in fact, this is rather good, as one always feels better afterward and learns what foods to avoid. It is my hope that students may learn what to avoid as early as possible.

For these reasons, I adopted the "benefit of the doubt" attitude and attempted an inclusivist focus to the subject of architecture. I believe that a tested and deeply contemplated inclusivist exposure (without any fear that we might perplex or even confuse the young) to the various channels of architectural creativity, through studio instruction and early in life, will become in a sense the agent of its own selectivity. This attitude will permit us to live within the framework of an evolutionary model, one that will help us reach our "inclusivist graduation" as early in life as possible. After all, all important architects before us did "graduate" to the richer and ever-evolving "inclusive" spheres of architecture.

As one grows older and more experienced, one finds oneself immersed in the realm of higher combinations of inclusivism. Then, as if by a miracle, the project is conceptualized through multilayered (or overlapping) levels of rationalization and expressed through sketches in a matter of seconds. The older one becomes, the broader the context of conceptualization, the faster the idea is conceived, the smaller the sketch of depiction. The wisdom and experience of inclusivist architects affords them the extraordinary advantage of being able to explore a greater number of alternatives than those who have not been trained inclusively, and to generate or reject solutions through their "human computer" with greater facility than others.

It does take time out of an architect's life to come to know when he or she is right, to gain confidence, to know when to stop. It is even more difficult for the beginner to know which way to go about searching and eventually finding oneself.

The poetics of architecture begins with the architect's mind; his or her creative life is a trip through inclusivity. All the rest, including immortality for the very few, will depend on the enthusiasm, imagination, and creativity of the beholder.

# Index